WOMEN, MINORITIES, & CR

A Multicultural Intersectionality Approach

Kendall Hunt
publishing company

Carla Miller Coates ⋮ Moneque Walker-Pickett

Cover image © Shutterstock.com

Kendall Hunt
publishing company

www.kendallhunt.com
Send all inquiries to:
4050 Westmark Drive
Dubuque, IA 52004-1840

Table of Contents

SECTION 3: Women and the LGBTQIA+

SECTION 4: Cybersecurity

Preface

The dialogue about women and minorities in criminal justice is currently one of the most "talked about" issues in a variety of social and political spaces. On any given day, topics related to use of force, bias in policing, unemployment, immigration, mass incarceration, women issues in policing, and crime, can be viewed on the Internet through the use of digital news reports accessed via web-based and mobile apps. Unlike traditional sources of media and news media, users can select topics of interest to them and not have to sit in front of the television and wait for the story that headlined and "got their attention" in the first place, including a story about crime. Although there has been a significant decline in the overall rates of incarceration in the United States, people of color represent more than 60% of the U.S. prison population.[1] Additionally, while it is well-known that males are more likely to be in incarcerated than their female counterparts, it should be noted that over the past several decades, women's rates of incarceration have increased dramatically. In fact, women have been the fastest growing prison population in the United States and women of color make up a disproportionate number of incarcerated women.

Over the past two years, there has been an upsurge in the number of incidents regarding police use of force. What is also trending is the unconscionable proportion of SWAT team raids on communities of color, which has resulted in the death of innocent people and the destruction of personal property. The shooting death of Breonna Taylor by Louisville police officers in 2020 has further highlighted how offenses like these languish in the system unless multiplicities hold law enforcement officers accountable. These issues are some of the topics that will be covered in this text as well as research on implicit bias, women and delinquency, foreign women in prison, criminal record and employment, domestic violence, minority judges, bullying, sexual harassment, women and leadership in criminal justice, LBGTQ issues in policing and crime, cybersecurity and cybercrime, and teaching in criminal justice, to name a few.

While the literature is replete with studies on women's pattern of offending that analyze factors such as race and ethnicity, women's economic vulnerability and marginalization, and social class background, less consideration has been given to the multiplicative influence of gender, racial and ethnic background, and social class from a multicultural and interdisciplinary approach. As such, the articles in this text provide a unique way of understanding how the intersection of gender, race and ethnicity, sexuality, and social class may influence women's involvement in the criminal justice system. The editors have collaborated with scholars from a range of institutions to provide a more comprehensive understanding of women, race and ethnicity, crime, sexual orientation, and the criminal justice system. The interdisciplinary nature of the text can be used by scholars from a variety of disciplines and may be utilized by both undergraduate and graduate students. The textbook, an anthology, is different from most textbooks on gender and crime as the aim is to touch on aspects

---

[1] Carson (2018).

of the gendered experience in various areas of the criminal justice system; from the entry in the system as an offender to the correction experience, through an examination of the intricacies of reintegration and recidivism. Using the lens of intersectionality, the text deviates from other texts on gender and crime by integrating an analysis of the "woman" experience in law enforcement and the courts (e.g., as attorneys, judges, probation, and administration). Although the focus is on women, there are accounts discussed within the text on the experiences of Black men and other men of color. Some of these discussions include the impact that having a criminal record has on employment opportunities and the treatment of a Black male business owner by police officers during a SWAT raid. While the aim of the text was not intended to directly resemble a text on racial inequality, discussions about race or racial differentiation cannot be avoided since many of the problems discussed in several chapters within the text involve issues of race and racial inequality, even though "race" may not be explicitly stated.

Students who take courses in criminal justice, sociology, and criminology should be exposed to ideas about race or how racialization impacts power relations in society. This includes, but is not limited, to encounters with the law and the legal system, access to employment, access to housing, and access to educational opportunities. The proliferation of "racial differentiation" remains omnipresent and used as a way of maintaining the status quo through social and economic processes. Racial differentiation is maintained through social, legal, and political controls (i.e., vestiges from slavery and Jim Crow laws) with the intended purpose of maintaining the social, political, cultural, and economic hierarchy whereby Whites are at the top and Blacks and other people of color are at the bottom. What is more complicated about the idea of racial differentiation is the multiplicative and simultaneous influence of race, gender, social class, and sexuality, or intersectionality. Intersectionality, which is the framework used by several authors in this text, explains how race, class, gender, and sexuality are often overlapping and creates multiple levels of social injustice. Thus, it is important that students understand the intersectionality framework when studying issues related to women and minorities in criminal justice.

© Niavani Michelle Grier

Carla Miller Coates and Moneque Walker-Pickett

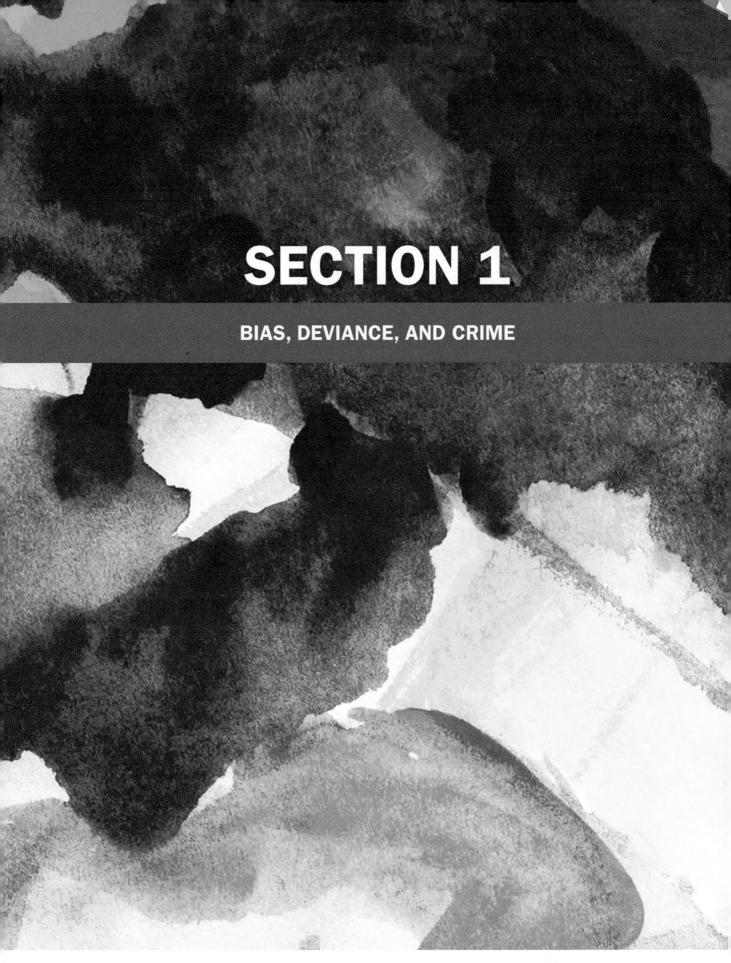

SECTION 1

BIAS, DEVIANCE, AND CRIME

CHAPTER 1

Light THEM Up and Shut "EM" Down: The Impact of a SWAT Raid on a Black Business in Virginia

Carla Miller Coates, Ph.D. | *North Carolina A&T State University*

"The boys in blue [are] at war with the citizens, they are supposed to protect... for Blacks, the war on terror hasn't come home...It's always been there" (McMichael, 2017, p. 115).

Overview

The purpose of this chapter is to introduce students to the increasing number of SWAT raids on communities of color. This chapter is important due to the lack of scholarly research in this area (McMichael, 2017). The primary goal of this chapter is to provide students with a brief history of the creation of SWAT units, paramilitary police practices, and a case study on a recent SWAT raid on a Black-owned business in South Hampton Roads, Virginia. Included in the case study are the actual police documents including the (1) search warrant, (2) incident report, (3) the SWAT policy for that police department, (4) photos, and (5) screenshots of actual text messages related to the case. To protect the individuals involved, pseudonyms are used, and personal information contained in the original search warrant, and other documents, have been redacted. The chapter begins with a discussion on officer-involved shootings and ends with thought-provoking discussion questions. Web links are also provided at the end of the chapter.

Chapter Outcomes

After reading this chapter, you should understand:

- The development of the Special Weapons and Tactics Team (SWAT).
- Research conducted on SWAT raids and the outcomes of those raids.
- The perception of bias in policing.
- Intersectionality.
- Solutions of change.

Say *"Their"* Names

In the wake of the controversies surrounding the officer- or citizen-involved deaths of *George Floyd, Breonna Taylor, Ahmaud Arbery, Rayshard Brooks, Eleanor Bumpers, Kendra James, Kathryn Johnson, Aiyanna Stanley Jones, Shereese Francis, Rekia Boyd, Miriam Carey, Michelle Cuseaux, Gabriella*

Nevarez, Tanesha Anderson, Sandra Bland (i.e., who died while in police custody), *Trayvon Martin* (i.e., an unarmed teenager who was murdered by George Zimmerman), *Freddie Gray Jr., Sam Dubose, Jordan Davis* (i.e., an unarmed teenager who was murdered by Michael Dunn), *Michael Brown, Eric Garner, Philando Castile, Terence Crutcher, Alton Sterling, Tamir Rice, Aki Gurley, Eric Harris, Walter Scott, William Chapman II, Jeremy McDole,* and *Jamar Clark*, to name a few,[1] there is a need to create national strategies regarding the use of force, the militarization of police (SWAT), the lack of police accountability, and bias-based policing (Kraska, 2007[1999]; Mummolo, 2018; Simckes, Hajat, Revere, Rowhani-Rahbar & Willits, 2019). For more than three decades, there has been a significant increase in the number of police-related deaths of unarmed citizens of color—throughout the United States. For example, according to an empirical study conducted by The Washington Post, approximately 986 people were shot by police in 2015, 962 in 2016, 986 in 2017, 998 in 2018, and 583 as of August 23, 2019 (Somashekhar & Rich, 2016). In fact, the daunting number of fatalities involving unarmed individuals has prompted citizens across the nation to question police culture and police tactics, this is not an easy task. More importantly, in order to get answers regarding the fatal shootings of citizens by police officers, social and legal justice leaders are using multidimensional strategies to bring about change. Some of those strategies include but are not limited to (1) advocating for social change through the use of peaceful protests,[2] (2) lobbying for change in legislation regarding police behaviors and police tactics including defunding the police and police reform, and (3) creating global networks (i.e., Black Lives Matter) to address the systemic and pervasive inequalities within the American system of justice (see Table 1 for a full list of social and legal justice organizations). While officer-involved shootings are replete in a variety of media platforms, the massive transformation in American policing (i.e., militarization) is not. Defined, *militarization* is "the social process in which society organizes itself for the production of violence or the threat thereof" (Kraska, 1999, p. 208; Kopel, 2000).[1]

© boyphare/shutterstock.com

© arcdelta.art/shutterstock.com

The Correlation Between Special Weapons and Tactics (SWAT) Teams and Social Justice Movements

The recent use of SWAT teams or heavily armed police officers in "battle armor" (Mummolo, 2018, p. 1) at public protests has garnered much attention since the murder of George Floyd. Yet, there is a lack of research that explores the harm associated with SWAT raids within communities of color (Mummolo, 2018). Prior to the killing of George Floyd during the COVID-19 pandemic in 2020, perhaps the most widely publicized officer-involved shooting within the past five years, was the shooting of an unarmed

[1]*At the time of this article's publication, cities across the United States enter their 31st day of protest of the killings of unarmed citizens. In fact, several protesters have been injured, beaten, tear gassed, and/or shot with rubber bullets, even while peacefully protesting. Many of the peaceful protests were organized by the "Black Lives Matter" (BLM) Global Network. BLM is a movement advocating for non-violent civil disobedience in protest against incidents of police brutality against African people.*

Black man in Ferguson, Missouri (Hayes, 2015; Mummolo, 2018). On August 9, 2014, Darren Wilson, a Ferguson police officer at the time, fatally shot 18-year-old Michael Brown. The findings from the investigation conducted by the Department of Justice (DOJ) revealed that Wilson fired 12 shots, shooting Brown approximately 8 times, including the fatal gunshot to Brown's head. Mike Brown's death resulted in a series of public demonstrations as citizens across the nation "took to the streets" to protest yet another shooting of an unarmed Black male. While protestors chanted "hands up, don't shoot," and voiced their opinions regarding police brutality and racial injustice, SWAT units and the National Guard were deployed. As onlookers from across the world watched the events unfold, it was clear that the militarization of police was "real," as evidenced by the arrival of armored vehicles and police officers pointing assault rifles at Black and Brown protestors (Mummolo, 2018). Consequently, on August 11, 2014, a crowd gathered on West Florissant Avenue in Ferguson and SWAT units dispersed tear gas on the citizens protesting (Araiza, Strum, Istek & Bock, 2016). Unfortunately, the Ferguson protest was only one of multiple accounts of the use of SWAT teams against citizens who "exercised their right to assemble" (Araiza, Strum, Istek & Bock, 2016, p. 309). Given the events that occurred in Ferguson a recent report found that the deployment of SWAT teams can be viewed as a controversial practice (Kraska, 1999; Kopel, 2000).

The Creation of SWAT Teams

In the mid-1960s, a Special Weapons and Tactics (SWAT) Team (originally coined by Daryl Gates, who was the former Chief of the Los Angeles Police Department (LAPD), as the Special Weapons Assault Team) was created as a response to "a series of high-profile incidents" that required police to use varying levels of force (Balko, 2013; Klinger & Rojek, 2008, p.1; Kopel, 2000). This highly specialized unit was developed to provide assistance to police officers during high-risk situations including (1) an active shooter, (2) hostage situations, (3) heavily armed suspects, or (4) a barricaded subject incident. SWAT members are police officers who receive special training in weapons and tactics. This paramilitary unit receives more intense training offered during basic training at the police academy. Their appearance resembles military special forces (i.e., militarized) and they are heavily armed (Kappeler & Kraska, 2015; Kraska & Kappeler, 1997). They are typically equipped with a sidearm, a Kevlar jacket (i.e., a heavy-duty bullet-proof vest), and a Kevlar helmet. Some other standard equipment includes a gas mask, an assault rifle, gas grenades, and flashbangs. In most police departments, SWAT team members volunteer to serve and must pass a physical fitness test, a marksman test, and participate in an interview process. The caveat, however, is that the type of equipment and process to become a SWAT team member varies from jurisdiction to jurisdiction.

It has been postulated that the first "deployment" of SWAT was in 1969 during a protest initiated by the Black Panthers (Bennett, 2010, para 6). In fact, a report issued by the Los Angeles Police Department, revealed that there were four critical incidents that prompted the development of SWAT (IACP National Law Enforcement Policy Center, 2011):

- the Watts Riots, which forced department members into tactical situations they were ill-prepared for;
- the emergence of snipers as a challenge to civil order;
- the appearance of the political assassin; and
- the threat of urban guerrilla warfare militant groups (p. 2).

The primary goal of SWAT, however, was to support police operations during high-risk situations and to reduce the number of casualties among police and citizens (IACP National Law Enforcement Policy

Center, 2011). While the incident between SWAT and the Black Panther Party put the LAPD SWAT team on the map, "it was the Comprehensive Drug Abuse Prevention and Control Act (DAPCA) of 1970 and President Richard M. Nixon that laid the foundation for most of the SWAT work that has occurred over the 40 years that followed" (IACP National Law Enforcement Policy Center, 2011, p. 2). Additionally, by 1975, there were approximately 500 SWAT teams nationwide and by the end of 1996, "89 percent of police departments in medium to large cities had a paramilitary police unit" (Balko, 2013; Kraska, 1999, p. 142). It is important to mention that for more than four decades, the use of SWAT units has increased significantly (Kraska, 2007; MacDonnell, 2016, p. 135; Mummolo, 2018).

© Nova Patch/Shutterstock.com

The increase in SWAT units through the years has contributed to the "war on drugs" (MacDonnell, 2016). Thus, according to Kraska (1997), a great proportion of SWAT callouts (75% to 85%) were related to search warrants—as opposed to their original intended purpose of responding to a hostage situation, a barricaded subject, heavily armed suspects, or an active shooter.

Although police militarization is not a new phenomenon, the recent upsurge in the use of paramilitary tactics is problematic (Kraska, 1999). In fact, in an interview on the evolution of police militarization in Ferguson and Beyond (2014), Kraska suggested "even though I was the first academic to identify, research, and write about these trends, even I would not have predicted the extent to which the military model would overtake the community policing reform movement so rapidly" (Li, 2014, para. 9). Furthermore, additional issues surrounding the deployment of SWAT teams include the excessive problems with search warrants (i.e., entering the wrong house) and mistaking legal substances (i.e., natural herbs) for illicit drugs (Whitehead, 2011). According to Dansky (2014), each year, there are approximately 45,000 SWAT raids on 124 homes per day (p. 2). For example, in a study conducted by the American Civil Liberties Union (ACLU), *War at Home: The Excessive Militarization of American Policing,* "nearly 80% of SWAT raids are [conducted] to search homes, usually for drugs, and disproportionately, in communities of color" (Dansky, 2014, p. 2). The latter is problematic, particularly given the overwhelming lack of support for the effectiveness of the "war on drugs" and the widespread research supporting its epic failure. An abundance of research suggests that this failed policy disproportionately impacts communities of color, particularly Blacks, which disenfranchises communities of color specifically, and Black men in particular. In fact, between 2011 and 2012, 79% of SWAT teams were used to serve search warrants for drugs as opposed to its primary mission. Consequently, only 7% of SWAT deployments were actually used for the "primary mission" as described above (ACLU, 2014, pp. 2–4).

The ACLU (2014) study targeted 260 law enforcement agencies. Law enforcement leaders were asked to submit all of their reports regarding SWAT team deployments between 2011 and 2012 (p. 8). By 2013, the ACLU received approximately 3,844 records from those law enforcement agencies from 26 states. The agencies responded to the following questions:

1. What was the number, race, ethnicity, and sex of those impacted?

2. How many children were present during the raid?

3. Were any mentally ill individuals impacted?

4. How many officer-related deaths or injuries were there?

5. Was forcible entry involved?

6. Was a flashbang grenade or other distraction device used?

7. What was the purpose of the SWAT deployment (i.e., to execute a search warrant, in response to a barricade, hostage, or active shooter scenario, etc.)?

8. Was it a no-knock warrant?

9. Was the warrant issued in conjunction with a drug offense?

10. Were any weapons found?

11. Were drugs and/or other contraband found?

12. Did the deployment result in property damage? (p. 8)

The Bleak Picture of SWAT Invasions

This next section highlights several SWAT invasions that were featured in the ACLU 2014 report, War Comes Home: The Excessive Militarization of American Policing. The purpose of this section is not to restate all of the detailed facts of each case, rather the goal is to paint the "bleak" picture of the excessive militarization of American policing and harm that these tactics cause.

Case 1: In January 2008, Lima, Ohio SWAT officers killed an unarmed 26-year-old, Black woman named Tarika Wilson, as she was "holding her infant son" (ACLU, 2014, p. 5). While the victim was not a suspect, she was shot and killed when SWAT officers entered the premises and opened fire. The baby was injured but he survived. Officers entered Tarika's home searching or her boyfriend. Tarika was the mother of six.

Case 2: Huntington, West Virginia. In 2011, SWAT team members threw a "flashbang" into a home during the execution of a search warrant involving a drug case. Inside was a child, a pregnant woman, and a man. While the report did not include the race and ethnic background of these individuals, according to the ACLU report, "the majority of the Huntington SWAT deployments the ACLU studied were conducted in connection with drug investigations, and the majority of the people impacted were Black" (ACLU, 2014, p. 6).

One major problem revealed in the ACLU (2014) report is the lack of consistency of SWAT reports. According to the study, many of the reports were flawed and "the incident reports lacked information… [and] officers failed to provide reports that were consistent."

Case 3: Eurie Stamps, a 68-year-old man, was a grandfather of twelve and resided in Framingham, Massachusetts. In January 2011, Stamps was "in his pajamas watching a baseball game" when his home was invaded by SWAT. According to the ACLU report, SWAT used a "battering ram and threw a flashbang grenade" into his home (p. 9). According to the report, Stamps was ordered to "lie face down on the floor with his arms above his head" (p. 9). Stamps died in this position even though he was not a suspect. The police were actually looking for his girlfriend's son who they suspected of selling drugs. What is more perplexing about this case was that the suspect had already been arrested prior to SWAT entering Mr. Stamps' home. Yet, SWAT still decided to enter the home and killed an innocent man.

Case 4: In 2014, in a home on the outskirts of Atlanta, Georgia, a family of six who had just relocated from Wisconsin fell prey to a SWAT invasion. According to records, SWAT team members entered a room where the family was sleeping and one of the officers threw a flashbang grenade into the room. The flashbang landed in the baby's crib. The report indicated that SWAT team members were unaware that a family resided in the home. Unfortunately, the baby suffered from third-degree burns from the blast (ACLU, p. 14). The backstory of the home invasion is described below:

> The SWAT team was executing a "no-knock" warrant to search for someone who did not live in the home that was raided. Police were searching for Bounkaham's (the victim's father) nephew, who was accused of making a $50 drug sale (p. 14).

> According to Alecia, (the victim's mother), "after breaking down the door, throwing my husband to the ground, and screaming at my children, the officers—armed with M16s—filed through the house like they were playing war... this [the SWAT raid] is all about race. You don't see SWAT teams going into a white-collar community throwing grenades into their homes" (p. 14).

Subsequently, there were no guns or drugs found in the home and no arrest was made. The suspect that the SWAT team was originally searching for was arrested at another location. As for the baby, "he was still in a medically induced coma when the report was written" (p. 15).

Case 5: Jose Guerena, a military veteran, was shot 22 times in 2011 while in his Tucson, Arizona home. According to the ACLU (2014) report, Guerena heard noises and saw a shadow outside of his home. Guerena grabbed his rifle, and told his wife to hide in the closet with their 4-year-old son while he investigated the situation. SWAT team members fired 71 shots. Guerena was found dead in his kitchen with 22 gunshot wounds. Guerena did not receive any medical attention. Guerena's home was one of two homes raided that night. There were no drugs found in Guerena's home.

Case 6: On June 23, 2012, a SWAT team raid was deployed at a home in Gwinnett County, Georgia at approximately 6:00 am (ACLU, 2014). According to the report, the initial raid was abandoned but later reinstated because the officers involved decided that there was probable cause. SWAT team members believed the home was occupied by a convicted felon. SWAT entered the premises despite knowing that an elderly citizen and children were in the home.

Several studies and digital media suggest that a large proportion of SWAT deployments are the result of search warrants as police look for drugs (see Kilnger & Rojek, 2008). In a recent report regarding a botched SWAT raid in Chicago, Illinois, a police officer shot 12-year-old Amir Worship (a Black male) during a SWAT raid before dawn (Melendez, 2019, para 1). When officers entered Crystal Worship's home searching for her boyfriend, who was in the home at the time SWAT entered, they carried exploding flash grenades and automatic rifles. The Worship family filed a lawsuit in the Circuit Court of Cook County. The family is suing for $50,000 in damages for alleged (1) negligence, (2) willful and wanton conduct, (3) assault, (4) battery, and (5) false imprisonment. Crystal Worship and her three sons, Amir, Eric (13 years old), and Robert (18 years old) were asleep when the SWAT raid occurred (Melendez, 2019, para. 2). Ms. Worship's boyfriend, Mitchell Thurman, was arrested and charged with drug possession. However, the charges against Mr. Thurman were later dismissed.

Unfortunately, the cases related to SWAT raids do not end here. There are too many stories in the ACLU (2014) report to enumerate. However, the results of the study indicate the following:

1. Policing and Militarism: Policing, particularly through the use of paramilitary teams in the United States has become excessively militarized, mainly through federal programs that create incentives for state and local police to use unnecessarily deadly weapons and aggressive tactics designed for the battlefield.

2. Lack of Transparency and Oversight: The militarization of policing in the United States has occurred with almost no public oversight.

3. The Purpose of SWAT: SWAT teams were often deployed unnecessarily and aggressively to execute search warrants in low-level drug investigations; deployments for hostage or barricade scenarios occurred in only a small number of incidents.

4. The Use of Paramilitary Weapons and Tactics: When paramilitary tactics were used in drug searches, the primary targets were people of color, whereas when paramilitary tactics were used in hostage or barricade scenarios, the primary targets were white.

5. Use of Violent Tactics and Equipment: SWAT deployments often and unnecessarily entailed the use of violent tactics and equipment, including APCs (armored vehicles); use of violent tactics and equipment was shown to increase the risk of bodily harm and property damage (pp. 21–37).

The Case of a Black-Owned Music Studio

In 2017, Lynsey Reed agreed to assist her son, Tre, with his business ventures. Tre is an aspiring artist with multiple talents. In fact, he designs web pages, owns a t-shirt business, designs clothing, sings, and writes music. Although he had many career aspirations, he always dreamed of owning his own music studio. For several months, Tre searched for the perfect location. He wanted a space that would meet his professional goals; a place where he could manage all four of his talents. Finally, after three long months, Tre found a commercial rental property located in a prominent business district in South Hampton Roads, Virginia. Tre submitted an application to rent the commercial property. Although Tre had a good Fair Issac Corporation (FICO) score, the owner refused to rent to him. While we cannot definitively state why his credit application was denied by the owner, Tre believed that his application was denied because of his race, gender, socioeconomic status (or what Crenshaw would explain as intersecting identities), age, and/or lack of employment history (although he had owned his own business for four years, possessed a business license, and had income tax records). Although Tre did not use criminological, sociological, or psychological words to describe his experiences, what he articulated was what Crenshaw (1994) explained as intersecting identities. In this regard, Tre's experiences reflected how Black men are perceived through those intersecting identities as threatening, criminal, or violent, as if Black men are their own monolithic group and not part of the larger heterogeneous population. Often, when these intersecting identities converge, they create greater risks for people of color to experience a number of disadvantages and discrimination, as seen in Tre's case.

© Pressmaster/Shutterstock.com

Since Tre was denied an opportunity to rent the commercial property, his mother agreed to rent the suite for him. The owner was aware that Tre would be the occupant and Tre's mother Lynsey would act as the guarantor. Tre's mother was a professional. She wanted to see her son accomplish his dreams. She knew that she would be taking a risk financially because new businesses without the proper financial cash flow has a greater probability of failing within the first two-years of business (Leonard, 2018). In fact, according to Leonard (2018, para 1) some of the primary reasons that businesses fail during the first two years include: (1) weak or no business plan, (2) lack of capital or startup capital, (3) no marketing strategy, and (4) lack of material to actually produce the product (e.g., ink for the t-shirt press and other office supplies). The risk for Lynsey did not matter. She was elated by the fact that she could help her son. During Tre's first year of business, he focused on building his brand. He began to acquire investors and subsequently partnered with a close friend. Tre's father also invested in the business as he was also eager to help. Since Tre had multiple business ventures, he spent the majority of his time operating his painting business, while his business partner managed the music studio, which included managing the property, booking studio time, and managing their online presence. Additionally, since Lynsey was the guarantor, she advised Tre to be cognizant of the type of traffic (i.e., people) that the music studio could attract. While many patrons do not have any "ill intent," music studios have a reputation of becoming a place for people to "hang out" and smoke marijuana. This behavior may garner the attention of the police; Lynsey did not want any trouble with the police as she was well aware of the glaring inequalities in policing. As a matter of fact, during Tre's first year of operation, he did not have any encounters with the police, but this would change in early 2018.

© pixelheadphoto digitalskillet/Shutterstock.com

In February of 2018, law enforcement officers were called to the property. When they arrived, they informed Tre that they had received a noise complaint. While there, the officers said that they "smelled marijuana" as soon as they approached the building. They asked Tre if they could enter the premises and he agreed. Tre stated that he had nothing to hide. Typically, Tre would not have let the police in without a search warrant. However, since he had never had any issues with the police, he thought that by granting them access to the suite, they could see what type of establishment he ran. Tre hoped that his willingness to comply would help build a rapport between him and the officers assigned to that jurisdiction. He was very aware of the negative publicity and public outcry for police accountability and as a Black man, he was socialized not to trust "the police." In fact, one could argue that Tre's willingness to "get to know the police" was important given the overwhelming research and national attention related to police misconduct; killing of unarmed Black men, women, and children; and the excessive misuse and deployment of SWAT units (United States Department of Justice, para. 2; ACLU, 2014).[2]

Police Encounters of the "Third Kind"

Around March 2019, Tre was notified by mail that two new business tenants would be moving into the business complex. Ironically, both of the businesses just happened to be "music recording studios" and both of the owners just happen to be Latino men. Of note, the two men were not related. As mentioned earlier, Tre was busy establishing his painting company. Therefore, he had not been spending much time at the studio. However, he did stop by twice a week to check things out. On March 15, 2019, Tre went to the studio. At this time, he noticed a significant change in the environment. More specifically, he noticed heavy traffic and a lot of cars and people hanging around the front and back of the other studios. There were motorcycles driving around and women twerking to music coming from parked cars; it was like a big party. Tre did not pay much attention to it because it had nothing to do with him. It is worth noting that when Tre and Lynsey went to pick up the keys to their suite, the property owner warned about the "lady next door." The owner mentioned that she kept a watchful eye on the complex and that she had no problem calling the police if she deemed it to be necessary. Tre and Lynsey appeared "unbothered" by this warning because they knew that they would be operating a "legitimate" business.

---

[2]Please note that the police officers found no evidence of marijuana or any other drug.

However, the other tenants in the complex did not feel the same, particularly the lady next door who was an elderly White woman who had owned her business in that complex for more than 30 years. Keep in mind that prior to Tre and the new Latino tenants moving in, all of the business owners in the complex of about 30 professional suites were White. Tre, by the way, was the only Black business owner.

The lady next door was not happy about the loud noise, the smell of marijuana, and the number of people in the parking lot. To express her frustration, she called all of the property owners and complained and threatened to notify the police if the noise continued.

For several months, things went back to normal. The traffic decreased and the massive crowds of people declined. It was not until Tre had an issue with his former girlfriend did the real trouble begin.

In May of 2019, Tre terminated his relationship with his girlfriend Alysha. Alysha was upset and came to Tre's suite and knocked on the door. Tre was not there, but his business partner was. When the business partner came to the door, he advised Alysha that Tre was not there and to come back later. Alysha grew angry because she thought he was lying for Tre. As a result, Alysha went to her car and retrieved a screwdriver and attempted to enter the premises. When she could not pry open the door, Alysha began hitting the glass with the screwdriver until the glass shattered. When Tre's business partner noticed what she was doing, he called the police, and then he called Tre. Tre arrived a few minutes before the police did. After he assessed the damages, Tre called his mother and kept her on the phone while the police questioned Alysha about the damages. Alysha informed the police that she was the "property manager" and had the right to enter the premises. The police never asked her to present a key; the officer believed her and told Tre that he would have to take Alysha to civil court to resolve any professional disputes. The next day, the lady next door noticed the damage to the door and took a picture. She included the photo in her text message to the owner of the property. The owner contacted Lynsey and asked her to take care of the damage.

It does not stop here. The lady next door began to launch complaints about anything she could. She alleged that people from Tre's suite were throwing bottles on her roof. She also claimed that there were illegal vehicles parked in front of Tre's suite. The text messages did not stop. Each day, Lynsey would receive a message about one thing or another. There was even a report made to the city regarding the legitimacy of Tre's business license. Lynsey consulted with Tre and they decided to terminate their lease. The harassment was overwhelming and Lynsey did not want to deal with it any longer. In fact, in one of the text messages Lynsey received, the lady next door called the Black and Latino business owners "them people!" Taken together the constant complaints to the owner, the calls to the city, and the calls to the police, Lynsey realized what the lady next door was attempting to do. She wanted to drive "them people" out!

As Tre and his mother prepared to vacate the premises, Tre received a call from his business partner that a woman, who was a visitor of someone recording music, alleged that she was sexually assaulted by one of the men on the premises recording music. Tre was not in the suite at the time of the incident. However, his business partner informed him that the music engineer had a few people in the suite drinking and smoking marijuana. The ages of these men ranged between 19 and 30. Often, according to Tre, when the "guys" came to record music, they would bring their female companions with them. The women would hang out and listen to the music being recorded.

Once the assault was reported to the police, they came to the studio to conduct an investigation. When the police arrived, the individual accused of the offense was at the studio and claimed that it was not a sexual assault; according to the offender, the woman had given full consent. During the investigation, detectives canvassed the area seeking answers. They went to the suite next door. Although she had no knowledge of the assault and could not reference the incident directly, the lady next door told the detective that drugs were being sold from the music studio. She added that Tre and his partner did not possess the proper business license needed to operate the music studio. Consequently, after the police left the premises, the lady next door contacted the property owner to inform him of the alleged rape. The owner later contacted Lynsey to inform her, but she told him she was already aware of the alleged assault. Lynsey advised the lady next door that her son would be leaving the premises and asked her to please stop harassing him. Unfortunately, the lady next door did not comply and she kept making allegations and complaints against them. She began to contact the police regularly. Over the course of the next few days, the police were called several times a day. Finally, two weeks before the lease ended, Lynsey received a text from the lady next door, which stated that there was a SWAT team at the property and that she did not know what was going on because the police were not letting anyone in or out.

Unfortunately, Lynsey was at work and did not read the text message until two hours later. By that time, the raid had concluded. Lynsey was shocked! She had no idea why SWAT would enter the building. What were they searching for? The only logical answer Lynsey could come up with was that the lady next door had made more allegations in reference to the studio. The fact that the lady next door specifically listed the addresses that would be "hit" by SWAT in her text messages aroused suspicion. As such, Lynsey suspected that the lady next door played an integral role in submitting false information to the police, which subsequently led to the SWAT raid. The question is, if she was not directly involved, how would she have known specific details including the addresses and suite numbers of the businesses involved? The SWAT raid on Tre's business was devastating, particularly since the lease was going to be terminated in two weeks. The SWAT team entered the premises and caused significant structural damage and destroyed all of Tre's business equipment and personal belongings (see photos at the end of the chapter). The damage the police did was unconscionable. Lynsey knew that their actions were excessive. Lynsey wanted answers so she requested a copy of the original search warrant (see the appendix section). More importantly, Lynsey wanted to understand why the SWAT team was used to enter a legitimate business. Lynsey learned in college that SWAT should only be used if there was a hostage situation, an active shooter, a heavily armed individual, or a barricaded subject. When she read the search warrant, she found out that SWAT was used to search for:

1. Marijuana and paraphernalia.

2. A violation of Virginia State Code 18.2-250. 1 Possession of Marijuana.

The search warrant also stated that there were several complaints made against Tre's business regarding noise and the smell of marijuana. Lynsey also found out that the other two music studios owned by the Latino men were raided by SWAT as well. Tre's suite which was the largest of the three music studios in the area, was destroyed. The behavior of the police officers on the SWAT team appeared to have specifically targeted businesses owned and operated by men of color (i.e., Black and Latino). As stated in the ACLU's (2014) report, it is not necessary for SWAT teams to be deployed on search warrants that target low-level drug activity. This was the case with Tre's business. It is also worth mentioning that when SWAT entered Tre's music studio, there were three individuals inside. There was one White female and two Black males. Fortunately, they were not harmed. When SWAT detained the individuals in the suite and searched them, they found 3.5 grams of marijuana on the White female and 1 gram of marijuana on the Black male. The other individual did not possess any drugs on his person; however, when the police searched the trunk of his car, they found 3.5 grams of marijuana. Both males were issued a summons while the White female was permitted to leave. She was not issued a summons.

Similar to many of the cases contained in the ACLU (2014) study, The SWAT raid did not produce any evidence that the establishment was being used to sell narcotics. There was no evidence of illegal activity and there were no guns found. No arrests were made. SWAT not only damaged the contents within the building excessively, but they also told Tre's business partner to consider a "new profession". According to Tre's business partner, the police told him that if he continued to operate a studio at that facility, they would continue to show up! As evidenced by the photos at the end of this chapter, it appears that the SWAT teams excessive destruction of Tre's property was intentional and was done to send a message.

Conclusion

In 1964, SWAT was formed. By 1975, there were more than 500 SWAT teams nationwide and by 1999 all 50 states had SWAT units (Roth, 2001; Blau, 1994). While the initial goal of SWAT was to provide support for incidents involving hostage situations or barricades, SWAT units have primarily been used to execute search warrants, which is a traditional method of the SWAT team culture, to look for drugs. In fact, according to research, approximately 60% of SWAT deployments involved drug searches (ACLU, 2014). Thus, many cases included in the ACLU 2014 report on SWAT raids, similar to the case highlighted in this chapter, were unfounded and did not produce any evidence of drug sales or illegal activities in the homes and businesses targeted. Most of the time, the suspect(s) they were searching for was not in the home at the time of the raid, and if drugs were found, it was only a small amount (ACLU, 2014). The findings of the ACLU study highlight the critical need for citizens to "unite" and bring about systemic and systematic change regarding the militarized policing tactics used by law enforcement agencies. There needs to be a strategic plan in place that will produce legislation aimed at holding law enforcement accountable for their actions. More specifically, there needs to be (1) better documentation, (2) transparency, and (3) a reduction in the use of the paramilitary style of policing. What is more, the report suggested that SWAT raids tend to disproportionately impact communities of color and that SWAT teams were often deployed unnecessarily and aggressively to execute search warrants in low-level drug investigations and less likely to be used for hostage or barricade situations (ACLU, 2014, p. 5).

The case study presented in this chapter is an actual account of a SWAT team raid on the business of a young Black man in Virginia, with the pseudonym of Tre. On July 30, 2019 Tre and his mother moved the final items out of the building. Review the discussion questions and key terms at the end of this chapter. You be the judge!

Solutions for Change and Accountability

The following are solutions recommended by law enforcement agencies to assess the use of SWAT teams and minimize the harm of SWAT invasions:

1. Develop a forum that supports antiracist discourse and hire law enforcement officers that can articulate and demonstrate a "true" understanding of cultural sensitivity.

2. Reform must be systemic; the problems of overly aggressive policing are cultural and cannot be solved by merely identifying a few "bad apples" or dismissing the problem as a few isolated incidents (ACLU, 2014, p. 6).

3. Use or create a warrant risk assessment matrix that supports harm reduction and errors.

4. Use SWAT only in high-risk situations and use a variety of assessments (i.e., a three-step process and a threat assessment) that will determine if SWAT should be deployed (Police Use of Force Project, 2017, p. 20).

5. End employment as opposed to using transfer as a disciplinary action (Schlesinger, p. 25).

6. Hold police officers accountable. The data states that when police departments adopt strict use of force policies, there is a decrease in the number of officers involved shootings (Police Use of Force Project, 2017).

Key Terms:

Aggressive Policing

Barricaded Subject

Barricaded Suspect

Bias

Black Panther Movement

Cultural Sensitivity

Disproportionality

Intersectionality

Militarization

Paramilitary Style of Policing

People of Color

Police Use of Force

Policing and Militarism

Risk Assessment

Search Warrant

Tactical Team

Transparency

Use of Force

Discussion Questions:

1. Do you think that the lady next door was the individual alerting the police?

2. After reviewing the photos, do you think that the SWAT team intentionally destroyed the contents within the building?

3. After reading the search warrant, did the police establish probable cause?

4. How much money do you think it cost the city to conduct the raid?

5. Why do you believe that the White female who was in the building on the day of the SWAT raid was instructed to leave the premises?

6. After reading the incident report located in the Appendix section of this chapter, do you believe that the police could have planted the small amount of cocaine to make the raid "look good?"

Web Links:

https://www.c-span.org/video/?c4515732/kara-dansky-law-enforcement-poor-communities

https://www.aclu.org/report/war-comes-home-excessive-militarization-american-police

https://www.rutherford.org/publications_resources/john_whiteheads_commentary/swat_team_mania_the_war_against_the_american_citizen

https://www.thedailybeast.com/illinois-cop-shot-unarmed-black-12-year-old-in-bed-during-botched-raid-lawsuit

http://publici.ucimc.org/2007/10/home-invasion-racial-disparities-in-swat-raids/

http://www.pbs.org/independentlens/blog/the-evolution-of-swat-team-equipment-from-wwii-rifles-to-bearcats/

https://policeviolencereport.org/

Note: The web links provided are for educational use only. In order to assess the validity of the information contained within the links, students should cross-reference the material, and search for peer-reviewed documents regarding the information found on the website. Wikipedia is not a peer-reviewed resource.

References

Abbey-Lambertz, K. (2014). *How a police officer shot a sleeping 7-year-old to death.* Retrieved from https://www.huffpost.com/entry/aiyana-stanley-jones-joseph-weekley-trial_n_5824684?guccounter=1&guce_referrer=aHR0cHM6Ly93d3cuZ29vZ2xlLmNvbS8&guce_referrer_sig=AQAAAKKmV0hZhvblnomOwfyOigkeKmoz9c3nwynILNUefKV0PuG4gmD7Qw6lh659hf7323sV5NADw09ZMS_BBQ3d-k8M15Hv2kZ_lRrzn7vQspZ-oT5FW4xD822Kw3_BX7Nmr3UlRaS_nxzClrN7WMtkDflKOE2UZUk-LC0Lqr4VLOm_8

American Civil Liberties Union (2014). *War comes home: The excessive militarization of American police.* Retrieved from https://www.aclu.org/report/war-comes-home-excessive-militarization-american-police

American Civil Liberties Union (2019). *7-year-old girl accidentally shot by SWAT team.* Retrieved from https://www.aclu.org/other/7-year-old-girl-accidentally-shot-swat-team

Araiza, J. A., Strum, H. A., Istek, P. & Bock, M. A. (2016). Hands up, don't shoot, whose side are you on? *Cultural Studies-Critical Methodologies,* 16(3), 305–312.

Balko, R. (2013). Swatted. *The militarization of America's police.* Holidays. Retrieved from https://www.the-american-interest.com/2013/10/10/swatted-the-militarization-of-americas-police/

Balko, R. (2013). *Rise of the warrior cop.* Retrieved from https://www.wsj.com/articles/rise-of-the-warrior-cop-1375908008

Balko, R. (2013). Rise of the warrior cop: The militarization of America's police forces. New Your, NY: Public Affairs.

Bennett, C. (2010). *The birth of SWAT.* Retrieved from https://www.officer.com/investigations/article/10232858/the-birth-of-swat

Brenstein, M. (2013). *Memorial planned to mark 10-year anniversary of Portland police fatal shooting of Kendra James.* Retrieved from https://www.oregonlive.com/portland/2013/04/memorial_planned_to_mark_10-ye.html

Brown, E. (2014). *Timeline: Michael Brown shooting in Ferguson, MO.* Retrieved from https://www.usa-today.com/story/news/nation/2014/08/14/michael-brown-ferguson-missouri-timeline/14051827/

CNN (2009). *Ex-Atlanta officers get prison time for cover-up in deadly raid.* Retrieved from http://www.cnn.com/2009/CRIME/02/24/atlanta.police/

Crenshaw, K. (1991). Mapping the margins: Intersectionality, identity politics, and violence against women of color. Stanford Law Review, 43(6), 1241–1299.

Dansky, K. (2014). *Another day, another 124 violent SWAT raids.* Retrieved from https://www.aclu.org/blog/smart-justice/mass-incarceration/another-day-another-124-violent-swat-raids

Feuer, A. (2016). *Fatal police shooting in Bronx echoes one from 32 years ago.* Retrieved from https://www.nytimes.com/2016/10/20/nyregion/fatal-police-shooting-in-bronx-echoes-one-from-32-years-ago.html

Finders for Justice.org (2019). *Organizations addressing police accountability and racial justice.* Retrieved from https://fundersforjustice.org/organizations/

Hayes, F. W. (2015). War against the people: Killer cops and community terrorism. *Critical Sociology,* 41(6), 881–885. doi:10.1177/0896920515589725

International Association of Chiefs of Police National Law Enforcement Policy Center (2011, August 9). *Special weapons and tactics (SWAT).* Retrieved from https://www.theiacp.org/sites/default/files/all/s/SWATPaper.pdf

Klinger, D. A. & Rojek, J. (2008). Multi-method study of special weapons and tactics teams. U. S. Department of Justice. Retrieved from https://www.ncjrs.gov/pdffiles1/nij/grants/223855.pdf

Kopel, D. (2000). Smash-up policing. When law enforcement goes military. National Review, 44–46. Retrieved from http://davekopel.org/CJ/Mags/Smashup-Policing.htm

Kappeler, V. E. & Kraska, P. B. (2015). Normalising police militarization, living in denial. *Policing and Society,* 25 (3) 268–275. doi: 10.1080/10439463.203.84655

Kraska, P. B. (1999). Questioning the militarization of U.S. police: Critical versus advocacy scholarship. *Policing and Society,* 9, 141–155.

Kraska, P. B. (1999). Militarizing criminal justice: Exploring the possibilities. *Journal of Political and Military Sociology, 27,* 205–215.

Kraska, P. B. & Kappeler, V. E. (1997). Militarizing American Police: The rise and normalization of paramilitary units. *Social Problems,* 44 (1), 1–18.

Kraska, P. B. & Paulsen, D. J. (1997). Grounded research into U.S. paramilitary policing: Forging the iron fist inside the velvet glove. *Policing and Society, 7,* 253–270.

Leonard, K. (2018, August 8). Business financial problems. Chron. Retrieved from https://smallbusiness.chron.com/business-financing-problems-292.html

Li, S. (2014). *The evolution of police militarization in Ferguson and beyond.* Retrieved from https://www.theatlantic.com/national/archive/2014/08/the-evolution-of-police-militarization-in-ferguson-and-beyond/376107/

MacDonnell, T. C. (2016). When more is less—SWAT and procedural Justice. *Washington and Lee Journal of Civil Rights and Social Justice,* 23 (1), 135–180.

Marenin, O. (2016). Cheapening death: Danger, police street culture, and the use of deadly force. *Police Quarterly,* 19(4), 461–487.

McMichael, C. (2017). Pacification and police: A critique of the police militarization thesis. *Capital & Class,* 41(1), 115–132.

Melendez, P. (2019). Illinois cop shot unarmed Black 12-year-old in bed during botched raid: Lawsuit. Retrieved from https://www.thedailybeast.com/illinois-cop-shot-unarmed-black-12-year-old-in-bed-during-botched-raid-lawsuit

Mummolo, J. (2018). *Militarization fails to enhance police safety or reduce crime but may harm police reputation.* Proceeding of the National Academy of Sciences of the United States of America, 115, 9181–9186. https://doi.org/10.1073/pnas.1805161115

Police Use of Force Project (2017). *Police violence report.* Retrieved from https://policeviolencereport.org/

Simckes, M., Hajat, A., Revere, D., Rowhani-Rahbar, A. & Willits, D. (2019). A conceptualization of militarization in domestic policing. *Police Quarterly,* 1–28. doi: 10.1177/1098611119862070

Somashekhar, S. & Rich, S. (2016). *Final tally: Police shot and killed 986 people in 2015.* Retrieved from https://www.washingtonpost.com/national/final-tally-police-shot-and-killed-984-people-in-2015/2016/01/05/3ec7a404-b3c5-11e5-a76a-0b5145e8679a_story.html

Appendix

© *Carla Miller Coates*

One hour after the raid. This is the front structure of the building.

© *Carla Miller Coates*

Left side, post SWAT raid.

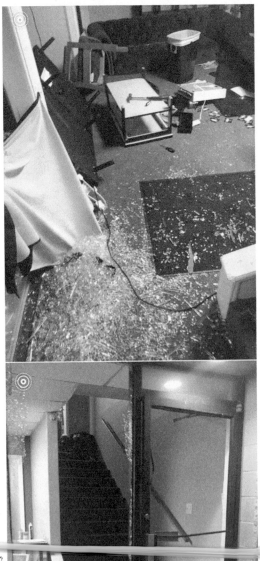

Inside of the property one hour after the
SWAT raid.

Cash register

© *Carla Miller Coates*

© *Carla Miller Coates*

Inside, post SWAT raid. Below, owner looking at the ceiling.

Another inside view.

© Carla Miller Coates

Parts of cash register

© Carla Miller Coates

Inside, flipped furniture

Music studio

Music studio

Warehouse

Warehouse

Searching for narcotics

Dumped out coffee, searching for narcotics.

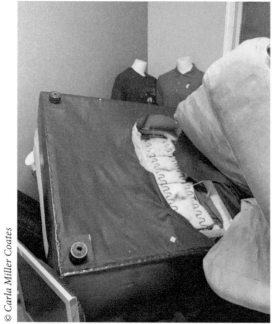

© Carla Miller Coates

Searching for narcotics. Ripped up bottom of sofa and flipped all of the furniture.

© Carla Miller Coates

Searching for narcotics

© Carla Miller Coates

Busted open speaker searching for narcotics

© Carla Miller Coates

Removed ceiling tiles to search for narcotics

Removed ceiling tiles to search for narcotics

Blinds and debris

Debris. Notice camera stripped from door/wall.

Damage to the front entrance. Notice the broken metal door frame.

© Carla Miller Coates

The aftermath of the SWAT raid. Debris and tossed furniture.

© Carla Miller Coates

The aftermath of the SWAT raid. Debris and tossed furniture.

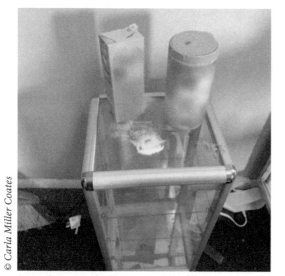

© Carla Miller Coates

Poured out carpet fresh searching for narcotics.

© Carla Miller Coates

The aftermath of the SWAT raid.

© Carla Miller Coates

Post raid cleaned building. Note missing glass.

AFFIDAVIT FOR SEARCH WARRANT

Commonwealth of Virginia   VA. CODE § 19.2-54

The undersigned Applicant states under oath:

1. A search is requested in relation to [X] an offense substantially described as follows:
[ ] a person to be arrested for whom a warrant or process for arrest has been issued
identified as follows: A violation of Virginia State Code 18.2-250. 1 Possession of Marijuana

[ ] CONTINUED ON ATTACHED SHEET

2. The place, person or thing to be searched is described as follows:

[ ] CONTINUED ON ATTACHED SHEET

3. The things or persons to be searched for are descibed as follows:
Marijuana, Paraphernalia

[ ] CONTINUED ON ATTACHED SHEET

4. The material facts constituting probably cause that the search should be made are:
See attached.

FORM DC -388 (MASTER, PAGE ONE OF TWO) 07/17

FILE NO.

AFFIDAVIT FOR SEARCH WARRANT

APPLICANT:

NAME

Master Police Officer
TITLE (IF ANY)

ADDRESS
Virginia

Certified to Clerk of _____ Circuit Court

_____
CITY OR COUNTY

on _____
DATE

_____
TITLE   SIGNATURE

Original Delivered
[ ] in person [ ] by certified mail
[ ] by electronically transmitted facsimile
[ ] by use of filing/security procedures defined
in the Uniform Electronic Transactions Act

to Clerk of _____
CITY OR COUNTY WHERE EXECUTED

Circuit Court on _____
DATE

_____
TITLE   SIGNATURE

5. The object, thing or person searched for [X] constitutes evidence of the commission of such offense [ ] is the person to be arrested for whom a warrant or process for arrest has been issued.

6. [X] I have personal knowledge of the facts set forth in this affidavit AND/OR

[X] I was advised of the facts set forth in this affidavit, in whole or in part, by one or more other person(s). The credibility of the person(s) providing this information to me and/or the reliability of the information provided may be determined from the facts:

See attached.

The statements above are true and accurate to the best of my knowledge and belief.

██████████ ██████████
APPLICANT

Master Police Officer
TITLE OF APPLICANT

Subscibed and sworn to before me this day.

7/9/19   4:00pm
DATE AND TIME

██████████ ██████████
[ ] CLERK [X] MAGISTRATE [ ] JUDGE

FORM DC -388 (MASTER, PAGE TWO OF TWO) 07/17

SEARCH INVENTORY AND RETURN

The following items, and no others, were seized under authority of this warrant:

1.
2.
3.
4.
5.
6.
7.
8.
9.
10.
11.
12.
13.
14.
15.

(CONTINUE AT RIGHT OR ATTACH ADDITIONAL PAGES AS NECESSARY)

The statement above is true and accurate to the best of my knowledge and belief.

_____
(DATE)

_____
EXECUTING OFFICER

Subscribed and sworn to before me this day

_____
(DATE)

[ ] CLERK [ ] MAGISTRATE [ ] JUDGE

[ ] NOTARY PUBLIC: My commission

FORM DC-399 5/84 (114:3-021 9/93)

EXECUTION

Executed by searching the within described place, person or thing.

7/18/29 1952 hrs
DATE AND TIME EXECUTED

██████████
EXECUTING OFFICER

Certified to
Circuit Court on _____
(DATE)

_____
(EXECUTING OFFICER)

Received on _____
(DATE)

by _____
CLERK, CIRCUIT COURT

4. The material facts constituting probable cause that the search should be made are:

This investigation began in June 2019 when this affiant recieved information about possible marijuana use occurring at ███████ in Virginia Suite ███████ . The information this affiant received stated that there frequently is an odor of marijuana coming from the suite ███████ as well as high amount of vehicle traffic and groups of subjects hanging out in the parking lot. This affiant was able to determine that ███████ studio, was operating out of ███████ in Virginia.

On 6/15/2019 officers from the ███████ Police Department responded to ███████ circle, Suite ███████ in Virginia in response to a rape that had allegedly occurred inside the business. During this investigation on 6/15/2019 Detective ███████ went inside the business to speak with employees about possible security video that may be pertinent to the rape investigation. While inside the business Detective ███████ stated that he was able to smell an odor of marijuana throughout the business.

On 6/29/2019 while officers from the ███████ Precinct Community Policing Squad were conducting surveillance ███████ in Virginia, Officer ███████ observed a verbal dispute begin in the parking lot. Two subjects that were involved in the dispute got into white Honda Civic bearing Virginia registration ███████ and attempted to drive from the area. The Honda Civic struck a parked vehicle prior to getting away from the area and the vehicle came to a stop. Officer ███████ responded to the scene and contacted the driver of vehicle (W/M, 1/20/███████). ███████ gave Officer ███████ consent to search his vehicle and during a search of the vehicle Officer ███████ located an open bottle of liquor as well as a quantity of marijuana. ███████ stated that he was inside ███████ studio recording music and he had received a quantity of marijuana from an unknown subject inside the studio. The affiant knows that ███████ studio is the recording studio located at ███████ in Virginia ███████ was subsequently charged with possession of marijuana, illegal drug possession of alcohol, open container of alcohol, DUI and refusal.

On 7/05/19 this affiant and other members of the ███████ Precinct Community Policing Squad responded to a call for service in Virginia. The complaint ███████ called into dispatch stating that a subject was outside banging on the front door of the business. When officers arrived on the scene, they contacted ███████ (B/M, 09/26/███████) who was standing in front of the business. During a consent search of ███████ Officer ███████ located and recovered a quantity of marijuana.

While Ofc. ███████ was speaking with ███████, I contacted the complaint, inside ███████ in Virginia. ███████ told me that he was the manager at ███████ studio, and the studio is owned by the subject named ███████ . This affiant was able to identify ███████ as ███████ (10/10/███████). While speaking with ███████ I was able to smell and odor of marijuana inside the business. ███████ stated that ███████ was inside the business earlier in the evening recording music and got upset when he wasn't allowed back inside the business. After ███████ was issued a summons for possession of marijuana ███████ allowed him to enter the business and wait for a ride.

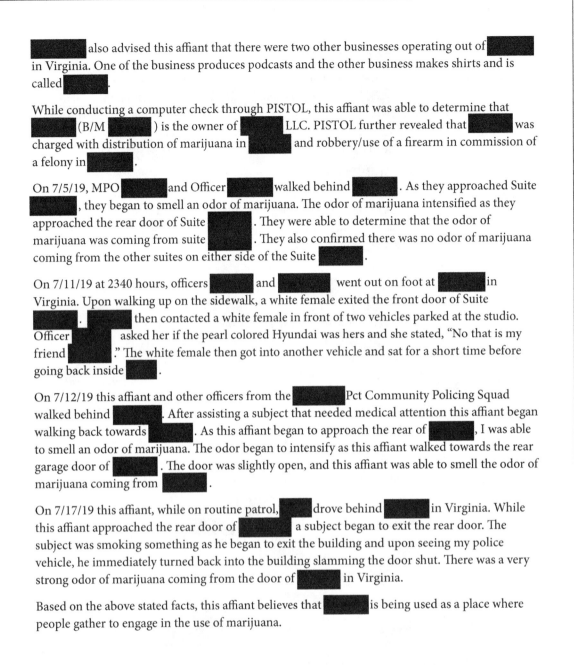

████ also advised this affiant that there were two other businesses operating out of ████ in Virginia. One of the business produces podcasts and the other business makes shirts and is called ████.

While conducting a computer check through PISTOL, this affiant was able to determine that ████ (B/M ████) is the owner of ████ LLC. PISTOL further revealed that ████ was charged with distribution of marijuana in ████ and robbery/use of a firearm in commission of a felony in ████.

On 7/5/19, MPO ████ and Officer ████ walked behind ████. As they approached Suite ████, they began to smell an odor of marijuana. The odor of marijuana intensified as they approached the rear door of Suite ████. They were able to determine that the odor of marijuana was coming from suite ████. They also confirmed there was no odor of marijuana coming from the other suites on either side of the Suite ████.

On 7/11/19 at 2340 hours, officers ████ and ████ went out on foot at ████ in Virginia. Upon walking up on the sidewalk, a white female exited the front door of Suite ████. ████ then contacted a white female in front of two vehicles parked at the studio. Officer ████ asked her if the pearl colored Hyundai was hers and she stated, "No that is my friend ████." The white female then got into another vehicle and sat for a short time before going back inside ████.

On 7/12/19 this affiant and other officers from the ████ Pct Community Policing Squad walked behind ████. After assisting a subject that needed medical attention this affiant began walking back towards ████. As this affiant began to approach the rear of ████, I was able to smell an odor of marijuana. The odor began to intensify as this affiant walked towards the rear garage door of ████. The door was slightly open, and this affiant was able to smell the odor of marijuana coming from ████.

On 7/17/19 this affiant, while on routine patrol, ████ drove behind ████ in Virginia. While this affiant approached the rear door of ████ a subject began to exit the rear door. The subject was smoking something as he began to exit the building and upon seeing my police vehicle, he immediately turned back into the building slamming the door shut. There was a very strong odor of marijuana coming from the door of ████ in Virginia.

Based on the above stated facts, this affiant believes that ████ is being used as a place where people gather to engage in the use of marijuana.

6. [X] I have personal knowledge of the facts set forth in this affidavit AND/OR
[X] I was advised of the facts set forth in this affidavit, in whole or in part, by one or more other person. The credibility of the persons providing this information to me and slash for the reliability of the information provided may determine from the following facts:

This Affiant has been employed by the ▮▮▮ Police Department since August 2002 and is currently assigned to the ▮▮▮. PCT ▮▮ Squad. This Affiant has attended additional training concerning the investigation of individuals and organizations involved in the trafficking of illicit narcotics, as well as in the methods and techniques used by drug dealers to conduct and conceal their illegal activities. This Affiant has been involved in numerous narcotic investigations that have resulted in the confiscation of assets, narcotics and the arrest and conviction of individuals involved in the use and distribution of narcotics, to include cocaine, heroin, marijuana, methamphetamine, and MDMA.

Detective ▮▮▮ has been a Sworn Police Officer with the ▮▮▮ Police Department since August 2006. Officer ▮▮▮ has been a sworn member of the ▮▮▮ since January 2015. Officer ▮▮ is currently assigned to the ▮▮▮ Precinct Community Oriented Policing Squad. Officer ▮▮ has received training in the recognition of illegal and illicit narcotics. Has been involved in numerous narcotic investigations that have resulted in the confiscation of illegal narcotics and the arrest and conviction of individuals involved in the use and distribution of illegal narcotics.

Officer ▮▮▮ has been a sworn member of the ▮▮▮ Police Department since April 2017. Officer ▮▮▮ is currently assigned to the ▮▮▮ Precinct Community Oriented Policing Squad. Officer ▮▮▮ has received training in the recognition of illegal and illicit narcotics. Officer ▮▮ has been involved in numerous narcotic investigations that have resulted in the confiscation of illegal narcotics and the arrest and conviction of individuals involved in the use and distribution of narcotics.

▮▮▮

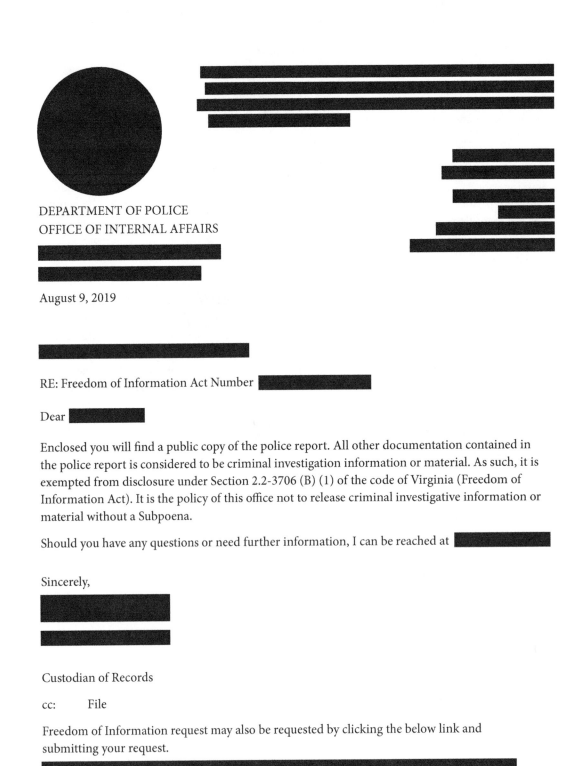

DEPARTMENT OF POLICE
OFFICE OF INTERNAL AFFAIRS

██████████████████████████
██████████████████

August 9, 2019

█████████████████████████

RE: Freedom of Information Act Number ███████████████

Dear ████████

Enclosed you will find a public copy of the police report. All other documentation contained in the police report is considered to be criminal investigation information or material. As such, it is exempted from disclosure under Section 2.2-3706 (B) (1) of the code of Virginia (Freedom of Information Act). It is the policy of this office not to release criminal investigative information or material without a Subpoena.

Should you have any questions or need further information, I can be reached at ████████████

Sincerely,

███████████████
███████████████

Custodian of Records

cc: File

Freedom of Information request may also be requested by clicking the below link and submitting your request.

████████████████████████████████████

	Police Department **INCIDENT REPORT** PUBLIC COPY	Case #: ███████

Location of Incident ████████████ ████████████	Zone: ████████ Neighborhood: ████████ ████████	Date / Time Reported: 07/18/2019 11:00 PM Last Known Secure: 07/18/2019 07:52 PM At Found: 07/18/2019 07:52 PM
Reporting Officer ████████ Supervisor ████████ Investigating Officer ████████	Case Status ████████ Date: 07/23/2019	Disposition NOT APPLICABLE Date: 07/23/2019

Crime# 1: DRUG/NARCOTIC VIOLATIONS (35A1) – Completed

Entry	Exit	Security Type	Premise: OFFICE BUILDING, COMMERCIAL How Left Scene?
1:	1:	1:	
2:	2:	2:	

Criminal Activity	Weapons/Tools　　(A) - automatic	Bias/Motivation
1: POSSESSING/CONCEALING	1:	NONE (NO BIAS)
2:	2:	
3:	3:	

Crime# 2: DRUG/EQUIPMENT VIOLATIONS (35B) – Completed

Entry	Exit	Security Type	Premise: OFFICE BUILDING, COMMERCIAL How Left Scene?
1:	1:	1:	
2:	2:	2:	

Criminal Activity	Weapons/Tools　　(A) - automatic	Bias/Motivation
1: POSSESSING/CONCEALING	1:	NONE (NO BIAS)
2:	2:	
3:	3:	

Modus Operandi:	Method of Entry	Trademarks

Victims and Others Involved

Code	#	Type	Name	Victim of Crime#s	Will Prosecute	Age	Sex	Race
VI	1	SOCIETY / PUBLIC	SOCIETY / PUBLIC	1,2	Y			
CO	1	Law Enforement	Restricted		Y			

Involvement Codes: CO=COMPLAINANT   DR=DRIVER   OW=OWNER   VI=VICTIM, OTHER
Race Codes: A=ASIAN OR PACIFIC ISLAND (ASIAN INDIAN, POLYNESIAN)   B=BLACK/AFRICAN AMERICAN
I=AMERICAN INDIAN/ALASKAN NATIVE   U=UNKNOWN

Property	Status	*Value	*Post Value	Quantity	Description
COCAINE (ALL FORMS EXCEPT "CRACK")	6			0.01 GM	COCAINE (ALL FORMS EXCEPT "CRACK")
DRUG/NARCOTIC EQUIPMENT	6	$10.00		2.00	DIGITAL SCALES
MARIJUANA	6			4.00 GM	MARIJUANA
Total Stolen Value: $0.00				Total Recovered Value: $0.00	

Property Statuses: 1=NONE   2=BURNED   3=COUNTERFEITED/FORGED   4=DAMAGED/DESTROYED/VANDALIZED   5=RECOVERED
6=SEIZED/IMPOUNDED/EVIDENCE   7=STOLEN   8=UNKNOWN   OTHR=OTHER/FOUND   SUSP=SUSPECT   TARG=TARGET VEHICLE/PROPERTY
Note: "Value" is $1 if Unkown. "Post Value" column displays value of property based on the condition at the time of recovery.

No RELATED VEHICLES
END OF REPORT
If you have additional information or questions regarding this incident, please contact the **Investigator** at ███████

Name of Organization	State
ABFE: A Philanthropic Partnership for Black Communities	National
ACLU of Arizona	Arizona
ACLU of New Jersey	New Jersey
Action Now	Illinois
Advancement Project	National
All of Us or None	California
Alliance of Californians for Community Empowerment	California
Alliance of Families for Justice	New York
Amnesty International	National
Anti-Police Terror Project	California
Anti-Violence Project	New York
Arab American Association of New York	New York
Arizona Center for Empowerment	Arizona
Asian American Legal Defense and Education Fund	National
Assata's Daughters	New York
Audre Lorde Project	New York
Baltimore Algebra Project	Maryland
Baltimore Bloc	Maryland
Baltimore United for Change	Maryland
Baltimore United for Change-Legal Bail Support for Baltimore	Maryland
Bill of Rights Defense Committee	National
Black Alliance for Justice Immigration	National
Black Lives Matter	National
Black Lives Matter Memphis	Tennessee
Black Organizing for Leadership & Dignity	National
Black Organized Project	California
Black Women's Blueprint	National
Black Youth Project	National
BlackOut Collective	California
BMAfunders	National
Bolder Advocacy	National
breakOUT	Louisiana
Bronx Defenders	New York
Brooklyn Movement Center	New York
Brotherhood/Sister Sol	National
Build People's Power Assemblies	National
CAAAV Organized Asian Communities	New York
California Families to Abandon Solitary Confinement	California

Call to Action for Racial Equality	West Virginia
CASA	Maryland
Causa Justa: Just Cause	Maryland
Center for Constitutional Rights	National
Center for Nuleadership on Urban Solutions	New York
Center for Social Inclusion	New York
Chhaya CDC	New York
Chicago Torture Justice Memorial and People's Law Office	Illinois
Child Welfare Organizing Project	New York
Cincinnati Black United Front	Ohio
Coalition Against Police Crimes & Repression	Missouri
Coalition for Police Accountability	California
Colorado Anti-Violence Project/Survivors Organizing for Liberation	Colorado
Colorofchange	National
Communities United Against Police Brutality	Minnesota
Communities United for Police Reform	New York
Communities United for Restorative Justice	California
Connecticut Community Organizing for Racial Justice	Connecticut
Council on American Islamic Relations- New York	New York
Creating Law Enforcement Accountability & Responsibility	New York
Critical Resistance	National
Demos	New York
Desis Rising Up & Moving	New York
Dignity and Power Now	California
Equality to Flatbush	New York
Families Against Stop and Frisk	New York
Families for Freedom	National
FEIRCE	National
Forward Together	National
Freedom Side	National
Funder's Committee for Civic Participation	National
Gay Man of African Decent	New York
Hands up United	Missouri
Helping Educate to Advance the Right of the Deaf	Washington D.C.
Highlander Research and Education Center	Southern U.S.
Immigrant Defense Project	New York
Highlander Research and Education Center	Southern U.S.
Immigrant Defense Project	New York
Ingoma Foundation	National
Ironbound Community Corporation	New Jersey
Jews Against Islamophobia	New York

Jews for Racial & Economic Justice	New York
Justice Committee	New York
Justice Teams Network	California
LatinoJustice PRLDEF	New York
Law Enforcement Action Partnership	National
Leaders of a Beautiful Struggle	Maryland
Leadership Conference for Civil and Human Rights	National
Legal Aid Society	New York
Living United for a Change in Arizona	Arizona
Local Progress	National
Los Angeles Community Action Network	California
Louisiana Justice Institute	Louisiana
Make the Road New Jersey	New Jersey
Make the Road New York	New York
Malcom X Grassroots Movement	New York
Manhattan Young Democrats	Report and Case Studies
Marijuana Communities United	New York
Maryland Communities United	Maryland
Millennials Activist United	Missouri
Million Hoodies Movement for Justice	National
Missourians Organizing for Reform and Empowerment	Missouri
Mothers Against Police Brutality	Texas
Movement Strategy Center	National
NAACP Legal Defense and Education Fund	National
National Coalition of Anti-Violence Programs/New York City Anti-Violence Project	New York
Neighborhoods Organizing for Change	Minnesota
New York Civil Liberties Union	New York
New York Harm Reduction Educators	New York
NJ Communities United	New Jersey
Northern Manhattan Coalition for Immigrant Rights	New York
NY Communities United	New York
Ohio Student Association	Rhode Island
Colleyville Neighborhood Association	Rhode Island
People's Justice for Community Control and Police Accountability	New York
Peoples Organization for Progress	National
Persist Health Project	New York
PICO National Network, Live Free Campaign	National
Picture the Homeless	New York
Poder in Action	Arizona
PolicyLink	National

Project NIA	National
Project South	Southern U.S.
PROS Network	New York
PRYSM	Rhode Island
Public Science Project	New York
Puente Movement	Arizona
Race Forward: The Center for Racial Justice Innovation	National
Racial Justice NOW!	Ohio
Resources, Information, Help for the Disadvantaged (RIHD)	Virginia
Right to the City	National/ New York
Safe Streets/ Strong Communities	California
Sankofa	National
School of liberty and Liberation	New York
Sistas and Brothas United/ Northwest Bronx Community & Clergy Coalition	New York
Southern Coalition for Social Justice	North Carolina
Southerners on New Ground	Southern U.S.
Streetwise and Safe (SAS)	New York
Sylvia Rivera Law Project	New York
TGI Justice Report	National
The Ordinary People Society (TOPS)	Alabama
The Organization for Black Struggle	Missouri
The Philanthropic Initiative for Racial Equality	National
The Security & Rights Collaborative	National
Trans Queer Pueblo	Arizona
Transgender Law Center	National
Tribeca for Change	New York
Trinity Lutheran Church	New York
Turning Point for Women and Families	New York
T'ruah: The Rabbanic Call for Human Rights	New York
US Human Rights Network	National
VOCAL-NY	New York
Wisconsin Jobs Now	Wisconsin
Women with a Vision	Louisiana
Workers Centers for Racial Justice	National
Young Activist United St. Louis	Missouri
Young Gifted and Black	California
Youth Justice Coalition	California
Youth Ministries for Peace and Justice	New York
Youth Represent	New York

CHAPTER 2

Asian American Women in Law Enforcement: Entry, Challenges, and Perspectives

Daisy Ball | Roanoke College

Introduction

In the U.S., tensions between law enforcement and communities of color remain high. This is largely due to recent, high-profile shootings of unarmed Black men by White law enforcement officers. Following such events, several social movements have arisen, the most vocal of which has been the Black Lives Matter movement. The movement seeks to direct attention to the experiences of minorities' criminal justice contact. Largely absent from these conversations are the voices of Asian Americans, including Asian American victims and perpetrators of crime, as well as Asian Americans working in the field of law enforcement.

This chapter shares findings from interviews with Asian American females in law enforcement, which is part of a larger project measuring the experiences of Asian Americans in law enforcement in the era of the Black Lives Matter movement. Based on in-depth interviews, I explore their entry into and experiences within the field. A central theme that emerges concerns the barriers and challenges they face due to their intersectional statuses: as Asian Americans, who are typically cast as the "model minority" (Hartlep 2013); as females, who are more often stereotyped as docile nurturers, and less often associated with enforcement of the law (Archbold & Schulz, 2012); and finally, as Asian American females, who are commonly stereotyped as passive, submissive, and/or exotic (Mukkamala & Suyemoto, 2018). Thus, my project seeks to better understand the experiences of Asian American females working in law enforcement in the era of the Black Lives Matter movement. What does it mean to be the "middleman minority" (Bonacich, 1973) employed in law enforcement? Does one experience privileged status, and possibly hostility from communities of color, for one's "model minority" (Lee, 2009) status? Or, to the contrary, does one face hostility from the racial majority, given one's "forever foreigner" (Tuan, 1998) status?

As this chapter goes to publication, our nation is reeling from yet another police killing of an unarmed Black man, George Floyd. This event has reinvigorated the Black Lives Matter movement, and has spawned a national conversation about how to move forward with policing in the U.S., including possibly defunding the police, reallocating police funds for more effective training, and/or eliminating the entity of police entirely.

The current chapter focuses on the experiences of Asian Americans in policing, and is therefore particularly relevant in light of Floyd's death, for which four officers have been charged. One of the four, Tou Thao, identifies as Hmong, and is only the second Asian American police officer to be associated with a high-profile killing of an unarmed Black person.

Chapter Outcomes

After reading this chapter, students should:

- Articulate tensions stemming from recent events involving law enforcement officers and communities of color.
- Understand the intersectional status of Asian American women in law enforcement, and the challenges they face due to their intersectionality.
- Identify interview respondents' typical paths of entry into the field of law enforcement.
- Explain interview respondents' perspectives on the Black Lives Matter movement.

Setting the Scene

The Black Lives Matter Movement

The Black Lives Matter movement began in response to the "not guilty" verdict in the *State of Florida v. George Michael Zimmerman* case in 2013 (Chase, 2018). Zimmerman, a Hispanic/Caucasian male, was patrolling his gated community on a February evening in 2012, as its neighborhood watch coordinator. During his patrol, he encountered Trayvon Martin, an unarmed African American high school student, who was returning home to the neighborhood on foot after purchasing snacks at a local convenience store. A scuffle ensued, and the encounter turned fatal for Martin, whom Zimmerman shot "in self-defense," citing Florida's Stand Your Ground Law (Barry et al., 2012). This incident, and the eventual acquittal of Zimmerman, sparked outrage across the globe, and thus the Black Lives Matter movement was born. Hailed as "more than just a civil rights movement," Black Lives Matter co-founder Opal Tometi proclaims:

> [The Black Lives Matter movement] is about the full recognition of our rights as citizens; and it is a battle for full civil, social, political, legal, economic, and cultural rights as enshrined in the United Nations Universal Declaration of Human rights…the movement is a struggle for the human rights and dignity of black people in the U.S., which is tied to black peoples' struggle for human rights across the globe. (2015)

Since its inception, the movement has grown, largely in response to a series of killings of unarmed Black men by Whites in law enforcement positions: the victims include Michael Brown, Philando Castile, Samuel DuBose, Eric Garner, Freddie Gray, and Alton Sterling, to name just a few. Today, the Black Lives Matter movement maintains a consistent hold in the eyes of the public (Chase, 2018).

The Case of Peter Liang

In 2015, Asian American "rookie" police officer Peter Liang shot and killed Akai Gurley, an unarmed Black man, in the stairwell of a New York City housing project (Kang, 2016). Liang and partner Shaun Landau were conducting a "vertical patrol"[1] of Brooklyn's Louis H. Pink Houses. Liang's gun went off, the bullet ricocheting off a wall and hitting Gurley, who was descending the stairs with his girlfriend (Nir, 2016). The single bullet pierced Gurley's heart, resulting in his death (Nir, 2016). The case was settled when Liang was found guilty of manslaughter and official misconduct, but served no jail time, which sharply divided the Asian American and African American communities. Asian Americans believed Liang was only charged *because* of his racial minority status (they characterized him as a scapegoat), whereas African Americans believed that had Gurley been White, Liang would have received a much harsher sentence (that is, they saw this as yet another example of excessive use of force by police against the Black community) (Kang, 2016).

© a katz/Shutterstock.com

Review of the Literature

The Model Minority Stereotype

The model minority stereotype of Asian Americans asserts that they are smart, hardworking, and conformists (Hartlep, 2013). While this might appear to be a positive stereotype, its "double-edged sword" nature has been widely documented in the literature (Zakeri, 2015). The model minority stereotype has been shown to be both ubiquitous (Kiang et al., 2017; Hartlep, 2013; Ng, Lee & Pak, 2007; Ng & Lee, 2007), and detrimental to those to whom it is applied (Kiang et al., 2017; Lee, 2009). Treating Asian Americans as a monolithic group (Lee, 1994; Yi & Musesus, 2015), it assumes Asian Americans to be academic "all-stars" or academic success stories (Assalone & Fann, 2017; Lee, 1994; Yi & Museus, 2015), thus holding them to a higher standard than members of other racial/ethnic groups, and downplaying the hardships faced by other racial/ethnic minorities (Lee, 2009; Yi & Museus, 2015). Asian Americans often internalize the model minority stereotype, using it as a measuring stick of their own progress and success. If they fail to live up to the platitudes contained in the stereotype, this causes them distress (Hartlep, 2013). Moreover, stereotypes associated specifically with Asian American females include the assumption that they are quiet, subservient, and/or exotic, sexualized beings (Mukkamala & Suyemoto, 2018).

---

[1] The policing tactic known as "vertical patrol" is a routine, up-and-down patrol of stairwells, primarily those in public housing buildings. The aim of the vertical patrol is to "keep criminals at bay" in public housing developments (Schwirtz, 2014).

Gender and Policing

The image of police work is decidedly male in nature, as policing has historically been a male-dominated profession in the U.S. (Chan, Doran & Marel, 2010; Archbold & Schulz, 2012). While affirmative action and equal opportunity hiring practices have increasingly opened the workforce to women, including in the field of law enforcement, challenges remain (Martin, 2006; Chan et al., 2010). Women face both resistance and barriers to their entry into police work (Doran & Chan, 2003; Silvestri, 2007; Martin & Jurik, 2006), for a multitude of reasons, including the nature of police work (Chan et al., 2010; Charles, 1982), the gendered nature of the institution of law enforcement (Martin & Jurik, 2006), the subculture of police work (Franklin, 2008), and the threat of women to the police image and men's identity (Chan et al., 2010).

According to the Bureau of Justice Statistics (BJS), in 1987, women constituted just 8% of full-time, sworn, local police officers (Reaves, 2015, p. 4). While the most recently available data (2013) shows that women now constitute 12% of police, female representation in policing remained relatively stagnant from 2007–2013 (Reaves, 2015, p. 4). In terms of managerial and supervisory positions, the BJS reports that in 2013, the percentage of females in first-line supervisory positions was a mere 9.5%, with only 3% of local police chief positions occupied by females.

Intersectionality

In a 1989 paper for the *University of Chicago Legal Forum*, scholar and activist Kimberle Crenshaw coined the term "intersectionality" as a concept via which the nuanced experiences of Black females can be understood. According to Crenshaw (1989), the feminist and racial/ethnic studies literature had overlooked the lived experiences of Black women due to the intersecting, oppressive statuses they experienced:

> Because the intersectional experience is greater than the sum of racism and sexism, any analysis that does not take *intersectionality* into account cannot sufficiently address the particular manner in which Black women are subordinated. (p. 140)

Taking issue with the "single-axis analysis" customary in traditional approaches to the social sciences, Crenshaw argued that without an intersectional approach, "Black women are theoretically erased" (p. 139). Today, the concept of intersectionality is a customary framework through which to view the experiences of humans with multiple, intersecting, oppressive statuses, including those tied to race/ethnicity, gender, sexuality, socioeconomic status, immigration status, and so forth.

Central Research Questions

Based on a review of the literature, and as part of a larger project assessing the experiences of Asian Americans working in the field of law enforcement in the era of the Black Lives Matter movement, the following research questions emerged:

1. How do Asian American females enter the field of law enforcement, and what corresponding reactions do they face from family members?

2. What challenges do Asian American females face in their law enforcement careers, given the intersection of two minority statuses they hold: Asian American and female?

3. Where do Asian American females stand in terms of the Black Lives Matter movement, and do they perceive that it has impacted them professionally?

Methodological Approach

This chapter shares findings from one branch of a larger, ongoing project on Asian Americans in law enforcement in the era of the Black Lives Matter movement. During the summer of 2018, in-depth interviews were conducted with Asian American females who work in the field of law enforcement. Study participants were recruited via a branch of the Asian American Law Enforcement Association (AALEA). I contacted the AALEA branch president and asked him to share a "Call for Study Participants" with members of his organization. He complied, and interested members contacted me. From there, study participants referred acquaintances to me. This technique is known as snowball sampling: as study participants refer you to others, your sample gradually builds (Auerbach & Silverstein, 2003). According to Noy (2008),

> A sampling procedure may be defined as snowball sampling when the researcher accesses informants through contact information that is provided by other informants. This process is, by necessity, repetitive: informants refer the researcher to other informants, who are contacted by the researcher and then refer her or him to yet other informants, and so on. Hence the evolving snowball effect. (p. 330)

While snowball sampling can be appropriate for a variety of endeavors, it is an especially useful technique when attempting to reach members of a group who are not immediately identifiable or accessible; it is also well-suited when studying sensitive or private issues (Biernacki & Waldorf, 1981, p. 141), both of which circumstances are applicable to the current project.

Interviews were conducted in person whenever possible, in locations including my faculty office and local coffee shops. When meeting in person was not possible given geographic distance, interviews were conducted over the phone. Interviews were digitally recorded and later transcribed. Pseudonyms were assigned to participants, and recordings were destroyed after transcription.

Interviews were semi-structured in nature, lasting between 45 minutes and 2 hours. Semi-structured interviews allow the interviewee to guide the interview based upon topics and themes that *they* deem of particular importance; in addition to the respondent playing a significant role in the shape the interview takes, this approach allows the researcher to learn about the subculture being discussed, which helps inform subsequent interviews.

The interview script asked participants to speak about their backgrounds, their education, their career trajectory, and racial/ethnic experiences they had had while employed in law enforcement. I then asked, specifically, about their perceptions of the Black Lives Matter movement, and if the movement had impacted them given their line of work.

The sample size (*n*=5) for this branch of the project is limited, as the project is ongoing, and the population is one that is not readily accessible: Asian Americans are underrepresented in the field of law enforcement,[2] as are females. In terms of racial/ethnic identification, all respondents identified generally as Asian American, with three respondents identifying as "Chinese American," one respondent identifying as "Korean American/Caucasian," and one respondent identifying as "Japanese American/Korean American/Caucasian." In terms of age, respondents ranged from 26 years to 54 years. All but one respondent had completed a four-year college degree; she was just one credit shy of completing her bachelor's degree at the time the interview took place. Two respondents worked for local law enforcement agencies (the same agency, an urban police department in the southern United States serving the city of "Mapleton," a city of approximately 100,000 residents); and three respondents held positions in federal law enforcement agencies. Three respondents resided on the East Coast of the United States, one on the West Coast, and one currently lived abroad. Of the five, three occupied mid-level positions, and two occupied senior-level positions. See Table 1 for demographic and career data of respondents.[3]

The sample is limited with regards to size and ethnic-group identification. Nonetheless, as the interviews progressed, stark patterns emerged, as similar sentiments and themes were expressed by my respondents. In several cases, respondents from very different backgrounds shared stories with me that were almost identical, give or take inconsequential details. This phenomenon is known as "theoretical saturation," and has its origins in Grounded Theory. Glaser and Straus (1967) explicate theoretical saturation as follows:

> The criterion for judging when to stop sampling the different groups pertinent to a category is the category's theoretical saturation. Saturation means that no additional data are being found whereby the sociologist can develop properties of the category. As he sees similar instances over and over again, the researcher becomes empirically confident that a category is saturated. He goes out of his way to look for groups that stretch diversity of data as far as possible, just to make certain that saturation is based on the widest possible range of data on the category. (p. 61)

Thus, while the project's limited sample size compromises generalizability of findings, the fact that saturation has already taken place lends credibility to the project, even in its early state. In qualitative research, theoretical saturation has come to be seen as essential, with Morse (2015, p. 587) referring to saturation as "[T]he most frequently touted guarantee of qualitative rigor offered by authors," and Guest, Bunce, and Johnson (2006) referring it as "the gold standard." A number of scholars have come to regard theoretical saturation as a rule or criterion for qualitative research (e.g., see Denny, 2009; Morse et al., 2002; Leininger, 1994; Morse, 1995; Sparkes et al., 2011).[4]

---

[2] According to the Bureau of Justice Statistics (BJS), in 2013, Asian Americans constituted just 2.4% of full-time sworn personnel in local police departments (Reaves 2015: 5), despite constituting over 5% of the U.S. population (U.S. Census Bureau 2010). The larger the population the police department serves, the more Asian American representation there is on the force. For example, according to BJS statistics from 2013, in local police departments serving 1,000,000 residents or more, Asian Americans constituted 4.4% of the force, whereas in departments serving 2,500–9,999 residents, they made up just 0.4% of the force.

[3] To protect respondents' identities, pseudonyms have been assigned, and exact title and organizational affiliation has been fictionalized in some cases.

[4] The concept of theoretical saturation is not without its critics. For example, scholars have critiqued inconsistency in terms of both its conceptualization and application (e.g., see Dey, 1999; Bowen, 2008; O'Reilly and Parker, 2013; Nelson, 2016; Francis et al., 2010).

TABLE 1: DEMOGRAPHIC AND CAREER DATA OF RESPONDENTS

Respondent's Pseudonym	Racial/Ethnic Identification	Age	Education	Current Level of Law Enforcement	Current Organizational Affiliation	Current Position
Celia Chang	Chinese American	49	Bachelor's Degree	Federal	U.S. Dept. of the Treasury	Assistant Special Agent
Anna Easton	Korean American/ Caucasian	28	Bachelor's Degree	Local	City of Mapleton Police Department	Police Officer II
Aurora Lai	Chinese American	47	Bachelor's Degree	Federal	U.S. State Department	Senior Special Agent
Gwyneth Rapp	Japanese American/Korean American/Caucasian	54	Bachelor's Degree	Federal	Drug Enforcement Administration	Special Agent
Eliza West	Chinese American	26	High School	Local	City of Mapleton Police Department	Detective

Findings[5]

Central Themes: Entry, Challenges, and Perspectives on Black Lives Matter Movement

Entry

Entry into the field of law enforcement for each of my respondents was not a given; rather, a chance encounter when an opportunity caused them to "notice" the field for the first time as a viable option for them, career-wise. In college, Chinese American respondent Celia majored in accounting and business administration. As she puts it, "I've always been into...the numbers part of it." Upon graduation, she hoped to get a job with a public accounting firm, but given the competitive job market at the time, she wasn't able to find a position. So, she ended up applying to the U.S. Department of the Treasury, and got a job working on the civilian side of the organization. After about five years, she was restless—she found the work tedious. A colleague mentioned the assistant special agent position within the Department; Celia applied and was hired.

Similar to Celia, Chinese American respondent Aurora "stumbled" into law enforcement. While in college, she completed an internship working security for the U.S. State Department, which sparked her interest in federal security "on the ground." As she explains, this career path had not been on her radar prior to the internship:

> I had not had a previous interest in law enforcement. My original intention was to...get a PhD in defense and arms control studies and work in the Pentagon or for a defense contractor doing POL MIL—political military analysis.

For Chinese American respondent Eliza, a chance happening caused her to discover the field. During her senior year of high school, having finished requisite classes early, she had the opportunity to take classes at a local community college. Although she was excited to sign up for an art class, alas, she was told there was no availability. She shared the following:

Eliza: [The admissions counselor said], "Well, we don't have any availabilities in [art], BUT, if you want to take *this* class you can." And it turned out to be a criminal justice class.

Daisy: Oh, how funny.

Eliza: So, I was like, [exasperated sigh], "Fine, whatever." [laughs] Whatever will...work towards my college degree! [laughs]...So... I took it and...my professor...was awesome...She really opened my eyes to the career field...for her class, [we did a ride along]...The officer that I rode with had a huge impact on me...after that I was like, "Oh, hey, I wanna be a cop!" [laughs]

Korean American/Caucasian respondent Anna, who majored in psychology in college, initially wanted to pursue a career in child psychology, and was bound for graduate school in both her eyes, and those of her parents. However, her mother was an attorney, and she worked part-time in her mother's law office during college, which provided her initial exposure to law enforcement. After several ride-alongs with officers she met through work, she put her graduate school plans aside, and became committed to pursuing a career in law enforcement.

---

[5] In order to protect respondents' identities, some inconsequential details from their narratives have been changed.

Japanese American/Korean American/Caucasian respondent Gwyneth explains that since high school, she's had an interest in working in law enforcement. During her senior year of high school, she took part in an exploratory career program with a local police department, which solidified her interest. After high school, she initially applied for employment with another federal agency, but several local police officers she knew "hated the FBI" and thus put a word in for her at the Drug Enforcement Administration (DEA): "'Please call this woman because we would hate to see her go with the FBI.' That's how I got my initial contact, which eventually led to me going with them." Gwyneth recounts that she would never have been considered for initial employment with the DEA if she had identified as Asian during the hiring process. Because of the design of a demographic information form, she ended up marking "Caucasian": "If I had not [marked Caucasian] I would not have gotten my interview in Baltimore because the person up there didn't want to interview anyone who wasn't White."

Familial Misunderstanding, Resistance, and/or Shame

During the course of the interview, I asked each of my respondents what their family's reaction was to the news that they'd entered the field of law enforcement. Each one of my respondents was met with some combination of misunderstanding, resistance, and/or shame from some family members. For example, Celia tells me there wasn't much of a reaction, because, "To this day, I don't think my Mom knows what it is I actually do. We don't really talk about that kinda stuff…she doesn't really understand, she wasn't born and raised here…She just thinks I look at books and records and stuff." I ask Celia what her mother would say if friends and family were to ask what field she was in:

> **Celia:** Accounting.
>
> **Daisy:** So, she wouldn't say law enforcement, or criminal justice, or something like that?
>
> **Celia:** Nope.

Thus, the association with law enforcement that is at the very core of Celia's professional identity is not understood, or acknowledged, by her mother.

Aurora, who works in the field of federal security for the U.S. State Department, says that her parents "did not understand at all" her decision to enter the field. Right after college, Aurora worked in the private Information Technology (IT) sector for several years, earning "good money." Thus, her career move into law enforcement represented to her parents both a "step down" in terms of prestige, and a "step into" questionable territory. Having grown up in Taiwan during the period of martial law, her parents "did not have a very positive view of police or military." Aurora elaborates:

> [T]hey grew up in Taiwan…during the reign of the White Terror—police were disappearing people from their homes…[They] knew people who'd been disappeared by the police, so they had an inherent distrust of police and security.

Aurora tells me that even though she's worked in federal security for several decades now, her parents struggle to understand, or celebrate, her career successes, of which there have been many. Although her parents have come to see some of the value in the work she does (namely, given the rise in prestige for military post-9/11, and given the fact that her public sector job was secure during the Great Recession of 2007) they don't fully understand or appreciate her profession. This has caused stress for all involved:

> They still tell people that I worked in [the IT] field…for the first…seven or eight years that I was in the State Department, every single time I called them my parents would offer, "Do you want to go

to law school? We'll help you pay for law school!" …At one point they blamed themselves—they blamed each other for my failings…

In terms of Gwyneth's family's response to her career path, it's been mixed. Her mother, who is of Korean and Japanese descent, pushed back:

> My mother's [pushback] was cultural…law enforcement is not looked at…in some Asian cultures as being…a desirable position… [because of] corruption…she was embarrassed by me going in there…she didn't tell her family what I was doing.

If her mother could have dictated a career path for her, she would have "preferred…a doctor or a lawyer." On the other hand, her father, a white male raised in the United States, was supportive: "He was just happy, like he couldn't have been more supportive."

Eliza, who entered law enforcement before finishing her bachelor's degree, tells me that her parents' reaction to her career move was mixed as well: her father, a Caucasian, was happy, whereas her mother was not:

> My mom, she's like the stereotypical Asian tiger mom: "Why aren't you going to finish school first?" And after that… "What are the benefits like?" …In Asian cultures, *schoooool* is super important…Having a good job…becoming a doctor…every Asian stereotype you can think of…that's… what my mom like projected onto me.

Anna, whose parents expected her to go to graduate school or law school, initially kept her application to become a law enforcement officer a secret: "It was kinda the first time I did something without telling them." Her parents' perception of law enforcement was that it was dangerous, a "down in the mud, getting your hands dirty" type of job. Although they supported her decision, they were surprised by it, as most of her other family members are doctors, lawyers, and professors. Her mother, a "stereotypical tiger parent," had "real reservations" due to safety concerns and wished that she would enter a more prestigious line of work.

Challenges

Each of my respondents recounted numerous challenges they faced given their intersectional status as Asian American females working in the field of law enforcement. Challenges included dealing with the at once mundane and grueling nature of the job, dealing with racism and sexism in the workplace, and experiencing ageism for being a young law enforcement officer. Eliza highlighted several of these from the very start of my query about challenges:

> **Daisy:** [H]ave there been challenges that you have faced [in your career]?

> **Eliza:** Yes: Being a young, Asian, female…Sucks [laughs]…If you've ever been around cops, you know…it's still a very male-dominated career field…when females come in…they're judged harder. And they're judged even harder by their female peers.

> **Daisy:** …[S]o, being a young Asian female—so females judge you harder?

> **Eliza:** Yeah…You know…you've gotten where you're at because you're an Asian female…. And I check two boxes off the list [laughs].

While above, Eliza is referring to her experiences with colleagues, she tells me she has experienced primarily ageism and sexism from the public, whereas she downplays the role race has played with the public. Although above she cites her race/ethnicity as a central challenge, she goes on to claim that she's been "lucky," for she's never been "insulted for [her] race":

> **Eliza:** [I've experienced] stigma from…the public more so [because of] my age…but…I see that with…my other [young] counterparts…I've never felt like it was specifically towards me 'cause I'm an Asian person—an Asian officer.
>
> **Daisy:** Right. It hasn't been specifically tied to race/ethnicity. OK.
>
> **Eliza:** No, um…guys are like [mocking voice], "Oh, you don't have a dick, you won't understand," …it's…comments like that…
>
> **Daisy:** OK.
>
> **Eliza:** I've honestly *never* been insulted for my race before.
>
> **Daisy:** Interesting. Like…since entering law enforcement?
>
> **Eliza:** Yep.
>
> **Daisy:** Ok, what about before that?
>
> **Eliza:** No, never…I've been pretty, pretty lucky. [laughs]

In Eliza's telling, she first states that she *has* faced race-based stigma; she then goes on to characterize herself as "lucky" for *never* having faced race-based stigma. This muddiness associated with one's description of stigma faced due to intersecting, marginalized statuses, was something I heard from several of my respondents; the literature suggests that within-interview contradictions "express individual ambivalences and indicate indecision" (Witzel & Reiter, 2012). Moreover, although racial/ethnic identity is something that is often discussed in "black and white" terms, the social science literature indicates that racial/ethnic identity is highly nuanced, including feelings of ambiguity and ambivalence (Harpalani, 2009; Ball, 2019).

When I asked Anna about challenges she's faced in the field, she tells me that she has faced numerous comments from male colleagues that question her "fit" in law enforcement: "Oh, you seem so smart… honor roll…why do you wanna work down in the mud with us?"; "You do a great job, but to be honest, if I was your size, I wouldn't want to do this job. What makes you wanna do it?" During academy, a White male applicant who was let go early in the process suggested in a group chat that Anna had only made it through because she was a minority female: "He [suggested] that me being a female minority officer… [was more] desirable demographically than he was as a white male…if you're a female officer, you're [perceived as] more desirable for the department, and you might get promoted faster."

> Anna tells me that she's also faced racism from the public:
>
> I've been called everything from a "chink-eyed bitch" to this one lady, who I was arresting for an assault…as she was going to jail, she was like "Oh, I bet you love…pork fried rice!" "We won the Vietnam War!" …It was just the most random barrage of like, Asian-centric insults.

Related, a central challenge raised by Celia surrounds respect, or lack thereof. While she's not certain that the lack of respect she's faced is due to her race/ethnicity, she's confident her gender has something to do with it: "You know, being a female—I don't know if being...Asian helps—...being a female to some of [my colleagues] ...that's been a big challenge." I ask Celia to clarify—being female is a challenge, but being Asian is an *asset*? She responds, but does not clarify; instead, she says that people can't be outwardly racist. She goes on to say that people also can't be outwardly sexist—sexist sentiments are there, but not explicitly. People "can't" say "Women shouldn't be in law enforcement," although she tells me that every now and then, they *have* said this to her. Added to this is the fact that some of the treatment she received in the past stemmed from ageism associated with her youth. Our conversation illustrates, again, the muddiness of the intersectional statuses my respondents hold—teasing apart what was said to them, by whom, and why, is labor-intensive, and there's not always a satisfying answer, or explanation, at the end.

When I ask Gwyneth about challenging experiences in the field, the first challenge she mentions is logistical: the work is taxing and time-consuming. For example, one year, during the pinnacle of her career, she was on the road 41 out of 52 weeks. Similar to other respondents, Gwyneth speaks about challenges related to race/ethnicity and gender. While both have presented a challenge, being female has been the bigger obstacle:

> [M]ore often it's [being] female [that presents a challenge] ...people...get punished for being a racist, [but] they don't get punished for being a sexist. Every day, people make comments that are inappropriate [regarding] women...Even just saying...to a bunch of guys, "Hey, ladies!"...I mean, would you say, "Hey, Asian people!"?...Every time I went to [training] I was the only woman...then [someone would say]..."Uh gentlemen, and lady"...I'd have to take them aside and say, "Please don't single me out"...as long as you don't drop the "C-word" we are good.

Nonetheless, Gwyneth acknowledges that her racial/ethnic status has resulted in numerous problematic occurrences, but insists, "...I always try to give people the benefit of the doubt first...unless [the racism] was blatant." I ask her to elaborate, and she shares this story:

> **Gwyneth:** In Pittsburgh...back when...we had the car-to-car radios...The agent [on the radio] was...trying to get through to me and... he called me a fucking gook on the [radio]. There were like six or seven agents that heard that and they were really upset...I *thought* I heard it but I was busy doing my thing...When they all got back to the customs house, several of the older guys came up to me...they didn't like him anyways...they were like, "You need to do something about him, like, end his career."

> **Daisy:** So...what happened to him?

> **Gwyneth:** Oh, I decked him! [exuberant laughter]...I said, "You hate me that much?...I just gave you a reason to take a swing at me, and if you don't...."...Well, I won't repeat what I said to him, but I said, "Look, you don't have to like me, but there are eight guys up there that want me to end your job and I probably should, but I'm not going to"...[N]ow me and him get along fine.

To Gwyneth, perhaps the most baffling aspect regarding racist and sexist remarks is the willingness of people to make such comments in front of her. As she puts it, "What the hell do you say when I'm NOT around?!" This includes misperceptions on the part of both the public and her colleagues, due to her race/ethnicity and gender. For example, she tells me she's had many "Mister Tibbs moments"[6]:

---

[6] "They call me Mister Tibbs": Refers to a scene in the film *In the Heat of the Night* (1967), in which character Virgil Tibbs (Sidney Poitier), a black police detective from Philadelphia, reprimands the chief of a small-town police department in rural Mississippi who refers to him, disrespectfully, by his first name.

I go to park in my government car—a little sports car or something—and I'll have a little guy roll up next to me and scream, "Can't you fucking read, this is police parking?!" ... I'm like, "Yeah, we come in all sexes and colors now...have a nice day!" [laughter]. That one day in D.C., I parked the car...went in...turns out that guy was a detective in the unit where I was going... [a colleague] went to introduce [us] and I said, "Oh, we met, he was helping me park." I could handle that with humor [laughter].

While her race/ethnicity and gender have presented obstacles for her on the job, Gwyneth asserts they have often proved advantageous when dealing with the public. During the early stages of her career, she worked in a city that was intensely segregated along White/Black lines, and in which there was "a lot of racial tension." She says she did very well working in this environment primarily *because* of her race/ethnicity and gender:

[I] can traverse into both sides...Whites looked at me like, "At least she's not Black," and...Blacks... like, "At least she's not White"...Color *does* matter...[you] cannot remove that [no matter] what side of the uniform you are on...A lot of the time I was more effective being with the non-White male because they were used to having a woman at the head of their household...a stronger woman...

Similar to Gwyneth, Aurora mentions the nature of the job when I ask her about the challenges she's faced, namely the "mundanity" of the work. She also cites challenges posed by her intersectional status: "So [racism and sexism were] a problem for everyone [at work] who was female and everyone who was not White. But because I was an Asian American female and the first one, I was particularly disliked. It wasn't really a great environment to be in."

Aurora experienced racism and sexism from the get-go, during training for her first post in federal security. She was one of four women (one Caucasian, one African American, and one Hispanic) in her cohort, which was (relatively speaking) a high number of women:

We were all harassed but I...got the worst of it...[T]he harassment... rapidly increased and became so problematic that a male student [in the cohort] reported it back to our office of professional responsibility...there was an investigation...I was getting threats... "watch your back" and that sort of thing.

Several male classmates took her aside and explained that not all the harassers were "bad people"; rather, they were "following the crowd." One classmate explained: "They're so upset with you...because you're female and...Asian and it really clashes with their view of what law enforcement is...[I]t's a blow to their testosterone." I asked Aurora why the intersection of her race/ethnicity and gender identities caused the situation to become particularly dire. She offered several reasons: 1) The other non-White women in her cohort had already developed strategies for handling racism and sexism, whereas she had not; 2) her female colleagues were so busy protecting themselves, they had little time to support or mentor her:

...The Hispanic woman...gave as good as she got...very verbally sassy. The African American woman did the angry Black woman thing...Her attitude helped her create an armor whereas I was not...verbally assertive in responding. I had no sense there was anyone there to help me or to tell me what to do....

A final race and gender-related challenge raised by Aurora concerns promotion: when she did not receive a promotion and post that she coveted, she learned that the person in charge of hiring had said: "She's a woman. She's going to get married and have babies and then she'll just leave..." Aurora also cites stereotypes associated with the "model minority" label as a reason she has not been promoted as she deserves:

"Being perceived as an Asian American female—not a gunslinger—more of an intellectual person—will slow down promotion into the more senior ranks."

Perspectives on Black Lives Matter Movement

The current project is part of a larger endeavor to learn about Asian Americans' experiences in law enforcement in the era of the Black Lives Matter movement. Thus, near the end of each interview, I asked my respondents their perceptions of, and experiences with, this movement. In my conversation with Gwyneth about Black Lives Matter, she offers the following commentary:

> …[T]here is a lot of anger pent up behind…Black Lives Matter…it puts people on the defensive… you have cops saying Blue Lives Matter and…people saying All Lives Matter…if you are going to [say] Black Lives Matter, you should be accepting and say All Lives Matter too…but they won't do that….[Q]uite frankly, if you don't want to lose people, then as a community you also need to make sure that your people behave in a certain way.

When I ask Gwyneth if she has been personally affected by the Black Lives Matter movement, and/or if it has changed the nature of her work, she seems unconcerned: "I haven't really had…much negative [outcome from the movement]…[interestingly] more people ask me… 'Oh my God… isn't that a hard job to do?'… 'Aren't you worried that you are going to be a target?'"

When I first ask Anna about her perceptions of Black Lives Matter, she responds with a heavy sigh. While she acknowledges that members of the movement have a "valid" cause, she goes on to characterize them as domestic terrorists:

> [sigh]…[T]hey have a valid cause…[but] just because the cause is justified doesn't mean the means are…justified…once you get to the point where you're burning police cars, civilian cars…you… undermine your own cause…you're making yourself look more like a domestic terrorism group than…peaceful, organized protesters…That's kinda frustrating because…after a shooting, even [a shooting] across the country, [people] will come at you on calls and be like, "I have my hands up, don't shoot!"

During our conversation, Anna is one of several respondents to espouse the "rotten apple" theory of police misconduct (Menifield, Shin & Strother, 2018; Haider-Markel & Joslyn, 2017; Mummolo, 2018): "In my mind, it's like a few bad police officers…in any profession, you get—doctors that get malpractice suits, teachers in high school who are sleeping with their students…police officers that [use] excessive force that shoot people and they're not justified…" As Anna puts it, people pay attention to police use of force to the exclusion of "all the days that…officers across the country are doing their jobs, and there are no shootings…"

When I ask Eliza about her perceptions of Black Lives Matter, she, too, is critical of the movement's approach and puts forth the "bad apple" theory noted above:

> …To me, the whole Black Lives Matter thing…I get it, to a certain extent…there are going to be racist cops out there. There are going to be bad apples who do immoral, unethical things. And, unfortunately…those things come to light and get blasted on media…subsequently…people get ahold of that information and they're angry…Granted…the matter in which they try to protest or convey themselves comes across poorly…[which] causes more tension between officers and protestors…

Eliza speaks about the mission of the Black Lives Matter, to support members of a variety of oppressed groups; she comments that support of people beyond the African American community is "missing" from the conversation: "I mean, it's *Black* Lives Matter…that's pretty specific…I can't think of a time… recently where…an Asian was advocated for…it seems like all the people here recently have been African American." When I ask Eliza if her job has been impacted by the Black Lives Matter movement, she says that it has, undeniably. As an example, and as noted by other respondents, she cites the increased tendency for black suspects to put their hands up, yelling "Don't shoot!" when coming into contact with law enforcement. She says since the onset of Black Lives Matter,

> People do that stupid shit all the time. Quite frankly, I ignore it…I don't care if you're White, Black, Asian, Indian, Hispanic—if you're mouthing off to me, I'm gonna tell you to shut the fuck up and sit down…You can slur whatever racial stuff that you want to at my career or you can do the whole "hands up, don't shoot" thing but…that doesn't faze me at all, at all.

When I ask Celia about the movement, she explains that given the nature of her position (she's not out in the community like local police are), she doesn't think Black Lives Matter has impacted her. I ask if she simply has an opinion on the movement; she tells me she does not. However, we circle back to the topic later in the conversation, and she makes the following comment, referencing the "rotten apples" theory of policing, among other things:

> I think a lot of times people use race as an excuse to deter from what actually took place…I'm not saying that…as law enforcement officers we are always right…it's tough, it's rough out there, on the streets, you know, the local cops, what they do day-to-day…part of our job as law enforcement officers is to enforce the law…and you know, I know there's bad cops out there, and there's good cops out there.

Of all of my respondents, only one, Aurora, tells me that she supports the Black Lives Matter movement. Although she claims no impact from it, she characterizes the controversy between communities of color and law enforcement as "regrettable." She goes on to state:

> I don't really understand why people just can't get along. If people could spend even half the amount of time being spent on race issues doing something more productive…this issue would resolve itself to a certain degree…

Of note, when Aurora and I discuss the mission of the movement (i.e., to give voice to marginalized populations, including various racial/ethnic minorities), she tells me she's surprised to learn that the mission refers to more than just the plight of African Americans. In her mind, contrary to the bulk of

TABLE 2: FINDINGS BY RESPONDENT

Respondent's Pseudonym	Reports Familial Misunderstanding/ Resistance/ Shame	Reports Racism	Reports Sexism	Supports BLM Movement
Celia Chang	Y	N/A	Y	N
Anna Easton	Y	Y	Y	N
Aurora Lai	Y	Y	Y	Y
Gwyneth Rapp	Y	Y	Y	N
Eliza West	Y	Y	Y	N

literature in Asian American studies, and contrary to her own race-related struggles outlined earlier in this chapter, Asian Americans are not a marginalized group:

> …I had no idea it was supposed to cover beyond Black…My feeling is that Asians are not perceived to be a marginalized group so even if Black Lives Matter [was] supposed to include all marginalized groups, I don't think it would include Asians because we are not typically perceived by either Blacks or Whites to be marginalized.

Discussion/Conclusion

Several noteworthy themes emerged in the course of my in-depth interviews with Asian American females working in the field of law enforcement in the era of the Black Lives Matter movement. See Table 2, below, for a breakdown of findings by respondent.

For each of my respondents, law enforcement was a career path they happened upon or fell into without much forethought. In Anna's case, a part-time job in her mother's law office caused her to rethink her plans to attend graduate school, whereas in Eliza's case, the unavailability of an art course at her local community college caused her to sign up for a criminal justice course, and the rest is history.

Each of my respondents faced some combination of misunderstanding, resistance, and/or shame from family members when they shared news of their career in law enforcement. In several cases, parents simply did not understand the nature of the work, and the consensus between parent and child seemed to be an unspoken "understanding to not understand." In two cases, parents indicated to family and friends that their child worked in a field *other* than law enforcement: for example, Celia's mother tells people she works in accounting, which is not accurate. In Aurora's case, her parents continue to mention her previous work in IT, at the exclusion of her current career in law enforcement. In the case of four of my five respondents, parents expressed explicit displeasure about their career choice, citing safety concerns, distrust of the police, and lack of prestige associated with the profession. Each one of my respondents espoused elements of the model minority stereotype in their discussion of parental expectations of them; for example, parents expected them to go to graduate school, or to law school, rather than enter the "lowly" field of law enforcement.

The central challenges faced by respondents stemmed from the intersection of two statuses they held associated with oppressed groups: Asian American and female. Four of my five respondents cited their racial/ethnic identification as posing a central challenge to them; all of my respondents cited their gender as posing a central challenge to them. The intersection of these two statuses compounded these challenges, as each respondent worked in a field that has been historically dominated by White males and continues to host a hyper-masculine climate. Each one of my respondents told stories of having been silenced, oppressed, challenged, and/or misunderstood by colleagues because of their racial/ethnic and/or gender identification.

In the course of each interview, I asked respondents to discuss their perceptions of the Black Lives Matter movement. Four of five respondents were not supportive of this movement; the fifth respondent, who did state she supported the movement, did not express particularly strong feelings about, or knowledge of, the movement. Three of my respondents stated that they had been personally impacted by the movement, for example, encountering suspects who react to them with some version of, "My hands are up! Don't shoot!" Three respondents espoused the "rotten apple" theory of police misconduct, stating that there are "bad apples" in any profession, and the public's attention to the "bad apples" in law enforcement was unjust. This runs counter to much of the criminal justice literature, which has reached an understanding in recent years that the "rotten apple" theory is at best a misunderstanding on part of the public (Menifield, Shin & Strother, 2018), and more precisely, a myth (Tator & Henry, 2006; Haider-Markel & Joslyn, 2017; Mummolo, 2018).

In sum, the current project sheds new light on Asian American females' experiences in the field of law enforcement during the era of Black Lives Matter. It adds to the literature in both Asian American studies and criminal justice by illustrating how the challenges associated with the intersection of membership in two distinctly marginalized groups are further compounded in the context of the male-dominated field of law enforcement.

That said, the current project brings with it significant limitations. The central limitation is sample size: as the project is ongoing, and as the study population is not easily accessible, the sample remains small, and thus my findings are not generalizable across the greater population of Asian American females in law enforcement. To be clear, in this project, I employ an ethnographic approach, which dictates the study of relatively small groups of people (Gray et al., 2007, p. 181). A strength of the ethnographic approach is its ability to produce rich and nuanced findings, whereas a weakness is lack of representativeness. The current project is also limited given the demographic profile of respondents (only certain categories within "Asian American" are represented), and the professional profile of respondents (only local and federal law enforcement agents are represented). Future work should attend to these and other limitations.

Key Terms:

Criminal Justice   **Asian American Studies**   **Black Lives Matter Movement**

Discussion Questions:

1. Briefly discuss the Black Lives Matter movement, including its history, mission, and implications.

2. Briefly discuss the model minority stereotype. What does this stereotype suggest? How does this stereotype impact the people to whom it is applied?

3. Discuss the methodological design of the current project, including its strengths and weaknesses.

4. How did respondents' identification as both Asian American and female, present challenges to them, given their line of work?

5. What were respondents' impressions of the Black Lives Matter movement, and why do you think they felt this way about the movement?

References

Assalone, A. E. & Fann, A. (2017). Understanding the influence of model minority stereotypes on Asian American community college students, *Community College Journal of Research and Practice*, 41(7), 422–435, doi: 10.1080/10668926.2016.1195305

Archbold, C. & Schulz, D. M. (2012). "Research on Women in Policing: A Look at the Past, Present, and Future," *Sociology Compass* 6(9): 694–706.

Ball, D. (2019). "America's 'Whiz Kids'? Ambivalence and the Model Minority Stereotype." *Sociological Spectrum* 39(2): 116–130.

Barry, D., Kovaleski, S. F., Robertson, C. & Alvarez, L. (2012). "Race, Tragedy, and Outrage Collide After a Shot in Florida." *The New York Times* (April 1).

Bonacich, E. (1973). "A Theory of Middleman Minorities." *American Sociological Review* 38: 583–594.

Chan, Janet, Doran, S. & Marel, C. (2010). "Doing and Undoing Gender in Policing," *Theoretical Criminology* 14: 425.

Charles, M.T. (1982). Women in policing: The physical aspect, *Journal of Police Science and Administration* 10(2): 194–205.

Chase, G. (2018). "The Early History of the Black Lives Matter Movement, and the Implications Thereof," *Nevada Law Journal* 18: 1091–1112.

Crenshaw, K. (1989). "Demarginalizing the Intersection of Race and Sex: A Black Feminist Critique of Antidiscrimination Doctrine, Feminist Theory and Antiracist Politics," *University of Chicago Legal Forum* 1(8): 139–167.

Franklin, C. 2007. Male peer support and the police culture, *Women & Criminal Justice* 16(3): 1–25, doi: 10.1300/J012v16n03_01

Gray, P. S., Williamson, J. B., Karp, D. A. & Dalphin, J. R. (2007). *The Research Imagination: An Introduction to Qualitative and Quantitative Methods*. New York: Cambridge University Press

Haider, D. P. & Joslyn, M. R. (2017). "Bad apples? Attributions for police treatment of African Americans." *Analyses of Social Issues and Public Policy* 17(1): 358–378.

Harpalani, V. (2009) Ambiguity, ambivalence, and awakening: A south Asian becoming 'critically' aware of race in America." *Berkeley Journal of African-American Law & Policy* 71 (2009); Chicago-Kent College of Law Research Paper. Available at SSRN: https://ssrn.com/abstract=2183234

Hartlep, N. D. (2013). *The model minority stereotype: Demystifying Asian American success*. Charlotte, NC: Information Age.

Kang, J. C. 2016. "How Should Asian-Americans Feel About the Peter Liang Protests?" *The New York Times* (February 23).

Kiang, L., Huynh, V.W., Cheah, C.S.L., Wang, Y. & Yoshikawa, H. (2017). Moving beyond the model minority," *Asian American Journal of Psychology* 8(1): 1–6.

Lee, S. (1994). Behind the Model-Minority Stereotype: Voices of High- and Low-Achieving Asian American Students. *Anthropology & Education Quarterly, 25*(4), 413–429. Retrieved from: http://www.jstor.org/stable/3195858

Lee, S. (2009). *Unraveling the "Model Minority" Stereotype: Listening to Asian American Youth.* New York, NY: Teachers College Press.

Martin, S. E. (2006). "The Effectiveness of Affirmative Action: The Case of Women in Policing," *Justice Quarterly* 8(4): 489–504.

Martin, S. E. & Jurik, N. C. (2006). *Doing Justice, Doing Gender.* Los Angeles, CA: Sage Publications.

Menifield, C. E., Shin, G. & Strother, L. (2018). "Do White Law Enforcement Officers Target Minority Suspects?" *Public Administration Review* 79(1): 56–68.

Mukkamala, S. & Suyemoto, K. L. (2018). Racialized sexism/sexualized racism: A multimethod study of intersectional experiences of discrimination for Asian American women. *Asian American Journal of Psychology, 9*(1), 32–46. http://dx.doi.org/10.1037/aap0000104

Mummolo, J. (2018). Modern police tactics, police-citizen interactions, and prospects for reform. *Journal of Politics* 80(1): 1–15.

Ng, J. C., Lee, S. S. & Pak, Y. K. (2007). Contesting the model minority and perpetual foreigner stereotypes: A critical review of literature on Asian Americans in education. *Review of Research in Higher Education,* 31, 95–130. doi:10.3102/00917 32X07300046095

Nir, S. M. (2016). "Officer Peter Liang Convicted in Fatal Shooting of Akai Gurley in Brooklyn," *The New York Times* (February 11).

Reaves, B. (2015). "Local Police Departments, 2013: Personnel, Policies, and Practices." *Bureau of Justice Statistics,* https://www.bjs.gov/content/pub/pdf/lpd13ppp.pdf

Silvestri, M. (2007). "'Doing' Police Leadership: Enter the 'New Smart Macho', " *Policing and Society* 17(1): 38–58.

Tator, C. & Henry, F. (2006). *Racial Profiling in Canada: Challenging the Myth of "A Few Bad 'Apples."* Toronto: University of Toronto Press.

Tometi, O. & Lenoir, G. (2015). "Black Lives Matter Is Not a Civil Rights Movement," *Time Magazine* (December 15).

Tuan, M. (1998). *Forever Foreigners or Honorary Whites? The Asian Ethnic Experience Today.* Rutgers: Rutgers University Press.

Yi, V. & Museus, S. (2015). "Model Minority Myth," in *The Wiley Blackwell Encyclopedia of Race, Ethnicity, and Nationalism,* Stone et al., eds. Hoboken, NJ: Wiley.

Zakeri, B. (2015). "A Double-Edged Sword: Side Effects of the Model Minority Stereotype on Asian immigrants in the U.S." In *Modern Societal Impacts of the Model Minority Stereotype,* Nicholas Hartlep, ed. Hershey, PA: IGI, pgs. 231–258.

CHAPTER 3

Female Police Officers and the Use of Force: Understanding When and How Much

Roddrick Colvin, Ph.D. | *San Diego State University*

Introduction

Even before the emergence of viral videos of officers using various force strategies to gain individual compliance, the use of force by police officers has been one of the most common areas of recent research across a number of fields, including criminal justice, psychology, law, public policy, and philosophy (Klahm, Frank, & Liederbach, 2014). As Legewie (2016) noted, law enforcement personnel are the only public servants authorized to use physical coercion to gain compliance from members of the community. With such state authority granted, we must be diligent in our oversight to ensure its appropriate application (Terrill, 2014). Thus, various scholars have studied the use of force, and applied discipline-specific understanding to this topic (Barkan & Cohn, 1998; Dick, 2005; Klahm & Tillyer, 2010; Lawton, 2007; McEwen, 1996; Ochs, 2011; Skolnick and Fyfe, 1993; Williams & Hester, 2003).

Chapter Outcomes

By the end this chapter students will:

- Understand why the use of force is challenging to study
- Understand how officer personal characteristics can affect when they use force during an incident
- Understand how male and female officers apply force differently
- Understand what female officers think about the use of force

Although there has been continued interests and research efforts about the use of force, there is no single, universally agreed-upon definition of the concept. The International Association of Chiefs of Police have described the use of force as the "amount of effort required by police to compel compliance by an unwilling subject" (2001, p.1). In addition to the lack of a universal definition, there is no agreement on the proper "amount of effort" required by police in any given situation. Although all police agencies in the United States have policies and provide training and guidance on the use of force, the complex nature of law enforcement and variability that occurs with each police community-member encounter make consistent or universal policies, guidance, and training difficult to establish. Because of this, most police agencies use a continuum model for guiding officers in the application of force. This model describes an escalating series of actions an officer may take to resolve a situation. The continuum generally has several levels, and officers are instructed to respond at "a level of force appropriate to the situation at hand, acknowledging that the officer may move from one part of the continuum to another in a matter of seconds" (National Institute of Justice [NIJ], 2019, p.5). Generally, the continuum often includes measures such as officer presence where no force is used, to lethal force where a weapon may be used to gain control of the situation (NIJ, 2019).

This research focuses on officers' personal characteristics (specifically gender), and their understanding of the use of force based on their personal experience, training, and the policies of their agencies. While officers' personal characteristics such as gender, race, age, and education will vary, such characteristics may help to explain the decision to use force, and the amount of force applied. Using nine distinct police scenarios, this research investigates police officers' gender and their decision to use force, in terms of when and at what amount. Police officers from a single department in upstate New York were presented with common encounters that occur under routine policing circumstances and asked their views on the use of force based on their personal experience and department training. In deciding whether to use force, women were more likely than men to decide not to use force. In situations where officers did decide to apply force (verbal persuasion to deadly), men started with lower levels of force. The results suggest that women may be less likely to resort to force, equal in their application of it, but more likely to initial at a higher level than men. It also suggests that officers in this department appear to have a shared understanding of the application of force appropriate to their agency's policies and training.

Literature Review

As several recent scholars have noted, variations among empirical studies—including data-gathering methodologies, study populations, geography, and research questions and hypotheses—explain some of the variation in results about the use of force by police officers (Smith, Kaminsky, Alpert, Fridell, Mac-Donald & Kubu, 2009). Others have noted changes in the field policing—including officer training—as well as conceptual and technological advances as contributors to the variations in research results (Lim & Lee, 2015; Terrill, Leinfelt, & Kwak, 2008). The lack of national standardized data has undoubtedly hindered the exploration of the use of force in a more concerted effort (Shane, 2016). Alpert and Dunham argued that "since the use of force and excessive force can be defined or measured in a variety of ways, it is impossible for researchers to state definitively the frequency with which the police use force justifiably or to excess" (Alpert and Dunham, 2010, p. 20).

Gender of the Police Officer

As more female officers have entered into law enforcement, studies have included gender as a possible distinguishing personal characteristic. Several studies have found little or no difference based on gender (Brandl & Stroshine, 2013; Dejong, 2005; Hoffman & Hickey, 2005; Paoline & Terrill, 2004). Paoline & Terrill (2005) found that women were no more or less likely to use force than men. Hoffman and Hickey (2005) found similar results. Their study of single department data from 1993 to 1999 found no statistical difference between men and women in the overall use of force. Schuck and Rabe-Hemp (2007) considered the use of violence against female officers. Reviewing nearly 65,000 arrests data from several different metropolitan areas, their work highlighted the importance of the situation in which officers find themselves, and its effect on the level force. They found that

© Carl ballou/Shutterstock.com

female officers were at higher risk of being assaulted in family conflict situations (2007). Furthermore, the results suggested that female officers were at the highest risk of being assaulted in family conflict situations when the community individual was under the influence of drugs or alcohol (2007). The authors posit that any variations in the use of force can be attributed to—in part—due to officers' responses this gender-based officer violence.

These studies differ significantly from other studies that found variation between men and women. Bazley et al. (2007) similarly considered the situation—in this case resistance from the suspect—to explore if there were variations by the gender of the police officer. Their examination of use of force reports showed that level of resistance to arrest was not related to the gender of the officers, but that female officers use a narrower range of force and are thus less likely to use lethal force (2007). McElvain and Kposowa (2008) echoed this sentiment in their research, which found that men were more likely to use deadly force than women. Finally, Lonsway, Wood, Fickling, De Leon, Moore, Harrington & Spillar (2002) summarized the literature on the use of excessive force and both civil liability cases (e.g., "police brutality" civil lawsuits) and citizen complaints about force in the United States. Compared with female officers, male officers were significantly more likely to have the excessive force complaints against them sustained.

Overall, the research—while varying in results—shows that there is still essential exploration about the subject that could help to explain if and how male and female officers decide to use force. Given the number of factors and the various situations that present themselves, it seems logical to assume that no single unified model will explain conclusively how and why officers react the way they do. From this perspective, additional analyses of various personal characteristics and situational factors may not settle the debates on force but will help to build our expanding knowledge about each factor.

Methodology

In order to understand the decision to use force, and what amount to be applied, police officers in this study were presented with nine common police community-member scenarios. Each scenario explained a situation where force may or may not be applicable. Officers were asked not to assume any facts that were not presented in the scenario.[1] The scenario approach was advanced by Phillips (2009), and Phillips and Sobol (2012). While Phillips (2009) focused on the characteristics of the suspects, this work applies the same approach to officers and their characteristics. Similar to Phillips (2009), and Phillips and Sobol (2012), these scenarios were developed in conjunction with law enforcement officials, and thus can be considered valid in their representation as realistic cases for officers to consider.

As the International Association of Police Chiefs (2019) noted, context matters, and police officers use any number of factors as they assess a situation. To minimize individual officer bias, each scenario was contextualized with basic information about the scene, including the time of day and temperature, height, weight, gender, strength, appearance, and build of the community-members involved in the incident, and if the community-member involved or location was known by the officer. The contextual information was provided in such a way as to convey to the officers that the scenarios provided should be considered at their face value, and that they should consider the incident as routine in every way possible.

After each scenario, officers were reminded of the continuum of force used by their department, and the definitions ascribed to each measure of force. If the officer believed that force *would* be applicable in the given scenario, the officer was then asked at what level she or he would apply it. If the officer believed that she or he would *not* have applied a level of force listed or had an alternative approach to gaining

---

[1] See Appendix A for each scenario and context

compliance, no level of force follow-up question was asked. This approach is similar to the approaches used by Barrett, Haberfeld & Walker (2009), and Smith, Kaminsky, Alpert, Fridell, MacDonald & Kubu (2009).

Police Department and Location

Police officers from a single police department in upstate New York participated in this study. Table 1 provides general details about the department and the community. At the time of the survey, the department had 152 sworn officers, plus 60 additional staff members, including school crossing guards, and community service officers. Given the nature of the study, only sworn officers were surveyed. The department was certified as an accredited agency by the New York State Law Enforcement Accreditation Council in 1993 (Accreditation Council, 2018).[2] In addition to calls for service and routine patrol, the department practices community-oriented policing through the Police and Community Together (PACT) program (NIJ, 2019).

© Keith Homan/Shutterstock.com

The community served by this department has a population under 100,000. It has an average household income of just over $73,000. The community is 64% White. The crime rate in 2016 was 18.11 per 100, which ranks this community in the top 25th percentile in terms of

TABLE 1: ABOUT THE NORTHEASTERN CITY AND THE DEPARTMENT

Demographics of the northeastern city		
	Population served	~80,000
	Race: White	46%
	Race: Hispanic	28%
	Race: Black or African American	18%
	Race: Other	~10%
	Crime rate (1000 in 2016)	18.11
	Median household income (2016 U.S. Census)	$73,187.00
Demographics of the northeastern city's police department		
	Number of sworn officers	152
	Race: White	75%
	Race: Black or African American	10%
	Race: Hispanic	13%
	Race: Other	<1%
	Sex: Women	9%

Population and Housing Unit Estimates Data (2020). The United States Census Bureau. Retrieved 3 February 2020, from https://www.census.gov/programs-surveys/popest/data.html, (2020). Police Employee Data. (2020). FBI. Retrieved 3 February 2020, from https://ucr.fbi.gov/crime-in-the-u.s/2016/crime-in-the-u.s.-2016/topic-pages/police-employees

---

[2] Accredited departments agree to meet particular benchmarks. In the case of force, it is a minimum of 11 hours of training as part of basic training for cadets.

Civilian complaints 2007–2015	2007	2008	2009	2010	2011	2012	2013	2014	2015
Force	4	6	6	2	2	1	2	1	2
Abuse of authority	10	14	16	9	10	4	6	8	6
Discourtesy	14	15	20	8	5	9	7	4	7
Ethnic slur	0	0	0	1	0	0	0	0	0
Miscellaneous	9	2	5	6	5	2	5	5	5
Totals	37	37	47	26	22	16	20	18	20

NYS Division of Criminal Justice Services. (2020). NYS Crime Reporting. [online] Available at: https://www.criminaljustice.ny.gov/crimnet/ojsa/crimereporting/ [Accessed 3 Feb. 2020].

safety (US Department of Justice, FBI, 2016). Table 2 provides an overview of internal and external complaints filed against police employees.

In the spring of 2016, the survey was administered to the department. The survey was made available at the front desk of the main office, and police officers were reminded—at roll call—four times over the course of a three-week period about the survey and its purpose. After three weeks, the department returned the completed surveys and consent forms. In total, 93 sworn officers of the 152 completed the survey and were included for analysis. This is a response rate of 61%.

Variables and Measures

The dependent variable in this study is the decision of officers to use force in each of the nine scenarios. The independent variable is the gender of the police officer. In the second analysis, the level of initial force is the dependent variable, and gender remains the independent variable. Basic descriptive statistics were calculated to determine levels of agreement among the survey responding police officers. In line with the literature on personal characteristics, this analysis assumes that gender—in conjunction with organizational, situational, and other factors—affects officers' perceptions and understanding of the use of force.

© John Roman Images/Shutterstock.com

Results

Table 3 shows the descriptive information about the 93 police officer respondents. Approximately 70% of the respondents were White, with the remaining 30% identified as ethnic or racial minorities. The average age was 40.5 years old. Ten percent of the respondents were women. A near majority (46.1%) of respondents have community college degrees, with an additional 27% possessing a bachelor's degree or higher. A supermajority of the officers are married (71.6%), with 10% being divorced.

TABLE 3: ABOUT THE SURVEY RESPONDING POLICE OFFICERS

	Number	Percent
Race		
White	65	69.9
Black / African American	12	12.9
Latino	6	6.5
Native Indian or Alaska Native	3	3.2
Asian	1	1.1
Other	3	3.2
Average age	40.55	
Female respondents	9	9.7
Education		
High school/GED	24	27
Community college	41	46.1
Undergraduate	19	21.3
Graduate	5	5.6
Relationship status		
Single	5	5.7
Divorced	9	10.2
Married	63	71.6
Relationship—not married	9	10.2
Other	2	2.3

Retrieved 3 February 2020, from https://ucr.fbi.gov/crime-in-the-u.s/2016/crime-in-the-u.s.-2016/topic-pages/police-employees

Table 4 shows the decision to use force by gender for each scenario. While officers agreed on whether or not to use force, women were less likely to decide to use force in eight of the nine situations. However, in only two of those eight situations, was the difference significant.[3] This occurred in scenario one where 59.4% of female officers versus 41% of male officers opted not to use force. In scenario five, 6.3% of female versus 1.8% of male officers opted not to use force. In one scenario (#9) were men less likely to use force than women. In that scenario, 8.9% of male officer versus 3.1% of female officers opted out of force.

Table 5 highlights the amount of force thought to be appropriate for each scenario. From "unarmed physical or body force" to "deadly force," officers had high levels of agreement on the initial level of force to be applied, however, male officers consistently applied *lower* levels of force than female officers. In six of the nine scenarios, the lower application of force by men was significant. In scenario one, three, four and five, the majority of male officers chose 'unarmed physical or body force' at a higher rate than female officers—who were spread among higher levels of force. In two cases (#8 and #9), male officers chose chemical agents at higher rates than female officers who were, again, spread over higher levels of force. In all three scenarios where, deadly force was selected (#5, #8, and #9), female officers selected it at higher rates than male officers.

---

[3] The threshold for both the decision to use force and the amount of force to be applied was 5%.

		No Physical Force	Physical Force
Scenario #1			
	Women	59	41
	Men	41	59
Scenario #2			
	Women	31	69
	Men	30	70
Scenario #3			
	Women	3	97
	Men	3	97
Scenario #4			
	Women	28	72
	Men	27	73
Scenario #5			
	Women	6	94
	Men	2	98
Scenario #6			
	Women	100	0
	Men	98	2
Scenario #7			
	Women	100	0
	Men	98	2
Scenario #8			
	Women	3	97
	Men	0	100
Scenario #9			
	Women	3	97
	Men	9	91

Retrieved 3 February 2020, from https://ucr.fbi.gov/crime-in-the-u.s/2016/crime-in-the-u.s.-2016/topic-pages/police-employees

What Female Officers Say About Force

Like most police forces across the United States, female officers do not constitute a large percentage of this force. Nationally, forces average about 12.5% female (U.S. Department of Justice, 2019). To augment the scenario data, qualitative data about female officers' views on the use of force and gender was also collected. The comments of female officers hew closely to the aggregated responses to the nine scenarios.

One female officer said, "*I saw the importance of how you respond verbally to a situation without using any of the tools on your belt, especially when the person doesn't have any weapon in their hand. . . . When it's those situations that you have to use your verbal skills to de-escalate a situation. . . . I think women are excellent at that.*"

TABLE 5: APPLICATION OF FORCE (BY PERCENT)

		Unarmed physical or body force	Chemical agents	Impact weapon	Deadly force
Scenario #1					
	Women	21.9	9.4	9.4	0
	Men	39.3	14.3	5.4	0
Scenario #2					
	Women	68.8	0	0	0
	Men	69.9	0	0	0
Scenario #3					
	Women	31.3	46.9	18.8	0
	Men	42.9	23.2	30.4	0
Scenario #4					
	Women	46.9	12.5	12.5	0
	Men	62.5	5.4	5.4	0
Scenario #5					
	Women	0	9.4	62.5	21.9
	Men	12.5	16.1	58.9	10.7
Scenario #6					
	Women	0	0	0	0
	Men	1.8	0	0	0
Scenario #7					
	Women	0	0	0	0
	Men	1.8	0	0	0
Scenario #8					
	Women	0	3.1	40.6	53.1
	Men	0	10.7	48.2	41.1
Scenario #9					
	Women	6.3	3.1	71.9	15.6
	Men	0	16.1	73.2	1.8

Retrieved 3 February 2020, from https://ucr.fbi.gov/crime-in-the-u.s/2016/crime-in-the-u.s.-2016/topic-pages/police-employees

Another officer said, "*Officers who don't fit the stereotype can defuse tense situations. There's a different approach when a female officer comes onto the scene. I experienced this myself. In stressful situations, sometimes it's a calming effect.*"

A third female officer said, "*I've always had to use my brains or try to talk the person down or talk them into the squad car or use other techniques to get the handcuffs on them . . .*"

Finally, a fourth female officer insightful said, "*Generally speaking, female police officers are more resilient than male police officers. Female officers often enter the law enforcement profession with very little upper body strength, limited tactical skills, and minimal exposure to a predominantly male-oriented work setting.*

Over time, female police officers develop physical strength, obtain tactical proficiency, and successfully assimilate into the male-oriented working environment.

However, after obtaining physical and tactical skills and becoming proficient with both lethal and less-lethal technology, female police officers never forget how to use their most valuable tool in law enforcement—their ability to prevent and/or defuse conflict rather than provoking it and/or responding to it."

Discussion

The results here suggest that there are important indicators related to the use of force and officers' gender. First and foremost, the results suggest some uniformity across this personal characteristic—gender—in terms of the decision to use force or not. While the percentages varied between men and women, there was consensus on when to use force. At this level, officers have a shared understanding when force is appropriate. This is most likely the result of training and department policies. For example, in scenario #5, one community-member has an ax handle and the officers witnesses her swinging it another person. As this classic scenario includes both a weapon (the ax handle) and a harm (swinging it at another person), most department guidelines - including for this department—would call for intervention. Overall, this research found little statistically significant variation between men and women in their understanding or decision to apply force. Using these measures, this work affirms the results of Hoffman and Hickey (2005) who found no statistical difference in the use of force by gender.

© Jack Dagley Photography/Shutterstock.com

There is much more variation when examining the amount of force that should be applied. Although men started with a low levels of force (for example, in the same scenario #5, 12.5 of men started with unarmed physical or body contact while no women started at that level), the officers' responses were usually spread over two or three categories, with majority agreement on only four of nine scenarios. Arguably, it is here where we see officer discretion as well as the possible influence of other factors, including other personal characteristics, contextual and situational factors. Like Bazley et al. (2007) who suggested that female police officers use the levels of force differently than male officers, we observe men applying lower levels but women applying more a more diverse range. Here, the comments of female officers is particularly useful. Their comments suggest a more nuanced approach to force, with includes understanding how to communicate differently, which may create opportunities for a broader range of force options.

We also observe women choosing no force or "no physical force" at higher levels by women. The results also suggest, as noted by Schuck and Rabe-Hemp (2007), that situations matter—especially in disturbance calls. For example, in the three scenarios where female officers skewed to higher levels of deadly force than men (scenarios #5, #8 and #9) all involved responding to disturbance calls. In the scenario #5, the call involves two women in a physical dispute. In scenario #8, the suspect is under the influence of drugs or alcohol—a more dangerous situation for women (Bazley et al., 2007). In scenario #9, the call involves intimate partner violence and the female victim has been injured. The responses to these scenarios suggest that female officers might intuitively or experientially understand the higher levels of risk for female officers in these situations. Again, the comments of female officer adds insights. As the fourth officer noted having less physical strength than the average male officer and developing tools (more intellectual strength) to compensate for muscle. The various contexts seem to require female to exercise a better-calibrated range of options than male officers. Female officers tend to apply lower level, and broader range—including deadly—use of force than male officers.

Conclusion

The decision and use of force by police continues to be a point of concern for police agencies and communities. In this study, using a more exploratory methods of scenario assessment, officers were given common policing situations and asked if force was appropriate. The body of literature suggests that the personal characteristics—such as the gender of the officer—may affect the use of force. Male and female officers in this single department showed a high degree of consistency in their decisions to use force or not. At this level, officers appeared to have a uniform understanding of when force is appropriate given a specific set of circumstances. We saw variation by gender when officers exercise discretion in determining the appropriate level of forces. Female officers were willing to use a broader range of options, including deadly force. Future research should consider how variations in the scenarios or situations are viewed differently by gender. Additionally, qualitative research on female officers and decision-making process would help to explain their comfort level with various types of force.

Appendix

Basic Context and Distinct Police Scenarios

Scenario 1 of 9: You arrive at a call for a dispute between two males. Upon arriving at the scene, you move the individuals away from each other to prevent a physical altercation and one of the males spits on you and says "get the hell away from me." You move to arrest, and he begins to yell and curse again.

Scenario 2 of 9: While on routine patrol in a vehicle, you are called to a store for a female being detained for stealing. As you enter the store you see the suspect being held by an employee. As you attempt to place the female under arrest, she yells "Get your hands off of me!" She refuses to engage in conversation, nor will she listen to your verbal commands.

Scenario 3 of 9: You respond to a call for an intoxicated male yelling and cursing at employees in a store. You approach the individual and ask him to leave the premises. The male refuses to leave and begins to push items off the shelves. While attempting to place the male under arrest he bites and scratches you.

Scenario 4 of 9: You receive a call from another officer for assistance placing an individual under arrest. When you arrive at the scene you are asked by the officer to assist in placing the suspect into the police vehicle. While attempting to place the handcuffed individual into the vehicle the suspect resists by stiffening his body and refuses to listen or respond.

Scenario 5 of 9: While conducting a routine patrol in a vehicle you observe two females on the street yelling at each other. As you approach the scene one of the females displays a stick (an axe handle without the blade) and threatens to hit you with it. As you attempt to talk to her, she swings the stick at the other woman, barely missing her head.

Scenario 6 of 9: An individual enters your precinct to speak to the officer who issued him a parking summons. The individual explains his discontent for receiving the summons and wishes to speak to the issuing officer. As you inform the individual that the issuing officer is out in the field and has not returned, the individual begins to shout and curse at you.

Scenario 7 of 9: You receive a call for a noise complaint at a residence. As you approach the location, loud music can clearly be heard coming from the specific location. You knock on the door of the home where the loud music is coming from and inform the individual that you received a call complaining about loud music. You ask the individual to lower the music, but the individual verbally refuses to lower the music and instead, starts complaining about his sensitive neighbor.

Scenario 8 of 9: You receive a call for a male in front of a building threatening to hit individuals walking by with a baseball bat. He may be under the influence of a substance. As you and your partner approach the male, he attempts to hit you in the head and narrowly misses.

Scenario 9 of 9: While on routine patrol in a vehicle, you are called to a domestic violence incident. As you enter the home you see a male punching a female on the ground. You quickly attempt to place the male suspect under arrest for assaulting the female. The male then wrestles with you and refuses to be placed under arrest.

Female and male police officers

Law enforcement

Scenarios

Use of force

1. In addition to gender, what other personal characteristics might affect an officer's decision to use force?

2. What is the use of force continuum?

3. Why do you think female officers are less likely to use force to gain compliance?

4. What is the difference between appropriate force and excessive force?

5. What can be done to improve diversity and inclusion in the police departments?

References

Accreditation Council (2018). NYS Division of Criminal Justice Services. Retrieved 26 July 2018, from http://www.criminaljustice.ny.gov/ops/accred/accred04.htm

Alpert, G. & Dunham, R. (2010). Understanding Police Use of Force: Officers, Suspects, and Reciprocity. London: Cambridge University Press.

Barkan, S. E., & Cohn, S. F. (1998). Racial prejudice and support by whites for police use of force: A research note. *Justice Quarterly, 15*(4), 743–753.

Bazley, T. D., Lersch, K. M., & Mieczkowski, T. (2007). Officer force versus suspect resistance: A gendered analysis of patrol officers in an urban police department. *Journal of Criminal Justice, 35*(2), 183–192.

Birks, S. (2008). Statistical Significance and Policy Significance. *SSRN Electronic Journal.* doi:10.2139/ssrn.1156166

Brandl, S. G. & Stroshine, M. S. (2013). The role of officer attributes, job characteristics, and arrest activity in explaining police use of force. *Criminal Justice Policy Review, 24*(5), 551–572.

DeJong, C. (2005). Gender differences in officer attitude and behavior. *Women & Criminal Justice, 15*(3–4), 1–32.

Dick, P. (2005). Dirty work designations: How police officers account for their use of coercive force. *Human Relations, 58*(11), 1363–1390.

International Association of Chiefs of Police. (2001). Police use of force in America 2001. Alexandra, VA.

International Association of Chiefs of Police (2019). Theiacp.org. Retrieved 6 April 2019, from https://www.theiacp.org/resources/critical-issues-use-of-force

Klahm, C. F., Frank, J., & Liederbach, J. (2014). Understanding police use of force. *Policing, 37*(3), 558-578.

Klahm, C. F., & Tillyer, R. (2010). Understanding police use of force: A review of the evidence. *Southwest Journal of Criminal Justice, 7*(2), 214–239.

Lawton, B. A. (2007). Levels of nonlethal force: An examination of individual, situational, and contextual factors. *Journal of Research in Crime and Delinquency, 44*(2), 163–184.

Legewie, J. (2016). Racial profiling and use of force in police stops: How local events trigger periods of increased discrimination. *American Journal of Sociology, 122*(2), 379–424.

Lonsway, K., Wood, M., Fickling, M., De Leon, A., Moore, M., Harrington, P., & Spillar, K. (2002). *Men, women, and police excessive force: A tale of two genders.* National Center for Women & Policing. Retrieved from http://womenandpolicing. com/PDF/2002_Excessive_Force. pdf.

Lim, H., & Lee, H. (2015). The effects of supervisor education and training on police use of force. *Criminal Justice Studies, 28*(4), 444–463.

McElvain, J. P., & Kposowa, A. J. (2008). Police officer characteristics and the likelihood of using deadly force. *Criminal Justice and Behavior, 35*(4), 505–521.

McEwen, T. (1996). National data collection on police use of force. Retrieved 26 July 2018, from https://www.ncjrs.gov/App/Publications/abstract.aspx?ID=160113

National Institute of Justice (NIJ). (2019). Police use of force. National Institute of Justice. Retrieved from https://www.nij.gov/topics/law-enforcement/officer-safety/use-of- force/pages/welcome.aspx

Ochs, H. L. (2011). The Politics of Inclusion: Black Political Incorporation and the Use of Lethal Force. *Journal of Ethnicity in Criminal Justice, 9(3), 238-26.*

Paoline, E. A., & Terrill, W. (2005). The impact of police culture on traffic stop searches: An analysis of attitudes and behavior. *Policing: An International Journal of Police Strategies & Management, 28(3),* 455–472.

Phillips, S. W. (2009). Using a vignette research design to examine traffic stop decision making of police officers: A research note. *Criminal Justice Policy Review, 20(4),* 495–506.

Phillips, S. W. & Sobol, J. J., (2012). Police decision-making: an examination of conflicting theories. Policing: *An International Journal of Police Strategies & Management, 35(3),* 551–565.

Schuck, A. M., & Rabe-Hemp, C. (2007). Women police: The use of force by and against female officers. *Women & Criminal Justice, 16(4),* 91-117.

Shane, J. M. (2016). Improving police use of force: A policy essay on national data collection. *Criminal Justice Policy Review, 1(21),* 128-148.

Skolnick, J. H. & Fyfe, J. J. (1993). Above the law: Police and the excessive use of force. New York, NY: Free Press.

Smith, M. R., Kaminsky, R. J., Alpert, G. P., Fridell, L. A., MacDonald, J., & Kubu, B. (2009). A multi-method evaluation of police use of force outcomes: Final report to the National Institute of Justice. *Survey Methodology, 3(1),* S178.

Terrill, W. (2014). Police coercion. In M. D. Reisig, R. J. Kane, & B. Bradford (Eds.), The Oxford handbook of police and policing (pp. 260-279). Oxford, UK: Oxford University Press.

Terrill, W., Leinfelt, F. H., & Kwak, D. H. (2008). Examining police use of force: A smaller agency perspective. *Policing: An International Journal of Police Strategies & Management, 31(1),* 57–76.

US Department of Justice, FBI. Crime in the U.S. 2017. (2019). Table 74. Retrieved 6 April 2019, from https://ucr.fbi.gov/crime-in-the-u.s/2017/crime-in-the-u.s.-2013/tables/table-74

US Department of Justice, FBI. Crime in the U.S. 2016. (2018). FBI. Retrieved 26 July 2018, from https://ucr.fbi.gov/crime-in-the-u.s/2016/crime-in-the-u.s.-2016

Williams, J. J., & Hester, G. (2003). Sheriff law enforcement officers and the use of force. *Journal of Criminal Justice, 31(4),* 373–381.

Web Links

These will be live in the eBook version

International Association of Chiefs of Police

National Institute of Justice (NIJ). Police use of force

Center for Policing Equity (https://policingequity.org/)

National Center For Women and Policing

Police Foundation

CHAPTER 4

Foreign Women in Prison

Biko Agozino | *Virginia Tech*

From African Journal of Criminology and Justice Studies, (AJCJS)
by Onwubiko Agozino. Copyright © 2008 by Onwubiko Agozino. Reprinted by permission.

Abstract

The imprisonment of women worldwide has always been a controversial issue. This is partly because women do not end up in prison as frequently as men and so discussions of prison populations most often focus on the experiences of male prisoners. Therefore, any attempt to focus attention on the experiences of female prisoners raises questions in the minds of most scholars as to whether the conditions of women in prison are harsh enough compared to male prisons and whether we should not be focusing on the more severe conditions in male prisons? However, the rate of increase of female prisoners far outstrips the rate of growth of male prisoners partly because of the relatively small number upon which the increases are calculated and partly because of increasing attempts by criminal justice officials to grant women equality with a vengeance. If we move beyond this numbers game and look at the incarceration of foreign women in prisons around the world, we could be in a position to consider the nature of prisons in general and the imprisonment of women in particular and question their relative essentialisms.

Introduction

Since the story of Eve, there has been a tendency to blame women for more than their share of the troubles on earth. This is known as the Eve syndrome. Many feminist writers have re-examined the narratives of the original sin to represent Eve as the mother of human rights. What she ate in the Garden of Eden was the fruit of knowledge and it is argued that knowledge is part of what makes us human and so it should not be censored, not even by God the Creator.

Without knowledge, we would be like the other animals rather than being fully human, in God's image, a likeness that provoked the jealousy of Lucifer who wanted all the creatures, including man, to be beneath the Divine rather than like the Divine, a pride that led to the fall of Satan to the lowly mission of trying to prove that it was a mistake to have made man with so much power that he would likely abuse when tempted, resulting in the fall of Lucifer from grace and the eventual loss of paradise by man. Yet, the image that is left in the minds of most believers is that Eve was responsible for bringing sin into the world and some try to corrupt her name to suggest that she was evil and that all women by extension are evil. 'It is the woman you made for me', cried Adam, 'she made me eat of the forbidden fruit because Satan made her eat it first and now we know that we are naked, that is why we are ashamed and in hiding', or something like that. Adam was being a typical man, he denied responsibility and blamed it all on the evil woman.

Was Eve framed in such a way because she was a foreign woman in Eden in the double sense that she was not there from the beginning (she was not the first woman, that one created at the same time that man was made, Male and Female made He They, the Bible said; and later, the story of a sedated Adam undergoing divine surgery to remove a rib and artificially make Eve for him, without telling us what happened to the first woman, a dark woman who was said to have refused to submit to the authority of Adam, According to Pfohl, 1994) and in the additional sense that she was was not there earlier when Adam was made with the other woman and was later made from the rib of man? If you go through the bible, you will notice that most of the bad women were foreign women from the Queen of Sheba who came from Africa to tempt the wise king Solomon to Delilah the Philistine temptress that emasculated Sampson the Strong.

Some may see Esther as a good foreign woman but I doubt if the wife of the King that she displaced or the King himself who also lost out as a result of her charms would agree with the elasticity of goodness in Esther or Ruth in foreign lands. Their roles, as narrated by male authors, present them in less reputable lights than, say Joseph the slave who resisted the temptations of the wife of his master and was the target of the false accusation and hell-knew-no-fury of a woman scorned. The interesting thing is that the woman's husband did not rush to kill Joseph, the honer man, as Trinidadians and Tobagonians would call the adulterous man, instead, he threw him in jail and seemed to forget about him until someone reported that there was a dream reader in prison who could help the Pharoh figure out how to save for a rainy day before the crash of the stock market and an economic depression. Maybe the man had heard such allegations too often before from his apparently insatiable wife or maybe Joseph was extra cute as the bible suggested, although we do not see evidence of other women rushing to throw themselves at him and he had to woo the daughter of the priest before he could get a wife. What the whole story illustrates, as central theme of the bible from beginning to end, is that of unconditional love and mercy from God to humanity. Despite all transgressions of the great men in the bible, Malcolm X reminds us that each one of them erred but was forgiven for the things they got right. This story of mercy as a form of justice is yet to be fully written but that will be for another day. The focus here is how especially foreign women are viewed in official penal discourse.

The only good foreign woman that I can think of was Mary the Mother of Christ who is worshipped across Europe as the Black Madonna. But despite her Holiness, she was portrayed as an unwed mother who could have been stoned to death if Joseph had rejected her, and like African women abroad, she could not get accommodation in any hotel nor in any home in Bethlehem, the home town of her husband, Joseph. So she had to give birth in a manger, the way pregnant foreign women are forced to give birth in prisons around the world. The sex worker from Jericho who hid the spies and lied about their presence could have been another example of a 'good' foreign woman in the bible but she was not foreign in Jericho and her role is hardly a good image for a woman to have — a whore and an unpatriotic one at that. The New Testament gave women more positive roles as Mary the mother of Christ and Mary Magdalene, Mary and Martha came to represent something holy but still none of them was given the privilege of writing any of the gospels despite their closeness and insight into the life of Jesus.

The negative perception of foreign women in the bible is not the cause of the treatment of foreign women around the world today but an indication that xenophobia is a long established tradition in the world. It is easier to blame a foreigner than to blame a fellow citizen for anything going wrong. The Salem witch craze was reported to have started when a slave from Barbados allegedly initiated some white American girls into witchcraft, although Stephen Pfohl (1994) interpreted the witch hunting as a product of the economic depression and threat of the withdrawal of the royal charter that the puritans faced at that time.

In the development of criminological theory, the role of the foreigner and the immigrant is prominent (Agozino, 2000). The Italian school of Lombroso almost explicitly blamed crime on foreigners by asserting that criminals were atavistic throw-backs to an earlier stage of evolution. Lombroso was describing the features of Sicilians as being closer to the features of Africans and Jews and as being signs of what he called atavistic stigmata or signs of the born criminal. The female criminal was to him a monster because she was doubly atavistic – with a clitoris that approximated the male phallus which supposedly explained her sexual promiscuity and tendency to commit sexual crimes. Perhaps some law enforcement agents in Italy today still believe that there is something pathological about the poor women from Africa who are trafficked there for prostitution. More about this later.

The Chicago school later tried to move away from explicit stereotyping of the immigrant. Immigration still featured in their research but they used it to prove that immigrants are not essentially criminal given that crime remained high in the zone of transition irrespective of which ethnic group provided the majority of immigrants who populated the high crime zone from time to time. They emphasized structural problems of social disorganization and called for the reorganization of society as the solution to high crime rates instead of engaging in immigrant bashing.

Gabbidon and Taylor (2005) reported that when official records of criminals started being kept in America, a constant feature was a report on foreign born criminals but after some years, that category was dropped from the official reports without explanation. The reason may be found in an article published in *The American Journal of Sociology* in 1896 by Hastings H. Hart. In the article, 'Immigration and Crime' the author rebutted another article by Mr. F.W. Hewes on 'Delinquents' which was published in *Outlook* of March 7, 1896. Whereas Hastings concluded that white immigrants committed twice as many crimes as native born whites per ten thousand, Hart argued that immigrants committed only two thirds of the crimes of natives per ten thousand of the population. He claimed that he left female prisoners out of the comparison because the US Census Bureau did not include the nationality of female prisoners in the official records and that since female prisoners were only nine percent of the prison population, his conclusions would not be threatened.

Throughout the world, women are less likely to end up in prison than men. The average proportion of women in prison in any country of the world is about seven per cent. In response to this fact, some malestream criminologists doubt whether women are more law abiding than men or whether they are able to conceal their wrongdoings from law enforcement agents or, whether the mostly male lawenforcement agents are more likely to pardon a women due to chivalry while the male offender is more likely to be arrested and charged. Lorraine Gelsthorpe (1986) suggested that it might not be the case that law enforcement agents are being chivalrous when they release girls with a warning while they detain boys. She suggested that due to socialization, girls are more likely to accept their responsibility and apologize while boys are more likely to deny responsibility and therefore could not be warned by police officers who could only issue warnings after the admission of guilt.

In a review of the literature, it is noticeable that some authors argue in support of the chivalry thesis while others question its existence and yet others wonder whether it is chivalry or paternalism that benefits married women as well as married men (Agozino, 1997b). However, there is evidence that women are more likely to be incarcerated when they are not offenders or suspects but due to their proximity to suspected men (Agozino, 1997). And even when they are accused of a crime and are convicted, their alleged offences are often not serious enough to justify what Julia Sudbury (2005) termed a program of *Global Lockdown*. The most interesting thing about Sudbury's edited book is that the chapters on women trafficking, drug trafficking and international prostitution indicated that the women were arrested and locked up to be deported like common criminals when they could be said to be victims of crime and patriarchal violence.

If only women who committed violent crimes went to prison, then there would be too few female prisoners to justify the amazing rates of increase in female prison populations and if the same principle was applied to male prisoners, then the prison as a repressive fetish of western modernity would be arrested in its growth and might even wither away with time. There might still be a need for places to confine those who did something more serious than picking their noses but the growth of a prison industrial complex would not be sustainable. This is one important lesson we could learn by studying the articulation of race-class-gender relations (Hall, 1980) concerning foreign women who are more likely to be detained for immigration offences than for committing a violent felony.

Foreign Women in UK Prisons

The Prison Reform Trust issued a briefing in May 2004 that looked at 'the startling increase over the last decade in the number of foreign national prisoners' in England and Wales, highlighting the disparate treatments and conditions of the foreigners compared to the natives. The briefing offered the following key facts and figures:

- There are 8,937 foreign national prisoners (defined as anyone without a UK passport), about one in eight (12 per cent) of the overall prison population. One in five women in prison are foreign nationals.

- They come from 168 countries, but over half are from just six countries (Jamaica, Irish Republic, Nigeria, Pakistan, Turkey and India). A quarter are Jamaicans, by far, the largest single group.

- There has been a 152 percent increase in foreign national prisoners in the last ten years compared to a 55 per cent increase in British nationals.

- In two prisons, the Verne in Dorset and the women's prison Morton Hall in Lincolnshire, foreign nationals make up half or more of the population. In sixteen prisons they make up a quarter or more.

- Despite their number the Prison Service does not have a dedicated policy or strategy to deal with foreign national prisoners.

- A recent prison service survey found that nearly 90 per cent of prisons holding foreign nationals are not making regular use of the available translation service.

- The vast majority of foreign national prisoners, four out of ten sentenced men and eight out of ten sentenced women, have committed drug offences, mainly drug trafficking. Six out of ten foreign national prisoners are serving sentences of more than four years.

- In 2003 eight foreign national prisoners committed suicide, out of a total of 94 suicides. In the past five years, 35, have taken their own lives.

The above report indicates how the war on drugs is primarily responsible for the huge increase in the number of women who are in prison. This pattern was already evident in the early 1990s with the conclusion that black women were still being subjected to colonial styles of control (Agozino,

1997; Chigwada, 1997; Carlen, 1998; Smart,1995; Kalunta Crumpton, 1999; and Worrall, 1990). It is evident that many innocent black women were subjected to criminal justice control because of their proximity to suspected black men who were their sons, husbands, boyfriends, fathers or brothers (Agozino, 1997).

It is rare to come across any male suspect who was arrested or attacked by law enforcement agents because of his proximity to suspected black women. The practice of what Agozino (1997) termed victimization as mere punishment seemed to be reserved for the black women and sometimes for Irish women but in the Irish case this was due to the war by the Irish Republican Army. These could be interpreted as instances of the attempts by the institutions of penalty to colonize the fields of victimization and represent them as part of the territory of penalty. This interpretation calls for the empire of punishment to be decolonized by recognizing what was being done to innocent black women as instances of victimization and not as cases of punishment (Agozino, 1997).

It is therefore surprising that a reform agency like the Prison Reform Trust could document thousands of cases of foreign women in prison but without identifying a single innocent person among them. On the contrary, Kalunta-Crumpton (1998) provides evidence that when black people make claims in court regarding their innocence, this was disregarded out of hand by the court officials and that even when diplomats supplied character witnesses for some of the defendants, the judges implied that the documents may have been forged due to what was seen as high levels of corruption in their countries of origin.

Note that the reference is frequently to England and Wales rather than the whole of the United Kingdom which would include Scotland and Northern Ireland as well as Gibraltar where many African immigrants are detained. This is because the other jurisdictions are smaller and the major locations of foreigners in the UK are found in England and Wales. At the same time, the statistics do not tell us how many of the sentenced foreign nationals are in England and how many are in Wales despite devolution to the Welsh Assembly and the Welsh Language Act that calls for legislation and legal proceedings to be made available in the Welsh language but without provisions for the separate listing of Welsh criminal statistics yet. The Home Office for England and Wales gave the population of foreign prisoners in England and Wales at the end of 2003 as follows:

SENTENCED FOREIGN NATIONAL PRISON POPULATION, 31 DECEMBER 2003 (HOME OFFICE RDS)

Offence Group	Male	Female	Total
Violence against the person	971	35	1,006
Sexual Offences	435	0	435
Burglary	238	8	246
Theft & Handling	220	16	336
Fraud & Forgery	309	46	355
Drug offences	2,383	533	2,916
Other	499	26	425
Not Recorded	48	2	50
Total	5,551	677	6,228

Source: Prison Reform Trust Briefing, May 2004.

The table suggests that 47% of sentenced foreigners were convicted of drugs charges with this category of offences covering nearly half the men under sentence (43%) and more than three quarters of the women (79%). By comparison only 13% of sentenced UK national men and 29% of sentenced female UK nationals were convicted of drugs offences. If drugs were legal, it means that nearly 80% of foreign women in prison would be free, the other cases of violence against the person, theft and fraud could also be drugs-related with the effect that there would be hardly any foreign woman in prison in England and Wales.

As indicated in the 1990s, Nigerian nationals were the single largest group sentenced for drugs offences but it was warned that given the small size of the Jamaican national population compared to that of Nigeria, it was alarming that they came a close second to Nigeria (Agozino, 1997). That warning is now borne out by the fact that Jamaicans are now reported to be the single most incarcerated group of foreign nationals in connection with drugs offences. The Prison Reform Trust reports that there were 2,500 Jamaicans incarcerated in 2003, nearly a quarter of all foreign nationals in prisons. Seventy per cent of Jamaican prisoners are there for drugs offences.

The Structural Adjustment Programs in Caribbean and African countries exacerbated the income inequality and unemployment situation in those countries, forcing many more of the poor to be tempted with the risky prospects of resorting to being used as drug mules to help their family to survive increasing hardship from the small but tempting fees promised by often threatening drug barons. Greater control at Jamaican points of departure through measures like the loaning of Scotland Yard officers to Jamaica and stricter visa controls have reduced the number of Jamaicans arrested in London but the numbers of other Caribbean nationals arrested in London, such as those from Trinidad and Tobago, have also increased prompting the country to also invite Scotland Yard officers to help with the social control in the country. The reports in Prison Statistics, England and Wales reveal these trends.

The organization, Rethink (2003) avoided challenging the criminalization of drugs after noting that 90% of Jamaican women in prison were there as first time offenders while Jamaican women made up 96% of women in prison in England and Wales. The organization argues:

> There are ethical and pragmatic reasons for the government to rethink policy on drug couriers, in particular the use of long terms of imprisonment. There is no question that Jamaican women who smuggle drugs are breaking the law. But they themselves are almost always pawns in a much bigger game. Long spells of imprisonment cause hardship for them and their families. On pragmatic grounds there are also good arguments for rethinking sentencing policy related to drug couriers. Giving drug couriers long prison sentences is not working as a deterrent. Given the significant levels of poverty in Jamaica, there will always be some who are prepared to risk imprisonment, are unaware of the consequences, or are coerced into importing drugs. At a time when the prison system is facing an overcrowding crisis, it makes little sense to compound the problem by pursuing a sentencing approach that is so manifestly failing (Rethink, 2003).

The Rethink organization went on to recommend that once arrested, drug couriers should be deported to face trial in their own country or if convicted they should be sent back to serve their sentences in their own country, or that the UK government should assist Jamaica in developing noncustodial sentences that might involve peer-to-peer education in the community. None of these punitive reforms would solve the problem of poverty that helps to recruit drug couriers in the first place. The policy of deportation that is being suggested here is actually tried and tested and proven to be largely ineffective.

Foreign Women in US Prisons

Many of the above observations about the UK are applicable to the US and this point is brought out clearly by recent statistics on US prisons. Larger in scale than the UK prison populations, the proportion of foreigners in US prisons is also larger than that of the UK. However, analyzing the prison population simply in terms of citizens versus noncitizens in the US would appear misleading given that African Americans, Native Americans and Puerto Rico prisoners are not fully treated as citizens. If you add these categories of nominal citizens to those officially categorized as non-citizens in the US, it will become clear that the prison industrial complex in America is there primarily for the control of others. A similar point can be made about the UK prison populations in the sense that those categorized as UK nationals are also disproportionately Black British nationals who are often discriminated against as if they were not UK nationals. Commenting on this Cheloitis and Liebling (2006: 288) state as follows:

> To take but a few examples, whereas one's race in France is perceived along the lines of being either a French citizen or a foreigner, with the latter representing and undergoing the exclusionary consequences of 'Otherness', 'the politics of race [in Britain] has historically been understood . . . in a more agonistic fashion, as one of belonging' (Bosworth 2004: 231). Irrespective of citizenship, Bowling argues, 'Englishness or another of Britain's national identities . . . privilege claims to *belong*, to be of Britain, "one of us," only to white British people' (1998: 11, original emphasis). This is not to be confused with a mere Black–White distinction which would fit somewhat better, but still not at all neatly, to the American paradigm.

Also similar to the UK is the fact that the war on drugs is the engine driving the over-representation of minorities in US prisons despite the fact that minorities are not more involved with drugs than Caucasians (Tonry, 1996) and despite the fact that the illicit drugs are safer than many legal substances (Reiman, 1979).

What was described as victimization as mere punishment refers to the fact that many of the black women who were subjected to social control were not suspects themselves but were simply proximate to suspected black men (Agozino, 1997). This finding was independently supported by Kemba Smith (2005), the young African American student who was sentenced to a long term in prison when her boy friend was found to be dealing in drugs. She was eventually pardoned by President Clinton in his last acts of clemency before handing over to George Bush, but Smith described her experience as akin to a modern day slavery driven by politically motivated drugs policies that disadvantage minorities in the US. Her analysis is indirectly supported by the US Bureau of Justice Statistics which state that:

> Immigration offenses drove the growing case load, BJS noted, increasing by an average annual 14 percent in immigration arrests and 25 percent in prison sentences for immigration convictions.

> Drug offenses were the felonies most frequently disposed of in federal district courts during the decade. There were 20,219 such cases during 1994 (with a 86 percent conviction rate) and 28,597 cases in 2003 (with a 92 percent conviction rate). There were 3,673 felony weapons cases disposed of in 1994 (85 percent conviction rate) and 8,147 cases concluded during 2003 (90 percent conviction rate).

> The number of non-citizens in the federal criminal justice system increased steadily from 1994 through 2003. The U.S. Marshals Service arrested and booked 131,064 suspects during 2003, of which 38 percent were non-citizens, compared to 27 percent in 1994.

All offences	Drugs offences				Drugs
Characteristics	1994	2003	1994	2003	Percentage
All inmates	84,253	152,459	50,555	85,789	
Gender					
Male	92.1%	93.1%	91.2%	92.0%	92%Male
Female	7.9%	6.9%	8.8%	8.0%	
Race					
White	62.1%	58.1%	61.9%	53.9%	54% White
Black	35.3%	39.0%	36.8%	44.5%	
Native Americ	1.5%	1.6%	0.3%	0.4%	
Asian	1.1%	1.3%	1.1%	1.2%	
Ethnicity					
Hispanic	25.1%	32.1%	31.3%	33.0%	
Non Hispanic	74.9%	67.9%	68.7%	67.0%	67% NonHi
Age					
Under 19	0.1	0.4	0.1	0.2	
19-20 years	1.3	3.3	1.0	3.2	
21-30	30.1	41.3	31.6	44.2	44% 21-30
31-40	35.9	33.0	36.4	32.3	
Over 40	32.6	22.1	30.9	20.2	
Citizenship					
US Citizen	77.5%	72.2%	71.8%	74.1%	74% US
Non-US	22.5	27.8	28.2	25.9	

Source: 1994: https://www.bjs.gov/content/pub/pdf/Pi94.pdf, 2003: https://www.bjs.gov/content/pub/pdf/p03.pdf

Unlike the UK, the US did not provide the number of the foreign nationals who were female but we can infer from trends elsewhere that they are more over-represented among female prison populations than male foreigners among male prisoners. The table below shows that whites, males and US citizens appear to be the only groups that dropped slightly while almost all the other categories recorded increases between 1994 and 2003. For instance, male prisoners recorded a slight drop while female prisoners recorded a slight increase in their proportions but the drop recorded by whites and the rise recorded by blacks were more dramatic. Note that this is only the tip of the iceberg represented by federal prisons and that including state prisons and county jails would be even more staggering as the US prison population exceeded two million during the period.

The role that immigration law plays in increasing the incarceration of foreign women, men and children is also highlighted by the above quotation more clearly than is the case with UK statistics where this connection is relatively concealed. In their essay, 'Remaking Big Government: Immigration and Crime Control in the United States', Rebecca Bohrman and Naomi Murakawa (2005) expose this link more radically in a way that unites immigrants rights and prison activists for once to call into question the use of incarceration to deal with immigration offences when finance capital is allowed to roam the world without boarders, often causing more harm by funding organized crime compared to the relatively harmless offence of being an undocumented immigrant.

Female Foreign Prisoners in Europe

In her contribution to the abolitionist discourse, Asele Angel-Ajani (2005) focused on the repressive policing of immigrant African women in Italy where the prison population rose by 50% in two years due to over-reliance on incarceration as a response to immigration pressures, drugs offences and sex workers who are forced into Europe in the first place by oppressive policies imposed by international financial institutions on poor countries (see also, Andall, 2000). In her essay, 'Victims and Agents of Crime: The New Crusade Against Trafficking', Kamala Kempadoo (2005) adds to the perspective of Asele by pointing out how the repressive policing of immigrant sex workers is done under the guise of protecting the immigrants as victims of trafficking. She quotes the Sex Workers Association of Nigeria as responding to such pretence by declaring 'We want workers rights, not bloody sewing machines.'

Manuela Ivone Perieria da Cunha (2005) demonstrated in her essay, 'From Neighbourhood to Prison' that it is not only immigrant women who are suspected of any drugs offences that are incarcerated but their female children are also locked up with them due to the fact that the Portuguese authorities rely on their colonial tactics of collective targeting of whole communities under the assumption of collective responsibility. This challenges us to acknowledge that the positivistic differentiation between the insiders and the outsiders with reference to the prison walls is misleading because this boundary, like the international boundaries that fortress Europe tries but fails to seal, is porous and blurred. In her essay, 'Latinas and the War on Drugs in the U.S., Latin America and Europe' Juanita Díaz-Cotto (2005) reminds us that the war against poor women in the guise of the war against drugs affects poor Latinas, many of whom are black women, in three continents.

Conclusion

The war on drugs is clearly a political project targeting minorities and foreign nationals, especially those of African descent. This is political in the sense that drugs do not cause public harm that is proportionate to the long sentences that are handed out to the mostly black prisoners who are often first time offenders. For instance, it has been stated that cocaine is less dangerous than tobacco which kills half a million citizens in America alone every year and yet it does not only remain legal, the government offers subsidies to the mostly white farmers who grow it. Marihuana is also reported to be less deadly than alcohol and aspirin but these lethal legal drugs remain available without prescription while hundreds of black women are being jailed for long periods for trying to market relatively harmless substances.

Howard Becker (1967) revealed long ago that the main reason for this ridiculous policy is that alcohol and tobacco are easy to tax whereas marihuana is almost impossible to tax because users could grow their own if it is legal and if they grew their own, big tobacco and alcohol merchants would lose sales to the far safer substance. He explained that this was why moral entrepreneurs went all out to paint marihuana as being a demon drug in order to make it illegal at a time that doctors were prescribing it for many kinds of ailment. Evidence in support of this is the fact that the first law against marihuana was called the Marihuana Tax Act of 1937. When they found that it was impossible to tax, they then made it completely illegal 20 years later. Today, doctors still want to prescribe it but politicians around the world refuse to consider the scientific merit.

Imagine what would have been the case if tobacco was grown exclusively in Columbia, Jamaica and Nigeria and then sold in America and the UK to cause hundreds of thousands of death every year. Not only would they be illegal but that would be an excuse for America and Britain to invade Columbia, Nigeria and Jamaica under the pretext of waging the war on terrorism and there would be no difficulty finding a smoking gun to justify the invasions. But since it is rich white men who dominate the billion dollar tobacco and alcohol businesses, they remain legal and are supported with tax-payers money while poor black women are being banged up for trying to make a living out of produce that are in high demand on the streets of Europe and North America. Jones (2004) observed that a government committee set up by Jamaica to review the law on Marihuana reached the same conclusion by calling for the drug to be decriminalized along the lines of policies in The Netherlands but the government ignored the recommendation of the official committee.

If the prohibition of drugs is lifted as was the case with alcohol, nearly 80% of the foreign women in prison and nearly half the men will be free on the streets making an honest living and paying taxes on their sales instead of being held at tax-payers expenses while big business peddles drugs of mass destruction under the monopolistic control of white men at the expense of the defenseless public. This is an example of what is known as the pyrrhic defeat theory which helps to explain why *The Rich Get Richer and the Poor Get Prison* (Reiman, 1979):

> …we have an anti drug policy that is failing at its own goals and succeeding only in adding to crime. First, there are the heroin and crack addicts, who must steal to support their habit. Then, there are the drug merchants who are offered fabulous incentives to provide illicit substances to a willing body of consumers. This in turn contributes to the high rate of inner-city murders and other violence as drug gangs battle for the enormous sums of money available. Next, there are the law enforcement officials who, after risking their lives for low salaries, are corrupted by nearly irresistible amounts of money. Finally, there are the otherwise law-abiding citizens who are made criminals because they use cocaine, a drug less harmful than tobacco, and those who are made criminals because they use marijuana, a drug that is safer than alcohol and less deadly than aspirin… All this occurring at a time when there is increasing evidence that what does work to reduce substance abuse is public education (Reiman 1979:37).

This is to suggest that drugs addiction should be treated as health problems just like the more deadly addiction to alcohol and tobacco and thereby contribute to the gradual abolition of prison sentences for non-violent offences. It is surprising that the Prison Reform Trust did not mention this simple solution in its recommendations, concentrating instead on the provision of language translators for the prisoners. Once upon a time, the world carried on for centuries without the repressive fetish of the modern prison and so, maybe some day the world would reinvent itself and do away with this fetish once more, contrary to the pessimism of even the best intentioned prison reformers (Agozino, 2005).

Instead of maintaining the current absurd situation which regards certain drugs as criminal for the benefit of the drug lords who make a huge profit from the artificially high prices of drugs and probably launder the huge profits through terrorist and corrupt practices, history proves that legalization and the reliance on education would prove more effective in deterring people from using drugs. For instance, both alcohol and tobacco are legal but many of us shun them as health risks whereas if government raises an army to wage war on alcohol, the mafia will welcome the opportunity to make a killing. If tobacco and alcohol are controlled by Nigerian and Jamaican drug dealers, they would probably remain illegal today but the government would have had to build 100 percent more prisons to accommodate the addicts and smugglers. The government would spend all that money and still fail woefully to control the drugs while only succeeding in making criminal syndicates more powerful and so that is a classic case of pyrrhic defeat. Hence Julia Sudbury (2005) calls for the complete abolition of the British prison industrial complex that keeps relatively harmless Jamaican women and others under *Global Lockdown* while more menacing actors roam the streets with impunity.

I have left issues like the child-care for the children of incarcerated foreign women, their nutritional needs, their isolation from family members who could bring them supplies and their lack of religious rights that citizens enjoy in many cases. These issues are often taken up by reform groups but it is more important to question the foundations of the incarceration of foreign women the way I have done here. In a related vein, Wood, Ken and Montaner (2007) question the 'global over-reliance on criminal justice approaches to illicit drugs' because such policies put the lives of drug users at risk of HIV infection especially in cases where the provision of needle exchanges for drug users could help to reduce the harm of exposure to HIV given that 'a substantial number of new infections' affect those who inject drugs.

We begin with a fascinating essay by Dr Obiozo on graffiti, a phenomenon which is commonly seen in criminology as evidence of social disorganization, along with broken windows, which must be cracked down upon by agents of social control, at least as aspects of hooliganism or antisocial behaviours that could escalate to more serious felonies if unchecked. The article reminds us of the theme of mercy with which this editorial started – that the exercise of authority is not always best expressed punitively and that sometimes, tolerance of the relatively harmless would be more productive for society articstically, educationally, linguistically and morally, as Durkheim implied in his doctoral dissertation, *The Division of Labour and Society*, where he argued that a moderate level of deviance is necessary and positive for the health of the collective conscience. Since graffiti are ubiquituous and antiquituous, despite ancient and modern attempts to confirm the repression hypothesis that Foucault dismissed with reference to the history of sexuality, should we not follow the example of the radically republican Igbo culture of Nigeria by learning to appreciate graffiti as an art form for which no one needs to risk incarceration or a criminal record as is the case in many industrialized countries where the ownership of private property and control of public property define away possible artistic spaces from exceptional individuals with meaningful communications? Perhaps, every major city in Africa should follow the example of the Onitsha market traders and dedicate public spaces where graffiti artists could feel free to express their creativity without fear and maybe even introduce annual competition and prizes to nurture talents.

As I suggested in this editorial, such a liberal approach to graffiti could be extended to drugs and prostitution given that we know that countries like The Netherlands which have liberalized the drugs trade have not fared worse than countries wasting money and lives on the war on drugs while states like Nevada and countries like Senegal which regulate rather than repress the sex trade have fared better in the prevention of sexually transmitted diseases than repressive states. Similarly, the prohibition of abortion in almost all parts of Africa and the Caribbean, has failed to prevent abortions while endangering the lives of women. This lesson is the message that this editorial tries to emphasize by calling on our criminologists and policy makers to attempt loving approaches that would increase the prosperity and happiness of our people while reducing violence and strife.

The article on graffiti is followed by another important one on HIV/AIDS and health, national security, crime and the administration of justice in Africa. Dr Meni's article could not have come at a better time as Africa battles this major pandemic that threatens our very survival as a people. Once again, there is evidence that harm-reduction works better than repressiveness given evidence that those using intravenous drugs and sex workers and their patrons who do not use condoms are more prone to infection. The message of this editorial is echoed here by suggesting that if our women and men are allowed to trade in the prohibited drugs that are less harmful than tobacco and alcohol and if sex work is regulated rather than repressed, we may be better able to protect the health of our people and reduce the harm of HIV in Africa and the Caribbean.

Wilson rounds off the main article section for us this month with insights into the International Court of Justice that African countries have embraced as an innovation in international jurisprudence that could help to reduce war crimes in international conflict. I am particularly pleased to note that the author is affiliated to a university in Cameroon, a country that could have gone to war with Nigeria over millimeters of colonial boundary in the area of Bakassi. Luckily for us, the leaders of the two countries resolved to accept the decision of the International Court of Justice and when the judgement went in favour of Camerron, Nigeria peacefully ceded the oil-rich peninsula back to Cameroon rather than risk war in which millions of our African brothers and sisters could have been killed. Although that judgement came from a different international court, I believe that it illustrates the point that Wilson is making about the potential benefits of the new court for world peace. The peaceful resolution of the Bakassi dispute also echoes the recommendation in this editorial that we should shy away from waging war against our own people in the form of war on drugs, war on crime, war on this and war on that. We should leave war-mongering nations to wage war against their own citizens for as Victor Hugo said in *Les Misrables*, the republic is not so rich in men that it could afford to waste them. Let us return to the philosophy of peace and love which our ancestors bequeted to us.

Finally Zoller and Onyeozili offer us a review of a book on social thought that should interest African scholars of justice given the emphasis on economic history and colonialism. However, the relative silence on African thinkers and African history in the book, judging from the review, should be seen as a challenge to African thinkers to be bold in the development of their ideas so that no such book could be complete in the future without adequate reflection on African issues.

Discussion Questions:

Stephen Pfohl, Images of Deviance and Social Control (McGraw-Hill, Upper saddle River, 1994), quoted Angela Davis as challenging us to:

Imagine a more humane world, a world without poverty, without exploitation, without prisons, without racism, without sexism, without homophobia and without war.

Imagine a more humane world, a world without poverty, without exploitation, without prisons, without racism, without sexism, without homophobia and without war.

1. Do you think that such a world is possible or do you reject it out of hand as a utopian or a perfect world? Put on your thinking cap and do a little bit of critical thinking.

2. Before Christopher Columbus got lost and was discovered by Indigenous Peoples who had abundance and were willing to share with the lost strangers hallucinating about going West to reach East, there was no poverty, exploitation, prisons, racism, nor homophobia, while wars were mere song and dance for thousands of years before Europeans arrived to impose those fetishes of capitalist modernity. Now do you think that you can imagine a world where these fetishes are abolished so that we can return to the principle of from all according to their abilities and to all according to their needs?

3. Can you imagine ways that racism also affects poor whites adversely, patriarchy also affects poor men adversely, and imperialism threatens all in such ways that we all should be fighting together to end all systems of oppression?

4. Have you ever opposed a bully even when you were not the one being directly targeted and how did you feel?

5. Do you support Black Lives Matter and if not why not?

References

Agozino, B. (1997) *Black Women and the Criminal Justice System: Towards the Decolonisation of Victimisation*, Aldershot, Ashgate.

Agozino, B. (1997b) "Is Chivalry Colour-Blind? Race and Gender Discrimination in the Criminal Justice System' in *International Journal of Discrimination and the Law*, Vol. 2, No. 3, 119-216.

Agozino, B. (2000) 'Beware of Strangers: The Myth that Immigrants are Most likely to Be Deviant' in B. Agozino, ed., *Theoretical and Methodological Issues in Migration Studies*, Aldershot, Ashgate.

Agozino, B. (2005) 'Nigerian Women in Prison: Hostages in Law' in J. Sudbury *Global Lockdown: Race, Gender and the Prison Industrial Complex*, New York, Routledge.

Andall, J (2000) Gender, Migration and Domestic Service: The Politics of Black Women in Italy. Aldershot: Ashgate.

Angel-Ajani, A. (2005) 'Domestic Enemies and Carceral Circles: African Women and Criminalization in Italy' in Sudbury, J. ed. (2005) *Global Lockdown: Race, Gender and the Prison Industrial Complex*, New York, Routledge.

Becker, H. (1963) *Outsiders: Studies in the Sociology of Deviance*, London, The Free Press of Glencoe.

Bohrman, R. and Murakawa, N. (2005) 'Remaking Big Government: Immigration and Crime Control in the United States' in in Sudbury, J. ed. (2005) *Global Lockdown: Race, Gender and the Prison Industrial Complex*, New York, Routledge.

Bosworth, M. (2004), 'Theorizing Race and Imprisonment: Towards a New Penality', *Critical Criminology*, 12: 221–42.

Bowling, B. (1998), *Violent Racism: Victimisation, Policing and Social Context*. Oxford: Clarendon Press.

Carlen, P. (1998) *Sledgehammer: Women's Imprisonment at the Millennium* (Basingstoke: Macmillan).

Cheloitis, A.K. and A. Liebling (2006) 'Race Matters in British Prisons' in *British* Journal of Criminology. 46, 286–317.

Chigwada, R. (1997) *Black Women's Experiences of Criminal Justice: Race, Gender and Class-A Discourse on Disadvantage*, London, Waterside Press.

Da Cunha, I.P. (2005) 'From Neighborhood to Prison: Women and the War on Drugs in Portugal' in J. Sudbury *Global Lockdown: Race, Gender and the Prison Industrial Complex*, New York, Routledge.

Diaz-Cotto, J. (2005) 'Latinas and the War on Drugs in the U.S., Latin America and Europe' in J. Sudbury *Global Lockdown: Race, Gender and the Prison Industrial Complex*, New York, Routledge.

Gabbidon, S. and Greene, H.T. (2005) *Race and Crime*, New York, Sage.

Gelsthorpe, L. (1986) 'Towards a Skeptical Look at Sexism' *International Journal of the Sociology of Law* 14(2):125-152.

Green, P. (1996) *Drug Couriers*, London, Howard League.

Hall, S. (1980). 'Race, articulation and societies structured in dominance.' In: *Sociological Theories: Race and Colonialism*. Paris: UNESCO.

Hart, H.H. (1896) 'Immigration and Crime' in *American Journal of Sociology*

Jones, Marlyn J. (2004) Crossing the Wrong Boundaries: The Dilemma of Women's Drug Trade Participation in Jamaica. In Anita Kalunta-Crumpton and Biko Agozino, *Pan African Issues in Crime and Justice*. Aldershot: Ashgate.

Kalunta-Crumpton, A. (1999) *Race and Drug Trials*, Aldershot, Ashgate.

Kempadoo, K. (2005) 'Victims and Agents of Crime: The New Crusade Against Trafficking' in Sudbury, J. ed. (2005) *Global Lockdown: Race, Gender and the Prison Industrial Complex*, New York, Routledge.

Pfohl, S. (1994) *Images of Deviance and Social Control*, Upper Saddle River, Wadsworth.

Prison Reform Trust (2004) 'Forgotten Prisoners – The Plight of Foreign National Prisoners in England and Wales' *PRT Briefing*, May.

Reiman, J.H. (1979) *The Rich Get Richer and the Poor Get Prison*, New York, John Wiley & Sons.

Rethinking (2003) A Bitter Pill to Swallow: The Sentencing of Foreign National Drug Couriers.

Smart, C. (1995) *Law, Crime and Sexuality: Essays in Feminism* (London: Sage).

Smith, K. (2005) 'Modern Day Slavery: Inside the Prison-Industrial Complex' in in Sudbury, J. ed. (2005) *Global Lockdown: Race, Gender and the Prison Industrial Complex*, New York, Routledge.

Sudbury, J. ed. (2005) 'Mules', 'Yardies' and Other Folk Devils: Mapping Cross-Border Imprisonment in Britain' in J. Sudbury *Global Lockdown: Race, Gender and the Prison Industrial Complex*, New York, Routledge.

Tonry, M. (1996) *Malign Neglect: Race, Crime and Punishment in America*, Oxford, Oxford University Press.

Wood, E., Ken, T. and Montaner, J.S.G. (2007) 'HIV treatment, injection drug use, and illicit drug policies' in *Lancet*, 7/7/2007, vol. 370, issue 9581, pp8-10.

Worrall, A. (1990) *Offending Women: Female Offenders and the Criminal Justice System* (London: Routledge).

CHAPTER 5

Black, Blue, & Bloody: An Examination of the Lautenberg Amendment's Effect on Black Women and Officer Involved Domestic Violence

Caitlin Charles | *Louisiana State University*

Chapter Outcomes

- Understanding the progression of laws intended to protect women from domestic violence.
- Examine the loopholes in the Lautenberg Amendment
- Display the discrimination faced by victims of domestic abuse at the hands of police officers

Introduction

When discussing the topic of violent crimes, the most egregious of these is murder. Lethal violence against women accounts for approximately 20% of the estimated annual homicide deaths worldwide. Women who are victims of domestic violence that are killed, two-thirds of them are killed by their current or former intimate partner (McPhedran, Eriksson, Mazerolle, & Johnson, 2018). With numbers this high, it has become increasingly imperative to address the problem of intimate partner homicide (IPH) as an important and lethal issue as

© Kzenon/Shutterstock.com

IPH accounts for about 3.5% of homicides globally (McPhedran et al., 2018). There are predictors of violent behavior that lead up to the climax of taking the life of another human being that can be found when analyzing and researching the circumstances behind these tragedies (Bailey et al., 1997; Campbell et al., 2003; Eke, Hilton, Harris, Rice, & Houghton, 2011). Taking the time to examine the past behavior of the accused and convicted can reveal commonalities among offenders that can be used to prevent future acts of homicide. In the case of domestic homicide, it is imperative to protect the victims of domestic violence to prevent a grave loss of life.

What we Know

The criminal justice system has deftly enhanced their scope on the topic of domestic violence, from a state of non-responsiveness to one of intervention laws that are mandatory to be carried out. Jurisdictions in different states use different terminology and classification systems when referring to domestic violence. For example, some jurisdictions use the term domestic violence (DV), while others use the term intimate partner violence (IPV). This distinction is potentially important because there are often different associations with either title, although both are used to explain violence that is suffered at the hand of one's spouse or intimate partner. Commonly, the definition is recognized as the physical abuse of a romantic partner by his or her significant other resulting in visible marks, bruises and bumps. Without the tangible repercussions of abuse, people often dismiss it. The true definition of intimate partner violence varies by territory, but encompasses physical, sexual, emotional, economic, and psychological harm-including threats and (cyber)stalking-all committed by a current or former intimate partner or spouse (Akyüz, Yavan, Şahiner, & Kılıç, 2012). The topic of guns is one that is highly debated in the United States, especially with gun violence being prevalent in news stories daily. Many Americans are adamant to keep access to guns because they have the legal right to and avert their attention to the cons of gun laws being so lax. Instead of abetting a feeling of protection, keeping a gun in the home is associated with increased risk of both suicide and homicide of women (Bailey et al., 1997). A domestically abusive household that contains readily available firearms, places a female at particularly high risk of homicide at the hands of her spouse or intimate acquaintance, or a close relative (Bailey et al., 1997; Campbell et al., 2003). This risk increases dramatically should your abuser be an officer of the law as the rate of domestic violence among police families is 2-4 times that of the general public (Ammons, 2004). This type of crime fits under a subgroup of domestic violence known as officer-involved domestic violence (OIDV), which is easily defined, but difficult to identify, study and build effective interventions for due to the lack of data (Klinoff, Van Hasselt, & Black, 2015). That it remains a struggle to study this phenomenon despite constant news stories of women being murdered by their law enforcement partners is an indication that current laws such as the Lautenberg Amendment have not succeeded (Toohey, 2017; Toohey, Discher, & Skene, 2018).

To fix a problem, you must first understand what the nature of the problem. This includes the current and historical context of the problem, who the problem affects, how the problem affects them and what solutions have been previously implemented to address this problem. That is the path we will take as we delve into some of the current gun laws and examine how they affect victims of domestic violence, perpetuate misconduct within the criminal justice system and provides a lackadaisical solution to reducing the number of domestic homicides by gun. This report is written to inspect the absence of adequate policing, monitoring and due justice for women of color in abusive relationships with police officers. This specification is important within the research because of the higher rate of exposure to violence from an intimate partner that is experienced by women of color (Violence Policy Center, 2018).

An attempt of the government to assist in this comes in the form of laws such as the Lautenberg Amendment to put stricter limitations on gun requirements and acquisition. The remainder of this essay is written to show that despite its intentions, the Lautenberg Amendment did not completely fulfill its duty to restrict abuser's access to guns as well as highlighting ways that domestic violence might be reduced.

History

The disproportionate burden of fatal and nonfatal violence borne by Black women has almost always been overshadowed by the toll violence has taken on Black men (Violence Policy Center, 2018). The proportion of African American women abused by a partner during their lifetime is 1.3 times that of

White women and 1.2 times that of Hispanic women (Cheng & Lo, 2016). Analysis of the domestic abuse experiences of African American women identified several challenges for the current criminal justice system. It is important to consider that in Black communities, the "values of family stability, community, self-determination, and protection of one's racial and ethnic culture" may be viewed as contradictory to addressing one's domestic violence situation outside of the home–especially to an authority (Robinson & Chandek, 2000). Analyses of the experiences of battered African American women compared with White women indicate there are immediate instances of oppression that they face due to their race, gender and class–which is often seen as lower and not as important (Violence Policy Center, 2018; West, 2004). With this oppression in mind, the dismissal of Black women is ever more present when abused by a police officer, their disadvantage already then clusters with the protective nature of law enforcement amongst one another (Ammons, 2004; Ávila, 2015).

Abused women are five times more likely to be killed if their abuser owns a firearm and domestic violence assaults involving a gun are 12 times more likely to end in death than assaults with other weapons or physical harm (Toohill, 2018). Research conducted by the Center for Disease Control and Prevention (2011: 11) on homicides among intimate partners, found that "the percentage of women intimate partners killed with firearms (64.1%) higher that the percentage of all other female homicides combined (47.5%), demonstrating the imperative need for a reduction in access to firearms within households that suffer from intimate partner violence." In 2015, there were 1,686 women murdered by men; and for victims who knew their offenders, 64% of female homicide victims were wives or intimate acquaintances of their killers, with 55% of them being killed by firearm (Violence Policy Center, 2018). Typically, the violence faced by African American women is often overshadowed by the violence and suffering of African American men. Compared to a Black man, a Black female is far more likely to be killed by her spouse, an intimate acquaintance, or a family member than by a stranger. In a 2015 study of Black victims who knew their offenders, 58% (221 out of 381) were wives, common-law wives, ex-wives, or girlfriends of the offenders (Violence Policy Center, 2018). There is a subgroup of domestic violence known as officer-involved domestic violence, which is easily defined, but difficult to create effective interventions for due to there being very little information. The arrest of an officer can reflect negatively on the department and potentially undermine legitimacy and erode public confidence, especially during this time of public mistrust in law enforcement (Zavala & Melander, 2018). Looking at the risk factors that lead to domestic abuse, it is often seen that there is a desire for control their victim as well as having a lot of job-related stress (Anderson & Lo, 2011; Gibson, Swatt, & Jolicoeur, 2001). Both factors can be associated with the job requirements of police work which places them in a higher bracket for committing this offense.

Police abusers are different from the common abuser because they have "the advantages of their training, their badge, their gun, and the protection of their tight-knit culture" in their repertoire (Ammons, 2004). This makes a big difference because these advantages make them more efficient batterers and could increase their likelihood to begin abusing their romantic partner. Studies over the past two decades have found the rate of DV among police families to be somewhere between 22% and 41%, which is 2-4 times that of the general population (Ammons, 2004). In the case of African American women, there is a disproportionate risk for them experiencing domestic violence at a rate of 2.4 times that of their White counterparts (Hampton, LaTaillade, Dacey, & Marghi, 2008). It is a struggle for researchers to get a grasp on the extent of the problem with any accuracy, despite stories of women being murdered by their law enforcement partners continuing to appear in the news. This would seem to indicate that current laws, such as the Lautenberg Amendment, have not been successful in its practice. Furthermore, it stands to reason that the Lautenberg Agreement is not solely responsible for the lack of progress. There are other laws that preceded this one to prevent further gun violence and harm done against women at the hands of their romantic partner. The history of these impacts is listed below.

Laws

Gun Control Act of 1968

In 1968, after the assassinations of President John Kennedy and Dr. Martin Luther King, Jr., the Gun Control Act of 1968 was prompted into being passed due of the ease of the mail-order rifle that was used to shoot the former president. These acts of violence fueled an inferno of outrage in the public that demanded congressional action. This act was passed as an amendment to the National Firearms Act and contained even more significant restrictions on firearms. The act set its sights on helping the states enforce their own firearm laws by harshly restricting mail-order rifles, shotguns and ammunition—thus making it impossible to order long guns from an out-of-state gun mail-order house—as was done by the

man who assassinated President Kennedy. The act even includes a one-week waiting period so that state authorities have a chance to check the credentials of the purchaser to ensure that he can own the weapon that he has ordered. Gun salesmen who do not abide by this law are faced with a maximum penalty of a $10,000 fine and ten years in jail. In 1993, the Brady Handgun Violence Prevention Act (1993) was passed, that created a background check system which required licensed sellers to inspect the criminal history of prospective clients. Within the Gun Control Act, the Brady Act also created a list of individuals who are prohibited from buying firearms, thus creating stricter licensing and regulations on firearms. This allowed dealers to withhold access—including possession and the ability to purchase—from prohibited individuals such as fugitives, anyone convicted and imprisoned for more than a year, and people of low mental competence (Nathan, 2000). Within the confines of this law, a haven was created for government officials, military and law enforcement personnel by exempting them from its indictment under the guise of their weapons being for "official use."

Violence Against Women Act of 1994

The subject of domestic violence has often been listed as a 'personal family problem' to be dealt with inside of one's home between the individuals in that domain. Those feelings of resistance became feelings of unease with the rising violent crime rate, including women as constant victims of violence. During the 1970s period of radicalism, concern began to grow for the climbing violence against women. This became a public outcry for a shift in the attitudinal behaviors presented by societal blaming of victims and ignoring the violence against them in their own home. This led to data collection on family violence and the consideration of family violence as a crime rather than an intimate matter of little importance (Sacco, 2014). With the number of abused women and intimate partner homicide growing, Congress enacted landmark legislation to serve as a legal protector to these acts of immense violence. The Violence Against Women's Act was the first federal law that addressed domestic violence crimes and allowed the government precedence in the prosecution and punishment of these crimes, as well as the treatment and protection of the women affected (Conyers, 2007). The Violence Against Women Act (VAWA) was originally passed by Congress as Title IV of the Violent Crime Control and Law Enforcement Act of 1994 (Mennicke & Ropes, 2016; Sacco, 2014). The intentions of the act were to change public attitudes toward domestic violence, foster an awareness of domestic violence and sex crimes, improve services and provisions for victims, and revise the manner in which the criminal justice system responds to criminal proceedings of this nature (Sacco, 2014). VAWA enhanced the investigation process and prosecutions of sexual offenses, as well as provided several grant programs to address violence against women from a different angle on the topic that included law enforcement, public and private entities, service providers and victims of crime (Sacco, 2014). Over time, VAWA has been reauthorized and expanded to become more inclusive of every victim of domestic violence such as including the Battered Immigrant Women Protection Act into VAWA in 2000. This provided benefits to immigrants who were being abused by their U.S. citizen spouse or significant other, children in an abusive household and noncitizen spouses of government and military officials (Conyers, 2007). These laws provided a specific light to be shed on the violence against women and took steps to prevent it, although a specific kind of violence against women still lingered.

Lautenberg Amendment (1996)

The Lautenberg Amendment was created as an addendum to the Gun Control Act of 1968. The Lautenberg Amendment states that it is unlawful for any individual who has been previously been convicted of an offense that qualifies as a "misdemeanor crime of domestic violence," and to transport, ship, possesses or receive firearms or ammunition in or affecting commerce (Halstead, 2001; Skakun III, 2008). A "misdemeanor crime of domestic violence" is defined as, "an offense that is a federal, state, or tribal law misdemeanor and includes the use—or attempted use—of physical force or where threatened use of a deadly weapon as an element of the crime (Skakun III, 2008). It is also a requirement of the amendment that the offender's relationship to the victim must be in line with one or more of the following criteria: must be a current or former spouse, parent, or guardian of the victim, share a child with the victim; be a current or former cohabitant with the victim as a spouse, parent, or guardian; be similarly situated to a spouse, parent, or guardian of the victim(Halstead, 2001; Toohill, 2018). This amendment casts a wider net on who could be considered within the realms of possible offenders, which now included government officials, such as the police and military personnel. This was done to close the loophole in the Gun Control Act, which enabled domestic violence offenders to evade an additional felony conviction for gun possession by getting domestic violence felony charges reduced to misdemeanors.

Loopholes

Research reveals holes within the law such as, a loophole that excludes government officials such as police and senators from having to give up their weapons; the law not applying to abusers of non-spouse partners; the states having to create varying additions to this law that differ depending on where the victim is located. These are only three of the many gaps in the law that are presented by this amendment that was rushed into the law. To examine this deeper, I will draw on a detailed compilation of the law document, along with the subsequent state policies for some states, along with studies that provide a deeper context as to why the lack of consistency and complacency of lawmakers is serving to promote rather than impede domestic violence in one's personal home and within the realm of government workers who are flying under the radar in their weapons possession and abusive behavior. This law was intended to prevent access to purchasing and owning firearms for convicted domestic abusers, but has significant limitations to its proficiency, which is listed below as stated by the Giffords Law Center (2018):

- **Does not apply to many abusers who victimize non-spouse partners**. Domestic violence can affect people whose relationship falls outside of the protections of federal law. Such as dating partners that are not cohabitating or have a child together. A study of applicants for domestic violence restraining orders in Los Angeles found that the most common relationship between the victim and abuser was a dating relationship.

- **Does not apply to abusers who victimize a family member other than a partner or child**.

- **Does not apply to convicted stalkers and others subject to a protective order**.

- **Failure to require domestic abusers to surrender their firearms.** Federal law does not require domestic abusers to turn in their firearms once they are convicted of a crime of domestic violence or become subject to a restraining order.

- **Not all states report all prohibit abusers.** For background checks to prevent abusers from obtaining guns, states must report abusers who fall within prohibited categories to the proper databases.

- Federal law does not require a background check to be performed before every sale of a gun, including sales by unlicensed, private sellers. In states that require a background check for every handgun sale, 38% fewer women are shot to death by intimate partners.

Configuring a solution to states having laws that do not prohibit gun ownership or usage for individuals convicted of domestic violence, is critical to reducing the number of domestic homicides by gun. Law makers within some states have taken it upon themselves to create broader laws that cover the holes left by the Lautenberg Amendment as mentioned above, but it is not a requirement by law to do so. Several states have made some attempt to close the gaps in the law by applying their own solutions, in ways such as: broadening their definition of what is legally classified as domestic violence to include: former and current dating partners, someone who has had a romantic relationship with the offender, as well as any present or former household member or cohabitant of the offender (Toohill, 2018). California, Connecticut, Hawaii, and New York prohibit the purchase and possession of firearms or ammunition by anyone convicted of assault, battery, or stalking without regard to the victim's relationship to the offender (Toohill, 2018). With these adjustments, some states have experienced a notable reduction in the number of intimate partner homicides. Although there is support for policies that attempt to more comprehensively protect victims of domestic violence exist, it is problematic when every state has a fluctuating definition and differing additional policies that do not translate across state lines.

Police Handling of Domestic Violence

When approaching the stereotyped and biased views that police and society place on Black women, there is a lackluster approach–if any at all–to responding to domestic violence calls from poor ethnic-centered neighborhoods. Due to the level of power held by officers of the law, they are granted discretion of who

© FrameStockFootages/Shutterstock.com

they arrest and why both of which can lead to an abuse of power. This level of discretion becomes problematic when they consistently base their decisions on a suspect's race, gender or other attributes such as the normative view of Black women not being civilized enough to be protected within the bounds of the law (Jacobs, 2017; Wetendorf & Davis, 2015). Actions such as these can easily lead to institutionalized racism and sexism, all of which does not bode well for women of color in domestically abusive relationships

(Wetendorf & Davis, 2015). Police dichotomize the Blacks in high poverty areas as having an atypical family structure, drug problems and a history of habitual negative behavior within the context of the stereotypes. These principles along with the presence of systematic racism, can create a lack of responsiveness to the calls and pleas of those suffering from domestic violence—especially if the abuser in question is a police officer. There is a very ill-advised view by the police for women who are in abusive relationships, believing that they would leave or press charges if they really wanted to or if it was really that bad. The responses of abuse victims to intervention tactics are frequently to retract the charges against her abuser, refuse to testify against him and take him back. What happens to women who are in relationships with police offers is contrary to what officers portray. Instead women are being abused and cannot see a way out. Their complaints and calls for help often go unreported, ignored or covered up due to a dull understanding and consideration of the cycle of violence and the resulting trauma.

Research published in July 2017 by the Centers for Disease Control and Prevention found that, "Homicides occur in women of all ages and among all races/ethnicities, but young, racial/ethnic minority women are disproportionately affected." (Violence Policy Center, 2018). The article concluded, "The racial/ethnic differences in female homicide underscore the importance of targeting prevention and intervention efforts to populations at disproportionately high risk (Violence Policy Center, 2018). African Americans are economically and socially disadvantaged, which places them at greater risk for IPV. Although femicide is the seventh leading cause of premature death among women overall, Black women's marginalized status makes them particularly vulnerable. As evidence, murder by intimate partners is the leading cause of death among young African American women between the ages of 15 and 45, with risk levels increasing by a multiple of three if there are one or more guns in the home. (Bailey et al., 1997; Violence Policy Center, 2018; West, 2004)

When looking at an issue as large as domestic violence, and a subset as specific as officer-involved domestic violence, seeing the whole scope of the issue is imperative in fixing it properly. Using the information provided above sets up the platform to breed change and reform in an even larger way. Diffusing prejudices and monitoring the risk factors that police present opportunities for police families to stay safe and informed while acknowledging abusers' consequences both within a precinct and a court room.

Possible Solutions

The legal misrepresentation, disdain and abuse of Black women is a structural issue, as well as one that is considered dubious within police departments. A formal solution to this problem that would better serve the individuals that it is meant to protect, would be to approach change from both a macro and micro level. By conducting reform in this way, it allows for a more inclusive perspective that attempts to cover as many of the issues as possible.

© Rena Schild/Shutterstock.com

Legal & Systematic

Beginning at the top of the structural being, the creation of an inclusive law amendment that would cover every state, all forms/types of domestic abuse, and ensures that the law is carried out especially in government positions—to ensure that there is no collusion to subdue the crimes of offenders. Seeing as every state has their own classification and definition of what is considered domestic violence, it would be imperative to create a standard definition. By constructing an amendment that contains the following elements, it would prevent the amount of leeway toward abusers and the neglect of a victim's cries:

- A cohesive definition of what intimate partner violence is
- Who would be eligible to classify as an offender and/or a victim?
- What actions are associated with that—including behaviors such as stalking and assault.

Along with this amendment, it would be helpful to create a national database of offenders with a requirement to use and update it. This would be useful in maintaining firearm dealers and sales transaction legitimacy as well as providing a means to oversee the legal proceedings that occur in cases of domestic violence. The database could even be monetized by having all registered arms dealers and police stations to be required to have a subscription to it, which could provide a simpler process for updating abuser profiles and checking the buyer before a gun is sold.

Having a more detailed and comprehensive legal document, would prohibit the purchase and possession of firearms and ammunition by people who have been convicted in any court of a misdemeanor crime of domestic violence, stalking or battery. Having a guideline of who is included in participating states, as well as expounding on the protective orders under the law's jurisdiction, would serve as a more inclusive attempt at intimate partner homicide prevention. A group effort to stop officer-involved domestic violence would prove to be beneficial not only for the spouses being affected, but also the communities who have lost faith in the protecting and serving of the police to its neighborhood and people.

The largest problem is the protective system built into police stations that offer safeguard for officers involved in domestic violence. By having a separate group installed into the station that is unbiased in nature and completely of their own accord to inform and prevent OIDV. The creation of a nonpartisan task force that could be an open, neutral and completely confidential ear within the organization, could potentially draw forth some cooperation from the abused women in relationships with officers. Florida has a similar format with their task force within their model policy that includes, "multi-media tie-ins for all agencies, such as posters and brochures for roll call rooms and agency displays, and outreach to educate officers' families about domestic violence" (Oehme & Martin, 2011). This is important in informing officers and their families, as well as creating a safe space for the conversations to be had. An addendum to be made within the creation of the task force, would be important to make sure that there is as much diversity visible as possible, so that every female of any race or ethnicity that is being abused can feel comfortable in coming to the 'group'. A subset goal of this group would be specifically targeted at rooting out the violence hidden and dismissed by police and the ones associated with protecting them.

Local Police & Communities

In looking at a smaller scale of local police, it is imperative to mention the day-to-day interactions and application of how officers handle officer-involved domestic violence within their own communities. Within a neighborhood, sometimes there are resources that are available to victims of domestic violence. When resources are presented as part of police work, some studies find that it creates an awareness and opportunity for having conversations regarding this behavior. The International Association of Chiefs of Police (IACP) created a model policy in 1999 explaining how agencies should respond to officers who have been accused of domestic violence, and they recommended that every agency adopt such type of policy (Mennicke & Ropes, 2016). While some states have adopted policies guided by the IACP model, without any level of accountability or requirement, most states around the country lack regulatory frameworks that address OIDV scenarios. For example, Louisiana currently has no policies on OIDV. Currently, states with model policies do not bind individual law enforcement departments or mandate their adoption; state model policies merely serve as guidelines for agencies to create their own directives (Ávila, 2015). This lack of directive involvement has been ineffective, leaving many agencies with little to no actual classification or policy enforcement of OIDV. While litigation has developed in some areas to allow victims of police abuse to access legal solutions, courts have been reluctant to incorporate OIDV into their line-of-duty jurisprudence (Ávila, 2015). As an example of in-house treatments, the state of Florida, they use a model policy within the guidelines of IACP to encourage departments to create and utilize innovative programs for prevention, early intervention, training, and targeted assistance to officers and their families on this critical issue (Oehme & Martin, 2011). Line-of-duty misconduct is classified as any unlawful actions taken by the police while carrying out their official responsibilities. When citing this as an offense the statue is conveyed as "illegal activity conducted by police officers acting under 'color of law'; all of which must be regulated distinctively because the potential for abuse of power is greater when the wrongdoer is "clothed" with the authority of state law (Ávila, 2015). National and local legislators need to enact laws that push individual departments to adopt policies that treat OIDV as line-of-duty crime and give officers clear instructions on how to respond to and investigate these cases (Ávila, 2015).

Conclusion

During this research of the laws and policies, it has been revealed the underlying issue with police officer abusers preventing and regulating the issue of OIDV. Most state laws do not specifically manage prevention and intervention training regarding officer-involved domestic violence. To adequately protect these victims–who are already at a much higher risk for both domestic abuse and homicide–there needs to be some form of mediation. A collaboration of lawmakers, police officers and advocacy agencies would be ideal in coming up with solutions that could be consistent and effective.

Key Terms:

Gun Violence	Lautenberg Amendment	Officer-Involved Domestic Violence

Discussion Questions:

1. Compare and contrast the Lautenberg Amendment and domestic violence law between two U.S. states of your choosing.

2. In what ways could advocacy groups and scholars contribute to the conversation about protecting women from violence?

3. What criteria would you use to assess the local police force in your area?

4. Considering the current climate of the country, give two examples of officer-involved domestic violence.

5. Have you ever known anyone who suffered intimate partner violence? Was there any support that they received from the police in their neighborhood? Why or why not? Discuss the methodological design of the current project, including its strengths and weaknesses.

References

Akyüz, A., Yavan, T., Şahiner, G., & Kılıç, A. (2012). Domestic violence and woman's reproductive health: a review of the literature. *Aggression and Violent Behavior, 17*(6), 514–518. https://doi.org/10.1016/j.avb.2012.07.005

Ammons, J. (2004). Batterers with Badges: Officer-Involved Domestic Violence. *Women Lawyers Journal*, (Issue 5), 28.

Anderson, A. S., & Lo, C. C. (2011). Intimate Partner Violence Within Law Enforcement Families. *Journal of Interpersonal Violence, 26*(6), 1176–1193. https://doi.org/10.1177/0886260510368156

Ávila, A. (2015). When the Batterer Wears a Badge: Regulating Officer-Involved Domestic Violence as a Line-of-Duty Crime. *American Journal of Criminal Law, 42*(3), 213–239.

Bailey, J. E., Kellermann, A. L., Somes, G. W., Banton, J. G., Rivara, F. P., & Rushforth, N. P. (1997). Risk Factors for Violent Death of Women in the Home. *Archives of Internal Medicine, 157*(7), 777–782. https://doi.org/10.1001/archinte.1997.00440280101009

Campbell, J. C., Webster, D., Koziol-McLain, J., Block, C., Campbell, D., Curry, M. A., … Laughon, K. (2003). Risk Factors for Femicide in Abusive Relationships: Results From a Multisite Case Control Study. *American Journal of Public Health, 93*(7), 1089–1097. https://doi.org/10.2105/AJPH.93.7.1089

Centers for Disease Control and Prevention. 2001. *Surveillance for Homicide Among Intimate Partners —United States, 1981–1998* (Vol. 50 No. SS-3). Atlanta: Centers for Disease Control and Prevention.

Cheng, T. C., & Lo, C. C. (2016). Racial Disparities in Intimate Partner Violence Examined Through the Multiple Disadvantage Model. *Journal of Interpersonal Violence, 31*(11), 2026–2051. https://doi.org/10.1177/0886260515572475

Conyers, J. (2007). The 2005 Reauthorization of the Violence Against Women Act: Why Congress Acted to Expand Protections to Immigrant Victims. *Violence Against Women, 13*(5), 457–468. https://doi.org/10.1177/1077801207300650

Eke, A., Hilton, N., Harris, G., Rice, M., & Houghton, R. (2011). Intimate Partner Homicide: Risk Assessment and Prospects for Prediction. *Journal of Family Violence, 26*(3), 211–216. https://doi.org/10.1007/s10896-010-9356-y

Gibson, C. L., Swatt, M. L., & Jolicoeur, J. R. (2001). Assessing the Generality of General Strain Theory: The Relationship Among Occupational Stress Experienced by Male Police Officers and Domestic Forms of Violence. *Journal of Crime and Justice, 24*(2), 29–57. https://doi.org/10.1080/0735648X.2001.9721133

Halstead, T. J. (2001). *Firearms Prohibitions and Domestic Violence Convictions: The Lautenberg Amendment* (CRS Report for Congress No. RL31143). The Library of Congress. Retrieved from https://www.everycrsreport.com/reports/RL31143.html

Hampton, R. L., LaTaillade, J. J., Dacey, A., & Marghi, J. R. (2008). Evaluating Domestic Violence Interventions for Black Women. *Journal of Aggression, Maltreatment & Trauma, 16*(3), 330–353.

Jacobs, M. S. (2017). The Violent State: Black Women's Invisible Struggle Against Police Violence. *William & Mary Journal of Women & the Law, 24*(1), 39.

Klinoff, V. A., Van Hasselt, V. B., & Black, R. A. (2015). Homicide-suicide in police families: An analysis of cases from 2007-2014. *Journal of Forensic Practice, 17*(2), 101–116. https://doi.org/10.1108/JFP-07-2014-0019

McPhedran, S., Eriksson, L., Mazerolle, P., & Johnson, H. (2018). Victim-focussed studies of intimate partner femicide: A critique of methodological challenges and limitations in current research. *Aggression and Violent Behavior, 39*, 61–66. https://doi.org/10.1016/j.avb.2018.02.005

Mennicke, A. M., & Ropes, K. (2016). Estimating the rate of domestic violence perpetrated by law enforcement officers: A review of methods and estimates. *Aggression and Violent Behavior, 31*, 157–164. https://doi.org/10.1016/j.avb.2016.09.003

Nathan, A. J., student author. (2000). At the intersection of domestic violence and guns: the public interest exception and the Lautenberg Amendment. *Cornell Law Review, 85*(3), 822–858.

Oehme, K., & Martin, A. (2011). A practical plan for prevention and intervention: Florida's new Model Policy on officer-involved domestic violence. *Criminal Justice Studies: A Critical Journal of Crime, Law & Society, 24*(4), 395–408. https://doi.org/10.1080/1478601X.2011.626152

Robinson, A. L., & Chandek, M. S. (2000). Differential Police Response to Black Battered Women. *Women & Criminal Justice, 12*(2/3), 29–61. https://doi.org/10.1300/J012v12n02_04

Sacco, L. N. (2014). *The Violence Against Women Act: Overview, Legislation, and Federal Funding* (Congressional Research Service Report No. R42499) (p. 43). Washington D.C.: Library of Congress. Congressional Research Service. Retrieved from https://digital.library.unt.edu/ark:/67531/metadc332968/

Skakun III, J. M. (2008). Violence and Contact: Interpreting "Physical Force" in the Lautenberg Amendment. *The University of Chicago Law Review, 75*(4), 1833.

Toohey, G. (2017, August 2). Domestic violence killings in Baton Rouge reach "epidemic proportions" as homicides surge overall. Retrieved March 3, 2018, from http://www.theadvocate.com/baton_rouge/news/crime_police/article_7ca3b4e8-77d2-11e7-8bec-33a1fb466247.html

Toohey, G., Discher, E., & Skene, L. (2018, January 6). As Baton Rouge homicide rate exceeds Chicago's in 2017, an in-depth look at how, why. Retrieved March 3, 2018, from http://www.theadvocate.com/baton_rouge/news/crime_police/article_ddc03060-f173-11e7-90ea-9f16d6e9dbe8.html

Toohill, K. (2018). Domestic Violence & Firearms [Giffords Law Center]. Retrieved March 1, 2019, from https://lawcenter.giffords.org/gun-laws/policy-areas/who-can-have-a-gun/domestic-violence-firearms/

Violence Policy Center. (2018). *When Men Murder Women: An Analysis of 2016 Homicide Data* (Annual Study) (pp. 1–27). Washington, DC: Violence Policy Center.

West, C. M. (2004). Black Women and Intimate Partner Violence. *Journal of Interpersonal Violence, 19*(12), 1487–1493. https://doi.org/10.1177/0886260504269700

Wetendorf, D., & Davis, D. (2015, January). The Misuse of Police Powers in Officer-Involved Domestic Violence. Diane Wetendorf, Inc. Retrieved from https://vawnet.org/material/misuse-police-powers-officer-involved-domestic-violence

Zavala, E., & Melander, L. A. (2018). Intimate partner violence perpetrated by police officers: Is it self-control or the desire-to-be-in-control that matters more? *Journal of Aggression, Maltreatment & Trauma.* https://doi.org/10.1080/10926771.2018.1531960

CHAPTER 6

Recognizing Implicit Bias in the Criminal Justice System: Does It Result in Covert Discrimination?

Beverly Ross, Ph.D., C.S.P. | *Mathilda Spencer, Ph.D.*

Contributed by Beverly Ross. Copyright © Kendall Hunt Publishing Company.

Overview

Current research suggests that some individuals or groups receive disparate treatment by the criminal justice system. We suggest that to some degree, varying levels of implicit bias contribute to this disparity. Although there is extensive data that has examined the presence of implicit bias regarding race and to some degree gender, there is a dearth in the literature investigating the role of implicit bias and how it might influence the perceptions of criminal justice practitioners. Specifically, we will explore how implicit bias develops over the life course as well as to examine how it may be a factor for differential treatment in categories of race and gender. Using stories based on personal experience by some practitioners, we intend to illustrate this phenomenon and to raise greater self-awareness for those who will interact with minorities in the justice system. Accordingly, concluding sections will offer corrective measures to identify and potentially mediate these practices.

Chapter Outcomes

- Examine the relationship between gender and crime
- Consider the ways in which gender impacts justice practices
- Describe statistical inequities that are related to gender and disparate treatment
- Recognize how disparate sentencing results in covert discrimination
- Assess the significance of addressing and decreasing implicit bias in justice practitioners

Background/Research Questions:

Implicit or unconscious bias may be the reason why we hold a preference or an aversion for a particular group of people. Psychologists have identified this phenomenon through a variety of social interactions. Therefore, it is likely that implicit or unconscious bias would also contribute to disparate treatment of individuals in our criminal justice system. While there is extensive study of how an offender's race might impact the outcome of all phases of his or her interaction with the American justice system, the gender of the individual assessing the offender is less likely to be explored. We seek an understanding of the following questions: 1) how implicit bias develops over the life course and specifically, what are the cognitive processes that contribute to disparate treatment, 2) why practitioners might unintentionally practice gender or race discrimination, 3) what is the evidence or statistical support for these assumptions and, 4) how might these approaches be exposed and corrected?

Implicit Bias and Life Course Development

Unconscious bias is also referred to as implicit social cognition. Although early in the 1900's, many social psychologists assumed that development of stereotypes was a conscious process. Thus, later in the 20th century, through the work of Banaji and Greenwald (1995), it became evident that both attitudes and stereotyping are more likely the result of unconscious cognitive processing that is formed by past experiences. This development involves unconscious recollection of prior experience or exposure that will influence perceptions in three major categories. Categories include attitudes, self-esteem, and stereotypes. Our primary focus for this exploration will examine how attitudes and stereotypes that are informed through social cognition may result in a degree of unrecognized discrimination.

An implicit attitude is one that exists about a particular person or object. For example, if one has developed a negative attitude toward a specific religion or race, it is likely that this attitude will carry over to any member of that group without deliberate consideration otherwise. Social psychologists consider humans to be cognitive misers who do not take the time to deliberately process all types of information when formulating an opinion. It is much easier to generalize by using implicit social cognition (*Online dictionary.com*, 2015).

The process of stereotyping is very similar. It has been shown that single words can trigger attitudes about other individuals. This tendency has been identified as effortless automatic social cognition (Greenwald & Banaji, 1995). A second concept, called priming, utilizes a prior memory to form a quicker recognition of something. Although both of these processes can be generalized to most decision-making, our focus is to identify the way in which implicit bias influences racial and gender stereotyping.

Implicit Bias of Gender and Race

There are several studies that seek an understanding of the ways in which implicit bias impacts evaluation and behavior. Consistent with our exploration, it is important to illustrate evidence-based research and in two key domains, race and gender. For example, in Greenwald & Banaji (1995), findings from external studies revealed that White respondents were more likely to respond quickly when the pairings of words

© Rob Wilson/Shutterstock.com

were White-positive rather than Black-positive, specifically, the terms were *White-smart* versus *Black-smart*. Similarly, studies designed to evaluate gender, revealed that when respondents assessed authors who were perceived to be male, they were appraised more favorably than those they believed to be female (Greenwald & Banaji, 1995). Both of these examples elucidate the concept of priming. Moving beyond our illustration of the way in which social implicit cognition apprises perceptions and attitudes is an examination of the sentencing differences that indicate racial and gendered bias.

Disparate Treatment and Covert Discrimination

We expect that given the universal probability that all individuals will develop implicit bias to some degree that evidence of this will be recognizable in justice professionals not only acquiring these attitudes and stereotypes but also that their actions will likely create a cumulative disadvantage in all stages of adjudication. As we mentioned in our background statement, race in general and disparate treatment has been widely studied. However, we suggest that the attitudes of justice professionals toward females are different than for males and are influenced by implicit bias. Additionally, we assert that there is a secondary consideration for race that exposes the way in which justice professionals assess and process minority females versus minority males. We offer support for this position through the following research studies.

Disparate Sentencing

As previously indicated, disparate treatment of certain demographic groups has been widely studied. Goulette, Wooldredge, Frank, and Travis (2015) utilized 3,593 felony cases that were referred to prosecution in 2009. These researchers introduce relevant concepts that may explain why females are treated more leniently than their male counterparts. Goulette et al., (2015) suggest that one reason may be the chivalry/paternalism hypothesis that effectively results in justice professionals approaching these females with the same perspective as they would their own female family members.

© Skyward Kick Productions/Shutterstock.com

Specifically, this hypothesis argues that judges in particular view females as needing their protection rather than punishment. In their study, (Goulette et al., 2015) theorized that females would receive more lenient treatment than males needing punishment, which would include lower bonds amounts, less likely to be incarcerated pre-trial, more likely to receive suspended sentences, and shorter prison sentences overall. In our second research question, we sought to determine whether minority females would receive different treatment than their Caucasian counterparts. Therefore, the researchers in this study expected that White females would have cumulative advantages over Black females (Goulette, et al., 2015). The research sample included an appropriate cross section of defendants with age, gender, and racial representation. As Goulette et al., (2015) predicted, females in general were more likely to receive suspended sentences than males. The defendant's gender did not impact the length of sentencing if they were ordered to jail but Black females were more likely to receive prison sentences than White females.

In another study by Veysey (2015) gender role incongruence was examined as it related to criminal responsibility. Data from 4,842 cases provided by the Insanity Defense Reform Project was utilized to examine whether or not gender was a correlating variable to conviction outcomes. Veysey (2015) expected that women were more likely to be found not guilty by reason of insanity (NGRI) than males for similar crimes. This outcome was controlled by the relationship to the victim and specifically, whether or not the victims were members of the defendant's own family. The exception to this theory is whether or not the victim was the spouse of the defendant. In this scenario, women and men fare equally in successfully using the NGRI defense (Veysey, 2015). The results of the study supported the suggestion that gender would impact whether or not females are more likely to be successful in a NGRI defense than males as long as their victims were their own children or other family members. Women who used this defense for their spouses fared similarly to their male counterparts, concluding that their original theory supported gender disparity in the NGRI defense when victims were family members other than spouses (Veysey, 2015).

Finally, in one other study that examined gender disparity in sentencing sexual offenders, Weinsheimer, Wolwod, Coburn, Chong, and Connolly (2017) reviewed 4,237 cases of sexual abuse. From these, 70 cases were identified that named female defendants. The authors compared these 70 cases with a random sample of 70 male defendant cases and provided the following conclusions. First, female accusers went to court faster than males, in fact male defendant cases took twice as long. Plus, females received shorter sentences after controlling for the type of offense Weinsheimer, et al., 2017).

Policy Implications

According to Goulette et al., (2015) one of the remedies for the lack of uniformity created by implicit bias would be the use of mandatory sentencing guidelines resulting in fewer options for judicial discretion. Specifically, women that are more likely to receive probation than sentencing would have equal punishment.

Although these external measures would help to facilitate a more egalitarian approach to the way in which both males are females are processed in the American criminal justice system, it is likely that justice practitioners should utilize a parallel focus to address awareness of implicit bias. Weinsheimer et al., (2018) recommend gender-responsive programming that is designed to meet the specific needs of male and female juveniles. Perhaps a similar training approach should be developed to address gender disparities for practitioners working in all areas of the justice system.

In the final section of this paper we provide specific examples of implicit bias in practice as well as anecdotal information and insight.

Examining Gender, Race and Criminal Justice Practitioners'

The criminal justice system is comprised of three entities: law enforcement, courts, and corrections. There is a substantial amount of attention paid to the impact of race, gender, and class on criminal justice processing and sanctioning of the defendant. As we offered in the background statement, we anticipated that we would see some level of disparate treatment between males and females, and specifically minority females. The following sections provide anecdotal information on these three domains.

Law Enforcement

Federal law enforcement includes the FBI and U.S. Secret Service. State level agencies include the state or highway patrol. It is at the local level that we find those that are primarily conducting the arrest that result in prison and this includes the police and sheriff departments.

According to the Bureau of Justice Statistics (2018) more than 12,000 local police departments were operating in the United States during 2016. A 2013 survey, conducted by the National Association of

Women Law Enforcement Executives, found that there were only 169 women in management positions (Balsamo, 2017). The under-representation of women impacts contemporary law enforcement problems such as police brutality and the inadequate police response to violence against women.

Implicit bias is often cited as the reason for a disconnect between law enforcement and communities of color. On September 16, 2016 in Tulsa, Oklahoma, Officer Betty Jo Shelby fatally shot Terrance Crutcher, an unarmed motorist. This shooting, unfortunately one of many involving a white officer and a black unarmed citizen, received national attention. While most of the incidents involved White male officers, this incident involved a White female. Officer Shelby was tried and acquitted of first-degree manslaughter. Although acquitted, the jury questioned her judgment and suggested that serious consideration for Officer Shelby's return to practicing law enforcement should be considered (Becker, 2018). Did Officer Shelby's gender and Terrance Crutcher's race intersect and result in this deadly encounter? Officer Shelby continues to defend her action and has stated that race had nothing to do with it, but still felt the need to use deadly force despite describing Crutcher as intoxicated and exhibiting "zombie-like" behavior (Becker, 2018). If indeed Crutcher was exhibiting "zombie-like" behavior, could less lethal means have been utilized to subdue Crutcher? Upon viewing the videotape, I was shocked and appalled by the actions of this officer. I had a strong expectation, perhaps my implicit bias, that a female would be more understanding and less impulsive when encountering a Black male, but Officer Shelby's action was consistent with other actions by White female law enforcement officers. This most likely indicates that women are influenced through the same social cognition as men. Was implicit bias a factor in Office Shelby's actions? Although we have no way of knowing for certain, statistics as well as other examples would indicate that it was a factor.

Courts

The American Bar Association (2018) reports that 64% of attorneys are male and 36% are female. Additionally, their statistics indicate that 85% of attorneys are White and 5% are Black. While women make of half of the enrolled law students, less than one-third of state judges are women. Vanderbilt University (2016) created the first-of-its-kind database of more than 10,000 current state judges. The demographics reveal that the judicial representation is not consistent with the demographics of the constituents they serve. Currently, the Supreme Court is setting the tone for better demographic representation. For the first time in United States history, three of the nine sitting justices are women. More than half of the state trial and appellate judges are White men. For people of color, the statistics are abysmal, with two in ten judges being a racial minority and women of color being the most underrepresented in state courts (George & Yoon, 2016). Starting with the way that district attorney's select juries to imposition of sentences post-conviction, there are serious implications for the justice system if individuals are sanctioned differently based on gender. Attorneys often keep gender in mind if a case, especially a case involving violence against a woman, is coming to trial. Studies indicate that in rape cases, male jurors are less likely to convict than female jurors (Hegger, 2015). When selecting a jury, both the defense and the prosecution may remove potential jurors using an unlimited number of challenges for cause (e.g., stated reasons such as bias) and a limited number of peremptory challenges (i.e., do not need to state a reason). Prosecutors often remove jurors, based on their race or gender, if they perceive that the juror may be sympathetic to the defendant. In 1986, however, the Supreme Court ruled it unconstitutional to dismiss jurors based upon race (*Batson v. Kentucky,* 1986). In 1994, based upon the Batson decision, the Supreme Court upheld that the decision also applies to gender (*J.E.B. v. Alabama,* 1994). Although the Supreme Court called attention and eliminated these practices, attorneys have continued to seek a jury who are biased and swayed by their emotions.

As we assert there may be serious implications for individuals sanctioned differently based on gender. Sentencing guidelines have been developed to mitigate the influence of bias. The case of Judge Donna Jo McDaniel sheds light on how reasoned judgments can be impacted and detrimental. With primary oversight of the domestic violence and sex offender courts, Judge McDaniel, especially in my experience was always firm but fair. I was shocked to find out that Judge McDaniel had come under the scrutiny of the Superior Court of Pennsylvania using three cases where she was accused of bias when sentencing sex offenders. Accused of relying on unsubstantiated accusations, the sentences on sex offender cases reportedly exceeded the sentences recommended in the sentencing guidelines. In November 2018, the Superior Court of Pennsylvania, citing "unjustified bias" (Commonwealth of Pennsylvania v. Anthony McCauley, 2018) removed Judge McDaniel from three cases that were appealed based upon review the Superior Court. The court determined that as a trial judge, Judge McDaniel repeatedly refused to follow the mandates of the appellate court and that a pattern of bias had emerged (Ward, 2018). After 33 years of being a Common Pleas judge, Donna Jo McDaniel resigned. Judge McDaniel's bias manifested when sentencing sex offenders. While Judge McDaniel's support of crime victims is admirable, it led to explicit bias. The plaintiffs in her courtrooms were victims of domestic violence and sexual assault, thus primarily women and children. It is easy for the general public to support her bias when the defendants are accused of rape of a child or result in the permanent disability of the victim. With an emerging pattern of partiality, and the scrutiny of the Pennsylvania Superior Court, Judge Donna Jo McDaniel, a woman that I greatly admire, resigned. As a female judge witnessing a parade of male defendants and female victims her bias ultimately influenced her judgment. An accomplished professional, her court decisions reflect a gendered response that favored the victims and resulted in longer periods of confinement for the defendants.

Corrections

In May 2018, Louisiana State Rep. Kenny Havard said that a pay raise for prison guards was necessary in part, to reduce the number of women employed as security personnel at state facilities (O'Donoghue, 2018). With this statement, Rep. Havard demonstrated that there is work to be done if women are to receive the same respect and parity as their male counterparts in the correctional environment.

Although not every defendant that is convicted of a felony ends up in prison, they often end up on community supervision. According to the Bureau of Justice Statistics (BJS), 53.6% of Probation officers & correctional treatment specialists are female; making them the more common gender. Additionally, 68.4% of the most common race/ethnicity for Probation officers and correctional treatment specialists are White. Representing 23.5% of Probation officers & correctional treatment specialists, Black or African Americans are the second most common race or ethnicity in this occupation (Bureau of Justice Statistics, 2019).

I can say with confidence from my personal experience that discrepancies exist within the criminal justice system specifically according to gender. While completing my dissertation, I surveyed Pennsylvania adult probation officers (POs) supervising domestic violence offenders. One of the unexpected outcomes of my study was the influence of gender. Most of the studies on gender differences in supervision methods have focused on the offenders' desire to control the female PO and the need for the female PO to take a strong stance when supervising offenders (PCADV, 2003; Petrillo, 2007; Reddick & Chaplin, 1999).

Based upon current literature and the results of my study, I suspect that female POs have a heightened awareness of the needs of the DVO and may feel in need for greater support through than their male counterparts. Although the contributing variables to this phenomenon are yet to be confirmed, my research supports the rationale to explore the relationship of gender and its potential impact on offender supervision (Spencer, 2015).

It is important to state that as a probation officer, I was not impervious to my bias. As a juvenile probation officer, I worked with juvenile sex offenders. My male partner and I ran a cognitive- behavioral group. Our newest member was a female who had molested the males that she was babysitting. Our supervisor came to observe and noticed that wherever the female sex offender sat in the group, my partner and I sat on either side of her. Were we protecting her from the rest of the offenders? It was then that I became aware and acknowledged my own bias.

Interventions and Mediations

In Implicit Bias in the Court Room, Kang et al. identify interventions that might help mitigate the impacts of implicit bias by acknowledging its existence and regularly questioning our objectivity (2015). Practitioners' recognition of their bias is the only solution to improving our criminal justice system. Recognizing the existence of implicit bias in our decision-making is not to condemn a practitioner but to simply acknowledge how it might motivate decision-making. Once recognized, psychologists believe that through a gradual process of de-biasing techniques we can unlearn the implicit biases that are housed deep within our subconscious (Pittaro, 2018).

De-biasing refers to the techniques that will reduce our cognition distortions. Techniques using cognitive restructuring change how the problem is conceptualized, motivates change in incentives or punishments, as well as the use of technology to assist in problem-solving. All of these are designed to lessen and or potentially eliminate the cognitive distortions in decision-making (Pittaro, 2018). The implicit bias that resides in the subconscious of a criminal justice professional can have a negative influence on our real-world behavior resulting in adverse consequences for those whose fates lie at the mercy of criminal justice practitioners.

Conclusion

Our focus for this chapter was to introduce the reader to the concept of implicit bias/social cognition. We identified that reveal a tendency by criminal justice practitioners to evaluate women and men differently. This approach is supported by statistical support and augmented with on the job experience.

We posed a series of questions concerning the way in which implicit bias is formed, how it informs decision making, who is likely to be impacted, and what we should do to address its presence in our justice system. Given its incidence all of three bodies of the American criminal justice system, we agree that following strict mandatory sentencing guidelines would help to mitigate these practices. In addition, development of a more standardized system that includes a risk assessment model supplemented with external oversight would ensure a more equitable outcome for all. This intervention could be developed from an interdisciplinary approach using not only criminal justice practitioners but would also include psychologists and educators familiar with behavioral modification and implementation.

Covert discrimination   Disparate sentencing   Social cognition

De-biasing   Implicit bias

Discussion Questions:

1. What is meant by implicit bias and in what are some examples based on current social issues?
2. Explain the theories that inform deferential treatment of females.
3. In what way is the peremptory challenge relevant to implicit bias?
4. What is meant by the term de-bias?
5. What are some of the strategies or interventions that might be implemented to mitigate covert discrimination?

Web links (Mathilda)

The Gavel Gap: Who sits in judgment on state courts? http://gavelgap.org/pdf/gavel-gap-report.pdf

ABA National Lawyer Population Survey 10-Year Trend in Lawyer Demographics Year 2018 https://www.americanbar.org/content/dam/aba/administrative/market_research/National_Lawyer_Population_Demographics_2008-2018.pdf

Batson v. Kentucky 476 U.S. 79 (1986)

J.E.B. v. Alabama 511 U.S. 127 (1994)

References

American Bar Association (2018). ABA National Lawyer Population Survey 10-Year Trend in Lawyer Demographics Year 2018. Retrieved from https://www.americanbar.org/content/dam/aba/administrative/market_research/National_Lawyer_Population_Demographics_2008-2018.pdf

Balsamo, M. (2017). Growing number of women leading police departments. *Concord Monitor.* Retrieved from https://www.concordmonitor.com/Growing-number-of-women-leading-US-police-departments-7910926

Bureau of Labor Statistics, U.S. Department of Labor, Occupational Outlook Handbook, Probation Officers and Treatment Specialist. Retrieved at https://www.bls.gov/ooh/community-and -social -service/probation-officers-and-correctional-treatment-specialists.htm

Carson, E.A. (2018). *Prisoners in 2016.* Washington, DC: Bureau of Justice Statistics; Retrieved from the Bureau of Justice Statistics https://www.bjs.gov/content/pub/pdf/p16.pdf

Cognitive Miser. (2019). Online Dictionary. Retrieved from: http://www.oxfordreference.com/view/10.1093/oi/authority.20110803095622297

Commonwealth of Pennsylvania v. Anthony McCauley (PA SUP 339 2018) Retrieved from http://www.pacourts.us/assets/opinions/Superior/out/j-a20031-18o.pdf#search=%22Donna%20jo%20mcdaniel%20%27Superior%2bCourt%27%22

Correll, J, Judd, C.M., Wittenbrink, B., Sadler, M.S., Keesee, T. (2007). Across the thin blue line: Police officers and racial bias in the decision to shoot. *Journal of Personality and Social Psychology, 92*(6). doi: 10.1037/0022-3514.92.6.1006

Dagan, D. (2018, March 30). Women aren't always sentenced by the book. And maybe they shouldn't be. *Fivethirtyeight.com.* Retrieved from https://fivethirtyeight.com/features/women-arent-always-sentenced-by-the-book-maybe-men-shouldnt-be-either/

George, T. E., & Yoon, A. H. (2016). *The gavel gap: Who sits in judgement on state courts?* The American Constitution Society for Law and Policy. Retrieved from http://gavelgap.org/pdf/gavel-gap-report.pdf

Greenhouse, L. (1994, April 20). High court bars sex as standard in picking jurors. *The New York Times.* Retrieved from https://www.nytimes.com/1994/04/20/us/high-court-bars-sex-as-standard-in-picking-jurors.html

Greenwald, A., & Banaji, N. (1995). Implicit social cognition: Attitudes, self-esteem, and stereotypes. *Psychological Review, 102*(1), 4-27 doi: 10.1037/0033-295x.102.1.4

Hegger, J. (2015). *How gender affects offenders and officers in the criminal justice system.* Community Corrections Insights. Retrieved April 13, 2019 from https://www.correctionsone.com/probation-and-parole/articles/9508420-How-gender-affects-offenders-and-officers-in-the-criminal-justice-system/

Helfgott, J. B., Gunnison, E., Murtagh, A., & Navejar, B. (2018). BADASSES: The Rise of Women in Criminal Justice. *Women & Criminal Justice, 28*(4), 235. Retrieved from https://search-ebscohost-com.proxy-calu.klnpa.org/login.aspx?direct=true&AuthType=sso&db=edb&AN=133507529&site=eds-live&scope=site

J. E. B. v. Alabama ex rel. T. B., 511 U.S. 127 (1994)

Kaeble, D. (2018). *Probation and Parole in the United States, 2016.* Washington, DC: Bureau of Justice Statistics. Retrieved from the Bureau of Justice Statistics. https://www.bjs.gov/content/pub/pdf/ppus16.pdf

Kang, J., Bennett, M., Carbado, D., Casey, P., Dasgupta, N., Faigman, D., & Mnookin, J. (2012). Implicit Bias in the Courtroom. UCLA Law Review. 59.

O'Donoghue, J. (2018, March 19). Louisiana lawmaker on prison guards: "You don't need a bunch of ladies guarding men". *The Times-Picayune.* Retrieved from https://www.nola.com/politics/2018/03/louisiana_lawmaker_on_prison_g.html

Pennsylvania Coalition Against Domestic Violence. (2003). Domestic violence intervention and supervision model for *Commonwealth of Pennsylvania adult probation and parole departments.* Harrisburg: Pennsylvania Commission on Crime and Delinquency.

Petrillo, M. (2007). Power struggle: Gender issues for female probation officers in the supervision of high-risk offenders. *Probation Journal, 54*(4), 394–406. https://doi.org/10.1177/0264550507083538

Pittaro, M. (2018, November 21). Implicit bias within the criminal justice system. Retrieved from https://www.psychologytoday.com/us/blog/the-crime-and-justice-doctor/201811/implicit-bias-within-the-criminal-justice-system

Rabe-Hemp, C. E., & Miller, S. L. (2018). Special Issue: Women at Work in Criminal Justice Organizations. *Feminist Criminology, 13*(3), 231–236. https://doi.org/10.1177/1557085118763391

Reddick, C., & Chapin, D. (2002, July 17). *Domestic violence: A parole officer's perspective.* Retrieved August 17, 2009, from GWC, Incorporated: https://news.illinois.edu/view/6367/640610

Springer Science+Business Media. (2013, February 19). We know when we're being lazy thinkers: Human thinkers are conscious cognitive misers. ScienceDaily. Retrieved from www.sciencedaily.com/releases/2013/02/130219102202.htm

Smeal, S.M. (2018, April). What women bring to corrections. *Voices.* Retrieved from https://www.governing.com/gov-institute/voices/col-women-corrections-safety-operations-communication-security.html

Spencer, M. (2015). Community Supervision of the Domestic Violence Offender. (Doctoral dissertation). Retrieved from https://knowledge.library.iup.edu/etd/947/

Strickler A. (2015, July 20). Judges key to closing trial counsel gender gap. *Law360.* Retrieved from https://www.law360.com/articles/680493/judges-key-to-closing-trial-counsel-gender-gap.

The Sentencing Project (2018). *The incarceration of women and girls* [Fact sheet]. Retrieved from https://www.sentencingproject.org/publications/incarcerated-women-and-girls/

Wade, S. (2015). *The Justice Women: The Female Presence in the Criminal Justice System 1800-1970.* [N.p.]: Pen and Sword History. Retrieved from https://search-ebscohost-com.proxy-calu.klnpa.org/login.aspx?direct=true&AuthType=sso&db=e000xna&AN=1102467&site=eds-live&scope=site

Ward, P. R. (2018, December 19). Superior Court sends another sex offender case back for resentencing, removes Judge Donna Jo McDaniel. The Post-Gazette. Retrieved from https://www.post-gazette.com/local/city/2018/12/13/Judge-Donna-Jo-McDaniel-resigns-Allegheny-County-sex-offenders/stories/201812130201

Wolf, A. (2016, June 22). Massive database shows state judges are not representative of the people they serve. *Vanderbilt News*. Retrieved from https://news.vanderbilt.edu/2016/06/22/massive-database-shows-state-judges-are-not-representative-of-the-people-they-serve/

Zeng, Z. (2018). *Jail Inmates in 2016*. Washington, DC: Bureau of Justice Statistics; Retrieved from the Bureau of Justice Statistics https://www.bjs.gov/content/pub/pdf/ji16.pdf

CHAPTER 7

Succeed Like A Man: Scarcity and Gendered Deviance and Crime under the One-child Policy in China

Ting Wang | The University of North Carolina at Greensboro

Have you watched the actual-event-based movie *The Saga of Anatahan*? If not, have you heard of the story about the 'Queen Bee of Anatahan'—a Japanese woman, Kazuko Higa, trapped with 31 men on a deserted island (called Anatahan) for seven years as a result of World War II? If this is the first time you have heard of the sketch, what image comes to your mind? Is it an Asian version of *The Crown*, a crowded version of *I am not an Easy Man*, or an excitingly raunchy version of *Game of Thrones*? If commodity goods are in short supply, intuitively and economically, the scarcity should endorse them decent market values (e.g., a high price). But is that also true while being applied to human beings?

Before you google the story yourself, I want to warn you of the sadness and absurdity that happened on "Queen" Higa in her "wonderland-like kingdom." Being the only woman on that Pacific island, few benefits did Higa enjoy; however, she was descended to a wifely object drawn into men's rivalries over power. Eventually, the non-stop competition led to jealousy, aggression, violence, and deaths. She, consequentially, was turned against by her quondam lovers and wooers with death threats as the alleged culprit of the chaos that was caused by men. Higa's story was, undoubtedly, an accidental tragedy, and it premises this chapter for the topic of sex composition, gender construction, and their impacts on crime.

Another relevant story has directly changed the birth and life of one in five people on the earth for over 35 years and counting.

Influenced by Malthusianism, the Chinese central government announced the one-child policy on September 25, 1980 and had since implemented the strictest population control approach in human history till 2016 when the policy was revised to the "two-child policy" under the pressure of aging problems in China. The original and most important intent of the one-child policy was to control fertility rates and curb the then fast-growing population, thereby concentrating limited resources to enhance population quality and eventually eliminating poverty in China. The content of the policy varied from province to province, but sharing general guidelines: For people who were Han ethnicity (comprising over 90% of the Chinese population), every urban couple could only have one child regardless of its sex; every rural couple, because of the manual labor demand in agricultural production, could have two children but only if the first was a girl, or only one if the first was a boy (Wang, 2019). This policy, officially named as one of the "basic national policies" and mingled with the strong executive capacity of socialist governments[1], swept the whole country and generated nationwide effects on cultural and social structure.

Working as designed, the one-child policy has successfully bridled the growth and shrunk the total population by over 400 million as an estimate given by the Chinese National Health and Family Planning Commission in 2013. Correspondingly, the average fertility rate in China dropped from over six births per woman in 1960s to less than 1.5 in and after 1990s that was much lower than the widely recognized replacement level[2]. Working as undersigned but perhaps expected, the policy solidified the cultural sexism[3] and worsened the offspring sex selection in practice, which resulted in the imbalance of sex ratio at birth (calculated as the number of boys per girl) shortly after its announcement (see Figure 1). As a response to the conflict between culture and the policy, some practical methods were used to circumvent the policy's influence on the traditional preference of a child's sex. Among all such methods, prenatal sex selection was the most popular option. Especially after the introduction of ultrasound for prenatal inspection in the early 1980s, fetal sex identification followed by gender-specific induced abortion was pervasive. According to a medical project covering eight provinces and cities in 1986, the sex ratios among 500 and 1,226 aborted sex-identifiable fetuses in rural and urban areas were 94.6 and 96.8, respectively (Zeng et al., 1993). These ratios are demonstrative for the impact of offspring sex selection while being compared with the real sex ratio of living birth that year, which was 107.7.

The pervasive sex selection eventually shrank the marriageable population by the extremely low fertility rate and raised tension in the marriage market after the one-child generations grew up. Hesketh and Zhu estimated that there were up to 34 to 41 million "missing females" in China by the end of 2000 (2006). This number was even higher, according to Nobel laureate Amartya Sen's estimate that there were 50 million "missing women" in China alone by the end of the 1980s (1990). These staggering numbers of missing women eventually brought about 32 million surplus men among the one-child generations by 2005 (Zhu, Lu, & Hesketh, 2009) and a deficit of one million marriageable

---

[1] To carry out this policy, propaganda and necessary practices were widely adopted including contraception (including distributing free condoms and sterilization surgeries for either men or women) and abortion to achieve the goal of controlling fertility rates. Troops of family-planning enforcers employed by local governments cooperated with community workers or village cadres to educate newlywed couples, monitor pregnancy, and register unborn and newborn babies. All pregnancies were tightly followed and meticulously guided since the first trimester with necessary assistance from clinic and hospitals. Only the registered unborn would have a Birth Approval Certificate (which was renamed as Family-planning Service Certificate) that was required if the expecting mother wanted to have pregnancy tests and gave the newborn a *hukou* (household registration) after she/he was born. If violating the policy and having more children than allowed, the couple would face severe sanctions including forced abortion before the birth or heavy penalties (called "social upbringing fee," ranging from three to ten times the regional average income or the household's actual annual income, whichever was greater). They would also be fired from public employment (covering most jobs in China especially before the state-owned enterprise reform in 2005) after the birth. If rejecting the penalties, the extra child would never have a *hukou*, which meant she/he would lose access to education, occupation, medical care, or even have problems getting married and having legalized children. This group is called "black-market children" (*hei haizi*). As estimated, there are about 13 million black-market children in China caused by the one-child policy (Fong, 2016), who live like illegal immigrants without any documents in their home country for a lifetime.

[2] Replacement level fertility rate is the average number of children born per woman in her lifetime, at which a society can replace its population and keep the size stable across generations endogenously without migration. The acknowledged replacement rate is around 2.1 in developed countries, while higher in developing countries to compensate the higher mortality rates.

[3] The one-child policy went against the cultural preference for sons in China. Under the influence of Confucianism, Chinese people valued boys more than girls because of the prevalent desire to "raise sons to provide for one's old age" under the patrilocal and patrilineal customary practices (Chen & Silverstein, 2000, p. 44). For a long time, sons were perceived as the future of a family and the guarantors of their parents' security in China. In contrast, daughters were regarded as debt or an economic burden because women were doomed to join another family upon marriage, thereby ceasing to take responsibilities for care for their parents when they were ill or elderly (Hesketh & Zhu, 2006)

Figure 1

Sex Ratio at Birth* in China (1953–2015)

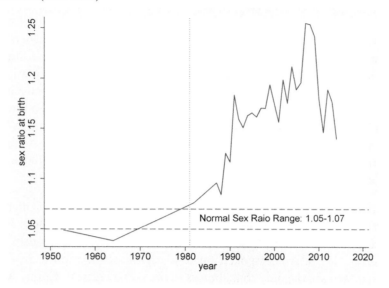

* Sex ratio at birth is calculated as the number of newborn boys per girl.

Adapted from: Chinese population censuses (1953, 1964, 1982, 1990, 2000, 2005, 2010), *Chinese Population & Employment Statistics Yearbooks* (named as *Chinese Population Statistics Yearbook* before 2000) (1987–2015), and *China Statistics Yearbooks* (2000–2015).

Figure 2

Female Share of Offenders** in China (1972–2014)

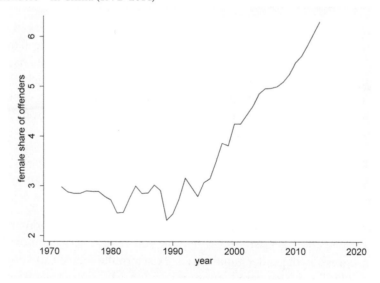

** Female Share of Offenders is calculated as (# female offenders / # total offenders).

Because of data inaccessibility, the female share of offenders equals the female share of prison inmates from 1972 to 1992 and from 2003 to 2014, and equals the female share of convicts from 1994 to 2001.

Adapted from: Department of Correction in China (1981–1985), Supreme Court in China (1986–1992), *Chinese Yearbooks of Court of Justice* (1994–2001), *China Statistics Yearbooks* (2003–2012), and a BBC news report (Hatton, 2015).

women in the first-marriage market per year after 2010 (Tuljapurkar, Li, & Feldman, 1995). Men occupied about 97% of all unmarried people at ages 28 to 49 in China (Hudson & Den Boer, 2002). Therefore, for the nearly 1.4 billion people, it is not just a story but their lives; it also sets the research context of this chapter.

When we think about crime, what would happen under such a circumstance where a striking population imbalance exists between genders? Most research has connected the increasing crime rates with a large proportion of unmarried men who are subject to adverse marriage market conditions (e.g., Edlund, Li, Yi, & Zhang, 2013). But limited by data accessibility, previous research has adopted a gender-blind approach in explaining crime and ascribed the increase in crime rates to the fierce competition among men. A substantial amount of literature links high delinquency rates with a large population of young, unmarried, and competitive men through psychological, biological, financial, and sociological processes (Nigel Barber, 2003; Cameron, Meng, & Zhang, 2016; Cheatwood & Block, 1990; Mesquida & Wiener, 1996; Wilson & Daly, 1985).

Accordingly, most criminological forecasts predicted the male percentage of offending in mainland China would go up when numerous single men could not find wives (Den Boer & Hudson, 2004; L. Edlund et al., 2013; Lena Edlund, 2005; Lena Edlund, Li, Yi, & Zhang, 2010; Hudson & Den Boer, 2002, 2004; Tuljapurkar et al., 1995). An unspoken but underlying assumption shared by criminological research studies is that men are the only contributors to the rising crime in China. As a result, this gender-blind or male-only simplification has sacrificed the gendered influence of the policy on ideologies and socialization. Without understanding the effects on genders from both sides, we cannot comprehensively estimate how substantial and fundamental changes the policy has brought about to Chinese society, which may be long-lasting or even irreversible regardless of whether still valid or not the policy is. Therefore, this chapter adopts the feminist perspective to explore the relationship between gender and crime in the context where women are scarce but not invisible.

Change in Crime Rates

One of my studies caught the trend in gendered crime rates over the past decades in China (see Wang, 2019). By applying multiple sources of data, my dataset showed a fast-growing female percentage of crime outpacing its male counterpart (see Figure 3). Specifically, after 14 years of enactment, the lagged effect of the one-child policy appeared when the first one-child generation reached the age of criminal responsibility.[4] Or in other words, the artificial and exogenous sex ratio imbalance generated more female offending that is even faster than the growth rate of male offenses; moreover, this effect emerged when the generation under the policy grew up.

This phenomenon is contradictory to the previous criminological explanations and predictions, in which women have been perceived as the "hot cake" or beneficiary of the imbalanced marriage market and therefore assumed to be distanced from criminal involvement.

In addressing the incongruousness between the rising female crime phenomenon and theoretical predictions, this chapter explores how gender would be built and rebuilt in a paradoxical context where the progression and retrogression of gender equalization exist simultaneously and how the dynamics of gender construction would influence gendered crime and deviance by aiming at answering the question: What caused the rising female crime in China under the influence of the one-child policy?

---

[4] From the first version (1979) through the last version (2015), Chinese criminal law consistently defines sixteen as the age for comprehensive penal responsibility, fourteen to sixteen partial penal responsibility for index offenses only, and younger than fourteen no responsibility.

Figure 3

Relationships between crime and deviance

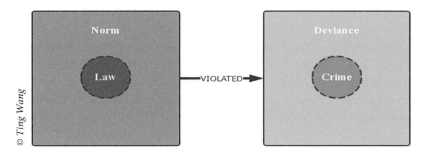

Scarcity, Gender, and Crime

Relationships between Gender Composition and the Gendered Crime

Gender composition of the population, according to demographers (e.g., Van Bavel, 2010), includes the sex ratio and absolute cohort size. It has been verified to be influential to gender norms and gendered behaviors in Guttentag and Secord's (1983) seminal work through marriage squeezes on population (Caldwell, Reddy, & Caldwell, 1983; Hvistendahl, 2011; Trent & South, 2011). In a high-sex-ratio society, the heterosexual marriage squeeze is likely to happen on men, which means they face a shortage of suitable female partners; on the other hand, women experience the squeeze when marriageable men are scant.

Moreover, birth rates and corresponding cohort sizes may catalyze or buffer the squeeze pressure of imbalanced sex ratios on gender roles and the gender gap in crime (Guttentag & Secord, 1983; Hvistendahl, 2011) Because a traditional age gap exists between heterosexual spouses, such as an older husband and younger wife, the influence of the sex ratio imbalance is mediated by the corresponding age cohort size. In a society with a surplus of men but a deficit in women, an expanding cohort weakens the marriage-squeeze effect of the imbalance, and a shrinking cohort intensifies the effect on the contrary. Conversely, in a society with a surplus of women but a deficit in men, an expanding cohort size intensifies the effect of imbalance, whereas a shrinking cohort weakens the effect.

Because of the corresponding pressure on the marriage market, gender composition has a profound influence on gender roles and norms in society (Guttentag & Secord, 1983). A patriarchal society with marriage squeezes on men (i.e., a high sex ratio or a shrinking marriageable cohort size) tends to impose traditional constraints on women. When in short supply, women are highly valued as the marriageable partners and after that as mothers and homemakers (Angrist, 2002; South & Messner, 1987). This is a result of counteracting forces of *dyadic* power in interpersonal relationships and *structural* power in societal relationships between genders (Guttentag & Secord, 1983). Although women's dyadic power is likely to be enhanced in a society with an imbalanced gender composition where they are scarce, the overwhelming structural power owned by men limits the ways how women's potential dyadic power can be exercised. As a result, women in societies with higher sex ratios (such as India, Qatar, and Saudi Arabia) tend to marry at a younger age to complement the bride supply and therefore invest less in education and career development. It is more common for women to stay at home and work as full-time homemakers with constrained extrafamilial goals in those societies than in societies with a lower sex ratio or a more expanding marriageable population. According to this theoretical paradigm, therefore, people expect to see more traditional gender norms and roles in a society scarce in marriageable women and, therefore, less female offending; and vice versa.

Following this demographic theory, South and Messner (1987, 2000) have posited a negative association between the sex ratio of the population and female involvement in criminal offending. Because women are likely to be constrained more in traditional gender roles in a society with higher sex ratios, their activities primarily center around family and domestic issues. Therefore, they have less ability and chance to commit crimes. Conversely, women in lower-sex-ratio societies tend to be more delinquent due to more extrafamilial activities providing them with opportunities to become involved in crime. Using the female share of property crime as the dependent variable and the sex ratio for ages 15 to 49 as the key explanatory variable, this hypothesis has been supported by a cross-national empirical study covering 60 countries (South & Messner, 1987).

Campbell, Muncer, and Bibel have linked the sex ratio with female violent crimes to an evolutionary perspective (2001). In their model, a low sex ratio in a region tends to strain male-partner resources, which is likely to induce more female crime, especially intra-female assaults, for competing for male partners and future paternity and paternal investment (Buss, 1994). This proposition has also been applied to explain increasing Black female crime in the United States. Due to race-specific mass incarceration and the increasing economic marginalization of Black men, women in the Black communities have to face the shortage of suitable male partners, who are expected to hold a higher socioeconomic status than themselves (Becker & Posner, 2009). The regional low sex ratio leads to a significant increase in the proportion of female-headed households and female crimes consequentially (Taylor, Chatters, Tucker, & Lewis, 1990).

Little empirical research has been done regarding the cohort size change except for the causal effect of a shrinking cohort on the sex ratio imbalance (Das Gupta & Li, 1999; Hvistendahl, 2011). But following the logic of Guttentag and Secord's theoretical paradigm, it should have similar effects as the sex ratio imbalance on gender norms and, correspondingly, the gendered behaviors.

What Has the Demographic Theory Missed?

Guttentag and Secord's (1983) theory connects gender structure and gender roles at a macro level and has generated considerable empirical support (Barber, 2000a, 2001; Messner & Sampson, 1991; Pedersen, 1991; Porter, 2007; South, 1988; Trent & South, 1989). Some research applied this theory in explaining criminal offending and found a negative causal relationship between the sex ratio and female crime (South & Messner, 1987), or positive for male crime (Barber, 2000b; Edlund et al., 2013). Regardless of the strong empirical support, however, this theory has oversimplified the endogeneity of the gender composition of society by setting it as the cause or at least as one crucial causal factor of gender norms. Gender composition as a demographic feature of a society is also a product of its cultural and social structures. Usually, an imbalanced sex ratio is accompanied by some specific culture and structure biases toward one gender. For example, a society with a sex ratio higher than normal[5] probably has a culture favoring sons and a structure empowering men (Becker & Posner, 2009; Das Gupta et al., 2003). Meanwhile, the culture and structure of the society are also the determinants of gender norms and roles. Therefore, the relationship between the demographic sex ratio of the population and gender norms, as well as the gendered behaviors, is just like two apples on one tree—they are

---

[5] Calculating from developed countries' statistics, the true sex ratio at birth without social, behavioral and disease-induced interference is around 106 males per 100 females, which is biologically stable (Johansson & Nygren, 1991). Therefore, a sex ratio at birth ranging from 105 to 107 is practically regarded as normal (Hesketh & Zhu, 2006; Hudson & Den Boer, 2002; Sen, 1990; Zeng et al., 1993).

both outcomes of a society's culture and structure. The direct relationship between the sex ratio and gender norms/gendered behaviors tends to be spurious unless we find causal logic supporting it or the tree trunk generating them both. However, since they are both products of culture and structure, it is hard to find exogeneity of either.

Another problem of the current demographic theory is that it omits the social change that may have taken place in gender ideologies. In the original monograph, Guttentag and Secord applied their theory to explain several worldwide historical events in which the gender compositions of populations were imbalanced for some reasons (1983). However, limited by the time of the work, they missed the newer episodes featured in gender ideology vicissitude. Logically, without external intervention, a society with equalized gender norms should have a balanced sex ratio close to the natural range. But the possibility for the imbalanced cases still exists in the modern era because we have not yet fulfilled the equalization between genders. Those latter-day cases for sex ratio imbalance mingled with gender ideology change can provide a venue to explore the relationship between gender and crime in a more dynamic and vivid way.

Adler (1975) and Simon (1975) have ascribed the rise in female crime to women's emancipation, including more liberated gender roles and more abundant extrafamilial activities, which facilitate women's involvement in crimes. Their pioneering works have inspired feminist criminologists and attracted scholarly and public attention to the social change of gender ideologies. Influenced by globalization and mass media, the ideologies of gender, especially of women, have been changing worldwide (Savolainen et al., 2017). Women have gained more access to all fields that traditionally were exclusively or predominantly occupied by men; according to Adler (1975) and Simon (1975), this change increases women's inclination and opportunities to commit crimes. Therefore, the higher female participation in economic production may play a role in changing the gender ideologies and eventually, the gender norms and gendered deviance.

Previous research has emphasized either gender-composition imbalance or liberated ideologies to explain the change in gendered crime but has failed to take the interrelation of these two causes into consideration. One reason for this deficiency is the endogenous counteraction between these two phenomena. Should the high sex ratio be an outcome of sexist ideologies, for instance, liberated and less biased gender ideologies are likely to decrease the imbalance against girls; in other words, liberated gender ideologies can naturally correct the imbalance in the gender composition of the population. Understandably, therefore, it is hard to capture the symbiosis of these two phenomena.

From the perspective of a quasi-experiment, the Chinese female offending under the influence of the one-child policy was a unique historical exception. Not only did it externalize the gender composition of the population, but also embraced the social change in gender ideologies through processes of economic reform and marketization while still largely retaining cultural sexism that has been concreted by the one-child policy. Therefore, it provides us with an extraordinary opportunity to explore the etiology of the increase in female crime, which may also boost our understanding of the rising female crime phenomena happening across the globe.

On the Shoulders of Giants: Theoretical Framework of Current Study

The demographic theory captures the relationship between the gender composition and gender norms but overlooks ideological change, especially in our modern era, along with economic development. Current criminological theories, conversely, focus on the etiological reasoning of the involvement of crime but fall short of explaining the structural influence of gender composition. This is because they have been primarily used in explaining the criminal phenomena in the "mainstream" advanced Western countries where the gender compositions have been being relatively stable in the contemporary age. By contrast, in past decades, China has experienced dramatic changes in both economic and social structures. In addition to the one-child policy, the economic reforms and marketization that began in 1978 have brought changes to every field in China. Therefore, there should be substantial variations in gender ideologies, gender compositions, and gendered crime for us to detect the latent relationships between them. To comb through the intricate relationships, this chapter reconstructs a theoretical framework to connect the influential factors pertaining to sex composition, gender ideologies, and crime together and then utilizes an online survey that was carried out in the summer of 2017 in China to unfold the effects of the policy[6].

Deviance, Criminality, and Gender Ideologies

Criminologists define deviance as behavior violating expected rules and social norms. It is not necessary to be criminal unless the rule it impinges on is a law (see Figure 4). Crime is the most definite and serious deviance because the trespassed norm is codified and ratified by the legal authority; correspondingly, the deviant is punishable by the officially endorsed judicial machinery.

However, non-criminal deviance occupies much more general activities than the criminal counterparts and contains countless examples. For instance, wearing bright colors to a funeral is deviance in most cultures, but it is not a crime. The offended family may give the eccentric dirty looks, curses or even kick the person out but they may not be able to call the police over this behavior (they can, but the case is likely to be ignored or dropped in most situations). Another example of deviance that is always taken by students of SOC 101 course to test. They feel the power of norms by standing in a crowded elevator backwards. This minor breach, according to most students, triggers uncomfortable feelings because they receive annoyed or sneering reactions from the surrounding, but no student has reported that she/he has been charged for this behavior. Therefore, the non-criminal deviance is much more common in our daily lives than crime, because it is more trivial and less costly, although it is not easy to attract attention from the public as is the crime.

Nevertheless, deviance provides a terrific alternative to criminality that is usually very difficult to measure because it is analogous to crime in the nature of attaining instant gratification. Scholars have found that deviant people are much more prone to commit crime than their non-deviant counterparts; conversely, criminals are usually deviant in activities including non-criminal deviances (Gottfredson & Hirschi, 1990; Perrone, Sullivan, Pratt, & Margaryan, 2004; Widom, 2014). The advantage of surveying deviance rather than criminal involvement, furthermore, is the possibility to generate higher data quality than directly collecting information regarding crimes. The latter usually deters respondents from revealing their actual participation in crime (Thornberry & Krohn, 2000) and tends to produce inflation of null answers considering general low crime rates in society.[7]

---

[6] The survey recruited 2,006 adult respondents aging from 18 to 80s. The age and gender distributions are highly representative for the one-child-policy-oriented study. There were 908 respondents born after 1980, the announcement year of the policy, and 1,098 born before that year. Women were the majority (63.5%) of the respondents across generations (see Table 1). Identified by the IP addresses, the responses covered 31 Chinese provinces and municipalities occupying 97.1 % of the total geographic region. The questionnaire contained 46 multi- and single-response questions and seven self-rating scales (see appendix for the survey instrument).

[7] The United States has notoriously high crime rates among developed countries, the rate of prisoners and unsentenced detainees in total of which is 820.5 per 100,000 people in 2016 for instance. China has much lower rate that is 133.4 per 100,000 people in the same year (data source: UNODC, 2018, https://dataunodc.un.org/).

Whichever it is, notwithstanding, crime or deviance has been equalized to masculinity for a long time (see Figure 4). Almost in any patriarchal society, people tolerate boys' deviance much more than girls with the earful excuse "Boys will be boys." Influenced by the familial and extrafamilial environments, boys are pulled and pushed to learn how to fight, smoke, drink or join in a variety of deviant activities to show their fit in with the standard of the hegemonic masculinity, the most prized and prestigious gender identity in the whole society (Connell, 2005). As early as in the 1960s, sociologist Edwin Sutherland (1960) posited sex role theory and ascribed the high criminal involvement of men to the way how we construct masculinities in patriarchal societies. Boys can, should, and do learn deviance from a very young age. Although this theory has been criticized for its biological reductionism and essentialism, it is in accordance with people's intuition of the reason why men occupy the predominant position in the criminal world.

© Miami beach forever/Shutterstock.com

This belief is also deeply rooted in China. Among the respondents, over 21% of the men defined masculinity as aggressively; 9% of them believed that being a man should seek pleasure and immediate gratification; nearly half of the male respondents equalized masculinity to the control of women or the control of power over others.

Influenced by the established standards of how to be a "real man," it is natural to expect a prominent and stable gender gap in deviance (which means the gender difference in deviance) across generations. The survey outcomes, however, tell us a different story when we compare the self-rated deviance across genders and generations.

In the survey, one question asked respondents to rate their deviance from one (completely not deviant) to ten (very deviant) before the age of eighteen. Following the question, the definition of deviance was given with examples of the typical deviant behaviors: "We usually define deviance as the behavior that violates the socially accepted standards. Examples include smoking, drinking, fighting, getting something by force, shoplifting, deliberately damaging private or public property, having early sexual activities, and disobeying orders of parents, teachers, or other authorities including law and regulations" (Bao, Hass, & Tao, 2017).

The responding rate was 100% for this question. The dispersion of the self-rated deviance is stretched fully from the minimum one to the maximum ten with 4.6 as the mean and 2.4 as the standard deviance. The mode score is five, so the majority believed themselves as the average while comparing their deviance to the societal level. However, while being differentiated by genders and generations, a very interesting trend showed up.

The modes are consistently five in all four groups; however, when comparing the second most frequently self-rated scores (termed as "secondary mode") for deviance between groups, it is instructive to compare the generational changes: Both the "secondary modes" for the one-child generation men and women are two, drifting from six and one, respectively, from the pre-one-child generations. Moreover, the gender gap in deviance that was rated higher than five was narrowed from 4.7% for the pre-one-child generations to 3.9% for the one-child generations,[8] which shows a convergent trend of deviance between genders.

---

[8] The gender gap in deviance is calculated as 50%—[women's ratio/(women's + men's ratio) * 100%]. The larger the rate is, the wider is the gap correspondingly. For the equalized situation, women's and men's ratios should be the same, therefore, the rate is 50%—[1/2*100%] = 0, which means no gender gap there is.

This finding corresponds to the change of crime rates, both of which describe a similar image that both gender gaps in crime and deviance are shrinking in China across generations; or in other words, Chinese young women and men are converging in terms of their deviant propensities and behaviors, criminal or non-criminal. Why?

Changes in Socialization and Gender Ideologies under the One-child Policy

Doubtlessly, sons are culturally preferred in China (and many other patriarchal societies) for thousands of years. This partiality is rooted in a prevalent desire to "raise sons to provide for one's old age" (Chen & Silverstein, 2000) which derived from Confucian culture and traditional social structure. First, men were the primary labor in the agrarian age, so they traditionally held higher social and family positions than women. Then, the tradition of patrilineality (descents inherit fathers' family names) and patrilocality (married couples reside with or near husbands' parents) caused married daughters to be regarded as outsiders who were culturally believed to belong to other families upon marriage and would take care of their in-laws rather than their parents. And last, the lack of a public pension system in old China resulted in self-remedy so (male) offspring were the only providers of security for the elderly. These beliefs survive to this day and profoundly influence the sex preference for children. The one-child policy, however, turned this preference luxury and "luck-based." Families without such "luck" and only having daughters have to face the cruel reality—"who can provide for us when we are in need?"

To prevent the sex selection effect, since the very beginning of the policy implementation, extensive propaganda designed to educate people that girls are as valuable and promising as boys have been distributing nationwide. Colorful and vivid posters, banners, pamphlets, and wall paintings were not unfamiliar even to the outside world. From 1980 to the new millennium, the content and technologies have been changed, but the theme is the same that illustrates women as competent in any occupations as men or better in caring their parents than men. Some propaganda elicits that daughters are also inheritors of families who can shoulder the hope and attain the dream,9 which is strikingly different from the traditional Chinese belief.

Moreover, being mingled with the economic reform and marketization, attainment and success have been fossilized to a unidimensional definition—to be monetarily rich. Combining with the new family structure under the one-child policy, we, therefore, may expect a dramatic change in socialization practices, especially in families without boys.

Socialization Process and Gendered Outcomes

Control Theories

Deviance, according to control theorists, requires no skills. It may be the easiest or most expedient way for individuals to satisfy their needs and desires. What requires explanation, however, is why people conform. Control theories argue that people conform because of the controls to which they are subject

---

9 Under the influence of Confucianism, individual attainment in China is not a personal issue, however, it is shared by the family or even the clan. Specifically, success, in Chinese context, means not only personal achievement but also bringing glory on one's ancestors and the families sharing the same ancestors (guangzong yaozu). Therefore, Chinese respondents might understand family hope as the expectation of their family pinned on them optimistic for their recognizable attainments and prosperity, which has been acknowledged as a significant factor influential to parenting practices (Huang & Gove, 2015).

(Gottfredson & Hirschi, 1990; Hirschi, 1969; Kornhauser, 1978; Sampson & Laub, 1995). The controls can be categorized into three types: 1:) social control or external control (Hirschi, 1969), 2:) stake in conformity (Briar & Piliavin, 1965; Toby, 1957), and 3:) self-control or internal control (Gottfredson & Hirschi, 1990). Also, power control theory is another strand that specifies the relationship between family control and offspring offending from an inter-generational perspective.

External controls largely manifest as the fear of sanctions from others for deviant behaviors. The "others" include family, friends, school officials, employers, colleagues, neighbors, and the police. External controls can be enhanced if the others set clear rules forbidding deviance, monitor the individual's behavior, and consistently sanction violators in a meaningful manner (Agnew, 2009; Gottfredson & Hirschi, 1990).

Stake in conformity can be found in some individuals who are less likely to engage in deviant activities because they have more to lose for engaging in them. In particular, they have strong emotional bonds to conventional others, like families and friends, that may be jeopardized by deviance (Sampson & Laub, 1995). Investment in conventional activities, such as getting an education, can increase the stake in conformity. For example, adolescents who are doing well in school, devoting more time in homework, and anticipating obtaining a good education and job are less likely to engage in deviance because it is more costly for the potential peril to their accomplishment and life plans (Giordano, Cernkovich, & Rudolph, 2002; Smith & Paternoster, 1987).

Another restraint over deviance is the individuals' abilities and beliefs, keeping them from responding to temptations and provocations, which is defined as the internal control or self-control. People who are less likely to conduct defiantly usually had more external controls when they were young. Or in other words, they were taught to be conforming, and they accepted it as a "right" way to behave. Therefore, self-control is partly a result of the absorption of external controls, and after that, an internalization of the controls into one's traits (Gottfredson & Hirschi, 1990).

Gottfredson and Hirschi ascribed men's higher rates of crime commission than women to the fewer controls men are subject to (1990). Boys are less likely to be sanctioned by families, teachers, and the public for their aggressive and deviant behaviors than are girls. Compared with women, men are less likely to condemn crime but more likely to internalize pro-criminal definitions (Burton, Cullen, Evans, & Dunaway, 1994; Warr & Stafford, 1993). Moreover, resorting to violence and engaging in deviant activities, to some extent, is a way of demonstrating traditional masculinities (Messerschmidt, 1993, 2000), which in turn produces positive returns to their social identities. These gender-specific differences in crime involvement are, therefore, a consequence of the distinct socialization of women and men, which result in the gender stratification of controls (Lagrange & Silverman, 1999) derived from different social expectations for genders.

"Parents tend to socialize children to accept society's values and thereby develop their conscience" (Kempf, 1993, p. 145). However, social values and beliefs are different over genders. As a result, women are socialized differently from their male counterparts since the day of birth and are expected to be more submissive than men in patriarchal contexts. Besides its impact on internal control, the family also functions fundamentally in shaping the stratification of external controls. Women tend to be more closely monitored and controlled from their childhood through adulthood than their male counterparts (Steffensmeier & Allan, 1996), which limits opportunities for deviance and crime (Canter, 1982; Hagan, Gillis, & Simpson, 1985; LaGrange & White, 1985; LaGrange & Silverman, 1999). These gender-specific differences also exist in other institutions of socialization, including schools, peers, and the workplace. Having experienced a distinctively higher amount of controls, women are therefore much less likely to engage in crime than their male counterparts.

In addition to traditional control theories, Hagan, Simpson, and Gillis (1987) proposed power control theory to explain the inter-generational influence of gender power dynamics on offspring's delinquency. Wives have much less power than their husbands in patriarchal families in which husbands are employed in authority positions while wives as full-time homemakers; correspondingly, daughters enjoy much less freedom than their brothers in this type of families. The former power imbalance explains the latter; whereas the latter imbalance explains the reason why girls traditionally commit much less crime than do boys. On the one hand, the gender division of domestic work imposes more social controls on daughters; on the other hand, patriarchal families tend to socially reproduce daughters to focus their future around domestic labor and consumption following the model of their mothers, while reproducing sons to prepare for participating in direct production following the mode of their fathers (Hagan et al., 1987; McCarthy, Hagan, & Woodward, 1999).

Since the feminist movements for equal rights and opportunities between genders, more women have been joining the labor force. It has created a drive to rebalance the family power structure. This change results in the formation of more egalitarian families, in which the consumption and production spheres are undivided by gender. Relatively equal power between parents leads to the similar treatment of daughters and sons. Boys are encouraged to reject the traditional masculine norms that usually support risk-taking activities and deviance, and girls are encouraged to be independent and ambitious. As a result, the gender gap in deviance is narrower in egalitarian families than that in patriarchal families because of the generational decrease in men's and the increase in women's offending (Hagan et al., 1987; McCarthy et al., 1999).

Anomie/Strain Theory

Different from control theories, anomie/strain theory explains the reason why people offend. Emile Durkheim (1897/1951) ascribed crime and deviance to the imbalance between norms or values that have been previously held and the ones that newly evolve. Durkheim called this imbalance anomie, which may gestate people's criminality in searching for a more stable environment. Building on anomie theory, Robert Merton (1938) developed a more specific theory to explain the origin of crime. He refined the imbalance that Durkheim focused on, theorizing it to be the mismatch between the socially accepted goal and the means to the goal, which may cause frustration and other negative feelings. People may deal with strain through deviance so that they can accomplish their goal, or they turn to deviance as an outlet for negative feelings.

Messner and Rosenfeld (1997) applied this theory in explaining the reason why the United States suffers extraordinarily high crime rates compared to its peer nations. They ascribed the root to the prevalence of the "American dream" that overemphasizes economic success but with limited means to fulfill the dream, especially for the underclass. Meanwhile, institutional anomie intensifies the disparity with the societal overemphasis on economic success. The economy dominates over other social institutions, such as family and school, which should otherwise create external controls over individuals' deviant behaviors. Therefore, those who lack legal means to the cultural goal and necessary social controls from institutions are more likely to turn to illegal means alternatively. Therefore, anomie/strain theory successfully connects individual experience with the institutional structure at the macro level to explain motivations for deviance, though, gender-blindly.

Broidy and Agnew (1997) extended general strain theory to explain the gender difference in criminal drives. Women are traditionally perceived to have much less strain than their male counterparts because of different requirements of gender roles. Traditionally, women are believed to be insulated from the pressure of public life, especially the stress from economic and social status achievements

(Applin & Messner, 2015). The ideal image of women is often "sugar and spice," so that the female role is assumed to be less demanding than the male, which is alleged to generate less strain and therefore less deviance correspondingly (Naffin, 1985). Moreover, differences in types of strain exist between genders, which mediate the influence of strain on behaviors and emotions reacting to it (Moon & Morash, 2017). Compared to men, women tend to suffer strain more from relational conflicts than their male counterparts who are more likely to subject to strain from struggles in pursuing monetary success and extrinsic attainment (Broidy & Agnew, 1997). More concern with relational issues causes women to be constrained more by various social controls from families, friends, and colleagues and to have more social supports as well, all of which, corresponding to control theories, reduce the occurrence of deviance, especially serious and aggressive criminal offenses. Therefore, the different amount and type of strain experienced by women and men, various emotional reactions to strain, and distinctive conditioning factors between strain and responsive behaviors are the contribution of general strain theory in explaining the gender gap in deviance.

Learning Theory of Deviance

Peer influence is another correlate that has been frequently used to explain gender differences in deviance (Jensen & Akers, 2017). Over interaction with intimate personal groups, definitions favorable or unfavorable to deviance are learned with the assimilation of legal conscience (Matsueda, 1982; Sutherland, 1947). The differential association effect has been widely found in the interactions with friends, which has been developed to explain the gender-specific effect of peers on criminal involvement (Alarid, Burton, & Cullen, 2000; Covington, 1985).

As one gender-oriented derivation of learning theory, Giordano and her colleagues have affirmed that girls tend to be more deviant and delinquent within mixed-sex peer groups, while boys will be so when they are typically associated with same-sex companions (Giordano, 2009; Giordano & Cernkovich, 1979; Giordano et al., 2002). These mixed-sex peer groups play a role in taking the learning channel into effect, from which women can learn about and engage in deviant activities with the maximal opportunities to interact with men and deviance-analogous masculinity. As a result, women's deviance is "group influenced in a way that is similar to the pattern of male deviance" (Cernkovich & Giordano, 1979, p. 474).

In contrast, men are less aggressive when they are around women, which has been supported by the civilizing perspective (Lauritsen & Heimer, 2008). The increasing presence of women is expected to bring up a civilization effect restraining men's deviance to some extent. In this way, women act as men's "moral guardians" or at least as some form of informal control over men's delinquent and criminal behaviors (Lauritsen, Heimer, & Lynch, 2009; Rosenfeld, 2000). Both gender-specific contentions are derivations of learning theory and are consistent in nature. By setting men as the role model for deviance but women as the opposite, interaction with men may increase the involvement in crime and occurrence of deviance, while interaction with women may decrease. Therefore, the gendered perception of cross-sex friendship connects gender roles and learning theory of deviance together (Cernkovich & Giordano, 1979).

Reformulate Gendered Pathways to Deviance

As you have seen, gender is a factor having been embedded in criminogenic theories, that is because gender probably is the most consistent etiological element observed in predicting crime across time and place. Therefore, to be a competent and persuasive theory, it has to make some sense in expounding the fact why men predominate the criminal world. However, without taking a comprehensive and systematic perspective, most theories treat criminogenic factors and their relationships with deviance flatly without differentiating the structural positions held by each explanatory variable. As a result, those theories have developed separate and rival analytic paradigms explaining substantial effects of gender on deviance respectively. Those paradigms have generated different schools in criminology and, moreover, much confusion for learners – which theory is correct? And which theory is more correct? In fact, not only has competition been caused by independent research paradigms, but also contradiction happens between theoretical interpretations. For example, in the egalitarian families where mothers spend less time on supervising children, the external controls experienced by either girls or boys, tend to be less intense than that in the patriarchal families. The lessened family control should increase offspring's deviance in the light of social control theory, which derives contradictory prediction on boys' deviance with power control theory.

In no way can any research map the reality of the world; nevertheless, a good theoretical framework should at least consider its complexity of the object to some extent. Every social and cultural factor does not exist in a vacuum; they are intricately pertinent to each other (Parsons & Shils, 2001), and thereby, compose a multilayered intertwining effect network influencing people's behaviors and decisions. To reflect our society more accurately, therefore, we must distinguish the effects of each variable on deviance as well as on other potentially relevant factors. For this reason, this chapter reformulates extracted variables from the three strands of theories introduced above and configures a synthetic framework explaining the gendered pathways to deviance.

All variables are categorized into three groups based on their features and onset stages. The first category represents socialization processes within three primary institutions: families, peers, and schools, including family control, family hope, parents' power dynamics, bonding with family members, peer interaction, and school life. The second category, reflecting individual-level cognitive traits, includes self-control, life goal, and gender role perceptions. The societal-level gender structures, corresponding to the institutional means to realize individual expectations, are contained in the last category of variables.

Compared to the structural category, cognitive traits are more individual and likely to vary from person to person. Nevertheless, they should be outcomes of the societal settings of gender ideologies that shape the socialization practices in every corner of the society, which is beyond the individual's agency. Moreover, the effects of socialization practices on deviance are intermediated by individuals' cognitive traits; or in other words, individuals, even though having grown to maturity in similar environments, may make different decisions on criminal engagement still. In this process, personal traits play as a receptor and translator of external forces to behavior (Giordano et al., 2002).

Those three categories of variables influence individual deviance directly and indirectly, and an alteration in anyone may ripple over to other variables and deviance eventually.

Empirical Evidence from A Nationwide Survey

The survey recruited 2,006 respondents from mainland China that covered over 97% of the geographical distribution identified from their IP addresses. To reveal the gendered influence of the policy, those respondents are grouped into four categories according to their ages (born before or after 1980) and genders. Thence, they are one-child-generation men (OCG men), One-child-generation women (OCG women), pre-one-child-generation men (POCG men) and pre-one-child generation women (POCG women). Table 1 demonstrates the composition and the corresponding number of each category of respondents.

	Pre-one-child generations	One-child generations	Total
Women	638	636	1,274
Men	460	272	732
Total	1,098	908	2,006

Applying the synthetic pathway model, I reformulate pertinent variables extracted from the survey questions and show how the policy has influenced them as well as how their changes affect the gender differences across generations.

Layer I: Socialization Practices

Sibling care is assessed by two questions. One concerned the number of siblings, and the other was about the time spent in sibling care for the participants who were not single children. The responsibility of sibling care cultivates the conventional bonding within the family; thus, it is expected to decrease deviance (Hirschi, 1969). Encompassing the responses, the sibling care variable is binary (1 = need to care; 0 = no need). As anticipated, the inter-generational difference is significant that there was a higher proportion of the POCG responsible for their siblings' care (mean = 0.55) than the OCG counterparts (0.39). Unanticipatedly, however, this responsibility has skewed toward women over time. More young women shouldered the responsibility of sibling care than their male counterparts (mean = 0.41 for women and 0.34 for men); in contrast, fewer POCG women had to take the chore than did their male counterparts (mean = 0.52 for women and 0.59 for men). This gender-specific change might be a direct reflection of the policy's intervention. Families that had the "fortune" of having a boy as the firstborn would stop childbearing and comply with the policy. Whereas, families without such "fortune" would not be satisfied with the single child and tend to have a larger family, in which the first child turned to be an elder sister and likely the babysitter of her younger sibling(s). Consequently, the one-child generation women and men have been largely freed from the sibling-care responsibility, yet are they liberated equally.

Parent's power dynamic is gauged by the parents' relative positions at home. Respondents were asked who had the final say at their homes (1 = mother, 2 = mother for the major things and father for the less important, 3 = the same, 4 = father for the major things and mother for the less important, 5 = father). The higher is the number, therefore, the more patriarchal the family was where the respondent grew up. The mean is 3.24. This variable is not statistically different between generations, neither genders.

Family hope combines the scales for father's and mother's hope (0 = no, 1 = somewhat, 2 = yes, for either); therefore, it ranges from 0 to 4. A higher score in family hope means the respondent was burdened more by parents with the family dream. The mean is 2.84 for total but significantly different between genders. Men shouldered more family hope than women (mean = 3.00 for men and 2.75 for women). Moreover, the gender gap has shrunk across generations (the gender difference is 0.31 for the POCG, whereas 0.23 for the OCG). A higher proportion of young-generation women are also perceived as the bearers of the family dream by their parents when few alternatives there are available.

Family control is seized by the question whether the respondent would receive sanctions from the family if they were deviant or intractable when they were young (1= no, 2 = not always, 3 = yes). Compared to the older-generation counterparts (mean = 2.35), the OCG people (mean = 2.42) generally received more sanction from the family against their defiance. Moreover, there was no significant gender difference among the young generations. In contrast, the POCG men were subject to more disciplinary control than were their female counterparts. The intergenerational differences may be ascribed to lowered fertility rates and smaller family sizes that concentrates parents' attention on their only heir. It also echoes the increasing family hope anchored on the new generations.

Cross-sex friendship plumbs the learning effects on deviant behaviors (Lei, Simons, Simons, & Edmond, 2014), which is apprehended by the response to the question "Is friend's gender a concern when you are making friends?" (0 = no, 1 = somewhat, 2 = yes.) The mean is 0.75. Compared to men, women were concerned more about their friends' genders (mean = 0.80 for women, and 0.66 for men); noteworthily, however, this gender difference only exists among the POCGs, which reflects a permissive trend in making (male) friends for the young Chinese women. Also, women are more likely to be around male peers for the new generations than before when we consider about the extreme sex ratio imbalance (a surplus of men and deficit of women) for these cohorts, which is also supported from the responses regarding the ratio of cross-sex friends in their close network.

School effect shows via the scale of the self-reported school performance (1 = bad, 2 = below average, 3 = average, 4= above average, and 5 = good). The mean is 3.56, and no significant differences between generations nor genders show up though, one consistency across generations is that girls' self-perceived performance is better than boys.

In sum, either boys or girls of the one-child generations are more at the center of families (Bao et al., 2017). They are more freed from sibling care responsibility, pinned with more hope and more controlled by their families than the former generations because of their parents' low fertility rates. Nevertheless, the inter-generational change was not consistent between genders. On the one hand, the gender gap was narrowing in terms of socialization. Women have received relatively more family hope and controls and been more open to make male friends than were they before. On the other hand, however, some family chores, such as sibling care, has skewed to women. Overall speaking, the socialization practices have significantly changed over generations under the influence of the one-child policy; moreover, the change is gender-specific.

Layer II: Cognitive Traits

Legal conscience reflects the level of self-control and the internalization of the external controls. This variable adopts the responses to the question whether the respondent agreed on unconditional compliance with laws and regulations (1 = no; 2 = yes for most except the unpunishable; 3 = yes for most except the unreasonable; and 4 = yes). The mean is 3.32, with no difference between genders nor generations.

Masculinity and femininity reflect the effect of socialization on individual gender roles. They are evaluated in two ways: first, as the interaction between the definition of gender ideologies and the self-rated scale by either gender and second, as the comparison between the respondent's same-sex parent and themselves. Both definitions are gauged with 16 items, similar to those in previous studies (Kaufman & Taniguchi, 2006; Lei et al., 2014). Masculinity was defined by male respondents based on a multi-response question, including being independent, enterprising, aggressive, physically strong, emotionally repressed, controlling, pleasure-seeking, economically successful, muscular, sporty, tough, adventurous, sagacious, powerful, assertive, and knowledgeable. Based on the constructed definition, the male respondents were asked to rate their masculine level from 1 (not masculine) to 10 (very masculine). Correspondingly, femininity was defined by female respondents with options including being elegant, affectionate, delicate, sociable, submissive, family-centered, dependent, chaste, kind-hearted, quiet, cautious, sensitive, considerate, cultured, neat, and pure.

Parallelly, the respondents were also asked to rate their feminine score from 1 (not feminine) to 10 (very feminine) after constructing the femininity definition. Therefore, the scale of masculinity and femininity both range from 0 to 160 and positively relate to persons' self-perceptions of their gender ideologies. It is worth noting that the self-rated femininity significantly decreases over time (mean = 7.05 for the POCG and 6.24 for the OCG), but there is no discernible inter-generational change among men. Correspondingly, the interaction is significantly higher for the OCG women than that for their older counterparts but not different between male groups. Another gauging is the parent-child comparison of masculinity and femininity (1 = I am more masculine/feminine, 2 = the same, 3 = my father/mother is more masculine/feminine). The mean is 1.99 for the masculine difference and 1.95 for the feminine, which means both genders believed their parents as more cis-gender, and this perception was consistent across generations.

Life goal is composed of two parts. One is the definition of success, and the other is the aspiration to achieve economic success specifically. The respondents were asked to construct their definition of success from ten diverse items—being economically abundant, politically powerful, reputable, popular, knowledgeable, healthy, or having many friends, a happy family, outstanding children, and making the world a better place. Compared to the older generations who had a diverse spectrum in defining success, more of the OCG people, both women and men, disproportionately defined success as economic abundance (1 = yes, no = 0; mean = 0.49 for the POCG and 0.66 for the OCG; see also Dutton, 2005; Shen, 2015). Moreover, the gender difference has shrunk across generations (no difference among the OCG but a significant gap among the POCG). This pattern is consistent with the trend of aspiration for economic success (0 = no, 1 = somewhat, 2 = yes). The OCG people rated their desire to achieve success economically higher than their older counterparts (mean = 1.59 for the POCG, and 1.74 for the OCG). In particular, a higher proportion of single children among the new generations defined success economically (0.75 versus 0.62) and aspired for economic success (1.81 versus 1.70) than their peers who had siblings. This discrepancy perhaps is a result of being the "only hope" of their families for the single children who take full responsibility for glorifying and providing for their parents.

In sum, a higher proportion of the OCG people defined success as the monetary abundance and aspired for such success than the older generations. Moreover, femininity has been reduced over time, but no change in masculinity. Therefore, individual gender role expectations are different across generations. There are fewer gender differences for the newer generations in terms of life goal and gender ideologies in the modern era.

Layer III: Gender Structure

Gender structures are determined in four ways as the gender differences experienced by the respondents in family, school, workplace, and from the general income level to reflect the societal level of gender structure.

Family inequality is gauged by the responses to the question about whether their parents told or implied that "It is harder for women to succeed than that for men" (0 = no, 1 = somewhat, 2 = yes). The mean is 0.63. The parents of the OCG people less emphasized gender differences to their children as did their older counterparts (mean = 0.68 for the POCG and 0.56 for the younger). Compared to women, men's parents were more likely to transfer the chauvinist message to promote their sons' confidence in their gender. However, this gender difference is largely from the older generations, which is not observed among the one-child generations.

School inequality is assessed similarly as the family inequality, except for the gender-discriminatory messengers switched from parents to teachers (0= no, 1= somewhat, 2= yes). The mean is 0.57. Regardless of the consistency that women perceived themselves better in schooling than their male counterparts, gender discrimination has been strengthened over generations. A significantly higher proportion of young women (mean = 0.61) experienced such discrimination at schools than did their older counterparts (mean = 0.54). Besides the teachers' belief, more OCG respondents recalled that their teachers favored boys over girls because of the deep-rooted stereotype that girls are better in simple knowledge (e.g., arts and humanities) in junior years but boys in sophisticated knowledge (e.g., STEM) and able to overtake girls in senior years.

Job inequality is plumbed by the promotion prospect for women and men. Respondents were asked to predict the outcome of a scenario in which "A man and a woman are working at the same position. One day, the boss has a mind to promote one of them. Who do you think is more likely to get the promotion (1 = the woman, 2 = the same, 3 = the man)?" The mean is 2.22, which means the man got the most votes from the respondents. Notwithstanding, fewer OCG women agreed with the man getting the opportunity than did their male counterparts (mean = 2.18 for women and 2.31 for men). Interestingly, the gender difference is inversed for the POCG, among whom more women predicted the man to be promoted than their male counterparts (mean =2.28 for women and 2.13 for men). This inter-generational change shows that the younger-generation women have more emulative attitudes in jobs than the former generations and believe (or hope) they can overtake their male competitors.

Income inequality is explored by the perception of who have a higher income on average (1 = women, 2 = the same, 3 = men). The mean is 2.46, which means that more respondents regarded men as the winner in income. More important, the unequal perception has been reinforced over generations. More OCG people believed men's average income higher than women's than did the POCG. Like the job inequality, however, the OCG women are more optimistic than their older counterparts in the gender equality of earning, which reflects the dynamics of individual gender role expectations.

In general, regardless of the equalized family socialization and individual gender role perceptions, the societal gender structure turned out to be even more unequal than before, especially in school and on the general income. Compared to other socialization agents, families have the least gender discrimination toward the younger generations. As a result, women who have been socialized with such equality correspondingly expect equal treatment from other institutions after they step out of their original families and step in the societal arena. However, those institutions keep or even strengthen gender disparity, and eventually fail these hopeful young women.

Control Variables

Besides the modeled variables, three demographic control variables are gauged by singe-response questions. In addition to gender and age variables, childhood residence has also been collected and coded as 0, non-country, and 1, country, with 60- and 40- percentage distributions. From the IP addresses, the overwhelming responses were from economically advanced cities. However, the information revealed by the IP addresses is vague and impossible to seize more residential details after childhood. Combining with the fact of massive rural-to-urban migration in China happened over past decades (Lo, Cheng, Bohm, & Zhong, 2018; Solinger, 1999) and the relatively inconvenient infrastructural conditions in rural areas, there was a high probability that the internet-based survey respondents who had spent childhoods in the countryside moved out after they grew up.

Results

Guided by the synthetic path model, multiple technologies are employed to detect relations between variables.[10] The results for aggregated data without categorization over gender or generation show that the cognitive variables tightly tie in with deviance. High conscience is a good predictor of low deviance; whereas the aspiration for economic success increases deviance. These two variables are the results of socialization. Except for the sibling care responsibility, all other five socialization variables positively influence cognitive traits. Among all socialization institutions, family plays the most important role in shaping self-control and life goal through the external controls, hope anchoring, and power structure between parents. Nevertheless, the direct effects of family socialization largely diminish after controlling its indirect effects on deviance, which means family plays a big part in shaping the cognitive traits, which greatly affect behaviors, rather than intervenes behavioral decisions directly. The effects of school socialization are salient, either directly or indirectly. The acceptance of cross-sex friends influences self-control. Compared to their older counterparts, the one-child generations are more eager for economic success.

Growing up in the rural plays a role in reducing success aspiration and self-control simultaneously, which may be ascribed to unequal regional resource distributions and loosened parent-to-children relationships due to the massive labor force migrations from rural to urban that took away their parents from them when they were young.[11] After including all variables into the model, the effect of generation is not significant, which means the inter-generational differences have been explained. Furthered by differentiating gender and generation, a refined set of outcomes tells us a more interesting story regarding how the policy has affected gendered deviance by comparing the results between groups. Facilitated by the specification in gender, cognitive variables incorporate two gender role indexes also. Gender and generation, correspondingly, are removed from the control.

The results show salient differences between generations and genders in the etiological paths to deviance. Among the socialization variables, patriarchal family, family control, and school performance are the only three variables influential to deviance for all groups with consistent effects. The patriarchal family, where the mother has a lower position than the father, decreases the deviance of its daughters but increases that of sons on the contrary. This finding supports power control theory. Besides, girls from a more patriarchal family have a higher level of self-control, which deters deviant activities; whereas, boys tend to have a higher level of masculinity, which promotes the sense of toughness and eventually, deviance. Family control plays a role in reducing deviance for four groups through indirect paths. For male groups, family control significantly promotes the self-control and thereby reduces deviance. Distinctively, family control decreases the deviance level of POCG women by increasing their sense of (traditional) femininity. Moreover, both mechanisms can be found among the OCG women, whose experience of strict family control increases their femininity and legal conscience.

---

[10] Student's t-test is used to compare between genders and generations for every modeled variable. Pearson correlation tests and structural equation modeling are used to explore the statistical relationships between variables. The former target on bivariate correlations and the latter path models.

[11] The rural-to-urban migrations are an outcome of the persistence of China's *Hukou* (a household registration) system, adopted since 1958, and the inequality in regional resource distributions (Lo, Cheng, Bohm, & Zhong, 2016). Attracted by the greater amount of occupational opportunity in cities, over 260 million rural-registered people (Chinese National Census, 2010) migrated to urban areas for better payoffs (Jordan, Ren, & Falkingham, 2014). Restricted by the *Hukou* status, however, they are unable to enjoy same welfare benefits including the subsidized medical care and free public education for their children in their working cities. As a result, most of them have to leave children in their home villages to be taken care of by other family members. Those children share a name in China, "the left-behind kids."

School performance has a strong effect on deviance prevention. Except for the POCG women whose school performance indirectly decreases their deviance via the increase in femininity, good school performance directly reduces the deviance for the other three groups. This finding is consistent with the conformity stake theory that deviance is "costlier" for the better school performers.

The exclusiveness of same-sex friend network shows the gender-specific effects on deviance. Women's deviance tends to be higher if they are willing to make male friends, which is consistent across generations. The effect, however, is reversed for the OCG men. The deviance of an OCG man is higher if he tends to make friends with only men and lower if with women. This finding supports learning theory, including the mixed-sex association effect on women's deviance (Giordano & Cernkovich, 1979) and the civilizing effect on men's (Lauritsen et al., 2009). Being burdened with family hope has no effect on the POCG women's but plays a part in affecting the OCG women's and all men's deviance via indirect paths. For the OCG people, the family hope enhances legal conscience and therefore reduces deviance. The family hope placed on young women particularly increases their aspiration for economic success, so it has an extra positive effect on their deviance, which, however, is buffered by the effect of increased conscience. For the POCG men, the family hope enhances not only the conscience but also their masculinity. After counteracting, the deviance level of this group positively pertains to the family hope. The responsibility of sibling care, though has been decreased strikingly as a benefit to the OCG people, has no significant effect on their deviance.

Among the cognitive variables, the parent-child difference in femininity or masculinity is the only factor significantly affecting deviance for all four groups. Consistent with the predictions that masculinity encourages aggression while femininity on the other side (Connell & Messerschmidt, 2005; Lei et al., 2014; Messerschmidt, 1993), the decreased femininity promotes the deviance of the OCG women, and the decreased masculinity restrains the deviance of men conversely. Therefore, the opposite changes in individual gender ideologies narrow the gender gap in deviance that men are less deviant, but women more than before. Another index for gender roles, the self-rated femininity/masculinity, is significant for the POCG women and both male groups. Consistent with the effect of the inter-generational gender role change, a lower score in femininity or a higher score in masculinity boosts higher deviance for either gender. Conscience consistently decreases deviance among the OCG women and both male groups, which supports self-control theory (Burton, Cullen, Alarid, & Dunaway, 1998; Gibbs, Giever, & Martin, 1998; Perrone et al., 2004). Noteworthily, the aspiration for economic success specifically heightens the OCG women's deviance only. If a young Chinese woman longs for financial affluence as her life goal, her deviance level is likely to be higher than her counterparts who have no such goal.

Concerning gender inequalities, structural variables only influence women's deviance (regardless of generations), which is sensible for the fact that women disproportionally experience gender inequalities in a patriarchal society. If a POCG woman experiences gender discrimination in the family, she is likely to be more deviant than the ones who are protected from such experience by parents. Whereas for the OCG women, income inequality plays a more important role in increasing their deviance, which empirically supports strain theory with a positive effect of the success aspiration on deviance. Young women bearing with the dream to succeed will find themselves short on legitimate means to the goal when they enter the patriarchal society with stratified gender structure. Even if they have a paid job, they are still more likely to confront the disadvantages of the "double shift" (Zhang, 2014) and few chances to promotion than their male counterparts (Applin & Messner, 2015), which expose them further to the anomic pressure associated with the success-oriented goal.

Growing up in rural areas is positively consonant with deviance as a control variable for all groups except for the OCG men. It increases deviance via the indirect paths by decreasing the legal conscience.

Also, living in the countryside shrinks the success aspiration for the OCG women and femininity for the POCG women, respectively. The former plays a role in reducing deviance, but that is too weak to offset the positive effect of the lowered legal conscience.

The findings for the one-child generations, either women or men, are stable after being tested with data disaggregated by single or non-single children status, although the success-inequality strain effects are more significant among the single-children group. The perception of income inequality has a positive effect on OCG women's deviance, including the single children and the ones who have siblings, but not on their male counterparts'. For the single male children, more skewed income distribution toward men, in contrast, decreases their deviance for the obvious reason. Men are more likely to succeed through legitimate channels in a more patriarchal society benefited from an inclining earning structure. Thus, the one-child policy has changed not only the socialization for the single children and, correspondingly, their gender roles and the gendered pathways to deviance but also the other people who belong to the special generations. The single children, the ones directly influenced (and for most of them, even created) by the policy, have initially changed the generalized attitudes toward gender that in turn affect the gender ideologies of other peers in society. Despite the differences in the definition of or in aspiration to success between single and non-single children, what we can expect is that the difference will gradually fade out when the policy effects ripple out over time.

Discussion

The pathways to deviance are distinctive for every group representing each combination of gender and generation. Most explanatory factors are the same between male groups, except for the stronger peers' and weaker family interaction's effects on the deviance of the OCG men than on that of their older counterparts. For female groups, the inter-generational differences are more striking. The pathways to the OCG women's deviance reflect the features of both deviant pathways for their older counterparts and male counterparts; or in other words, the OCG women are in the middle between the POCG women and the OCG men in terms of the behavioral formation. Similar to men, family hope and legal conscience affect Chinese younger-generation women's deviance, both of which are not significant in the POCG women's pathways, nevertheless. However, school performance, a prominent factor deterring men's deviance, also plays a direct role in reducing deviance in the OCG women's pathways while only indirectly relates to the POCG women. As in the POCG women's model, moreover, the patriarchal family structure, and same-sex friendship also decrease the younger-generation women's deviance. In addition to the generational differences, the distinctions between genders are also prominent. Compared to men, women are subject to the gender inequality embedded in the social structure, which promotes their deviance across generations. For POCG women, gender discrimination from the family is substantial in enhancing their deviance. However, for the OCG women, income inequality between genders drives deviance up, especially when they have the aspiration for economic success.

This finding is consistent with strain theory. Although the OCG women have been socialized more equally with their male counterparts at home by their parents, they are still suffering from gender discrimination and inequalities in extrafamilial institutions. Women bearing with the dream to succeed monetarily will find themselves short of legitimate means to their dream when they entered the patriarchal society with stratified gender structure. Because of such a lag between the relatively equalized family socialization and the still-unequal societal attitudes toward gender with corresponding factual structures, Chinese young women are subject to the specific strain caused by the disparity between their newly instilled dream and the relentless reality in which the (legitimate) opportunities are still unequally rooted in the persistently hierarchical gender divisions.

In addition to testing the applicability of the mainstream criminological theories, I also examined the relative explanatory power of variations derived from them. For all four groups, control theories have gained the most support, especially social control and stake in conformity theories. Learning theory is also functional in the pathways to deviance for all respondents except for the POCG men. Whereas, strain theory only explains the deviant pathways for the OCG women that may be because they are the only group exposed to the strain rooted in the mismatch between the equalized life goals and unequal means associated with the hierarchical gender structure, as a result of the external policy.

Another extensive finding is in line with learning theory. For the OCG men, same-sex friendship demonstrates a positive connection with masculinity and thereby the level of deviance. However, the effect is antithetical for women's deviance that is, however, boosted by the opposite-sex friendship. Despite the contrary direction in the gendered pathways, the effect of friendship is consistent on deviance to some extent: male friends play as a deviant model in peer interaction and a socialization agent for definitions and motives favorable to delinquency regardless whether their friends are male (same-sex friendship) or female (cross-sex friendship). Moreover, such a peer effect on male and female deviance could have been enlarged by the imbalanced sex ratio among the one-child generation. It should be easier for women making friends with men than before but harder for men making friends with women while taking the huge deficit of women among the young generations into consideration. Thus, the increase in women's deviance perhaps is partially a consequence of the enhanced association with the mixed-sex peer groups caused by the imbalance in the sex composition.

As a result, the gender gap in deviance has been narrowed over generations. Moreover, this convergence is primarily a result of the increase in women's deviance. There are few differences between male groups inter-generationally because they are always "dream bearers" through history with constant socialization practices correspondingly preparing them for the mission.

In sum, unique socialization practices experienced by the one-child generations have improved the individual attitudes toward gender roles, which has equalized the life goal of the younger generation between genders. Nevertheless, the hierarchical gender structure is persisting and untouched, which limits women's means to their life goal and therefore, creates the strain specifically faced by Chinese young women.

Conclusion

The one-child policy has been strictly implemented for over 35 years and affecting the birth and life of one-fifth people in the world. As an unexpected result, it also has reshaped a society's culture and social structure externally and therefore provides an extraordinary chance to explore the underlying mechanisms and effect paths to gendered delinquency. Contrary to the prevalent predictions, however, the imbalanced sex ratios and scarcity of women do not endow them with more value, at least no more value as workers or producers in society. The gender gap in deviance has been converged but is not for the increase in gender equality as indicated (Lauritsen & Heimer, 2008; Lauritsen et al., 2009).

In general, two mechanisms function in narrowing the gender gap in deviance. On the one hand, women are less feminine than before; meanwhile, masculinity is decreased inter-generationally, which converge the gender difference in deviance together. However, this change is different from the "masculinization" of women or "feminization" of men because the pathways to deviance continue being distinctive between genders. If it is a simple neutralization of gender roles, the gender differences in other realms should also fade, and the deviant pathways should be "degendered." However, the findings still indicate strong differences between genders in almost all domains.

On the other hand, the equalizing progress in societal gender structure lags behind that in gender ideologies, which also contributes to the convergence by increasing women's deviance. The one-child policy has changed the socialization, especially family socialization of gender, and therefore altered the definition of what is normative femininity but untouched the existing hierarchical gender structure in the society. Even as stereotypes are modified, however, the cultural shift may still leave structural inequalities in place. This mismatch produces the gender-specific strain for Chinese young women, especially those who have been instilled in gender equality and pinned with the dream by their families. Therefore, the new-generation women are no longer "immune from the criminogenic institutional forces" (Applin & Messner, 2015, p. 4) but turn to be as likely as their male counterparts to exhibit support for the values associated with economic achievement. Eventually, deviance functions as an outlet and a reaction after their dream has been struck by the unequal means when they enter the real world.

Consequently, the rising female deviance and crime is not an outcome of liberalization; on the contrary, it is manifesting the toxic effect of persistent gender inequalities. The scarcity of one gender, moreover, is in no way to correct chronic and structural inequalities automatically; after all, the number is never the cause for inequality, but the result. Were we in an utterly equal society, would crime rates for either gender be higher or lower than the current situation?

Key Terms:

Sex composition imbalance	The gender gap in deviance and crime	Gender-specific strain
		Socialization

Discussion Questions:

1. Can you think other examples of non-criminal deviance, and what norms do they violate?

2. Compare social controls (e.g., in families, schools, or other places) you and one of your opposite-sex siblings/cousins/friends have experienced, who has had more controls? Is there any difference in deviant propensities/behaviors between you two?

3. What would happen in a society where men are scarce? What about sex composition imbalances happen in a matriarchal society (the opposite social arrangement to patriarchal societies where women hold the primary power position in social structure and control properties)? (If you are curious about the answers, a book *Too Many Women? The Sex Ratio Question, written by Guttentag and Secord, is highly recommended.*)

4. The rising female crime is a global phenomenon nowadays. After reading this chapter based on a demographic policy in one country, try to explain the reasons for the increases in other countries without such a policy.

5. What will be the trend of crime rates for either gender when equality is fully achieved?

References

Adler, F. (1975). *Sisters in Crime: The Rise of the New Female Criminal*. New York: McGraw-Hill.

Agnew, R. (2009). The contribution of "Mainstream" theories to the explanation of female delinquency. *The Delinquent Girl* (pp. 7–29). Philadelphia: Temple University Press.

Alarid, L. F., Burton, V. S., Jr., & Cullen, F. T. (2000). Gender and crime among felony offenders: Assessing the generality of social control and differential association theories. *Journal of Research in Crime and Delinquency, 37*(2), 171–199.

Angrist, J. (2002). How do sex ratios affect marriage and labor markets? Evidence from America's second generation. *Quarterly Journal of Economics, 117*, 997–1038.

Applin, S., & Messner, S. F. (2015). Her American Dream: Bringing gender into Institutional-anomie theory. *Feminist Criminology, 10*(1), 36–59.

Bao, W., Hass, A., & Tao, L. (2017). Impact of Chinese parenting on adolescents' social bonding, affiliation with delinquent peers, and delinquent behavior. *Asian Criminology, 12*, 81–105.

Barber, N. (2000a). On the relationship between country sex ratios and teen pregnancy rates: A replication. *Cross-Cultural Research, 34*(1), 26–37.

Barber, N. (2000b). The sex ratio as a predictor of cross-national variation in violent crime. *Cross-Cultural Research, 34*(3), 264–282.

Barber, N. (2001). On the relationship between marital opportunity and teen pregnancy: The sex ratio question. *Journal of Cross-Cultural Psychology, 32*(3), 259–267.

Barber, Nigel. (2003). The sex ratio and female marital opportunity as historical predictors of violent crime in England, Scotland, and the United States. *Cross-Cultural Research, 37*(4), 373–392.

Becker, G. S., & Posner, R. A. (2009). Sex selection. In *Uncommon sence: Economic insights, from marriage to Terrorism* (pp. 31–36). Chicago, IL: University of Chicago Press.

Briar, S., & Piliavin, I. (1965). Delinquency, situational inducements, and commitment to conformity. *Social Problems, 13*(1), 35–45.

Broidy, L., & Agnew, R. (1997). Gender and crime: A general strain theory perspective. *Journal of Research in Crime and Delinquency, 34*, 275–306.

Burton, V. S., Jr., Cullen, F. T., Alarid, L. F., & Dunaway, R. G. (1998). Gender, self-control, and crime. *Journal of Research in Crime and Delinquency, 35*, 123–147.

Burton, V. S., Jr., Cullen, F. T., Evans, T. D., & Dunaway, R. G. (1994). Reconsidering strain theory: Operationalization, rival theories, and adult criminality. *Journal of Quantitative Criminology, 10*(3), 213–239.

Buss, D. (1994). *The evolution of desire: Strategies of human mating*. New York: Basic Books.

Caldwell, J. C., Reddy, P. H., & Caldwell, P. (1983). The causes of marriage change in South India. *Population Studies, 37*(3), 343–361.

Cameron, L. A., Meng, X., & Zhang, D. (2016). China's sex raios and crime: Behavioral change or financial necessity? *IZA Discussion Papers, 9747*.

Campbell, A., Muncer, S., & Bibel, D. (2001). Women and Crime: An evolutionary approach. *Aggression and Violent Behavior, 6*(5), 481–497.

Canter, R. J. (1982). Family correlates of male and female delinquency. *Criminology, 20*, 149–167.

Cernkovich, S. A., & Giordano, P. C. (1979). Delinquency, Opportunity, and Gender. *The Journal of Criminal Law and Criminology, 70*(2), 145–151.

Cheatwood, D., & Block, K. J. (1990). Youth and homicide. *Justice Quaterly, 7*(2), 265–292.

Chen, X., & Silverstein, M. (2000). Intergenerational social support and the psychological well-being of older parents in China. *Research on Aging, 22*(1), 43–65.

Chesney-Lind, M., & Shelden, R. G. (2014). *Girls, Delinquency, and Juvenile Justice* (4th ed.). Southern Gate, Chichester: John Wiley & Sons, Inc.

Connell, R. W. (2005). Change among the gatekeepers: Men, masculinities, and gender equality in the global arena. *Signs: Journal of WOmen in Culture and Society, 30*(3), 1801–1826.

Connell, R. W., & Messerschmidt, J. W. (2005). Hegemonic Masculinity: Rethinking the concept. *Gender and Society, 19*, 829–849.

Covington, J. (1985). Gender differences in criminality among Heroin users. *Journal of Research in Crime and Delinquency, 22*(4), 329–354.

Das Gupta, M., Jiang, Z., Li, B., Xie, Z., Chung, W., & Hwa-Ok, B. (2003). Why is son preference so persistent in East and South Asia? A cross-country study of China, India and the Republic of Korea. *The Journal of Development Studies, 40*(2), 153–187.

Das Gupta, M., & Li, S. (1999). Gender bias in China, South Korea, and India 1920-1990: Effects of war, femine and fertility decline. *Development and Change, 30*, 619–652.

Den Boer, A., & Hudson, V. M. (2004). The security threat of Asia's Sex ratios. *SAIS, 24*(2), 27–43.

Durkheim, E. (1951). *Suicide*. New York: Free Press.

Dutton, M. (2005). Toward a government of the contract: Policing in the era of reform. *Crime, Punishment, and Policing in China*, 189–233.

Edlund, L., Li, H., Yi, J., & Zhang, J. (2013). Sex Ratios and Crime: Evidence from China's One-Child Policy. *The Review of Economics and Statistics, 95*(5), 1520–1534.

Edlund, Lena. (2005). Sex and the city. *Scandinavian Journal of Economics, 107*, 25–44.

Edlund, Lena, Li, H., Yi, J., & Zhang, J. (2010). *Marriage and crime: Evidence from China's rising sex ratios*.

Fong, M. (2016). *One child: The story of China's most radical experiment*. Boston, MA: Houghton Milfflin Harcourt.

Gibbs, J. J., Giever, D., & Martin, J. S. (1998). Parental management and self-control: An empirical test of Gottfredson and Hirschi's general theory. *Journal of Research in Crime and Delinquency, 35*, 40–70.

Giordano, P. C. (2009). Peer Influences on Girls' Delinquency. In *The Delinquent Girl* (pp. 127–145). Philadelphia: Temple University Press.

Giordano, P. C., & Cernkovich, S. A. (1979). On-complicating the relationship between liberation and delinquency. *Social Forces, 26*(4), 467–481.

Giordano, P. C., Cernkovich, S. A., & Rudolph, J. L. (2002). Gender, crime, and desistance: Toward a theory of cognitive transformation. *American Journal of Sociology, 107*(4), 990–1064.

Gottfredson, M. R., & Hirschi, T. (1990). *A general theory of crime.* Palo Alto, CA: Stanford University Press.

Guttentag, M., & Secord, P. F. (1983). *Too Many Women? The Sex Ratio Question.* Beverly Hills, California: Sage Publications.

Hagan, J., Gillis, A. R., & Simpson, J. (1985). The class structure of gender and delinquency: Toward a power-control theory of common delinquent behavior. *American Journal of Sociology, 90*, 1151–1178.

Hagan, J., Simpson, J., & Gillis, A. R. (1987). Class in the household: A power-control theory of gender and delinquency. *American Journal of Sociology, 92*, 788–816.

Hesketh, T., & Zhu, W. X. (2006). Abnormal sex ratios in human populations: Causes and consequences. *PNAS, 103*(36), 13271–13275.

Hirschi, T. (1969). *Causes of Delinquency.* Berkeley: University of California Press.

Huang, G. H., & Gove, M. (2015). Confucianism, Chinese families, and academic achievement: Exploring how Confucianism and Asian descendant parenting practices influence children's academic achievement. In *Science Education in East Asia: Pedagogical Innovations and Research-informed Practices.* New York: Springer.

Hudson, V. M., & Den Boer, A. (2002). A surplus of men, a deficit of peace: Security and sex ratios in Asia's largest states. *International Security, 26*(4), 5–38.

Hudson, V. M., & Den Boer, A. (2004). *Bare Branches: The security implications of Asia's surplus male population.*

Hvistendahl, M. (2011). *Unnatural selection: Choosing boys over girls, and the consequences of a world full of men.* New York: BBS Public Affairs.

Jensen, G. F., & Akers, R. (2017). The empirical status of social learning theory of crime and deviance: The past, present, and future. In *Taking Stock* (pp. 45–84). New York: Routledge.

Johansson, S., & Nygren, O. (1991). The missing girls of China: A new demographic account. *Population and Development Review, 17*(1), 35–51.

Jordan, L. P., Ren, Q., & Falkingham, J. (2014). Youth education and learning in twenty-first century China disentahling the impacts of migration, residence, and hukou. *Chinese Sociological Review, 47*, 57–83.

Kaufman, G., & Taniguchi, H. (2006). Gender and marital happiness in later life. *Journal of Family Issues, 27*(6), 735–757.

Kempf, K. L. (1993). The empirical status of Hirschi's control theory. In *Advances in Criminological Theory: Vol. 4. New Directions in Criminloogical Theory*. New Brunswick, NJ: Transaction Publishers.

Kornhauser, R. R. (1978). *Social sources of delinquency: An appraisal of analytic models*. Chicago, IL: University of Chicago Press.

LaGrange, R., & White, H. (1985). Age differences in delinquency: A test theory. *Criminology, 23*, 19–45.

Lagrange, T. C., & Silverman, R. A. (1999). Low self-control and opportunity: Testing the general theory of crime as an explanation for gender differences in delinquency. *Criminology, 37*(1), 41–72.

Lauritsen, J. L., & Heimer, K. (2008). The gender gap in violent victimization, 1973-2004. *Journal of Quantitative Criminology, 24*, 125–147.

Lauritsen, J. L., Heimer, K., & Lynch, J. P. (2009). Trends in the gender gap in violent offending: New evidence from the national crime victimization survey. *Criminology, 47*(2), 361–399.

Lei, M., Simons, R. L., Simons, L. G., & Edmond, M. B. (2014). Gender equality and violent behavior: How neighborhood gender equality influences the gender gap in violence. *Violence and Victims, 29*(1), 89–108.

Lo, C.C., Cheng, T. C., Bohm, M., & Zhong, H. (2016). Rural-to-urban migration, strain, and juvenile delinquency: A study of eighth-grade students in Guangzhou, China. *International Journal of Offender Therapy and Comparative Criminology, 62*(2), 334–359.

Lo, Celia C., Cheng, T. C., Bohm, M., & Zhong, H. (2018). Rural-to-urban migration, strain, and juvenile delinquency: A study of eighth-grade students in Guangzhou, China. *International Journal of Offender Therapy and Comparative Criminology, 62*(2), 334–359.

Matsueda, R. L. (1982). Testing control and diffential association theories: A causal modeling approach. *American Sociological Review, 47*, 489–504.

McCarthy, B., Hagan, J., & Woodward, T. S. (1999). In the company of women: Structure and agency in a revised power-control theory of gender and delinquency. *Criminology, 37*, 761–788.

Merton, R. K. (1938). Social structure and anomie. *American Sociological Review, 3*, 672–682.

Mesquida, C. G., & Wiener, N. I. (1996). Human collective aggression: A behavioral ecology perspective. *Ethology and Sociobiology, 17*(4), 247–262.

Messerschmidt, J. W. (1993). *Masculinities and crime: Critique and reconceptualization of theory.*

Messerschmidt, J. W. (2000). *Nine lives: Adolescent masculinity, the body, and violence*. Boulder, CO: Westview Press.

Messner, S. F., & Rosenfeld, R. (1997). Political Restraint of the Market and Levels of Criminal Homicide: A cross-national application of institutional-anomie theory. *Social Forces, 75*(4), 1393–1416.

Messner, S. F., & Sampson, R. J. (1991). The sex ratio, Family Disruption, and rates of violent crime: The paradox of Demographic structure. *Social Forces, 69*(3), 693–713.

Moon, B., & Morash, M. (2017). Gender and General strain theory: A Comparison of strains, mediating, and moderating effects explaining three types of delinquency. *Youth & Society*, *49*(4), 484–504.

Naffin, N. (1985). The masculinity-Femininity Hypothesis. *British Journal of Criminology*, *25*(4), 365–381.

Parsons, T., & Shils, E. A. (2001). *Toward a General Theory of Action*. Piscataway, NJ: Transaction Publishers.

Pedersen, F. A. (1991). Secular trends in human sex ratios. *Human Nature*, *2*(3), 271–291.

Perrone, D., Sullivan, C. J., Pratt, T. C., & Margaryan, S. (2004). Parental efficacy, self-control, and delinquency: A test of a general theory of crime on a nationally representative sample of youth. *International Journal of Offender Therapy and Comparative Criminology*, *48*(3), 298–312.

Porter, M. (2007). *The effect of sex ratio imbalance in China on marriage and houseold bargaining*. Chicago: University of Chicago Press.

Rosenfeld, R. (2000). Patterns in adult homicide: 1980-1995. In *The Crime Drop in America*. New York: Cambridge University Press.

Sampson, R. J., & Laub, J. H. (1995). *Crime in the making: patyhways and turning points through the life course*. Cambridge, MA: Harvard University Press.

Savolainen, J., Applin, S., Messner, S. F., Hughes, L. A., Lytle, R., & Kivivuori, J. (2017). Does the gender gap in delinquency vary by level of patriarchy? A cross-national comparative analysis. *Criminology*, *55*(4), 726–753.

Sen, A. (1990). More than 100 million women are missing. *The New York Review of Books*, *1990*, 1–15.

Shen, A. (2015). *Offending women in contemporary China: Gender and pathways into crime*. New York: Palgrave MacMillan.

Smith, D. A., & Paternoster, R. (1987). The gender gap in theories of deviance: Issues and evidence. *Journal of Research in Crime and Delinquency*, *24*, 140–172.

Solinger, D. J. (1999). *Contesting Citizenship in Urban China: Peasant Migrants, the State, and the Logic of the Market*. Los Angeles, CA: University of California Press.

South, Scott J., & Messner, S. F. (1987). The sex ratio and women's involvement in crime: A cross-national analysis. *The Sociological Quarterly*, *28*(2), 171–188.

South, Scott J., & Messner, S. F. (2000). Crime and Demography: Multiple linkages, reciprocal relations. *Annual Review of Sociology*, *26*, 83–106.

South, S.J. (1988). Sex ratios, economic power, and women's roles: A theoretical extension and empirical test. *Journal of Marriage and the Family*, *50*, 19–31.

Steffensmeier, D., & Allan, E. (1996). Gender and crime: Toward a gendered theory of female offending. *Annual Review of Sociology*, *22*, 459–487.

Sutherland, E. H. (1947). *Criminology*. Philadelphia: Lippincott.

Taylor, R. J., Chatters, L. M., Tucker, M. B., & Lewis, E. (1990). Developments in Research on Black Families: A Decade Review. *Journal of Marriage and the Family*, *52*(4), 993–1014.

Thornberry, T. P., & Krohn, M. D. (2000). The self-report method for measuring delinquency and crime. *Criminal Justice, 4*(1), 33–83.

Toby, J. (1957). Social disorganization and stake in conformity: Complementary factors in the predatory behavior of hoodlums. *Jounral of Criminal Law, Criminology and Police Science, 48*, 12.

Trent, K., & South, S. J. (1989). Structural determinants of the divorce rate: A cross-societal analysis. *Journal of Marriage and the Family, 51*(2), 391–404.

Trent, K., & South, S. J. (2011). Too many men? Sex ratios and women's partnering behavior in China. *Social Forces, 90*(1), 247–268.

Tuljapurkar, S., Li, N., & Feldman, M. W. (1995). High sex ratios in China's future. *Science, 267*(5199), 874.

UNODC. (2018). *United Nations Office on Drugs and Crime Statistics.* Retrieved from https://www.unodc.org/unodc/en/data-and-analysis/statistics.html

Van Bavel, J. (2010). Choice of study discipline and the postponement of motherhood in Europe: The impact of expected earnings, gender composition, and family attitudes. *Demography, 47*(2), 439–458.

Wang, T. (2019). Fewer women doing more crime: How had the one-child policy affected female crime in China? *The Sociological Quarterly, Online first*, 1–20.

Warr, M., & Stafford, M. (1993). Age, peers, and delinquency. *Criminology, 31*, 17–40.

Widom, C. S. (2014). Varieties of violent behavor. *Criminology, 52*(3), 313–344.

Wilson, M., & Daly, M. (1985). Competitiveness, risk taking, and violence: The young male syndrome. *Ethology and Sociobiology, 6*(1), 59–73.

Zeng, Y., Tu, P., Gu, B., Xu, Y., Li, B., & Li, Y. (1993). Causes and Implications of the recent increase in the reported sex ratio at birth in China. *Population and Development Review, 19*(2), 283–302.

Zhang, H. (2014). Domestic violence and its official reactions in China. In *The Routledge Handbook of Chinese Criminology.* London, UK: Routledge.

Zhu, W. X., Lu, L., & Hesketh, T. (2009). China's excess males, sex selective abortion, and One Child Policy: Analysis of data from 2005 National Intercensus Survey. *British Medical Journal, 338*.

Chapter Outcomes

The scarcity of women does not endorse them more value or equalize them to men; on the contrary, it works in a delicate way to press women to focus on reproduction rather than production and thereby strengthens the gender hierarchy in society.

The one-child policy has changed the family socialization of gender but left the existing hierarchical gender structures untouched. The change brings about two effects on the gender gap in deviance. On the one hand, women are less feminine than before; meanwhile, masculinity is decreased inter-generationally, which converge the gender difference in deviance together. However, this change is different from the "masculinization" of women or "feminization" of men because the pathways to deviance continue being distinctive between genders.

On the other hand, the equalizing progress in societal gender structure lags behind that in gender ideologies, which produces the gender-specific strain for the new-generation Chinese women, especially for those who had been instilled in the belief of gender equality and pinned with the family dream aspiring for economic achievement but disappointed by the gender hierarchy in society.

Therefore, the narrowed gender gap in deviance/crime is not an outcome of female liberalization; on the contrary, it is precisely manifesting the toxic effect of the persistent gender inequality that has been permeating every pore of all social institutions.

CHAPTER 8

Minority Female School Safety Agents' Identification of Adolescent Bullying

G. R. Paez | *University of Tampa*

Overview

Although the literature on the use of school-based law enforcement enhancing overall school safety continues to grow, little attention has been given of how officers are utilized to identify and prevent adolescent bullying. Moreover, literature has not explored how minority women in school-based policing identify bullying incidents and perceive their importance in bullying prevention. This study uses responses from a survey of minority female NYPD school safety agents to explore the influence of individual factors, their perceived importance in bullying prevention, and their identification of bullying incidents on their likelihood of intervention. Multivariate logistic regression results indicate that the survey responses support the assumption that minority female school safety agents who identified instances of bullying were more likely to intervene in cases of bullying. However, the results did not fully support the other assumptions proposed in this study. Implications for future research and practice are also discussed.

Chapter Outcomes

- Identify and describe bullying
- Discuss the significance and role of women in law enforcement
- Understand the significance of law enforcement in schools

Introduction

Despite research on the use of law enforcement in school safety, little work has explored how school-based law enforcement officers identify and intervene in instances of bullying (see e.g., Hindjua & Patchin, 2015). Exploring how school-based law enforcement officers identify instances of bullying is an area in critical need of investigation since these officers observe and interact with students outside of the classroom, where most forms of bullying actually occur. Research also lacks the exploration of how female minority school-based officers identify bullying incidents and perceive their importance in bullying prevention. These women encompass a smaller proportion of the overall amount of law enforcement officers. Examining how female minority officers in schools recognize bullying may also provide unique perspectives on bullying since these officers are part of a distinctive group in law enforcement.

This exploratory study seeks to understand whether minority female school safety agents recognize instances of bullying. Second, it explores the influence of individual factors of these officers and perceived importance in bullying prevention – on agents' likelihood to intervene in cases of bullying. To this end, three hypotheses are considered: (1) minority female school safety agents can identify instances of bullying when presented with facts of the case, (2) agents' individual factors will affect their likeliness to intervene in instances of bullying, (3) agents' perceived importance of their role in bully prevention will affect their likeliness to intervene.

Literature Review

Concern over school safety in the U.S. continues to develop as a result of violent acts like mass shootings. The tragic events that occurred at Sandy Hook Elementary and Stoneman Douglas High School forced schools to focus on safety strategies to protect students, teachers, and staff members. A noted strategy that continues to receive support is the use of school-based law enforcement officers (Devlin & Gottfredson, 2018; Jennings et al., 2011; Raymond, 2010; Thomas et al., 2013). However, the effect of school-based officers to prevent adolescent crime, violence, and behavioral issues has not been consistent. The use of law enforcement has trade-offs. Schools may curtail violence, crime and delinquency when officers are present, but they also run the risk of criminalizing certain behaviors and increasing the likelihood that youth come into contact with the criminal justice system (Jennings et al., 2011; May et al., 2015; Na & Gottfredson, 2011; Theriot, 2009). This extends to using school-based law enforcement officers to detect and prevent adolescent bullying (Crawford & Burns, 2016; Devlin et al., 2018; Raymond, 2010, Robles-Piña & Denham, 2012; Sampson, 2012).

Bullying and its Impact on Children

Bullying is conceptualized by three essential components that include: (1) intentionally harmful behavior that (2) usually occurs with some repetitiveness or highly likely to be repeated and (3) is aimed at an individual who lacks the ability to defend against such harm (Hutzell & Payne, 2012; Olweus, 1991; Popp, 2012). Bullying also encompasses hurtful behaviors that aim to cause harm to victims through physical, verbal, or psychological attacks or intimidation (Farrington & Ttofi, 2009; Olweus, 2011). Bullying is embedded in a social context, making school settings an ideal site for bullying to occur (Popp, 2012). The most significant aspect of bullying is that it establishes an imbalance of power when a more powerful individual (or child) torments a less powerful child over a period of time. That power imbalance is derived from physical stature, strength, or psychological influence that a child possesses and uses to fit in or because he/she feels that he/she is better than his/her victim (Oweus, 2011; Farrington & Ttofi, 2009; Ttofi & Farrington, 2008). An imbalance of power based on disparities of physical, mental, and verbal strength is necessary for an instance of bullying to transpire (Olweus, 2011; Ttofi & Farrington, 2008).

Bullying is divided into one of four categories: physical, verbal, social, and cyber (Farrington & Ttofi, 2009; Olweus, 2011; Patchin & Hinduja, 2015). Physical bullying involves the intentional use of force on a weaker person, which often results in physical harm (Olweus, 2011). Physical bullying embodies acts of violence during which an adolescent hits, pushes, kicks, slaps, or spits on another peer (Menard & Grotpeter, 2011; Olweus, 2011). Verbal bullying includes name-calling, taunting, teasing, and threatening. Bullies use words to degrade others and display dominance over peers (Olweus, 2011). Social bullying involves hurting another individual's character or social status by excluding him/her from a group, spreading rumors, or humiliating an individual publicly (Menard & Grotpeter, 2011; Olweus, 2011). Finally, cyberbullying is deliberate and recurrent harm is inflicted through internet-enabled devices such as computers, cellular phones, and other devices (Patchin & Hinduja, 2015). These devices allow a child to send hurtful messages and content (e.g., pictures, video, and text) to a victim or public sites accessible to third parties (Paez, 2016; Patchin & Hinduja, 2015).

The emotional and psychological effects of bullying are well noted, including short- and long-term internalizing/externalizing behaviors on both perpetrators and their victims such as sadness, low self-esteem, depression, aggression, drug use, and violence (Litwiller & Brausch, 2013; Olweus, 2011; Popp, 2012; Ttofi & Farrington, 2008; Turner et al., 2013). Bullying can also negatively impact the physical health of both perpetrators and their victims (Menard & Grotpeter, 2011; Popp, 2012; Ttofi & Farrington, 2008, Turner et al., 2013). Studies show that bullies have an increased likelihood to engage in risky and delinquent behaviors such as drinking, smoking, drug use, truancy, vandalism, bringing weapons to school, and violence (Hutzell & Payne, 2012; Menard & Grotpeter, 2011; Olweus, 2011). A strong relationship has also been noted between bullying and negative outcomes for victims such as low self-esteem, depression, and suicidal ideation (Litwiller & Brausch, 2013; Olweus, 2011; Popp, 2012; Turner et al., 2013). In response to the negative impact of bullying on children, school prevention efforts that includes law enforcement has emerged in literature.

Women in Policing

Although women have been involved in law enforcement in various capacities throughout the U.S. since the late 19th century, by the early 20th century the role of women in policing shifted from social welfare or protective assignments to more inclusive police work (Archbold & Schulz, 2012, Penzler & Sinclair, 2013; Schuck, 2017). The passages of the Civil Rights Act of 1964 and the Equal Employment Opportunity Act of 1972 also forced state and local law enforcement agencies to recognize and eliminate discriminatory hiring practices (Penzler & Sinclair, 2013; Rabe-Hemp, 2008a; Schuck, 2017). It was also during this period that women in law enforcement began to seek promotions but experienced opposition from their respective agencies that led to several recognized lawsuits (Archbold & Schulz, 2012; Penzler & Sinclair, 2013). While the number of women in policing has grown over the last 50 years, they continue to make up a disproportionate amount[1] of the police workforce (Archbold & Hassell, 2009; O'Connor Shelly et al., 2011).

Research has looked to understand the causes of the disproportion number of women in policing as well as their unique experiences or insights in varying areas of this male dominated field (Archbold & Schulz, 2012; del Carmen et al., 2007; Cordner & Cordner, 2011; Shelley et al., 2011). Studies have identified institutional barriers centered around recruitment, retention and promotional opportunities that negatively impact women in this field (Cordner & Cordner, 2011; O'Connor Shelly et al., 2011; Rabe-Hemp, 2008a; Schuck, 2017). Women in policing also experience instances of sexual harassment, exclusion and isolation (del Carmen et al., 2007; Rabe-Hemp; 2008; Shelly et al., 2011). In a survey of officers in the Milwaukee Police Department, Stroshine and Brandl (2011) found that female officers (16% of the total department) as well as minority females officers reported higher levels of isolation in their work environment compared to White males. Additionally, minority females confront discrimination as a result of their race/ethnicity. Del Carmen et al. (2007) suggests that literature lacks the exploration of issues that minority female officers face that includes, but are not limited to: integration, isolation, stress,

---

[1] As of 2013, data from the Bureau of Justice Statistics shows that women account for 12% of full-time law enforcement officers (Reaves, 2015).

and job satisfaction. Finally, a lack of research exists that focuses on how gender impacts police behavior (Rabe-Hemp, 2008b), and more specifically how female officers operate in distinctive settings such as schools and their ability to recognize bullying.

The Roles of School Resource Officers in Schools[2]

Police agencies have provided services to schools to protect children from school crime and violence for over sixty years (Coon & Travis, 2012; Raymond, 2010). During the 1960s, police officers assigned to schools known as school resource officers, had the legal authority to make arrests, search and seize, and issue summonses on school grounds (Coon & Travis, 2012; Mckenna et al., 2016; Raymond, 2010). By the 1980s and early 1990s, school resource officers extended their purpose through their presence in curriculum-driven instruction such as D.A.R.E. (Drug Abuse Resistance Education) and G.R.E.A.T. (Gang Resistance Education and Training). By 1991, the National Association of School Resource Officers (NASRO) was founded on the triad model of school-based policing that assigned school resource officers' duties into three capacities that include an educator, informal counselor, and law enforcement officer. The inclusion of school resource officers in curriculum-driven programming strengthened their presence beyond their purview of preventing crime and ensuring school safety (Esbensen et al., 2012; McKenna & Pollock, 2014). By 2010, approximately half of all public schools in the United States had police officers assigned to their location, demonstrating their abundant use in public schools (Raymond, 2010).

School-based officers have become a new breed of public servants, a fusion of educational, correctional, and law enforcement officials who play a role in ensuring the safety of students and school staff members. Raymond (2010) posits that although the function of school resource officers varies among school districts, the most common roles of school resource officers include: (1) safety expert and law enforcer (2) problem solver and liaison to community resources and (3) educator. This description enforces the roles school resource officers play in protecting children and staff. Safety personnel is expected to ensure the safety of students and all personnel in a school by conducting periodic inspections throughout and around the school and must make students and all school personnel aware of safety issues. School safety personnel are an important part of instituting a bully-resistant environment (Robles-Piña & Denham, 2012; Sampson, 2012). Sampson (2012) argues that bullying affects students' sense of security and may force them to avoid school when they perceive their safety is threatened. Thus, law enforcement may influence an adolescents' perception of school safety (Robles-Piña & Denham, 2012; Sampson, 2012).

The expansion of school resource officers has also received criticism for an overreliance of law enforcement in schools which may result in arresting children for behavior that is not considered dangerous. This is often referred to as the "school-to-prison pipeline" (May et al., 2015; McKenna et al., 2016; Pigott et al., 2018; Wolf, 2013). Pigott et al. (2018) argue that an individual's initial contact with the criminal justice system may possibly progress to more interactions with the criminal justice system. Therefore, studies have examined whether increasingly punitive measures applied by schools or the presence of school resource officers increase the size of the school-to-prison pipeline. To date, outcomes of these inquiries have produced mixed results (Crawford & Burns, 2016; Na & Gottfredson, 2011; Jennings et al., 2011; May et al., 2015; Pigott et al., 2018; Theriot, 2009). Findings have presented inconsistent views on the impact that school resource officers have on crime prevention, school safety and outcomes for students. Further, the literature on school-based law enforcement discusses

---

[2] School resource officers differ from slightly from school safety agents. School safety agents are peace officers, similar to a police officer but are not equipped with a firearm. School resource officers are also sworn officers, but are also armed.

by what means these officers and other safety personnel in schools can prevent crime (Coon & Travis, 2012; Mckenna et al., 2016; Raymond, 2010). However, the use of school resource officers to mitigate instances of bullying has received minimal attention and thus warrants further exploration.

School Resource Officers and Bullying

Thus far, limited research has examined the impacts of school resource officers on bullying (Devlin et al., 2018; Gerlinger & Wo, 2014; Kupchik & Farina, 2016). While examining whether school resource officers influence the level of bullying in schools through the use of a difference-in-difference identification strategy aimed at schools that introduced, ceased or resumed officers use in schools (Devlin et al., 2018). Devlin et al. (2018) found no significant changes in the level of bullying in schools related to the introduction, discontinuation or continuation of officer use. In another study, Gerlinger & Wo (2014) examined the outcomes of school security measures on bullying victimization through the development of an index comprised of school security or police officer presence, metal detectors, secured entrances and exits, and locker inspections. The results demonstrated that the measures used in the study were not significantly related to physical or verbal bullying (Gerlinger & Wo, 2014). Kupchik & Farina (2016) also sought out to examine and the effects of security guards or police officers on bullying victimization. However, Kupchik & Farina (2016) found no significant relationship between the presence of security guards or police officers and bullying victimization in schools. Although these studies identified the limitation of their results, they provide insights into exploring effective strategies to prevent adolescent bullying that may include the utilization of school-based law enforcement.

The presence of school resource officers may act as a bullying deterrent if adolescents believe they are likely to be caught and punished (Devlin et al., 2018). For example, school resource officers may assist teachers and school administrators to enforce anti-bullying laws or policies. Devlin et al. (2018) suggest that school resource officer responses to instances of bullying may vary depending on what role type they focus on while in the school setting (e.g., law enforcement or education). A safe school environment is instrumental to the proper socialization and development of children. School resource officers provide a level of safety and may have an impact on the school climates. For example, an environment that supports bullying creates a climate of fear and develops students' aversion to school (Hutzell & Payne, 2012; Popp, 2012). Thus, school resource officers may offer a method to enhance a schools' climate, anti-bullying efforts and overall safety.

The NYPD and School Safety

The New York City Police Department (NYPD) oversees the School Safety Division that ensures the safety of approximately 1.1 million students and staff members in 1,800 New York City public schools. The New York City public school system is also one of the largest in the country and comprised of predominately minority students.[3] The NYPD is comprised of approximately 5,000 school safety agents, and roughly 200 sworn police officers. School safety agents are designated as peace officers who are appointed to maintain law and order, similar to a police officer but are not equipped with a firearm. School safety agents have the same primary role as school resource officers, which is to work closely with school officials to ensure the safety of students and staff members.

In addition to efforts made by the New York City Department of Education (DOE), the NYPD School Safety Division has made organizational changes to prevent bullying in New York City public schools.

---

[3] As of 2019, the New York City Department of Education reports that the racial or ethnic composition of the students enrolled is 40.5% Hispanic, 26.0% Black or African American, 16.1% Asian, 15.0% White.

Since 2012, the NYPD School Safety Division has partnered with Life Space Crisis Intervention (LSCI), a nationally recognized training and certification program, to train agents on conflict resolution and bullying prevention. The goal of this three-day training course is to provide school safety agents with a framework to establish positive relationships with youth. The course also includes a component that informs agents of various aspects of bullying, identification and reporting practices, the impact on its victims, and discussing a myriad of methods to assist victims.

The Present Study

In contrast to research that examines school resource officers as a strategy to prevent or reduce adolescent bullying in schools, this study examines how minority female school safety agents' characteristics, perceived importance in bullying prevention, and their identification of bullying cases influence their decision to intervene. Therefore, this study applies multivariate logistic regression to examine these relationships.

It is hypothesized that minority female school safety agents can identify instances of bullying when presented with a description of an incident. A primary viewpoint of this study is that school safety agents who can identify an instance of bullying might be more inclined to get involved. Moreover, several individual factors and their perceived importance in bullying prevention also might influence the likelihood of intervention based on their unique perspectives, experiences and backgrounds. Although these assumptions have not been explored in this literature, they build on previous work that explored the use of law enforcement in bullying prevention (Devlin et al., 2018; Gerlinger & Wo, 2014; Kupchik & Farina, 2016; Robles-Piña & Denham, 2012).

Methodology

Design

A cross-sectional survey design was used to collect the information of minority female school safety agents and their perceptions of importance in bullying prevention. Eight vignettes were also constructed to solicit agents' identification and decision-making with respect to instances of bullying. Construction of each vignette was based on scholarly work that classifies bullying into one of four categories: physical, verbal, social, and cyber (Hutzell & Payne, 2012; Olweus, 2011; Patchin & Hinduja, 2015; Popp, 2012). Four of the eight vignettes, included in the survey, described instances that are not bullying to demonstrate whether the respondents could accurately distinguish between both types of instances.

TABLE 1: VIGNETTES FOR SSA BULLYING SURVEY

Vignette Number	Vignette	Type of Bullying[4]
1	You are approached by a student who claims to have been punched and kicked by another student. The student says that he/she is attacked every day behind the school building during dismissal time. The student tells you that he/she is afraid to leave the building.	Physical

---

[4] Bullying is defined as intentionally harmful behavior that usually occurs with some repetitiveness and is aimed at an individual who lacks the ability to defend against such harm.

2	It is dismissal time and you walk outside to patrol the area surrounding the school building. During your patrol you notice a small group of students form a circle around one student. As you approach these children, you hear the group yell "you're gay" at the student who is surrounded. The student who was surrounded informs you that this is not the first time that this has happened.	Verbal
3	In the hallway you overhear a female student crying. You approach the student and she tells you that someone sent her a hurtful text message to her cell phone calling her a "slut and whore".	Not Bullying
4	You are walking down a hallway and you see one student spit on another student's face.	Not Bullying
5	It is lunchtime and you witness a group of children at a table tell another student "you can't sit here; the freaks sit over there".	Not Bullying
6	You are conducting a directed patrol of the stairways and you hear a male student call another male student a "bitch".	Not Bullying
7	While standing in front of your school, you notice a student crying. You approach the student to investigate. The student tells you that his/her classmates have posted cruel messages on social media sites for three months that describe the student as fat, ugly, and stupid.	Cyber
8	You are approached by a student who tells you that other students have been spreading rumors about him/her during the school year. The student then shows you various letters that have been left in his/her desk. The letters make fun of the way the student dresses and speaks.	Social

© G.R Paez

The vignettes appeared in no particular order. Additionally, the survey instrument did not include a definition of bullying. The purpose of omitting the definition of bullying was to minimize the biasing of the respondents and to explore whether the respondents could accurately identify instances of bullying.

Multivariate logistic regression analyses were applied to assess the influence of minority female school safety agents' characteristics, their perceived importance with regard to prevention, and identification of bullying on their likelihood of intervention in examples of bullying.

Sample

The study utilized convenience sampling to survey NYPD school safety agents during training sessions held at five New York City public school sites from December 24th to 31st, 2014.[5] School safety agents assigned to patrol New York City public schools regardless of their rank, age, sex, or length of employment with the NYPD School Safety Division were asked to participate in the study. The sampling frame in this study did not include agents who worked in other capacities such as administrative positions in the School Safety Division's main office. Paper-based surveys were administered in-person to approximately 4,700 school safety agents during the survey period. The initial administration of the survey yielded 882 completed responses. For the purpose of this study, minority females were selected from the initial dataset (n = 600) and are the unit of analysis.

---

[5] The survey was pre-tested on September 25, 2014 at the School Safety Division's main office.

Measures

Dependent Variable. Each vignette contains an instance of bullying based on literature that classifies bullying into one of four categories: physical, verbal, social, and cyber (Hutzell & Payne, 2012; Olweus, 2011; Patchin & Hinduja, 2015; Popp, 2012). As previously mentioned, four out of the eight vignettes were cases of bullying, according to the agreed-upon definition, maintaining the behavior is intentional and repetitive. This to see whether school safety agents could accurately distinguish between both types of instances, bullying and non-bullying. Each vignette described a scenario and then asked whether the agent would intervene. These responses were recoded into a dichotomous variable (0 = No, 1 = Yes) to be included in multivariate regression models to identify predictors of school safety agent's intervention in cases of bullying. Construction of the dependent variable merited the use of multivariate logistic regression to assess the relationship between indicators and the dichotomous outcome measure.

Independent Variables. Several variables were included in this study. *Age* was constructed as a continuous variable to capture the school safety agents age at the time of participation in this study. *Years of Experience* was composed as an ordinal variable and aggregated into four categories (1 = 1 to 5 years, 2 = 5 to 10 years, 3 = 10 to 15 years, 4 = Over 15 years). *Education* was aggregated into two categories (1 = High School Diploma, 2 = College Degree). *Rank* was constructed as a dichotomous variable to differentiate those in supervisory and non-supervisory positions (0 = Non-Supervisor, 1 = Supervisor). Operating in a supervisory position might compel school safety agents to identify and react to instances of bullying more than school safety agents in non-supervisory positions because of their status in the NYPD School Safety Division or based on requirements and expectations of their rank.

Perceived importance with respect to preventing bullying was constructed as a dichotomous variable (0 = No, 1 = Yes) based on the question: "Do you think you play an important role in preventing bullying in your school?" On the second part of the survey instrument, school safety agents were asked to read eight vignettes. Each vignette was followed by a question that asked school safety agents to determine whether it is an incident of bullying (i.e., "Is this an incident of bullying?"). This question was used to construct *Identification of Bullying* as a binary measure (0 = No, 1 = Yes) to assess how school safety agents identify incidents as either bullying or non-bullying related.

Analytic Strategy

Several analyses were conducted to explore the influence of minority female school safety agents' characteristics, perceived importance with respect to bullying prevention, and identification of bullying on their likelihood of intervention. Purposely, multivariate logistic regression was used in the eight vignettes constructed for this study, given the nature of the dichotomous outcome variable (*Intervention*) developed for the study.

Results

Descriptive Statistics

Table 2 presents the unique characteristics of the school safety agents who participated in this study. The data from Table 2 revealed the mean age of agents in the study was 43. The sample of SSAs in this study reported varying levels of experience with the majority ranging from 1 to 15 years of experience. Approximately 75% of the sample of respondents for this study held a high school diploma and were overwhelmingly non-supervisors (92.1%).

Age	Mean Age	43
Years of Experience	1 to 5 Years	25.8% (155)
	5 to 10 Years	32.2% (193)
	10 to 15 Years	26.0% (156)
	Over 15 Years	16.0% (96)
Education	High School Degree	75.0% (450)
	College Degree	24.5% (147)
	No Response	0.5% (5)
Rank	Non-Supervisor	92.1% (552)
	Supervisor	8.0% (48)
Perceived Importance	No	10.0% (60)
	Yes	89.0% (534)
	No Response	1.0% (6)

© G.R Paez

Figures in Table 3 indicate that overall, a significant amount of minority female school safety agents accurately identified actual cases of bullying outlined in the vignettes. This outcome suggests that the minority female school safety agents generally understand what constitutes bullying, including the four types found in the extant literature (i.e., physical, verbal, social, and cyber-based). However, there was also a lack of variation in the responses regarding minority female school safety agents' identification of actual cases of bullying and instances of non-bullying. Moreover, approximately 89% of the agents in the sample used for this study felt they played an important role in preventing bullying.

TABLE 3: MINORITY FEMALE SSAS IDENTIFICATION OF BULLYING INCIDENTS (N=600)

Response	Vignette 1 Physical Bullying	% of Response	Vignette 2 Verbal Bullying	% of Response	Vignette 3 Non-Bullying Incident	% of Response	Vignette 4 Non-Bullying Incident	% of Response
No	24	4%	67	11%	31	5%	242	40%
Yes	576	96%	533	89%	569	95%	358	60%
Total	600	100%	600	100%	600	100%	600	100%
Response	Vignette 5 Non-Bullying Incident	% of Response	Vignette 6 Non-Bullying Incident	% of Response	Vignette 7 Cyber Bullying	% of Response	Vignette 8 Social Bullying	% of Response
No	136	23%	309	52%	42	7%	61	10%
Yes	464	77%	291	48%	558	93%	539	90%
Total	600	100%	600	100%	600	100%	600	100%

© G.R Paez

Table 4 illustrates the multivariate logistic regression outcomes for the eight vignettes embedded in the survey used for this study. The results indicate that school safety agents who identified a vignette as an instance of bullying had a higher likelihood of intervention compared to agents who did not identify the vignette as bullying. The results from Table 4 also indicate a higher propensity for school safety agents to identify bullying throughout all the vignettes even in non-bullying cases.

Discussion

The present study adds to the existing literature by examining school-based law enforcement officers' identification of bullying and intervention. Specifically, this study focuses on the perception of minority female NYPD SSAs that operate in the New York City public school system. The findings partially supported the hypotheses tested in this study. For hypothesis 1 – that said minority female school safety agents can identify instances of bullying when presented with details of an instance, the relationship between the school safety agents' identification of an instance of bullying and intervention was found throughout the analyses in both bullying and non-bullying scenarios. This outcome suggests that minority female school safety agents who identify an instance of bullying have a greater likelihood of intervention.

Yet, despite the training provided to minority female school safety agents, intervention in cases where it was not necessary appeared in the results of this study. This outcome highlights a disjunction between identification of bullying and involvement from minority female school safety agents. A cause for this lack of variation might be a product of the NYPD School Safety Division's commitment to preventing bullying in New York City public schools by informing and training school safety agents on how to protect victims and report bullying. For example, the NYPD provides training that applies the Life Space Crisis Intervention model to assist school safety agents in identifying and preventing instances of bullying.

It is also plausible that the sensitive nature of bullying led to social desirability biases, which denotes the tendency of individuals to respond to questions in a socially accepted manner. This might be the cause of school safety agents who in this study overidentified non-bullying instances as bullying. Further, the overidentification of cases by minority female school safety agents that are not bullying related might be the result of heightened social attention to the issue of bullying. The hyper-awareness of minority female school safety agents intervening in non-bullying cases in this study may also be the result of overtraining or pressure from the New York City Department of Education to assist in public school's anti-bullying efforts aimed at prevention.

For hypothesis 2 – that said minority female school safety agents' individual factors will affect their likeliness to intervene in instances of bullying, the relationship between these factors had a limited influence on agent intervention in both bullying and non-bullying scenarios (see Table 4). These outcomes may be the result of outside factors that were not captured by the survey instrument used in this study. For example, female officers may take on more of a maternal or nurturing role that may have contributed to the overidentification of bullying incidents. However, Rabe-Hemp (2008b) criticizes the presumption that female officers consistently embody feminine traits in the course of their work. Proposing that gender roles or traits may cause female officers to be more perceptive of bullying is an overly simplified explanation of the outcomes of this study.

Finally, for hypothesis 3 – that said minority female school safety agents perceived importance of their role in bullying prevention will affect their likeliness to intervene, was found to be significant in only one of the four bullying related vignettes used in the study (See Table 4). This outcome may be the result

TABLE 4: LOGISTIC REGRESSION COEFFICIENTS REPRESENTING MINORITY FEMALE SSAS INTERVENTION IN BULLYING SCENARIOS

Dependent Variable

Independent Variables	Vignette 1 - Physical Bullying Scenario		Vignette 2 - Verbal Bullying Scenario		Vignette 3 - Non-Bullying Scenario		Vignette 4 - Non-Bullying Scenario		Vignette 5 - Non-Bullying Scenario		Vignette 6 - Non-Bullying Scenario		Vignette 7 - Cyber Bullying Scenario		Vignette 8 - Social Bullying Scenario	
	Intervention		Intervention		Intervention		Intervention		Intervention		Intervention		Intervention		Intervention	
	B(SE)	Exp(B)	B(SE)	Exp(B)	B(SE)	Exp(B)	B(SE)	Exp(B)	B(SE)	Exp(B)	B(SE)	Exp(B)	B(SE)	Exp(B)	B(SE)	Exp(B)
Age	-0.030 (0.042)	0.970	-0.018 (0.037)	0.983	-0.002 (0.029)	0.998	0.006 (0.023)	1.006	0.026 (0.021)	1.026	0.021 (0.016)	1.021	0.026 (0.029)	1.027	0.022 (0.024)	1.022
Years of Experience	-0.211 (0.419)	0.810	0.556 (0.390)	1.743	-0.064 (0.305)	0.938	-0.101 (0.219)	0.904	0.096 (0.206)	1.101	0.075 (0.159)	1.078	-0.053 (0.291)	0.949	0.052 (0.233)	1.053
Education	-0.691 (0.801)	0.501	1.943 (1.122)	6.977	-0.358 (0.547)	0.699	0.525 (0.469)	1.69	-0.069 (0.355)	0.933	0.118 (0.293)	1.125	-0.478 (0.518)	0.620	-0.101 (0.444)	0.904
Rank	-0.220 (1.029)	0.803	0.270 (0.905)	1.310	0.614 (0.908)	1.848	-0.048 (0.555)	0.953	0.240 (0.611)	1.271	0.728 (0.519)	2.070	-0.039 (0.793)	0.962	0.361 (0.662)	1.435
Perceived Importance	1.913 (0.757)[1]	6.777	0.352 (0.957)	1.422	0.595 (0.707)	1.813	0.863 (0.453)	2.371	0.339 (0.460)	1.404	-0.177 (0.427)	0.838	-0.058 (0.848)	0.943	0.685 (0.548)	1.984
Identification of Bullying	2.809 (0.783)[3]	16.596	3.829 (0.703)[3]	45.995	3.280 (0.518)[3]	26.569	1.888 (0.409)[3]	6.607	2.411 (0.315)[3]	11.145	2.524 (0.365)[3]	12.476	4.011 (0.479)[3]	55.204	3.253 (0.386)[3]	25.866
Nagelkerke R²	0.260		0.348		0.229		0.143		0.238		0.232		0.388		0.308	
N	600		600		600		600		600		600		600		600	

[1]p < .05. [2]p < .01. [3]p < .001.

© G.R Paez

of a variation in agents perceived and actual importance in their schools' anti-bullying efforts based on the contextual demands of the school environment in which they work. It is plausible that agents see themselves as having an important role, but might operate in a school environment that either under-utilizes them or exerts their intervention exhaustively.

Since 89% of the minority female agents in this study felt they played an important role in preventing bullying, it is possible that other factors could have contributed to the lack of influence this factor had on agent intervention in cases of bullying. This outcome also suggests that minority female school safety agents are aware of bullying and view themselves as holding a significant position in the prevention of bullying. However, this outcome might have been influenced by several factors. First, this outcome might be the result of efforts made by the NYPD's School Safety Division to train and inform school safety agents on various aspects of bullying and its negative consequences on children. Another factor that might have influenced minority female school safety agent's high degree of perceived importance with respect to bullying prevention is the increased social awareness of bullying in various areas. Adolescent bullying continues to receive media attention due to reports of victims who commit suicide or engage in violent behavior as a response of victimization. The increase in social awareness on bullying might have influenced how agents in this study perceived their importance with bullying prevention since they are in contact with children. It also provides them with the ability to prevent bullying from occurring.

Limitations

The sample collected for this study contains female and minority officers that have not commonly been identified in previous that focused on school-based officers (Rhodes, 2017; Robles-Piña & Denham, 2012; Wolf, 2013). Therefore, the effects the individual factors found in this study might be the result of this unique group of school-based law enforcement officers. However, generalizing the results of this specific group of officers to other female minorities in school-based law enforcement, might not be accurate. Yet, the unique factors of these school safety agents provide insight into female minority school-based law enforcement as well as the importance of bullying and bullying identification and intervention.

Implications for Research and Practice

Although the results of this study produced varying results, it did not provide strong support for the influence of perceived importance in bullying prevention on intervention. Therefore, future work should continue to explore how minority female school-based officers perceive the importance of their role in bullying prevention. Specifically, examining female officers' identification and responses to bullying warrants more exploration.

Officers who feel they enhance a school's anti-bullying effort may be more inclined to intervene and apply their established roles (i.e., safety expert and law enforcer, problem solver and liaison to community resource, and educator) to ensure the safety of students. However, these views may also differ based on sex or race/ethnicity. Individual perceptions, however, are also difficult to assess since a measurement of how individuals perceive themselves is a construct that may not be observed directly through a survey instrument due to the existence of biases. For example, all school safety agents exercise their authority on school grounds by enforcing rules set by the NYPD and the New York City Department of Education. This dichotomy may influence not only school safety agents' perceived importance with respect to bullying prevention but also other school-based law enforcement officers.

The outcomes of this study, specifically minority female school safety agents' identification and intervention among bullying and non-bullying scenarios, necessitates more work to explore this relationship. The officers' ability to identify cases of bullying is a pertinent subject of this study because how they identify instances of bullying is vital to maintaining and enhancing a schools' anti-bullying efforts and overall school safety. Subsequent work should also assess the effectiveness of school-based law enforcement officers in a schools' anti-bullying programming and strategies. Research in this area should look at the training methods used to assist officers in bullying identification and prevention, examine best practices of law enforcement inclusion in anti-bullying programming and strategies, and ways in which officers can enhance school climate and overall safety.

Previous studies suggest that more work is needed to assess how school-based officers are used in school environments (McKenna *et al.*, 2016; Rhodes, 2017; Robles-Piña & Denham, 2012; Thomas *et al.*, 2013; Wolf, 2013). In cases of bullying, school-based law enforcement intervention may not necessarily require an adolescent to have contact with the criminal justice system but instead, apply an inclusive and holistic strategy to ensure minimal harm to the children involved. Yet, these decisions may also vary based on the officer's sex or race/ethnicity and thus require further exploration. Regardless of an officer's sex or race/ethnicity, they should be viewed as an additional resource for students to report an instance of bullying as well as to enhance a school's anti-bullying strategies and programming.

Key Terms:

Bullying

Cross-sectional Survey

Dependent Variable

Independent Variable

Multivariate Logistic Regression

Non-probability sampling

NYPD

School Resource Officer

School Safety Agent

School-to-prison pipeline

Triad Model of School-based Policing

Vignette

Discussion Questions:

1. What are the key components of bullying?

2. What are the negative effects of bullying on children?

3. What hardships have women in policing confronted?

4. What are the roles of school resource officers?

5. How can school-based law enforcement prevent bullying in schools?

References

Archibold, C.A., & Schulz, D.M. (2012). Research on women in policing: A look at the past, present and future. *Sociological Compass, 6*(9), 694–706.

del Carmen, A., Greene, H.T., Nation, D., & Osho, G.S. (2007). Minority women in policing in Texas: An attitudinal analysis. *Criminal Justice Studies, 20*, 281–94.

Coon, J. K., & Travis, L. F. (2012). The role of police in public schools: A comparison of principals and police reports of activities in schools. *Police Practice and Research, 12*(1), 15–30.

Cordner, G., & Cordner A. (2011). Stuck on a plateau? Obstacles to recruitment, selection, and retention of women police. *Police Quarterly, 14*(3), 207–226.

Crawford C., & Burns, R. (2016) Reducing school violence: Considering school characteristics

and the impacts of law enforcement, school security, and environmental factors. *Policing: An International Journal of Police Strategies & Management, 39*(3), 455-477.

Devlin, D. N., & Gottfredson, D. C. (2018). The roles of police officers in schools: Effects on recording and reporting of crime. *Youth Violence and Juvenile Justice, 16*(2), 208-223.

Devlin, D. N., Santos, M. R., & Gottfredson, D. C. (2018). An evaluation of police officers in schools as a bullying intervention. *Evaluation and Program Planning, 71*, 12-21.

Esbensen, F., Peterson, D., Taylor, T. J., & Osgood, D. W. (2012). Results from a multi-site evaluation of the G.R.E.A.T. program. *Justice Quarterly, 29*(1), 125-151.

Farrington, D. P., & Ttofi, M. M. (2009). How to reduce school bullying. *Victims & Offenders, 4*(4), 321–326.

Gerlinger, J., & Wo, J. C. (2014). Preventing School Bullying: Should Schools Prioritize an Authoritative School Discipline Approach Over Security Measures? *Journal of School Violence*, 1–25.

Hinduja, S. & Patchin, J. W. (2015). Bullying Beyond the Schoolyard: Preventing and Responding to Cyberbullying (2nd ed). Thousand Oaks, CA: Sage Publications.

Hutzell, K. L., & Payne, A. A. (2012). The impact of bullying victimization on school avoidance. *Youth Violence and Juvenile Justice, 10*(4), 370–385.

Jennings, W.G., Khey, D. N., Maskaly, J. and Donner, C. M. (2011), Evaluating the relationship between law enforcement and school security measures and violent crime in schools, *Journal of Police Crisis Negotiations, 11*(2), 109-124.

Litwiller, B. J., & Brausch, A. M. (2013). Cyberbullying and physical bullying in adolescent suicide: The role of violent behavior and substance abuse. *Journal of Youth Adolescence, 42*(5), 675–684.

May D. C., Barranco R., Stokes E., Robertson A. A., & Haynes S. H. (2015). Do school resource officers really refer juveniles to the juvenile justice system for less serious offenses? *Criminal Justice Policy Review, 29*(1), 1-17.

McKenna, J.M., Martinez-Prather, K., & Bowman, S.W. (2016). The roles of school-based law enforcement officers and how these roles are established: A Qualitative Study. *Criminal Justice Policy Review, 27*(4), 420–443.

McKenna, J. M., Pollock, J. M. (2014). Law enforcement officers in schools: An analysis of ethical issues. *Criminal Justice Ethics, 33*(3), 163-184.

Kupchik, A., & Farina, K. A. (2016). Imitating authority: Students' perceptions of school punishment and security, and bullying victimization. *Youth Violence and Juvenile Justice, 14*(2), 147–163.

Menard, S., & Grotpeter, J. K. (2011). Peer influence, social bonding, physical and relational aggression: Perpetrator and victimization in an elementary school sample. *Victims & Offenders, 6*(2), 181–206.

Na, C., & Gottfredson, D. C. (2011). Police officers in schools: Effects on school crime and the processing of offending behaviors. *Justice Quarterly, 1*(1), 1–32.

Olweus, D. (2011). Bullying at school and later criminality: Findings from three Swedish community samples. *Criminal Behavior and Mental Health, 21*(2), 151–156.

Paez, G. R. (2018). Cyberbullying among adolescents: A general strain theory perspective. *Journal of School Violence, 17*(1), 74–85.

Patchin, J. W., & Hinduja, S. (2015). Measuring cyberbullying: Implications for research. *Aggression and Violent Behavior, 23*, 69-74.

Pigott, C., Stearns, A. E., & Khey, D. N. (2017). School resource officers and the school to prison pipeline: Discovering trends of expulsions in public schools. *American Journal of Criminal Justice, 43*, 120-138.

Popp, A. M. (2012). The effects of exposure, proximity, and capable guardians on the risk of bullying victimization. *Youth Violence and Juvenile Justice, 10*(4), 124–134.

Prenzler, T., & Sinclair, G. (2013). The status of women police officers: An international review. *International Journal of Law, Crime and Justice, 41*, 115–131.

Rabe-Hemp, C. (2008a). Survival in an "all boys club": policewomen and their fight for acceptance. *Policing: An International Journal of Police Strategies & Management, 31*(2), 251–270.

Rabe-Hemp, C. (2008b). Female officers and the ethic of care: Does officer gender impact police behaviors? *Journal of Criminal Justice, 36*, 426–434,

Raymond, B. (2010, April). *Assigning police officers to schools.* Report prepared for the U.S. Department of Justice, Office of Community Oriented Policing Services, Publication No. 10. Washington, DC.

Reaves, B. A. (2015). *Local Police Departments, 2013: Personnel, Policies, and Practices.* Report prepared for the U.S. Department of Justice, Office of Justice Statistics Services. Washington, DC.

Rhodes, T. (2017). School resource officer perceptions and correlates of work roles. *Policing: A Journal of Policy and Practice, 13*(4), 1–19.

Robles-Piña, R. C., & Denham, M. A. (2012). School resource officers for bullying interventions: A mixed-methods analysis. *Journal of School Violence, 11*(1), 38–55.

Sampson, R. (2012, May). *Bullying in schools.* Report prepared for the U.S. Department of Justice, Office of Community Oriented Policing Services, Publication No. 12. Washington, DC.

Schuck, A.M. (2017). Female officers and community policing: Examining the connection between gender diversity and organizational change. *Women & Criminal Justice, 27,* 341–362.

Shelley, T.O., Morabito, M.S., & Tobin-Gurley, J. (2011). Gendered institutions and gender roles: Understanding the experiences of women in policing. *Criminal Justice Studies: A Critical Journal of Crime, Law and Society, 24*(4), 351–367.

Stroshine, M.S., & Brandl, S.G. (2011). Race, gender, and tokenism in policing: An empirical elaboration. *Police Quarterly, 14*(4), 344–365.

Theriot, M. T. (2009). School resource officers and the criminalization of school behavior. *Journal of Criminal Justice, 37*(1), 280–287.

Thomas, B., Towvim, L., Rosiak, J. Anderson, K. (2013, September). *School Resource Officers: Steps to effective school-based law enforcement.* Report prepared for National Center for Mental Health Promotion and Youth Violence Prevention. Washington, DC.

Ttofi, M. M., & Farrington, D. P. (2008). Bullying: Short-term and long-term effects, and the importance of defiance theory in explanation and prevention. *Victims & offenders, 3*(2), 289–312.

Ttofi, M. M., Farrington, D. P., & Losel, F. (2012). School bullying as a predictor of violence later in life: A systematic review and meta-analysis of prospective longitudinal studies. *Aggression and Violent Behavior, 17*(5), 405–418.

Turner, M. G., Exum, M. L., Brame, R., & Holt, T. J. (2013). Bullying victimization and adolescent mental health: General and typological effects across sex. *Journal of Criminal Justice, 41*(1), 53–59.

Wolf, K. C., (2014). Arrest decision making by school resource officers. *Youth Violence and Juvenile Justice, 12*(2), 1–15.

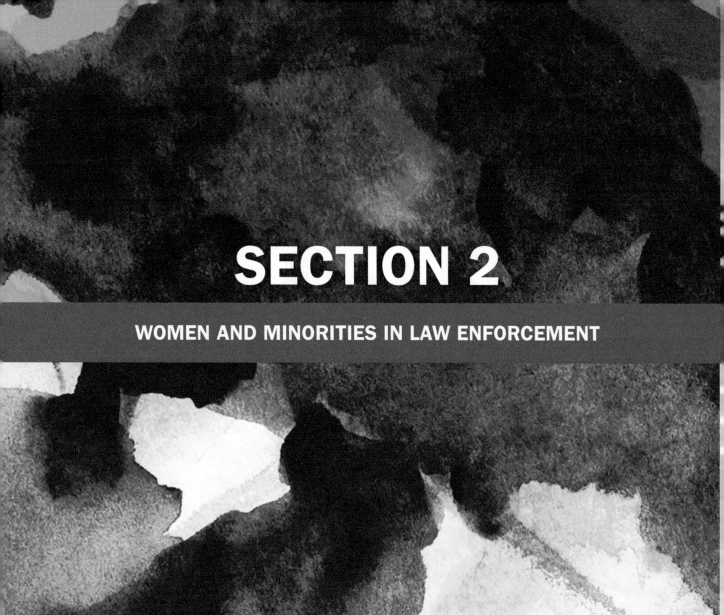

SECTION 2

WOMEN AND MINORITIES IN LAW ENFORCEMENT

CHAPTER 9

Women in Community Corrections: Supervision Styles and Decision-Making

Amber Wilson, MS | University of South Carolina
Barbara Koons-Witt, Ph.D. | University of South Carolina

Overview

During the 1970s, increased crime rates and a shift away from rehabilitation toward crime control measures precipitated dramatic increases in the corrections system at unprecedented levels. All parts of the corrections system were increasing, albeit some parts more than others (see Figure 1). By 2005, the prison population had expanded over 600% (Byrne, 2013). Although trends suggest that institutional populations are beginning to slightly decline, the most recent statistics indicate that there are 1.5 million Americans incarcerated in state and federal prisons (Carson, 2018). In response to the burgeoning corrections system and subsequent prison overcrowding, community corrections became increasingly utilized (Phelps, 2013), resulting in rapidly expanding the community corrections system. Since the 1980s, the community corrections area has experienced consistent growth, increasing 222% from a million people in 1981 (Bureau of Justice Statistics, 1982) to 4.5 million people in 2016 (Kaeble, 2018). In 2016, "1 in 55 adults in the United States was under [some form of] community supervision" (Kaeble, 2018, p.1).

As the community corrections field has grown, women have become employed by community corrections agencies at greater rates. Equal employment legislation in the 1970s resulted in increasing the number of women entering the field (Ireland & Berg, 2008), and the rate of female officers in community corrections departments has generally grown over the last few years (Bureau of Labor Statistics, 2018). As of 2018, there was a greater percentage of women working as probation officers than in any other area of the criminal justice field, including police officers, corrections officers, lawyers, and judges (Bureau of Labor Statistics, 2018; See Table 1). Despite their notable presence in the field, little is known about the experiences and decision-making of female probation and parole officers.

Instead, research on the gendered experiences of female practitioners within the criminal justice system has largely focused on police officers, corrections officers, and court workers. In this chapter, we focus on the decision-making efforts of probation and parole officers, including organizational-level factors and individual-level factors, with special attention to the research surrounding officer gender and the role it might play in officers' decision-making. Furthermore, we will discuss the importance of understanding potential links between officer gender and decision-making and make recommendations for future areas of research including the need to not only understand working experiences based on gender but also working experiences using an intersections perspective.

Figure 1

Number Of Persons Supervised By U.S. Adult Correctional Systems, 1980 – 2000 & 2006 – 2016

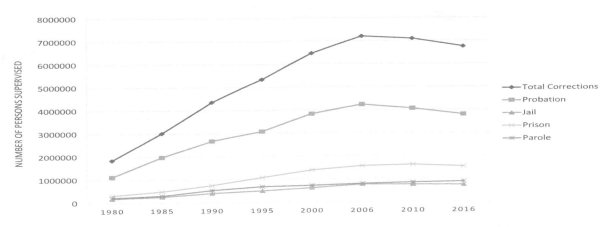

Adapted from Sources: Brown, Gilliard, Snell, Stephan, & Wilson, 1996; Bureau of Justice Statistics, 2000; Kaeble & Cowhig, 2018;

TABLE 1: SEX AND RACIAL/ETHNIC CHARACTERISTICS BY CRIMINAL JUSTICE EMPLOYEE

	Probation Officers	Lawyers	Judges	Police Officers	Corrections Officers
Sex					
Women	56.9%	37.4%	32.3%	15.4%	29.6%
Race					
African American	27.0%	5.5%	13.3%	12.7%	29.0%
Hispanic or Latino	15.9%	6.1%	6.7%	13.5%	13.7%

Adapted from Bureau of Labor Statistics, Employed persons by detailed occupation, sex, race, and Hispanic or Latino ethnicity dataset, 2018.

Chapter Learning Objectives

- Students should be able to describe how the corrections system has changed over the last several decades.
- Students should be able to explain what discretion CCOs have in supervising clients on their caseload.
- Students should be able to discuss both individual- and organization-level factors that impact CCOs' decision-making.
- Students should be able to identify the gaps in research on CCO supervision orientation.
- Students should be able to illustrate why an intersections perspective is useful for understanding the work experiences of CCOs.

History of Community Corrections and Supervision Models

Probation and parole are the most common forms of community corrections; however, community corrections can also include halfway houses, residential treatment facilities, and the use of day reporting centers (Alarid, 2019; Petersilia, 1998). The practice of community corrections has existed in the United States since the 1800s (Petersilia, 1998), but during recent decades we have seen major shifts in the use and expansion of community corrections. Like most criminal justice efforts, community corrections' policies and procedures often reflect the political and social climate of the times (Dean-Myrda & Cullen, 1998), and these ideologies often inform the way that probation and parole officers supervise clients.

When probation was first formalized, the emphasis of sentencing and corrections on rehabilitative efforts asserted that prosocial relationships between clients and community corrections officers (CCOs) could assist clients in desisting from engaging in criminal activities (Alarid, 2019; Lawrence, 1991; Viglione, 2018). This model of supervision, called the Caseworker Model (Lawrence, 1991), situated community corrections officers as case workers or social workers, and promoted their use of counseling when interacting with clients (Alarid, 2019). Some of the earliest listed qualifications for federal probation officers included some form of experience in social work (Alarid, 2019). Although supervision models within community corrections have changed over the decades (Alarid, 2019; Lawrence, 1991), it is noted that community corrections departments are still impacted by ties to their social work underpinning.

Today, community corrections departments focus on meeting the criminogenic needs of clients (Alarid, 2019; Viglione, 2018). These efforts are aimed at understanding the underlying reasons that clients commit crime and targeting those needs. To do so, CCOs must maintain prosocial relationships with clients while also ensuring that clients are abiding by the terms of their supervision. This professional relationship with clients requires a difficult balance for probation and parole officers, who must simultaneously work to meet their clients' needs while also supervising them and surveilling for non-compliance (Vissing, 2012). This dual role conflict contributes to the uniqueness of CCOs and understanding how they view their roles may be important when studying how officers make decisions at work.

Community Corrections Officers and Decision-Making

Despite a larger share of people being supervised in the community corrections area (as compared to institutional corrections), much remains unknown about officer decision-making. Studies completed to date have focused on officer attitude or orientation (Bolin & Applegate, 2018; Ricks & Eno Louden, 2015; Steiner, Travis, Makarios, & Brickley, 2011; West & Seiter, 2004), officer recommendations and referrals (Erez, 1989; Walsh, 1984), and supervision outcomes for clients (Bolin & Applegate, 2018; Kennealy, Skeem, Machak, & Eno Louden, 2012; Kerbs, Jones, & Jolley, 2009; Morash, Kashy, Smith, & Cobbina, 2017; Ricks & Eno Louden, 2015; Steiner, Travis, Makarios, & Brickley, 2011). Studies generally suggest that organizational factors may be most influential in shaping the types of decisions made by probation and parole officers (Kerbs et al., 2009; Steiner, Travis, Makarios, & Brickley, 2011; West & Seiter, 2004), however, individual- level factors may also be important, including officer gender and orientation (Steiner, Travis, Makarios, & Brickley, 2011; West & Seiter, 2004).

CCOs may be involved in the criminal justice process in both the pre-adjudication and the post- adjudication phases (see Figure 2). During the pre-adjudication phase, the judge may order that a defendant receive pre-trial supervision, which may include regular visits to a CCO or electronic monitoring during

Figure 2

Pre- and Post- Adjudication Officer Duties

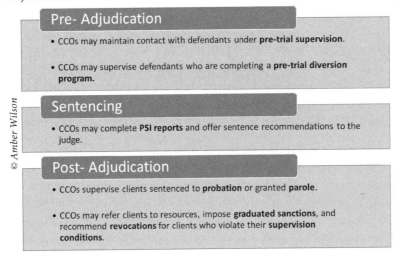

© Amber Wilson

Pre- Adjudication

- CCOs may maintain contact with defendants under **pre-trial supervision.**

- CCOs may supervise defendants who are completing a **pre-trial diversion program.**

Sentencing

- CCOs may complete **PSI reports** and offer sentence recommendations to the judge.

Post- Adjudication

- CCOs supervise clients sentenced to **probation** or granted **parole.**

- CCOs may refer clients to resources, impose **graduated sanctions,** and recommend **revocations** for clients who violate their **supervision conditions.**

or before trial (Alarid, 2019). Defendants who are granted participation in a pre-trial diversion program may be supervised by a community corrections officer for the duration of the program (Alarid, 2019). Before sentencing, some court jurisdictions may require, or the judge may request pre-sentence investigation (PSI) reports be completed by CCOs (Hawley, 2012; Steverson, 2012). The PSI report, including a sentence recommendation made by the investigating officer, is submitted directly to the judge to be considered during the sentencing hearing (Hawley, 2012; Steverson, 2012).

During the post-adjudication phase, CCOs are charged with the supervision of clients who are placed on probation (Hawley, 2012) or who have been granted parole (Vissing, 2012). While on probation or parole, clients have a list of terms that they agree to follow, known as their conditions of supervision. These conditions are set by the court for probationers or by the parole board for parolees. CCOs often experience broad discretion in how they supervise their clients (DeMichele & Payne, 2018). For example, officers are frequently required to address violations by clients regarding conditions of their community supervision (Swanson, 2012). Officers are generally able to determine independently how to respond to violations and may do so with limited departmental oversight (Klockars, 1972).

Sanctions that may be implemented by CCOs can range from referring a client to out-patient substance abuse treatment to arresting a client and recommending to the court or parole board that the client's probation or parole be revoked (Alarid, 2019; Zarse, 2012). For clients who are compliant with the terms of their supervision, officers can also recommend that these clients' supervision level be reduced, resulting in fewer contacts between clients and officers.

While supervising clients, CCOs are tasked with a range of areas for decision-making, including instituting or discontinuing curfews or allowing or denying clients' requests to travel across state lines (Klockars, 1972). CCOs often have broad discretion when making decisions regarding clients' supervision (DeMichelle & Payne, 2018; Kennealy et al., 2012; Ricks & Eno Louden, 2015). Kerbs and his colleagues (2009) believe that discretion is influenced by several converging factors including:

1. Individual beliefs and preferences;

2. Individual training and interpretation of the law;

3. Formal and informal workplace policies and practices;

4. Individual responses to offender characteristics; and

5. Available information at the time (p. 426).

More research is necessary to explain how officers use their discretion and make decisions that impact clients, the agency, and the wider community. CCOs' decision-making may impact their clients' supervision outcomes (Holmstrom, Adams, Morash, Smith, & Cobbina, 2017; Morash, Kashy, Smith, & Cobbina, 2015; Ricks & Eno Louden, 2015; West & Seiter, 2004) and create possible disparate outcomes for clients supervised by different officers or different departments (Kerbs et al., 2009). We next reviewed the literature on CCO decision-making, specifically focusing on factors at the organization- and individual-levels that tend to influence how officers use their discretion on the job.

Organization-Level Factors and Officer Decision-Making

Probation and parole services are situated in varying administrative settings sometimes together under a department of corrections or community corrections agency, and sometimes apart in separate departments or under the judiciary (Kerbs et al., 2009). Characteristics of the organization and policies mandated by the organization influence the decisions made by CCOs (DeMichele & Payne, 2018; Jones & Kerbs, 2007; Kerbs et al., 2009; Lutze, 2014; Steiner, Travis, Makarios, & Brickley, 2011). These features include administrative structure and department size, geographic location, and community setting (DeMichele & Payne, 2018; Kerbs et al., 2009; Ward & Kupchik, 2010). Organization-level policies addressed in the prior literature focus on caseload size and type, workload, and policies governing revocation decisions and their responses (Kerbs et al., 2009; Lutze, 2014; Matz, Conley, & Johanneson, 2018; Steiner, Travis, Makarios, & Meade, 2011; Turner, Braithwaite, Kearney, Murphy, & Haerle, 2012; West & Seiter, 2004).

Geographic location (e.g., southern vs. non-southern) and community setting are believed to influence the punitive nature of agencies and those individuals working in them. In their review of the sentencing literature on court context and setting, Kerbs and his colleagues (2009) found that southern states sentence defendants more harshly than other jurisdictions and surmised that these findings might translate to how community corrections agencies and their CCOs in different geographic areas might handle revocation decisions. Additionally, clients supervised in urban areas are subjected to closer surveillance and controls including more urinalyses and may be more likely to receive a revocation than their rural counterparts (Steiner, Travis, Makarios, & Brickley, 2011). In their study, however, Kerbs and his colleagues (2009) did not find significant differences in support for formal hearings to address revocations between officers from different geographic regions or from different community settings (rural vs. urban). It is also thought that the size of an agency can influence CCO decision-making. Research has found that agencies with a larger number of officers are less supportive of enforcement as a supervision goal (DeMichele & Payne, 2018) and are less likely to seek a formal hearing to address violations when responding to missed meetings, missed community service, and failed drug testing (Kerbs et al., 2009).

Caseload size and whether officers supervise a specialized client population are also believed to impact CCO decision-making (Kerbs et al., 2009; West & Seiter, 2004; Whitehead & Lindquist, 1992). In her discussion of the increased use of community corrections, Phelps (2013) explains that, while community corrections may serve to keep some clients from being sentenced directly to prison, some offenders who would have been given alternative sentences are being relegated to community supervision. Instead of lowering the overall numbers of individuals sentenced to incarceration, these shifts have instead increased the numbers of offenders under some form of state sanction (Phelps, 2013), a phenomenon that Morash and colleagues (2017) describe as a trend from "mass incarceration to mass supervision" (p. 4). Available data for the most recent eight years shows little growth in the number of probation officers (Bureau of Labor Statistics, 2018), which may indicate that officers' caseload sizes are growing (Randol, 2012). As caseload sizes increase, officers may be unable to dedicate time to address clients' individual needs (Teague, 2016; West and Seiter, 2004). Earlier research indicates that officers who supervise larger caseloads often have more punitive attitudes regarding supervision (Alarid, 2019; Whitehead & Lindquist, 1992), and West & Seiter (2004) assert that growing caseload sizes and having standard cases as opposed to specialized cases have resulted in officers being forced to focus on surveillance activities as opposed to social work activities that often require more time allotted for each offender. DeMichele and Payne (2018) find lower support for community reentry as a goal of supervision when caseload sizes are larger.

CCO's decisions are also governed by department policies and culture, some of which are meant to constrain the discretion of officers (Jones & Kerbs, 2007; Klockars, 1972; Lutze, 2014; Steiner, Travis, Makarios, & Meade, 2011; Turner et al., 2012). The use of risk and needs assessments to manage an increasingly serious offender population in the community is one example of how discretion has been impacted by policies implemented at the department level (Jones & Kerbs, 2007). Agencies can influence how probation and parole officers address supervision violations from offenders by either "inhibiting" formal responses or "pressuring" CCOs to officially respond under certain circumstances. Jones and Kerbs (2007) found that approximately 43% of the officers in their study felt external pressure to pursue formal action when they themselves did not want to, and 33% of officers felt restrained from pursuing formal action when they would have preferred to do so. Several states have implemented guidelines or policies containing structured responses to offender violations. In some cases, the intent was to reduce the number of offenders returning to prison for violations and burdening an already overcrowded prison system, and in other instances jurisdictions wanted to make responses more uniform across offenders and make sanctioned responses more rational (Steiner, Travis, Makarios, & Meade, 2011; Turner et al., 2012).

Jones and Kerbs (2007) contend that officer discretion is important and "provides a counterpart to a system embedded with a rigid set of rules" (p. 10). Klockars (1972) reminds us that the organizational context in which the probation officer works has limitations in controlling officers' behavior and decisions. He notes, "the rules, their application, and their dismissal are largely a matter of the discretion of the officer, who, with very little personal risk, may conceal or permit their violation" (p. 555). To appreciate why and how CCOs make decisions, we must move beyond organization-level factors and consider those factors that are specific to individual officers and how they approach their daily work.

Individual-Level Factors and Officer Decision-Making

In addition to organization-level factors, research indicates that individual-level factors also contribute to how CCOs supervise clients (Steiner, Travis, Makarios, & Brickley, 2011; West & Seiter, 2004). Officer orientation, which describes how a community corrections officer approaches his or her job, may not only influence how officers interact with and supervise clients, but also the decisions they make regarding graduated sanctions and revocations (Bolin & Applegate, 2018; Ricks & Eno Louden, 2015; Steiner, Travis, Makarios, & Brickley, 2011). Although fewer studies have focused exclusively on officer gender and its impact on decision-making (Erez, 1989; Ireland & Berg, 2008; Walsh, 1984), there is some

Figure 3

Community Corrections Officer Orientation Continuum

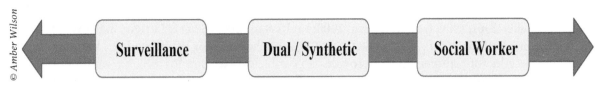

evidence that officer gender may also impact offender supervision (Ireland & Berg, 2008), potentially through an officer's adopted orientation.

Historically, several primary officer orientations have been identified within the community corrections literature: social work, surveillance, and synthetic (Bolin & Applegate, 2018; DeMichele & Payne, 2018; Erez, 1989; Klockars, 1972; Morash et al., 2015; Ohlin, Piven, & Peppenfort, 1956; Ricks & Eno Louden, 2015; Seng & Lurigio, 2005; West & Seiter, 2004; Whitehead & Lindquist, 1992). The social work orientation has focused on activities that encourage reentry and rehabilitation, such as helping clients find employment, referring clients to treatment programs, and offering other forms of prosocial support for clients (West & Seiter, 2004). Surveillance tasks may include conducting searches, participating in gang round-ups, and utilizing punitive responses to violations (West & Seiter, 2004). Research indicates that a blended or synthetic approach between surveillance and social work also exists, wherein officers attempt to provide services consistent with a social work orientation while also engaging in surveillance activities (see Figure 3) (Bolin & Applegate, 2018; DeMichele & Payne, 2018; Klockars, 1972; Morash et al., 2015; Ricks & Eno Louden, 2015; Whitehead & Lindquist, 1992).

Understanding officer orientation and how it may differ between CCOs is useful for determining how and to what extent CCO orientation impacts offender outcomes on supervision (Morash et al., 2015; Ricks & Eno Louden, 2015; West & Seiter, 2004). For instance, CCOs who maintain a synthetic or social work orientation may foster relationships with clients that reduce the likelihood of re-arrest or substance use (Holmstrom et al., 2017; Morash et al., 2015). Research finds that offenders with a dual diagnosis (offenders suffering both substance abuse and mental health issues) respond better to officers who utilize a social work approach as opposed to a surveillance approach (Morash et al., 2015), and officers who incorporate empathy and respect into interactions with clients report higher levels of offender compliance (Ireland & Berg, 2008).

Officer orientation can also adversely impact supervision outcomes for offenders. A CCO's emphasis on surveillance can actually increase noncompliance and offending behaviors (Morash et al., 2015), and when violations are detected, officers respond to those violations in a manner that appears to be in line with their own orientation (Ricks & Eno Louden, 2015). CCOs who adopt a surveillance orientation are more likely to pursue formal sanctions, including revocations, than officers who identify more with a social work orientation (Bolin & Applegate, 2018; Steiner, Travis, Makarios, & Brickley, 2011). Steiner, Travis, Makarios, and Brickley (2011) explain that surveillance-oriented officers may use sanctions as a punitive response to offender violations (such as a short-term jail incarceration for a positive drug screen), whereas social work-oriented officers may use sanctions as a way to increase contact with an offender or provide an offender with resources (such as increased drug screens or mandatory attendance to substance abuse classes).

While officer orientation has garnered much attention in the literature, other individual-level factors have not been given the same coverage—namely officer gender. This gap in the literature is surprising especially because women make up over half of all CCOs in the United States (Bureau of Labor Statistics, 2018). The extant literature has largely ignored the work experiences of women working in the probation and parole fields (Erez, 1989; Ireland & Berg, 2008; Kerbs et al., 2009; Seng & Lurigio, 2005; Walsh, 1984; Wells, Colbert, & Slate, 200 6; West & Seiter, 2004; Whitehead, 1986; Whitehead & Lindquist, 1992). The feminine ethic of care perspective provides a possible explanation for why we would expect the orientation and decision-making of women to be different from their male counterparts. Furthermore, feminine ethic of care has been important in framing gender discussions about social work (Freedberg, 1993), and it may be useful in understanding officer orientation given the field's social worker roots and emphasis on contemporary social worker-oriented activities. Although departmental policy and organizational culture likely influence officer decision-making, CCOs are often afforded a wide range of discretion in their decision-making (DeMichele & Payne, 2018; Ireland & Berg, 2008; Ricks & Eno Louden, 2015; West & Seiter, 2004), and it is possible that women might align themselves more with a social work orientation.

The existing research on women working in the probation and parole fields has been peripheral concerning officer gender and has been limited to PSI recommendations (Frazier, Bock, & Henretta, 1983; Walsh, 1984), referrals to programming and treatment (Erez, 1989), and revocation decisions (Kerbs et al., 2009), and has often led to mixed results. Considering PSI recommendations, one study found no indication that officer gender impacted recommendations (Frazier et al., 1983), while a second study did find differences in recommended sentences between male and female CCOs (Walsh, 1984).

Although focusing primarily on offender gender, Erez (1989) found that CCO gender did not impact which programs and activities officers recommended to clients (although offender gender did seem to matter). Studying officer orientation, DeMichele and Payne (2018) found no evidence that officer gender influenced an officer's orientation. In their study of the role of extralegal factors on officer decision-making, Kerbs and his colleagues (2009) found that officer sociodemographic characteristics did not influence officer decision-making regarding pursuing sanctions for technical offenses generally, except for failure to complete community service. Kerbs and his colleagues (2009) found that female officers were more likely to pursue formal sanctions in these cases as compared to male officers.

Other studies have found more conclusive evidence of officer gender differences, specifically when focusing on officer orientation. In their study of officer attitude and orientation, Whitehead and Lindquist (1992) found that female officers were generally less punitive than their male counterparts. In a later study, West and Seiter (2004) found that female officers spent more time focusing on social worker-oriented tasks than their male counterparts. Moreover, when studying how gender may interact with external factors of decision-making, West and Seiter (2004) found that, "despite caseload sizes, female [officers] still spend more time than males engaged in casework activities" (West & Seiter, 2004, p. 42). This study underscores the importance that gender may have when studying decision-making. While caseload size may impact officers' ability to focus on the specific needs of each offender, officer gender may influence supervision style.

Perhaps in the only study that has focused exclusively on the gendered experiences of female parole officers, Ireland and Berg (2008) observed that the female officers they interviewed felt strongly that gender impacted how they supervised clients and even how they maintained their own safety when working in the field. To gain compliance with clients, many of the women discussed the importance of respecting and building a positive rapport with clients and their families (Ireland & Berg, 2008). Several of the participants explained that building relationships through clear communication and respect with clients' family members often encourages family members to work with officers when their loved ones engage in criminal or harmful behavior (Ireland & Berg, 2008). Moreover, the female officers found that having a positive rapport with clients often resulted in safer arrests and more consistent compliance from clients (Ireland & Berg, 2008). Several of the women advised that they felt that their male counterparts relied less heavily on respectful interactions and positive relationships and more heavily on control, often resulting in less compliance and more use of force interactions (Ireland & Berg, 2008).

When comparing their interactions with clients to those interactions of male officers, the female officers all "shared a belief that male parole agents' overreliance on physical strength was counterproductive to personal safety" (Ireland & Berg, 2008, p. 483). CCOs establishing a positive rapport and supportive relationship with clients can lead to successful outcomes for them in the community (Kennealy et al., 2012; Morash et al., 2015).

Although less studied than other areas of community corrections, understanding individual level factors that may influence decision-making, especially officer orientation and officer gender, may allow researchers a better understanding of how officers make decisions in the field. In the next section, we discuss the importance of this research, especially as it relates to recidivism rates, supervision outcomes, and issues of fairness. We also reviewed possible policy implications and suggest topics that future research should address.

Discussion

Research on CCO decision-making and how officers approach their work remains limited in scope. The research to date provides us with a mixed picture, with some studies finding that officer orientation influences supervision outcomes for clients (Holmstrom et al., 2017; Morash et al., 2015; Ricks & Eno Louden, 2015; West & Seiter, 2004), while other studies indicate that officer orientation has a mixed or null effect on officers' behaviors (Bolin & Applegate, 2018; Steiner, Travis, Makarios, & Brickley, 2011). Moreover, little research focuses on the experiences of officers of color and how these officers may engage in decision-making, although theories of intersectionality suggest that both race and gender may contribute to how officers experience their careers and engage in decision-making. These unexplored areas warrant further investigation and could potentially have important policy and research implications.

As the community corrections offender population has grown, recidivism rates for these offenders continue to increase. "The number of parole violators who were revoked and readmitted to prison increased sevenfold between 1980 and 2000 (27,000 and 203,000, respectively)" (Kerbs et al., 2009, p. 425). In 2001, almost half of the probation population was revoked to either county jails or state prisons (Kerbs et al., 2009). Studies suggest that revocations have contributed to some states' recidivism rates (Morash et al., 2017; Petersilia, 1994). Although recent trends have called for the increased use of community corrections for offenders in attempts to decrease the prison population, practical outcomes may not reflect policymakers' intentions. Instead, the growth of community corrections may contribute to mass incarceration through net-widening (Alarid, 2019; Phelps, 2013).

While policy changes may ultimately be needed, understanding how CCOs contribute to or control the flow of offenders returning to jails and prisons is part of the recidivism puzzle impacting the corrections system and departmental resources (Ricks & Eno Louden, 2015). Community corrections agencies establish department-wide policies (Kerbs et al., 2009; West & Seiter, 2004), yet CCOs exercise a wide latitude of discretion in determining how they personally respond to offender behaviors (Kennealy et al., 2012; Ricks & Eno Louden, 2015). The discretion used by CCOs is often difficult for researchers to measure. Referred to by some as the "black box" of community corrections supervision, it often involves an inability to examine "out-of-view" interactions or informal responses to clients on their caseload (i.e., those that do not necessarily get recorded or included in agency information systems) as opposed to formally documented responses to offender behaviors (Bonta, Rugge, Scott, Bourgon, & Yessine, 2008; Bourgon & Gutierrez, 2012).

Although it has been argued that increased revocation rates reflect a shift in officer orientation that focuses on surveillance activities (West & Seiter, 2004), without further research, these connections cannot be explored. Furthermore, little is known about possible connections between officer gender and assumed officer orientation (Kerbs et al., 2009; Morash et al., 2015; West & Seiter, 2004). While little research has directly studied this relationship, researchers have found some evidence that officer gender is associated with a willingness to "reward offenders who completed supervision goals" (Steiner, Travis, Makarios, & Brickley, 2011, p. 916), an engagement in social work activities (West & Seiter, 2004), and may impact the types of violations that they feel warrant formal sanctions (Kerbs et al., 2009). Understanding possible relationships between officer gender and supervision outcomes may have important implications for explaining revocation and recidivism patterns.

Issues of fairness are also important if it is found that officer gender may impact supervision outcomes for offenders. If significant differences in supervision outcomes are found for clients supervised by female and male officers, it may be necessary to address possible issues of procedural justice (Kerbs et al., 2009). The importance of offender-officer relationships has been recorded in the literature (Holmstrom et al., 2017; Morash et al., 2015), and some supervision styles have been found to be protective against recidivism (Morash et al., 2015). If male and female officers have different outcomes, those disparities should be addressed.

Policy Implications

A better understanding of the links between gender, officer orientation, and supervision outcomes may have important policy implications, especially for hiring and training practices. If evidence suggests that female officers have better supervision outcomes, then it may be helpful for hiring practices to include attracting job candidates who are more willing to use nontraditional approaches to supervision (DeJong, 2005; Ricks & Eno Louden, 2015). Screening new hires for desirable traits, such as an emphasis on social work activities (Ricks & Eno Louden, 2015), may be practical for departments working to lower their recidivism rates, if such links between orientation and supervision outcomes are found.

This research could inform the development of new training for community corrections officers. If it is determined that officer orientation impacts supervision outcomes, then it may be helpful to implement training that teaches social work skills and emphasizes relationship-building with clients (DeJong, 2005; Kennealy et al., 2012; Morash et al., 2015). Although the question of whether or not orientation can be taught to officers exists (Kennealy et al., 2012), training may enhance these skills for officers who may have undervalued such skills and therefore have not cultivated them. Already utilized by some departments, communication skills training may be an important addition to departments who have not adopted similar training.

Recommendations for Future Research

Although CCO gender and decision-making is incredibly understudied (Erez, 1989; Ireland & Berg, 2008; Kerbs et al., 2009; Seng & Lurigio, 2005; Walsh, 1984; West & Seiter, 2004), the need for this research has not gone unnoticed. Researchers have consistently called for research to be conducted in this area (Kerbs et al., 2009; Morash et al., 2015; West & Seiter, 2004), as the possible impacts of officer gender have been uncovered and reported (DeJong, 2005; Ireland & Berg, 2008; Rabe-Hemp, 2008; Walsh, 1984; West & Seiter, 2004). Although officer orientation has been observed since the 1950s (Ohlin et al., 1956; Whitehead & Lindquist, 1992), extensive research of officer orientation and its impacts does not exist (Kennealy et al., 2012; Steiner, Travis, Makarios, & Brickley, 2011). Many factors may influence officer decision-making, and understanding these factors is important, especially as it relates to recidivism (Ricks & Eno Louden, 2015) and equal treatment among clients (Kerbs et al., 2009).

While studies that focus on the decision-making of female officers are lacking, there is even less research that considers the experiences of women generally in probation and parole (Ireland & Berg, 2006). The only study that exists that explores the gendered experiences of female officers in parole suggests that women experience their careers in community corrections differently than their male colleagues (Ireland & Berg, 2006). Future research should focus on further exploration of the broad experiences of female officers in probation as well as parole.

Future research should also utilize an intersectional framework to study how one's racial and gender identities shape their work experiences in community corrections. Crenshaw (1991) explains that it is important to consider a person's race, gender, and other characteristics, such as class, because those characteristics help create a person's identity. For example, a person is not only female but may have experiences from being Hispanic or being middle class that may affect her worldview. What Crenshaw (1991) calls the "intersection" of identity (where race and gender meet and affect a person's experiences) means that both race and gender matter when discussing a person's experiences. Although studies that have considered CCO race are few, research indicates that officer race may be associated with officer decision-making (Grattet, Petersilia, Lin, & Beckman, 2009). Since limited research exists considering CCO and race, it may be helpful to reference intersectional research from the policing literature. Some policing studies suggest that African American female officers have very different experiences from their White female counterparts and their Black male colleagues (Archbold, & Schulz, 2012; Greene, 2000; Hassell & Brandl, 2009; Martin, 1994; Pogrebin, Dodge, & Chatman, 2000). Evidence suggests, then, that both race and gender may impact officer decision-making, yet virtually no research exists in this area. Such research would be an important contribution to better understanding the experiences of women in community corrections.

Conclusion

In this chapter, we have focused on CCO decision-making, specifically the types of decisions officers make and organization- and individual-level factors that may influence those decisions. The current literature suggests that organization-level factors likely influence officer decision-making, especially department size and location, caseload size, and agency policies and culture. What has been explored to a lesser extent in the literature is the impact of individual-level factors on decision-making, specifically officer orientation and gender. To highlight the importance of these factors, we have reviewed the extant of the literature available on officer orientation and officer gender and have discussed available studies that include these variables. We have also emphasized the relevancy of this literature and explained the importance of this line of research, especially as it relates to policy implications and future research opportunities.

Criminogenic needs

Dual diagnosis

Dual role conflict

Dual/Synthetic orientation

Feminine ethic of care

Graduated sanctions

Intersections perspective

Net-widening

Officer orientation

Post-adjudication

Pre-adjudication

Presentence investigation
report (PSI)

Pretrial diversion program

Pretrial supervision

Revocation

Sanction

Social work orientation

Supervision conditions

Surveillance orientation

Technical violation

1. Although probation and parole are the most common forms of community corrections, community corrections can include other forms of justice involvement. List some of the other ways that clients can be involved with the criminal justice system through community corrections.

2. Identify and discuss how community corrections officers may be involved with clients during both the pre-adjudication and post-adjudication phases.

3. In what ways can the larger community corrections organization influence how CCOs use their discretion or make decisions concerning their clients?

4. What is officer orientation? Identify and discuss the three officer orientations reviewed in this chapter.

5. Although the research is mixed regarding the differences of male and female law enforcement officers, some studies suggest that female officers interact with clients and citizens differently than male officers. Identify and discuss some of these differences.

6. What does it mean to have an "intersection" of identity? Why might this be important when studying the experiences of community corrections officers?

Book Chapter – Web Links

The Association of Paroling Authorities International (APAI) http://apaintl.org/

Federal Probation and Pretrial Services https://www.uscourts.gov/services-forms/probation-and-pretrial-services

American Probation & Parole Association http://www.appa-net.org/eweb/

National Association of Pretrial Services Agencies https://napsa.org/eweb/startpage.aspx

National Institute of Corrections https://nicic.gov/

Bureau of Justice Statistics – Community Corrections https://www.bjs.gov/index.cfm?ty=tp&tid=15

References

Alarid, L. F. (2019). *Community-based corrections, 12th edition.* Boston, MA: Cengage Learning, Inc.

Archbold, C. A. & Schulz, D. M. (2012). Research on women in policing: A look at the past, present, and future. *Sociology Compass, 6*(9), 694-706.

Bolin, R. M. & Applegate, B. K. (2018). Supervising juveniles and adults: Organizational context, professional orientations, and probation and parole officer behaviors. *Journal of Crime and Justice.* Advance online publication.

Bonta, J., Rugge, T., Scott, T., Bourgon, G., & Yessine, A.K. (2008). Exploring the black box of community supervision. *Journal of Offender Rehabilitation, 47*(3), 248-270.

Bourgon, G., & Gutierrez, L. (2012). The general responsivity principle in community supervision: The importance of probation officers using cognitive intervention techniques and its influence on recidivism. *Journal of Crime and Justice, 35*(2), 149-166.

Brown, J. M., Gilliard, D. K., Snell, T. L., Stephan, J. J., & Wilson, D. J. (1996). *Correctional populations in the United States, 1994* (NCJ Publication No 160091). Retrieved from Bureau of Justice Statistics website: https://www.bjs.gov/content/pub/pdf/cpius94.pdf

Bureau of Justice Statistics. (2000). *Correctional populations in the United States, 1997* (NCJ Publication No. 177613). Retrieved from https://www.bjs.gov/content/pub/pdf/cpus97.pdf

Bureau of Justice Statistics. (1982). *Probation and parole, 1981* (NCJ Publication No. 83647). Retrieved from https://www.bjs.gov/content/pub/pdf/pp81.pdf

Bureau of Labor Statistics. (2018). *Employed persons by detained occupation, sex, race, and Hispanic or Latino ethnicity.* Retrieved from https://www.bls.gov/cps/cpsaat11.pdf

Byrne, J. M. (2013). After the fall: Assessing the impact of the great prison experiment on future crime control policy. *Federal Probation, 77*(3), 3-14.

Carson, E. A. (2018). *Prisoners in 2016* (NCJ Publication No. 251149). Retrieved from Bureau of Justice Statistics website: https://www.bjs.gov/content/pub/pdf/p16.pdf

Crenshaw, K. (1991). Mapping the margins: Intersectionality, identity politics, and violence against women of color. *Stanford Law Review, 43*(6), 1241-1299.

Dean-Myrda, M. C. & Cullen, F. T. (1998). The panacea pendulum: An account of community as a response to crime. In J. Petersilia (Ed.), *Community corrections: Probation, parole, and intermediate sanctions* (pp. 3-18). New York, NY: Oxford University Press, Inc. (Reprinted from *Probation, parole, and community treatment*, by L. F. Travis, Ed., 1985, Long Grove, IL: Waveland Press.

DeJong, C. (2005). Gender differences in officer attitude and behavior: Providing comfort to citizens. *Women and Criminal Justice, 15*(3), 1-32.

DeMichele, M. & Payne, B. (2018). Exploring probation officer styles and goals with individual, organizational, and social characteristics. *European Journal of Probation, 10*(3), 232-248.

Erez, E. (1989). Gender, rehabilitation, and probation decisions. *Criminology, 27*(2), 307-327.

Frazier, C. E., Bock, E. W., & Henretta, J. C. (1983). The role of probation officers in determine gender differences in sentencing severity. *The sociological quarterly 24*(2), 305-318.

Freedberg, S. (1993). The feminine ethic of care and the professionalization of social work. *Social Work, 38*(5), 535-540.

Grattet, R., Petersilia, J., Lin, J., & Beckman, M. (2009). Parole violations and revocations in California: Analysis and suggestions for action. *Federal Probation, 73*(1), 2-11.

Greene, H. T. (2000). Black females in law enforcement: A foundation for future research. *Journal of Contemporary Criminal Justice, 16*(2), 230-239.

Hassell, K. D. & Brandl, S. G. (2009). An examination of the workplace experiences of police patrol officers: The role of race, sex, and sexual orientation. *Police Quarterly, 12*(4), 408-430.

Hawley, F. F. (2012). Probation officers. In S. M. Barton-Bellessa (Ed.), *Encyclopedia of community corrections* (pp. 346-347). Thousand Oaks, CA: SAGE Publications, Inc.

Holmstrom, A. J., Adams, E. A., Morash, M., Smith, S. W., & Cobbina, J. E. (2017). Supportive messages female offenders receive from probation and parole officers about substance avoidance: Message perceptions and effects. *Criminal Justice and Behavior, 44*(11), 1496-1517.

Ireland, C. & Berg, B. (2006). Women in parole. *Women and Criminal Justice, 10*(1), 131-150.

Ireland, C. & Berg, B. (2008). Women in parole: Respect and rapport. *International Journal of Offender Therapy and Comparative Criminology, 52*(4), 474-491.

Jones, M. & Kerbs, J.J. (2007). Probation and parole officers and discretionary decision-making: Responses to technical and criminal violations. *Federal Probation, 71*(1), 9-15.

Kaeble, D. (2018). *Probation and parole in the United States, 2016* (NCJ Publication No. 251148). Retrieved from Bureau of Justice Statistics website: https://www.bjs.gov/content/pub/pdf/ppus16.pdf

Kaeble, D. & Cowhig, M. (2018). *Correctional populations in the United States, 2016* (NCJ Publication No. 251211). Retrieved from Bureau of Justice Statistics website: https://www.bjs.gov/content/pub/pdf/cpus16.pdf

Kennealy, P. J., Skeem, J. L., Manchak, S. M., & Eno Louden, J. (2012). Firm, fair, and caring officer-offender relationships protect against supervision failure. *American Psychological Association, 36*(6), 496-505.

Kerbs, J. J., Jones, M., & Jolley, J. M. (2009). Discretionary decision making by probation and parole officers: The role of extralegal variables as predictors of responses to technical violations. *Journal of Contemporary Criminal Justice, 25*(4), 424-441.

Klockars, C. B. (1972). A theory of probation supervision. *The Journal of Criminal Law, Criminology, and Police Science, 63*(4), 550-557.

Lawrence, R. (1991). Reexamining community corrections models. *Crime and Delinquency, 37*(4), 449-464.

Lutze, F.E. (2014). *Professional lives of community corrections officers: The invisible side of reentry.* Los Angeles, CA: Sage Publications.

Martin, S. E. (1994). "Outsider within" the station house: The impact of race and gender on black women police. *Social Problems, 41*(3), 383-400.

Matz, A.K., Conley, T.B., & Johanneson, N. (2018). What do supervision officers do? Adult probation/parole officer workloads in a rural Western state. *Journal of Crime and Justice, 41*(3), 294-309.

Morash, M., Kashy, D. A., Smith, S. W., & Cobbina, J. E. (2015). The effects of probation or parole agent relationship style and women offenders' criminogenic needs on offenders' responses to supervision interactions. *Criminal Justice and Behavior, 42*(4), 412-434.

Morash, M., Kashy, D. A., Smith, S. W., & Cobbina, J. E. (2017). Technical violations, treatment and punishment responses, and recidivism of women on probation and parole. *Criminal Justice Policy Review*, 1-23.

Ohlin, L. E., Piven, H., & Peppenfort, D. M. (1956). Major dilemmas of the social worker in probation and parole. *National Probation and Parole Association Journal, 3*, 211-225.

Petersilia, J. (Ed.). (1998). *Community corrections: Probation, parole, and intermediate sanctions.* New York, NY: Oxford University Press, Inc.

Petersilia, J. (1994). Debating crime and imprisonment in California. *Evaluation and Program Planning, 17*(2), 165-177.

Phelps, M. S. (2013). The paradox of probation: Community supervision in the age of mass incarceration. *Law and Policy, 35*, 51-80.

Pogrebin, M., Dodge, M., & Chatman, H. (2000). Reflections of African- American women in their careers in urban policing: Their experiences of racial and sexual discrimination. *International Journal of the Sociology of Law, 28*, 311-326.

Rabe-Hemp, C. E. (2008). Female officers and the ethic of care: Does officer gender impact police behaviors? *Journal of Criminal Justice, 36*, 426-434.

Randol, B. M. (2012). Probation: Administration models. In S. M. Barton-Bellessa (Ed.), *Encyclopedia of community corrections* (pp. 333-334). Thousand Oaks, CA: SAGE Publications, Inc.

Ricks, E. P. & Eno Louden, J. (2015). Relationship between officer orientation and supervision strategies in community corrections. *Law and Human Behavior, 39*(2), 130-141.

Seng, M. & Lurigio, A. J. (2005). Probation officers' views on supervising women probationers. *Women & Criminal Justice, 16*(1/2), 65-85.

Steiner, B., Travis, L. F., Makarios, M. D., & Brickley, T. (2011). The influence of parole officers' attitudes on supervision practices. *Justice Quarterly, 28*(6), 903-927.

Steiner, B., Travis, L.F., Makarios, M.D., & Meade, B. (2011). Short-term effects of sanctioning reform and parole officers' revocation decisions. *Law & Society Review, 45*(2), 371-400.

Steverson, L. (2012). Presentence Investigation Reports. In S. M. Barton-Bellessa (Ed.), *Encyclopedia of Community Corrections* (pp. 315-316). Thousand Oaks, CA: SAGE Publications, Inc.

Swanson, C. G. (2012). Case management. In S. M. Barton-Bellessa (Ed.), *Encyclopedia of community corrections* (pp. 33-37). Thousand Oaks, CA: SAGE Publications, Inc.

Teague, M. (2016). Profiting from the poor: Offender-funded probation in the USA. *British Journal of Community Justice, 16*(1), 99-11.

Turner, S., Braithwaite, H., Kearney, L., Murphy, A., & Haerle, D. (2012). Evaluation of the California parole violation decision-making instrument (PVDMI). *Journal of Crime and Justice, 35*(2), 269- 295.

Viglione, J. (2018). The risk-need-responsivity model: How do probation officers implement the principles of effective intervention? *Criminal Justice and Behavior.* doi: 10.1177/0093854818807505 (online first)

Vissing, Y. (2012). Parole officers. In S. M. Barton-Bellessa (Ed.), *Encyclopedia of community corrections* (pp. 297-299). Thousand Oaks, CA: SAGE Publications, Inc.

Ward, G., & Kupchik, A. (2010). What drives juvenile probation officers? Relating organizational contexts, status characteristics, and personal convictions to treatment and punishment orientations. *Crime & Delinquency, 56*(1), 35-69.

Walsh, A. (1984). Gender-based differences: A study of probation officers' attitudes about, and recommendations for, felony sexual assault cases. *Criminology, 22*(3), 371-387.

Wells, T., Colbert, S., & Slate, R. N. (2006). Gender matters: Differences in state probation officer stress. *Journal of Contemporary Criminal Justice,* 22(1), 63-79.

West, A. D. & Seiter, R. P. (2004) Social worker or cop? Measuring the supervision styles of probation and parole officers in Kentucky and Missouri. *Journal of Crime and Justice, 27*(2), 27-57.

Whitehead, J. T. (1986). Gender differences in probation: A case of no differences. *Justice Quarterly, 3*(1), 51-65.

Whitehead, J. T. & Lindquist, C. A. (1992). Determinants of probation and parole officer professional orientation. *Journal of Criminal Justice, 20,* 13-24.

Zarse, N. (2012). Offender supervision. In S. M. Barton-Bellessa (Ed.), *Encyclopedia of community corrections* (pp. 274-276). Thousand Oaks, CA: SAGE Publications, Inc.

CHAPTER 10

Do Women and Minority Judges Make a Difference?

Robert L. Bing III | *The University of Texas at Arlington*

Introduction

Judicial decisions are critically important and have major implications for anyone who enters the courtroom.

This chapter explores the literature on women and minority group members who serve on the bench in the courtroom. It attempts to answer the question: Do they make a difference? This question is predicated upon an assumption that women and minorities will bring their life experiences to the bench and that they will not be as punitive as their White male counter parts. The chapter also explores the extent to which there are differences and or similarities in judicial decisions by gender and ethnicity. It is predicated upon a perusal of select literature about the impact and or influence of women and or minority judges.

Why study female judicial decisions? The interest in female and minority judges is based upon a belief that female, Black and Hispanic judges will bring to the bench the totality of their lifetime experiences and a sensibility about judicial decisions, that will temper harsh judicial decisions made by their male counterparts. It has been suggested that by increasing minority and female representation on the bench, disenfranchised populations will receive better treatment in the courtroom (Spohn, 1990). Before exploring observations about the literature on this topic, the next section provides demographic data about the number of female judges in the United States.

The status of female judges. Although women represent 59% of the overall, U.S. workforce, some estimates reveal (that at the federal level), they comprise 15% of all federal judges. At the state level, according the National Center for State Courts (NCSC), the percentage is higher; NCSC data reveals that of the 18,006 state court judges, 5,596 or 31% are women. There is greater representation of females at the state level, than at the federal level. The impediments to female judgeships (at the federal and state level) relate to the perception of females as care takers of the family, along with lower levels of enrollment in law schools until recent decades. It is worth noting that there was a time when even Harvard Law School would not accept females. It is mentioned here as a historical fact.

Early History

To restate, the chapter explores research findings on female and minority judges and begins with seminal research about whether or not women or minority judges make a difference or engage in gendered judicial decisions.

Early History: The Influence of Spohn. In looking at the past research, Spohn suggests that "greater judicial representation of Blacks might reduce racism in the criminal justice system" (1990, p. 1198). This assumption is predicated upon the belief that minority judges are more liberal than their White male counter parts. Further, there is a pervasive assumption that minority judges will bring a certain sensitivity to the bench (Goldman, 1979). Going further, some have speculated that the perceived liberal views of minority judges will result in more support for the poor, and the "underdog" defendant (Spohn, 1990, p. 1198). In her seminal work, Spohn also found some early differences with respect to Black judges in Detroit. Despite assumptions about liberalism, race, and gender, using the research of Welch et al. (1988),

© Sirtravelot/Shutterstock.com

in the aggregate, the data from this case study suggest that Black judges were more likely than White judges to send White defendants to prison." By contrast, in the same study, Spohn observed that, "Black judges, but not White judges, favored defendants of their own race, when determining the length of the sentence" (1990, p. 1199). In another study referenced by Spohn, Gottfredson and Gottfredson (1980) found that Black and White judges decided differently in the appellate courts. Black judges, for example, were more likely to make liberal decisions that favored the defendant.

At the federal appellate level, Black judges were more likely to rule in favor of the claimant, when there was a sex discrimination case. And that some of the differences (in decision making) about the race and gender of a judge may be a function of past background, religion but not race. Spohn (1990) maintains that other variables (to be discussed) help explain some of the variation in findings with respect to decisions made by female and or minority judges.

The assumption of liberalism

According to Schumacher and Burns (1988) some individuals feel that female judges will be more liberal and are generally more compassionate. As such, the assumption is that the sentence put forth by female judges will be lighter (e.g., Schumacher & Burns, 1988; Kritzer & Uhlman, 1977). Concomitantly, there is an assumption that female judges are likely to be harsher on offenders who commit crimes of rape, because they can identify with the victim. Steffensmeier and Hebert (1999) suggests that the decisions of female and male judges may be behaviorally, cognitively, and emotionally different. Steffensmeier and Hebert (1999), citing Lehman and his 1993 research, states that "these unique differences purportedly lead men and women to take different approaches to a wide variety of issues and problems, including how they engage in occupational pursuits" (p. 179). The point to be made here is that female judges may be cognitively and behaviorally different than their male counterparts.

© Buncha Lim/Shutterstock.com

A case study. A look at the research of Steffensmeier and Hebert (1999), reveals interesting findings for this time period. The study is based upon research in the state of Pennsylvania. One major finding pertains to incarceration, that female judges were more likely than their male counter parts to imprison defendants, if the defendant had a prior criminal history. In the Pennsylvania study, female judges were 11% more likely to imprison defendants.

Surprisingly, in the same study, female judges were less likely to incarcerate female offenders, compared to male offenders. From the same study, female judges were more likely to incarcerate Black offenders, than White defendants or offenders. Similarly, female offenders, typically gave older offenders a break with respect to sentencing. In all, it appears that many female judicial decisions (in the Pennsylvania study) were influenced by a wide range of legal and nonlegal offender characteristics, including race. In other words, the race of the offender enhanced the likelihood of a sentence. The authors correctly assert that past research on the topic (see e.g., Spohn, 1990), has been based upon a small number of women judges. In other words, the Pennsylvania study improved upon the number of females in earlier studies. In the aggregate, however, these researchers conclude that women and male judges generally weigh cases alike, but exceptions do exist. The exceptions seem to occur with regard to race of the defendant and gender of the judge. Based upon this research, White female judges tend to be harsher in sentencing— offering longer periods of imprisonment than their White male counterparts. This research finding of punitive nature of female judges is consistent with earlier studies from the 1990s (see, e.g. Spohn, 1990). The next section explores the connection between the gender of the judge on sex discrimination cases.

Sex Discrimination Cases

There is limited literature on the topic of a judge's gender and sexual discrimination cases. Moyer and Haire (2015) conclude that female judges do react strongly to cases of sex discrimination. Martin et al., 2002 also found that exposure to *gender bias* in the workplace predisposes female judges to be more sensitive to cases of sex discrimination. In some cases, the *gendered roles* may be determined by the discrimination encountered while in law school (Wald, 1994). Glynn and Sen (2015), in their research also found that female judges behave differently, than their male counterparts with respect to sex discrimination cases. Similar findings can be found in the research of Boyd, et al. (2010), Presesie (2005) and Farhang and Wawreo (2004). Meanwhile, Martin and Pyle (2015) exploring judicial decision in divorce litigation found that female judges were more likely to vote in favor of women in divorce cases. Coontz, 2000 found that female judges in Pennsylvania were more likely to find male defendants guilty of assault than a female defendant with a similar offense. Meanwhile Songer, et al. (1994) found that female judges are more likely support victims in cases pertaining to discrimination in the workplace. Their analysis reveals that women judges have had an in impact on discrimination cases in the workplace. According to Boyd (2016) female judges are more likely than male judges to rule in favor of the plaintiff in sex discrimination cases. Lastly, Smith (2005) found that female judges were more likely to rule in favor of gay litigants than their male counterparts on the bench.

Minority Judicial Decision Making

There are myriad reasons, ranging from political affiliation, racial oppression, and life experiences to expect that Black judges behave differently. In an earlier study, Uhlman, (1978) found that Black trial court judges sentenced defendants more harshly than their White counter parts. By contrast, in a more recent study, Welch, Combs and Gruhl (2001) found that Black judges are more even handed in their approach to sentences. In more recent research, Boyd, et al. (2010) found that Black and female judges arrived at diversity cases differently. Some studies reveal that Black judges are more likely to rule favorably in race and sex discrimination cases (see e.g., Boyd, 2016). In another study, Steffensmeier and Britt (2010), found mixed results at the state trial court level. Bonneau and Rice (2009), found that Black judges (at the appellate court level), were less

© Africa Studio/Shutterstock.com

likely to overturn decisions, than White male counterparts. Farhang and Wawro (2004) found that while the presence of a Black judge on a judicial panel, had no effect; the presence of female judge of the panel at the state level in appellate courts had minor moderating effect in the review of appellate cases. It should be mentioned that differences were mostly minor and that for major criminal cases there is little variation in finding. This observation may be attributed to the vetting process. In other words, the vetting process creates in terms of ideology, a more homogeneous group of judges. The next section explores the influence of public opinion.

The Effects of Judge Gender, Public Opinion and Judicial Decision

The early research suggest that the public perceives the influence of female judges differently. Haire (2014) found that women and minority judges are likely to receive lower American Bar Association ratings, even when controlling for legal training. By contrast, Fix and Johnson (2017) when polling the public, found few differences in the public's opinions with regard to female versus male judges. According to Fix and Johnson (2017), men in public opinion surveys believed that the gender of the judge played a role in the female judicial decision making. Fix and Johnson (2017) also observe that some of the differences and public perception may be aligned along political party affiliation.

The current research. Abrams, et al., 2012 have found little differences between male and female judges, while earlier studies in heavily Black neighborhoods (e.g., Spohn, 1990), observed minor differences. In 2017, Boyd and Nelson (2017) found that female judges are more likely to actively seek approval and acceptance from their male judge counterparts. Boyd and Nelson (2017) in their analysis of female judges reveal that there is no evidence that male and female judges' sentence in fundamentally different ways. The literature reveals that female judges are more likely to settle a case and more likely to settle quickly (Boyd, 2016). These female judges do so more quickly than their male counterparts. It is also observed that women do not use their positions of power, in the same way as their male counterparts. The assumption here is that women are more likely to engage in more democratic styles, than their male counter parts (see, Boyd, 2016), even though they may arrive at the same decisions.

Discussion and Conclusion

The literature reveals interesting findings and observations about females and minority judges. In the aggregate, female judges' sentence in mostly the same ways, with some exceptions. Boyd and Nelson (2017) found that females are generally as harsh as their male counterparts. It is observed that some of the homogeneity in decision making may be related to female judges who are likely to seek approval from their male counterparts in some of their judicial decision making, but not in all of them.

Why the lack of variation of findings in major cases? One reason may be because the male dominated selection committee seeks to identify potential female judges who share similar values and expectations about how the criminal justice system should perform. According to Spohn (1990) the gender of the judge is typically offset by not only the selection, but also the socialization process. In other words, female judges become coopted by the court organization and they may adhere to the values of the courtroom workgroup (as explained below).

Courtroom work group. The courtroom work group generally consists of the judge, the district attorneys and defense attorneys. It is assumed that these individuals have specialized roles and positions of authority. The members of the workgroup have strong professional, economic and intellectual ties, etc. According to Eisenstein and Jacob (1977) this group has two functions: one is expressive and the other is instrumental. With regard to the expressive role, the members are concerned with creating the impression that *justice is being served*. With regard to the instrumental role, the work group concerns itself with moving cases along, which requires an awareness and acceptance of group values, influenced by the court bureaucracy. In other words, female and minority judges may be coopted by the prevailing values of norms of the male dominated work group.

Beyond the courtroom work group and liberal assumptions, Miller and Maier (2008), reference a survey of female judges about how they viewed themselves; their responses revealed some interesting statements about judicial identity, ranging from "I think you have some macho consideration with some of the younger men on the bench" (p. 548). "There are statutes that are pretty clear." "There's discretion but nothing that I see has anything that would be affected by gender." In this survey, most female judges downplayed their potential female gender roles. The female judges also denied that their life experiences impacted their decisions on the bench. The point to be made here is that most female respondents refused to see themselves as simply a female judge and this may also account for the overall lack of variation in judicial decisions. In all, the issue of whether women make a difference in the court room is settled; but there is variation in minor criminal and noncriminal cases. What is missing in the research, however, is a nation-wide study on female and or minority judges, as most studies continue to be limited to a handful of cities, which calls into question their generalizability.

Concluding remarks. In response to findings extrapolated from journal articles on the subject—having *more* females on the bench, might make a difference in sentencing, if female judgeships were proportional to the general population and if female judges were less influenced by the organizational values of the court bureaucracy. In the end, female and minority judges do indeed find themselves in a double bind. If a female judge conforms, then she is accused of being less than sympathetic. By contrast, females who do not conform, may be criticized for not making traditional decisions (Nelson, 2015).

Key Terms:

Courtroom-work groups	Gender bias	Liberalism
Female judges	Gendered justice	

Discussion Questions:

1. Based upon your reading, why is there an expectation that female and minority judges will decide differently in the courtroom?

2. What does the research suggest or reveal about female judges and sex discrimination cases? What are the limitations to these findings or observations?

3. What does the research suggest or reveal with regard to Black or minority judges? What are the limitations to these findings?

4. Based upon aggregate data, what is the general observation made about the differences, if any, between male and female decisions?

5. What is the criticism, if any, about the research on female or minority decisions?

6. What constraints, if any, influence the decisions made by female or minority judges?

Web Links

National Association of Women Judges https://www.nawj.org/statistics

Debate on Whether Female Judges Make A Difference: https://www.nytimes.com/2009/06/04/us/politics/04women.html

Hispanic Judges: https://www.fjc.gov/history/judges/search/hispanic

Ruth Bader Ginsburg. https://www.oyez.org/justices/ruth_bader_ginsburg

National Center for State Courts. https://www.ncsc.org/Information-and-Resources.aspx

Gender Bias and Judicial Decision Making. https://news.illinois.edu/view/6367/640610

References

Abrams, et al. (2010). "Do judges vary in their treatment of race?" *Journal of Legal Studies,* 41, 372–372.

Bonneau, Chris W. (2001). "The composition of state supreme courts, 2000." *Judicature,* 85, 26–31.

Bonneau, Chris. W and Heather M. Rice. (2009). "Impartial judges? Race, institutional context, and U.S state supreme courts." *State Politics and Policy Quarterly, 9*(4), 381–403.

Boyd, Christina L. (2016). "Representation on the courts? The effects of trial judges' sex and race." *Political Research Quarterly, 69*(4), 788–799.

Boyd, Christina. (2013). "She will settle it?" *Journal of Law and Courts,* 1, 193–219.

Boyd, Christina and Michael Nelson. (2017). "The effects of trial judge gender and public opinion." *Vanderbilt Law Review, 70*(6), 1819–1840.

Boyd, Christina L. (2016). "Representation on the courts? The effects of trial judges' sex and race." *Political Research Quarterly, 69*(4), 788–799.

Boyd, Christina, L., Lee Epstein and Andrew D. Martin. (2010). "Untangling the causal effects of sex on judging." *American Journal of Political Science, 54*(2), 389–411.

Coontz, P. (2000). "Gender and judicial decisions: Do female judges decide cases differently, than male judges?" *Gender Issue,* 18(4), 59–73.

Coontz, P. (1995). "Gender bias in the legal profession: Women 'see' it, men don't." *Women and Politics,* 15(2), 1–22.

Davis, Sue, Susan Haire and Donald Songer. (1993)." Voting behavior and gender on the U.S. court of appeals." *Judicature, 77,* 129–33.

Eisenstein, James and Herbert Jacob. (1977). *Felony Justice.* Boston: Little, Brown and Company.

Epstein, Cynthia Fuchs. (1988). *Deceptive Distinctions: Sex, Gender, and the Social Order.* Yale University Press.

Farhang, Sean and Gregory Wawro. (2004). "Institutional dynamics on the U.S. supreme court of appeals: Minority representation under panel decision making," *Journal of Law, Economics, and Organization,* 20, 299–330.

Fix and Johnson (2017). "Public perceptions of gender bias in the decisions of female state court judges." *Vanderbilt Law Review, 70*(6), 1845–1886.

Glynn, Adam and Maya Sen. (2015). "Identifying judicial empathy: Does having daughters cause judges to rule for women's issues?" *American Journal of Political Science, 59*(1), 37–54.

Gottfredson, Michael R. and Don M. Gottfredson (1980). *Decision making inCriminal Justice: Toward the Rational Exercise of Discretion.* Cambridge, MA: Ballinger Publishing Company.

Goldman, Sheldon. (1979). "Should there be affirmative action for the judiciary?" *Judicature.* 62, 488–94.

Gruhl, John, Cassia Spohn and Susan Welch. (1981). "Women as policy makers: The case of trial judges." *American Journal of Political Science, 25*(2), 308–322.

Haire, Susan and Laura Moyer. (2014). *Does Diversity Matter?* Charlottesville: University of Virginia Press.

Hurwitz, Mark and Drew Lanier. (2003). "Explaining judicial diversity: The differential ability of women and minorities on attain seats on state supreme and appellate courts," *State Politics and Policy Quarterly,* 3, 329–352.

Hurwitz, Mark and Drew Lanier. (2001) "Women and minorities on state and federal appellate benches, 1985-1999." *Judicature,* 85, 84–92

Kritzer, Herbert and Thomas Uhlman. (1977) "Sisterhood in the courtroom: Sex of judge and defendant in criminal case disposition." *Social Sciences Journal,* 14, 77–88.

Lehman, Edward. (1993). *Gender and Work: The Case of the Clergy.* State University of New York Press.

Moyer, Laura P and Susan B. Haire. (2015). "Trail blazers and those that followed: Personal experiences, gender, and judicial empathy." *Law and Society Review,* 49(3), 665–688.

Martin, Elaine and Barry Pyle. (2000). "Gender race, and partisanship on the Michigan supreme court." *Albany Law Review,* 631, 205–1225.

Martin, Elaine. (1990). "Women and men on the bench." Vive La Difference?" *Judicature,* 204–208.

McCall, Madhavi. (2003). "Gender, judicial dissent, and issue salience: The voting 1980–1998." *Social Science Journal,* 40(1), 79–97.

Miller, Susan and Shana L. Maier. (2008). "Moving beyond numbers: What female judges say about different judicial voices." *Journal of Women, Politics and Policy,* 29(4), 527–559.

National Center for State Courts. https://www.ncsc.org/Information-and-Resources.aspx

Peresie, Jennifer L. (2005). "Female judges matter: Gender and collegial decision making in the federal appellate courts," *Yale Law Journal,* 114, 1759–1790.

Schumacher, Paul and Nancy Burns. (1988). "Gender cleavages and the resolution of local policy issues." *American Journal of Political Science,* 32, 1070–95.

Smith, Fred O. (2005). "Gendered justice: Do male and female judges rule differently on questions of gay rights?" *Stanford Law Review,* 57(6), 2087–2134.

Songer, Donald, Sue Davis and Susan Haire. (1994). "A reappraisal of diversification in federal courts: General effect in the court of appeals." *The Journal of Politics,* 56(2), 425–439.

Songer, Donald R. and Kelley A. Crews-Meyer. (2000). "Does judge gender matter? Decision making in state supreme courts." *Social Science Quarterly,* 81, 750–752.

Spohn, Cassia. (1990a). "The sentencing decisions of black and white judges: Expected and unexpected similarities." *Law and Society Review,* 24 (5), 1197–1216.

Spohn, Cassia (1990b). "Decision Making in Sexual Assault Cases: Do black and female judges make a difference?" *Women and Criminal Justice,* 2, 83–105.

Steffensmeier, Darrell and Chester Britt. (2010). "Judges race and judicial decision making: Do black judges sentences differently?" *Social Science Quarterly,* 82, 749–64.

Steffensmeier, Darrell and Chris Hebert. (1999). "Women and men policy makers: Does the judges gender affect the sentencing of criminal defendants?" *Social Forces, 77*(3), 1163–1196.

Tiede, Lydia, Robert Carp, and Kenneth Manning. (2010). "Judicial attributes and sentencing: Do sex, race and politics matter?" *Justice System Journal,* 31(3), 125–148.

Uhlman, Thomas. (1978). "Black elite decision: The case of trial judges." *American Journal of Political Science, 22*, 884–895.

National Center for State Courts. https://www.ncsc.org/Information-and-Resources.aspx

Walker, Thomas G. and Deborah J. Barrow. (1985). "The diversification of the federal bench: Policy and process ramifications." *Journal of Politics, 47*, 596–617.

Welch, Susan, Michael Combs and John Gruhl. (1988). "Do black judges make a difference?" *American Journal of Political Science, 32*(1), 126–136.

Images. (please feel free to use them and or any others as you see fit)

https://www.shutterstock.com/image-photo/woman-judge-standing-court-room-110975876?src=5xqIPSCKI9EJxW-FcS45bg-1-61

https://www.shutterstock.com/image-photo/serious-judge-gavel-wearing-robes-court-245621431?src=5xqIPSCKI9EJxW-FcS45bg-1-89

https://www.shutterstock.com/image-photo/judge-about-bang-gavel-on-sounding-244312189?src=r4AdiYdZRBGFel4_VEHESQ-1-14

CHAPTER 11

Intersectionality in Correctional Contexts: Implications for Women under Supervision

Breanna Boppre | *Wichita State University*

Overview

The United States correctional system represents the processes and organizations that follow after an alleged crime has been handled by the police and court processing. More specifically, the correctional system carries out the court-ordered supervision or treatment conditions. The correctional system is comprised of community (pretrial diversion, probation, and parole) and institutional supervision (jails and prisons). Incarceration, or imprisonment, specifically refers to confinement under intuitional supervision.

As of 2014, nearly seven million Americans are under the supervision of the U.S. correctional system, with 2.2 million held in prisons or jails (Kaeble & Glaze, 2016). The U.S. is the world leader in imprisonment in general, but also in the incarceration of women with the highest rate in the world at 64 per 100,000 (see Figure 1; Walmsley, 2015). Although women comprise a relatively small proportion of the U.S. jail/prison population, about 9% (Walmsley, 2015), they are the fastest growing subpopulation of those incarcerated, at a rate double that of men from 1980 to 2016 (U.S. Sentencing Project, 2018).

Watch tower at a California State Prison

© Joseph Sohm/Shutterstock.com

However, the growth in women's incarceration has not been equal across intersectional subgroups. Minority women as well as LGBTQIA+[1] individuals, have been disproportionately represented in the U.S. correctional system at an alarming rate (Boppre & Harmon, 2017; Harmon & Boppre, 2015; Hartney & Vuong, 2009; Marksamer & Tobin, 2015). A disparity refers to a larger proportion of those incarcerated among a certain group on comparison to their representation in the general population or to other groups. Figure 2 portrays women's incarceration rates across racial groups from 1980-2012 (Boppre &

---

[1] LGBTQIA+ is used to describe persons who identify as lesbian, gay, bisexual, transgender, questioning or queer, intersex, asexual, and any other identity people with "non-mainstream" sexual orientation or gender identity.

Figure 1

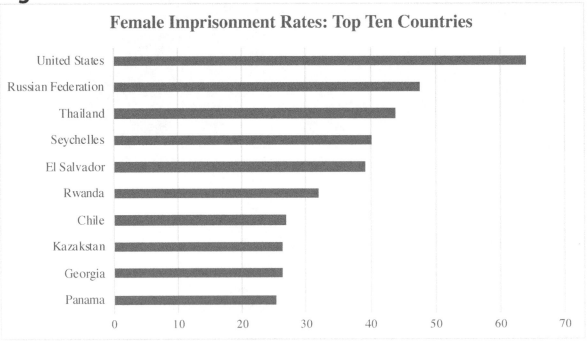

Female Imprisonment Rates: Top Ten Countries

Data Source: Walmsley, R. (2015). *World female imprisonment list*, 4th Edition. London: King's College London, International Centre for Prison Studies. Retrieved from: http://www.prisonstudies.org/world-prison-brief-data

Figure 2

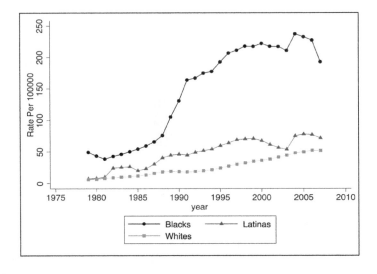

Source: Boppre, B.,& Harmon, M.G. (2016). "Examining Racial Disparity Among Women Offenders: The Effects of Sentencing Reforms on Black, Latina, and White Female Imprisonment." Poster Presentation. Poster Presentation. Western Association of Criminal Justice Annual Meeting, Las Vegas, NV.

Harmon, 2016). During this timeframe, women of color[2] were on average seven times as likely to be incarcerated in comparison to their White counterparts (Boppre & Harmon, 2016). Similarly, Latinas were 2.5 times as likely to be incarcerated in comparison to White women (Boppre & Harmon 2016).

Similar disparities were found among Native American women. The national rate of new admissions for Native American women in 2003 was 6.7 times that for White women (Hartney & Vuong, 2009). In more recent years, state-specific reports indicate such disparities among Native American women continue to persist. In Montana, for example, Native American women comprised approximately 6.5% of the state population yet represented 34% of the women's state prison population (Mehta & Rossi, 2018). Notably, these racial disparities are even starker among women in comparison to men (Harmon & Boppre, 2016; Hartney & Vuong, 2009; Mehta & Rossi, 2018).

Disparities extend among LGBTQIA+ persons as well. In 2012, 33% of women in prison and 26 % of women in jail identified as lesbian or bisexual—yet only 3.4 % of women in the general U.S. population identified as lesbian or bisexual (Meyer et al., 2017). Importantly, disparities are heightened with multiple forms of marginalization, such as being a woman of color or a Native American woman *and* transgender (Reisner, Bailey, & Sevelius, 2014).

With women at the margins disproportionately entering the correctional system, it is important that correctional interventions are inclusive and respond to women's intersectional needs. Just as intersectionality shapes women's experiences in general society, it also creates distinct social realities that lead women into the correctional system, and their experiences under supervision. The remainder of this chapter will discuss the challenges women at the margins face within U.S. correctional contexts followed by recommendations to make correctional settings more intersectionally-responsive.

Challenges Faced by Women at the Margins in the U.S. Correctional System

The U.S. correctional system is premised on contradictory goals related to punishment and rehabilitation (Cullen & Jonson, 2016). Punishment seeks to inflict pain and suffering whereas rehabilitation seeks to change law breaking behavior through the delivery of treatment and service. Importantly, most of the correctional strategies in the U.S. were designed with male prisoners in mind, and then generalized to women, as men make up 90% of the U.S. prison population (Walmsley, 2015).

© *Thawornnurak/Shutterstock.com*

Black woman's hands cuffed through prison bars.

The distinct contexts of correctional supervision in the U.S. create challenges for women at the margins who must exist in spaces that

[2] Potter (2015) suggested the preferred term for women who identify as Black or African American is "women of color." Crenshaw (1991) used the same term in her seminal piece.

were not designed with their needs and experiences in mind. These challenges include heightened social stratification and the neglect for intersectional needs in treatment and services. Such limitations can make it even harder for women at the margins to succeed within correctional environments.

Heightened Social Stratification

The organizational culture within institutional facilities (jails and prisons) typically emphasize dehumanizing tactics that do little to foster rehabilitation and holistic healing (Haney, 2012). Once women enter the correctional system, they are stripped of their identity through the assignment of a number in which they are then referred to by correctional staff (Boppre, 2018). Entrance into correctional facilities involves the mandatory removal of personal property, including clothing, jewelry, and hair products, which are often symbolic of one's cultural identity (Boppre, 2018).

The U.S. is stratified into categories of race, gender, social class, age, ability, religion, sexuality, and other distinctions. Social stratification represents differentiation in which groups vary based upon their social status. Certain characteristics are favored or normalized more than others, resulting in social inequalities (Coates et al., 2018). The same is true in correctional settings, and inequality can even be heightened due to the oppressive and competitive environment (Owen et al., 2017). Behaviors deemed "deviant" or against the norm can be subject to disciplinary sanctions. Yet, the determination of deviant stems from norms and hierarchies in general society where White, middle-class heterosexual values are prioritized.

Prior research indicated that women at the margins encounter decreased prison capital. Prison capital refers to resources for women to maintain safety while incarcerated (Owen et al., 2017). As minority women have less access to commissary and other goods reflective of social status, they may resort to various forms of misconduct (i.e., threats, violence, theft) while incarcerated to survive (Owen et al., 2017).

Additionally, incarcerated women face racial/homophobic stigmatization from staff and fellow prisoners in correctional settings (Boppre, 2018; Kerrison, 2018; McCorkel, 2013). Correctional environments are characterized by a distinct subculture that impacts the daily experiences of staff and prisoners. While in general women are less violent than men, the subculture in women's prisons is still competitive, racially segregated, and leads to tensions between prisoners and staff (Boppre, 2018).

Consequently, the behavior of those who violate typical middle-class, White, heterosexual norms are seen as a threat to traditional values, and are therefore labeled as deviant (Boppre, 2018; Kerrison, 2018). For instance, when women of color speak in loud assertive manners, in affinity with a strong Black woman identity, it can be taken as aggressive by correctional staff members (Boppre, 2018). This is problematic as aggression and defiance can result in disciplinary infractions.

The outcomes of disciplinary infractions are particularly pronounced in institutional settings, as administrative segregation is a commonly used sanction. A recent study by Tasca and Turanovic (2018) examined gendered and racial disparities among placement in restrictive housing placement while incarcerated. Their findings indicated that women of color, Latinas, and Native American women were more likely to be sent to administrative segregation than White women (Tasca & Turanovic, 2018). Women of color comprised the largest proportion of restrictive housing placements explained by security management.

Correctional settings assume binary gender identification and heterosexuality. Nonetheless, gender and sexuality are considered more fluid concepts than traditional conceptions. Gender dualism (Miller, 2014) neglects those who fall outside a traditional "woman" or "man" identity. This is important as institutional facilities in the U.S. are segregated by binary gender (Sumner & Jenness, 2014) through which persons are typically placed into housing based upon biological sex (Reuters, 2018). Thus, a person who identifies as a woman can be placed in an all-male prison (Sumner & Sexton, 2016).

Lesbian and trans prisoners are at particular risk for victimization, more so than straight women (Meyer et al., 2017). This risk is heightened for trans women who are racially marginalized (Reisner et al., 2014). Therefore, LGBTQIA+ prisoners can be placed in "protective custody." However, protective custody is essentially the same response to disciplinary infractions: administrative segregation (Meyer et al., 2017). Meyer and colleagues (2017) found that LGBTQIA+ prisoners were significantly more likely to be placed in administrative segregation in comparison to straight prisoners. Essentially, using administrative segregation equates one's sexuality to behaviors worthy of punishment. Segregating LGBTQIA+ prisoners is aimed to increase safety and security, yet this response further perpetuates "otherness" and the prisoners are at the losing end of this "solution" to gendered differences (Sumner & Sexton, 2016). The use of administrative segregation is especially problematic given the distinct psychological distress and isolation that can occur as a result of segregation (Metzner & Fellner, 2010).

In sum, minority women may face additional challenges under correctional supervision. They must exist in environments with heightened social stratification, racial tension, and homophobia (Boppre, 2018). Beyond such interpersonal and institutional disadvantages, minority women also have decreased access to relatable and representative treatment and services in correctional settings (Boppre, 2018; Pollock, 2000).

Lack of Attention to Intersectional Needs in Treatment and Services

Rehabilitation[3] and traditional correctional strategies as a whole claim generalizability, or applicability, across the majority of correctional subpopulations. This is because the theoretical foundation of rehabilitation is in general psychology, including social learning and cognitive behavioral theories. Accordingly, rehabilitation does not prioritize gender, race, and culture. Instead, such factors are secondary considerations related to individuals' treatment accessibility. While some research shows that genera is effective across race and gender (e.g., Usher & Stewart, 2014), some evidence exists to question the ability of generalized rehabilitation to translate across diverse clientele (e.g., Spiropoulos, Salisbury, & Van Voorhis, 2014).

© Tashatuvango/Shutterstock.com

---

[3] The most prominent rehabilitation model used in the U.S. is the Risk Need Responsivity Model (Andrews & Bonta, 2010). Thus, the critiques of rehabilitation largely reflect this model.

Also, actuarial risk assessments are tools to help correctional agencies predict future criminal behavior (also referred to as recidivism) and to assign clients to the appropriate supervision and treatment levels. Generalized risk assessments vary in their ability to predict recidivism across racial and gendered subgroups. In fact, some research shows that generalized assessments were more effective among White male clients (Folsom & Atkinson, 2007; Holsinger, Lowenkamp, & Latessa, 2003, 2006; Ostermann & Salerno, 2016).

Beginning in the 1990s, scholars argued that because gender-neutral theories and polices did not start with women in mind, they therefore neglect the treatment needs most relevant to women (Chesney-Lind, 2006; Salisbury, Boppre, & Kelly, 2016). Research shows that gender-responsive assessment and treatment are even more effective at reducing recidivism as well as mental health issues and substance abuse in comparison to gender-neutral treatment (Gobeil, Blanchette, & Stewart, 2016; Grella, 2008; Messina, Grella, Cartier, & Torres, 2010). Yet, evaluation research has not looked at potential racial or ethnic differences in gender-responsive assessment and treatment.

Ultimately, intersectional needs are not prioritized within gender-responsive correctional strategies. As the emphasis is on gender, such considerations are also an afterthought. Bloom and colleagues (2003) recognized "triple jeopardy" (i.e., interaction between gender, racial, and class), but they did not fully discuss how to address "triple jeopardy" in treatment. Consequently, correctional programming and services offered are often not truly representative of women at the margins (Boppre, 2018; Kerrison, 2018; Pollack, 2000). For instance, Pollack (2000) found that White women tend to better relate to programming aimed at building self-esteem and empowerment than Aboriginal or Black women. The programming in *Creating Choices* emphasized women's autonomy, yet women of color felt constrained through oppression and marginalization, that could not be addressed through this treatment approach.

Rehabilitation and gender-responsive programming emphasizes individual-level treatment. This places the responsibility for law-breaking behavior on the individual, despite the large body of evidence relating structural forces to crime (Goddard & Myers, 2017; Hannah-Moffatt, 2009). Intersectional and feminist research stressed structural and cultural environments that often compel or "entrap" women into situations leading to system-involvement (Pollack, 2000; Richie, 1996, 2012; Sered & Norton-Hawk, 2014). Ultimately, placing responsibility to change onto the client removes responsibility for crime away from society.

Additionally, actuarial risk assessments "launder" the criminal justice processes that preface women's entrance into the correctional system, including prior contact with police and other criminal justice practitioners (Goddard & Myers, 2017). Women of color often live in environments with increased social control (i.e., impoverished communities that are highly patrolled by police), leading to increased contact with the criminal justice system (Crenshaw, 2012; Harcourt, 2008). Assigning a risk score based upon criminal history may not actually reflect a woman risk of recidivism, but rather her life history that placed her in contact with the legal system (Harcourt, 2015; Paniagua, 2013). Individualized rehabilitative treatment also disregards larger reentry barriers, such as surviving impoverished or crime-ridden environments (Pollack, 2000; Grote et al., 2007).

To summarize, current correctional strategies for women de-prioritize and de-contextualize their intersectional experiences. The theoretical foundations and subsequent polices/practices were not developed with intersectionality in mind. Therefore, such approaches are not relatable or representative of diverse women. Further, problems exist within the individualized focus of rehabilitation that places responsibility for rehabilitation to the individual despite the multitude of structural barriers (e.g., poverty, systemic racism) that contribute to minority women's justice-involvement.

Recommendations for an Intersectionally-Responsive Approach

Boppre (2019), provides specific recommendations to correctional agencies to incorporate intersectional tenets. She uses the term "intersectionally-responsive" correctional strategies as those that recognize the interaction between gender, race, and other categories of difference that often impact persons' initial involvement in the criminal justice system, experiences on supervision and in treatment programming, as well as reentry in the community. Boppre (2019) acknowledges that the original socio-legal form of intersectionality seeks to dismantle the larger social structures that serve to oppress. Nonetheless, she uses intersectionality as a lens to account for multiple distinctions that jointly and holistically shape the needs and experiences of women who were or are incarcerated. Her recommendations are summarized as follows in three phases: prior to women's correctional-involvement, within correctional environments, and after, or beyond, correctional-involvement. Figure 3 summarizes the specific recommendations within each phase.

First, researchers, policymakers, and practitioners must consider potential variation in women's pathways into the criminal justice system. The recognition that more than gender alone shapes women's experiences is vital towards the adoption of an intersectionally-responsive approach. Various research has documented the distinct realities of minority women (e.g., Arnold, 1990; Cobbina, 2009; Flores, 2016; Holsinger & Holsinger, 2005; Jones, 2010; Miller, 2008; Potter, 2006; Richie, 1996, 2012) and these studies should be taken into account when developing programs and policy recommendations. Also, policymakers must consider the racial impacts of sentencing practices as historically women of color have been sentenced more harshly than their White counterparts (Boppre & Harmon, 2017).

Figure 3

Recommendations for an Intersectionally Responsive Approach (from Boppre, 2019)

Prior to Correctional-Involvement	Within Correctional Settings	After, or Beyond, Correctional-Involvement
Consider intersectional contexts in women's pathways to the criminal justice system Critically assess and reform sentencing practices	Shifts to organizational cultures and missions Assess and adjust actuarial assessments Address staff-client relations Ensure inclusive treatment and services	Consider intersectional contexts in women's reentry, including the provision of culturally-specific services/programs Modify typical evaluation research with a focus on participatory action research

Woman living on the streets.

Second, shifts must occur within correctional agencies. Correctional organizations must re-think their missions and values to prioritize inclusivity. Further, staff-client relationships can be improved through increased diversity. The majority of correctional staff across the U.S. are White, and more specifically, White men (Prison Policy Initiative, 2005; U.S. Department of Justice, 2003). However, women of color and other marginalized subpopulations are disproportionately represented within the U.S. correctional system (Harmon & Boppre, 2016). Therefore, cultural competency training must also be mandated. Additionally, correctional agencies must ensure the assessments and treatment programming utilized is relevant and inclusive of minority women. This can include culturally-specific treatment, mentoring, or support groups.

Moreover, supports must be put in place to identify and provide relevant services for minority women. The reentry needs of a White middle-class woman are far different from an impoverished Black woman. Reentry programming and services must reflect such differences and tailor release plans accordingly. More reentry services and programs must be provided to women to support desistance, as such services are lacking for women in general (Scroggins & Malley, 2010). These services/programs include parenting and childcare, healthcare, substance abuse treatment, counseling, housing and transportation, education, employment, and social support (Scroggins & Malley, 2010).

Finally, correctional agencies must move beyond traditional evaluation research to consider the differential impact their interventions may have on minority women. Boppre (2019) emphasizes the importance of participatory action research to involve and engage women directly impacted. Consulting with those directly impacted will ensure the relevance, usefulness, and inclusiveness of correctional programming. For example, The National Council for Incarcerated and Formerly Incarcerated Women[4] brings attention to the women-specific contexts and the consequences of incarceration. These incarcerated and formerly incarcerated women across the nation share their expertise with policymakers and other stakeholders. Their mission is to contribute to meaningful change to end the mass incarceration of women. Importantly, the National Council is led primarily by women of color who understand the intersectional contexts of incarceration firsthand.

---

[4] https://www.nationalcouncil.us/about/

Conclusion

Incarceration rates among women have increased at an alarming rate over the past four decades. However, the U.S. correctional system is disproportionately comprised of women at the margins. Nonetheless, the demographic composition of correctional staff and those who develop correctional programming and policies are not reflective of women who enter the system.

This chapter provided an overview of disparities in incarceration, the experiences of women at the margins in correctional settings, and recommendations for policymakers and practitioners. The female experience is not universal, and the pathways in and out of criminality look very different across intersectional subgroups. While the creators of gender-responsive strategies recognized the importance of race and class (e.g., Bloom et al., 2003), translating such complexities into correctional practice was never fully addressed. Increased recognition of the distinct and diverse experiences of women, including structural barriers to reentry, will help make correctional practices more relevant, inclusive, and accessible (Boppre, 2019).

References

Andrews, D. A., & Bonta, J. (2010). Rehabilitating criminal justice policy and practice. *Psychology, Public Policy and Law, 16*, 39–55.

Arnold, R. A. (1990). Processes of victimization and criminalization of black women. *Social Justice, 17*, 153-166.

Bloom, B., Owen, B., & Covington, S. (2003). *Gender-responsive strategies: Research, practice and guiding principles for women offenders*. Washington, DC: National Institute of Corrections, USDOJ.

Boppre, B. (2018). *Intersections between gender, race, and justice-involvement: A mixed methods analysis of women's experiences in the Oregon criminal justice system*. Unpublished doctoral dissertation. University of Nevada, Las Vegas.

Boppre, B. (2019). Improving Correctional Strategies for Women at the Margins: Recommendations for an Intersectionally-Responsive Approach. *Corrections: Policy, Practice, and Research.*

Boppre, B., & Harmon, M.G. (2016). "Examining racial disparity among women offenders: The effects of sentencing reforms on Black, Latina, and White female imprisonment." Poster Presentation. Western Association of Criminal Justice Annual Meeting, Las Vegas, NV.

Boppre, B., & Harmon, M. G. (2017). The Unintended consequences of sentencing reforms: Using social chain theory to examine racial disparities in female imprisonment. *Journal of Ethnicity in Criminal Justice, 15*, 394-423.

Chesney-Lind, M. (2006). Patriarchy, crime and justice: Feminist criminology in an era of backlash. *Feminist Criminology, 1*, 6-26.

Coates, R. D., Ferber, A. L., & Brunsma, D. L. (2017). *The matrix of race: Social construction, intersectionality, and inequality*. Thousand Oaks, CA: Sage Publications.

Cobbina, J. E. (2009). *From prison to home: Women's pathways in and out of crime*. Unpublished doctoral dissertation, University of Missouri, St. Louis.

Crenshaw, K. (2012). From private violence to mass incarceration: Thinking intersectionally about women, race, and social control. *UCLA Law Review, 59*, 1418-1472.

Cullen, F. T., & Jonson, C. L. (2016). *Correctional theory: Context and consequences*. Thousand Oaks, CA: Sage Publications.

Flores, J. (2016). *Caught up: Girls, surveillance, and wraparound incarceration* (Vol. 2). Oakland, CA: University of California Press.

Folsom, J. & Atkinson, J. L. (2007). The generalizability of the LSI-R and the CAT to the prediction of recidivism in female offenders. *Criminal Justice and Behavior, 34*, 1044-1056.

Gobeil, R., Blanchette, K., & Stewart, L. (2016). A meta-analytic review of correctional interventions for women offenders gender-neutral versus gender-informed approaches. *Criminal Justice and Behavior, 43*, 301-322.

Goddard, T. & Myers, R.R. (2017). Against evidence-based oppression: Marginalized youth and the politics of risk-based assessment and intervention. *Theoretical Criminology, 21*, 151–167.

Grella, C. E. (2008). From generic to gender-responsive treatment: Changes in social policies, treatment services, and outcomes of women in substance abuse treatment. *Journal of Psychoactive Drugs, 40*, 327-343.

Grote, N. K., Zuckoff, A., Swartz, H., Bledsoe, S. E., & Geibel, S. (2007). Engaging women who are depressed and economically disadvantaged in mental health treatment. *Social work, 52*, 295-308.

Hannah-Moffatt, K. (2009). Gridlock or mutability: Reconsidering gender and risk assessment. *Criminology & Public Policy, 8*, 209-219.

Haney, C. (2012). Prison effects in the era of mass incarceration. *The Prison Journal*, 1-24.

Harcourt, B. E. (2008). *Against prediction: Profiling, policing, and punishing in an actuarial age.* Chicago: University of Chicago Press.

Harcourt, B. E. (2015). Risk as a proxy for race: The dangers of risk assessment. *Federal Sentencing Reporter, 27*, 237-243.

Harmon, M. G., & Boppre, B. (2016). Women of Color and the War on Crime: An explanation for the rise in Black female imprisonment. *The Journal of Ethnicity in Criminal Justice*. DOI: 10.1080/15377938.2015.1052173

Hartney, C., & Vuong, L. (2009). *Created equal: Racial and ethnic disparities in the U.S. justice system.* Retrieved from http://www.nccdglobal.org/sites/default/files/publication_pdf/created-equal.pdf.

Holsinger, K., & Holsinger, A. M. (2005). Differential pathways to violence and self-injurious behavior: African-American and White girls in the juvenile justice system. *Journal of Research in Crime and Delinquency, 42*, 211–242.

Holsinger, A. M., Lowenkamp, C. T., & Latessa, E. J. (2003). Ethnicity, gender, and the Level of Service Inventory-Revised. *Journal of Criminal Justice, 31*, 309-320.

Holsinger, A. M., Lowenkamp, C. T., & Latessa, E. J. (2006). Exploring the validity of the Level of Service Inventory-Revised with Native American offenders. *Journal of Criminal Justice, 34*, 331-337.

Jones, N. (2010). *Between good and ghetto: African American girls and inner-city violence.* New Brunswick, NJ: Rutgers University Press.

Kaeble, D., & Glaze, L. (2016). *Correctional populations in the United States, 2015.* Washington, DC: Bureau of Justice Statistics. Retrieved from http://www.bjs.gov/index.cfm?ty=pbdetail&iid=5870

Kerrison, E. M. (2018). Risky business, risk assessment, and other heteronormative misnomers in women's community corrections and reentry planning. *Punishment & Society, 20*, 134-151.

Marksamer, J., & Tobin, H. (2015). *Standing with LGBTQIA+ prisoners: An advocate's guide to ending abuse and combating imprisonment.* Washington DC: National Center for Transgender Equality.

McCorkel, J. A. (2013). *Breaking women: Gender, race, and the new politics of imprisonment.* New York: New York University Press.

Mehta, S. & Rossi, S.K. (2018). Why are so many Indigenous people in Montana incarcerated? Retrieved from https://www.aclu.org/blog/smart-justice/parole-and-release/why-are-so-many-indigenous-people-montana-incarcerated

Messina, N., & Grella, C. (2006). Childhood trauma and women's health outcomes in a California prison population. *American Journal of Public Health, 96,* 1842-1848.

Metzner J.L, Fellner J. (2010). Solitary confinement and mental illness in US prisons: a challenge for medical ethics. *Journal of the American Academy of Psychiatry and Law, 38,* 104–108.

Meyer, I.H., Flores, A.R., Stemple, L., Romero, A.P., Wilson, B.D.M., & Herman, J.L. (2017). Incarceration rates and traits of sexual minorities in the United States: National Inmate Survey 2011–2012. *American Journal of Public Health, 107,* 234–240.

Miller, J. (2008). *Getting played: African American girls, urban inequality, and gendered violence.* New York: NYU Press.

Miller, J. (2014). Doing crime as doing gender? masculinities, femininities and crime. In G. Rosemary, & B. McCarthy (Eds.). *The oxford handbook on gender, sex, and crime.* New York: Oxford University Press

Ostermann, M., & Salerno, L. M. (2016). The validity of the Level of Service Inventory–Revised at the intersection of race and gender. *The Prison Journal,* 0032885516650878, 1-22.

Owen, B., Wells, J., & Pollock, J. (2017). *In search of safety confronting inequality in women's imprisonment.* Oakland, CA: University of California Press.

Paniagua, F. A. (2013). *Assessing and treating culturally diverse clients: A practical guide.* Thousand Oaks, CA: Sage Publications.

Pollack, S. (2000). *Outsiders inside: The social context of women's lawbreaking and imprisonment.* Unpublished doctoral dissertation, University of Toronto.

Potter, H. (2006). An argument for Black feminist criminology understanding African American women's experiences with intimate partner abuse using an integrated approach. *Feminist Criminology, 1,* 106-124.

Prison Policy Initiative. (2005). Analysis of census of state and federal adult correctional facilities, ICPSR 24642. Retrieved February 25, 2018, from https://www.prisonpolicy.org/graphs/US_staff_disparities_2005.html

Reisner, S. L., Bailey, Z., & Sevelius, J. (2014). Racial/ethnic disparities in history of incarceration, experiences of victimization, and associated health indicators among transgender women in the US. *Women & health, 54,* 750-767.

Reuters. (2018). U.S. rolls back protections for transgender prison inmates. Retrieved from https://www.reuters.com/article/us-usa-lgbt-prisons/u-s-rolls-back-protections-for-transgender-prison-inmates-idUSKCN1ID0O3

Richie, B. E. (1996). *Compelled to crime: The gender entrapment of Black battered women.* New York: Routledge.

Richie, B. E. (2012). *Arrested justice: Black women, violence, and America's prison nation.* New York: New York University Press.

Salisbury, E. J., Boppre, B., & Kelly, B. (2016). Gender-responsive risk and need assessment: Implications for the treatment of justice-involved women. In F. Taxman (Ed.), *Division on Corrections and Sentencing, Volume 1, Risk and Need Assessment: Theory and Practice*. London: Taylor and Francis/Routledge.

Scroggins, J. R., & Malley, S. (2010). Reentry and the (unmet) needs of women. *Journal of Offender Rehabilitation, 49*, 146-163.

Sered, S. S., & Norton-Hawk, M. (2014). *Can't catch a break: Gender, jail, drugs, and the limits of personal responsibility*. Oakland, CA: University of California Press.

Spiropoulos, G. V., Salisbury, E. J., & Van Voorhis, P. (2014). Moderators of correctional treatment success: An exploratory study of racial differences. *International Journal of Offender Therapy and Comparative Criminology, 58*, 835-860.

Sumner, J. & Jenness, V. (2014). Gender integration in sex-segregated U.S. Prisons:

The paradox of transgender correctional policy. In *Handbook of LGBT Communities, Crime, and Justice*. D Peterson & V. R. Panfill (Eds.), 229–59. New York: Springer.

Sumner J. & Sexton, L. (2016). Same difference: The 'dilemma of difference' and the incarceration of transgender prisoners. *Law and Law & Social Inquiry, 41*, 616–642.

Tasca, M., & Turanovic, J. (2018). Examining race and gender disparities in restrictive housing placements. Office of Justice Programs' National Criminal Justice Reference Service. Retrieved from https://www.ncjrs.gov/pdffiles1/nij/grants/252062.pdf

Usher, A. M., & Stewart, L. A. (2014). Effectiveness of correctional programs with ethnically diverse offenders: A meta-analytic study. *International journal of offender therapy and comparative criminology, 58*, 209-230.

U.S. Department of Justice. (2003). Bureau of Justice Statistics, Sourcebook of criminal justice statistics 2003. available at http://www.albany.edu/sourcebook/

U.S. Sentencing Project. (2018). *Incarcerated Women and Girls, 1980-2016*. Retrieved from https://www.sentencingproject.org/publications/incarcerated-women-and-girls/

Walmsley, R. (2015). *World female imprisonment list*, 4th Edition. London: King's College London, International Centre for Prison Studies. Retrieved from: http://www.prisonstudies.org/world-prison-brief-data

Correspondence concerning this article should be addressed to Breanna Boppre, Wichita State University School of Criminal Justice 1845 Fairmount St. Wichita, Kansas 67260
Email: breanna.boppre@gmail.com

This chapter was adapted from a full-length article: Boppre, B. (2019). Improving Correctional Strategies for Women at the Margins: Recommendations for an Intersectionally-Responsive Approach. Corrections: Policy, Practice, and Research.

Appendix

Chapter Outcomes

- Students should define what the U.S. correctional system is and identify recent trends in female imprisonment, including disparities.
- Students should identify how heightened social stratification in correctional settings can impact minority women.
- Students should distinguish how intersectional needs are neglected in treatment and services for women.
- Students should discuss methods to improve correctional strategies for minority women.

Key Terms:

Actuarial risk assessments	Incarceration	Rehabilitation
Disparity	Intersectionally	The correctional system
Gender-responsive correctional strategies	Prison capital	

Discussion Questions:

1. What is the U.S. correctional system? What are the recent trends in incarceration among women? What disparities exist in female imprisonment in the U.S.? Why do you think these disparities exist?

2. What are some issues related to the U.S. correctional system in relation to the supervision and treatment of women at the margins?

3. Do you think the correctional system should take intersectionality into account? Why or why not?

4. What are some ways to improve correctional strategies for minority women? Can you think of additional recommendations that were not mentioned in the chapter?

5. Consider the realities of two women who recently were released from prison after serving 3 years for drug-related offenses:

Renee is a 25-year-old Black woman whose family comes from a lower-class background. She lived with her family prior to her conviction and planned on returning to their apartment in a public housing unit. However, due to restrictions on public housing for those with a felony record, she is unable to live with her family. She must live in a shelter until after she finds employment and saves up enough money for a deposit on a place of her own. She also has a 5-year-old son who is in the foster care system because no one was able to care for him when she went to prison. She keeps applying for jobs but it seems as though no one will hire her. Her family emphasizes the importance of being strong and independent. However, Renee is struggling and worries she will permanently lose custody of her son due to her circumstances. She has no personal transportation and must travel over an hour on the bus to make it to her appointments with her parole officer. She has already been late to a few appointments and worries she may go back to prison on a revocation if she misses appointments. Her parole officer does not seem empathetic to Renee's situation. She feels hopeless and living downtown in the shelter, she has easy access to drugs. She is afraid she may relapse and resort to selling drugs in order to survive.

Marie is a 25-year-old White woman whose family comes from a middle-class background. Marie moves in with her family after release. Her family cared for Marie's 5-year-old son while she was in prison. Marie is happy to be able to live with her son and care for him once again. They provide her with groceries and anything she needs. A family friend offers Marie a job at a locally-owned grocery store. She begins working soon after release. The grocery store is located very close to her home and her family typically drives her to work. They also drive her to her appointments with her parole officer. Her parole officer, also a White woman, is very supportive of Marie and praises her for all her accomplishments thus far. Marie still fights the urge to use drugs, but keeps her mind off using with her job and taking care of her son.

Identify how Renee and Marie's reentry experiences are shaped by their intersectional identities. How are their financial, familial, and social circumstances different? How do the intersections of gender, race, and social class impact their access to resources needed to remain crime-free? Who do you think is at risk to return to prison? Is this risk something either woman can control? Why or why not?

CHAPTER 12

Women and Policing - Inside the Patriarchy: What Is It Like to Be a Female Correctional Officer?

Daniela Barberi | *George Mason University*
Lindsay Smith | *George Mason University*

Overview

The criminal justice system reflects a patriarchal system where males are entitled to a higher position than women (Blackburn, Fowler, Mullings, & Marquart, 2011; Castle & Martin, 2006). The work of correctional officers is not an exception. This male-dominated position has portrayed itself as a rigid and dangerous role unsuitable for women. As more women continue to choose this career path, it is important for researchers within the field of corrections to explore the experiences of female officers. The problem is that research on these women have mixed results (Armstrong & Griffin, 2004; Brough & Williams, 2007; Farkas, 2000; M. S. Gordon, 2006; Griffin, 2006; Griffin, Armstrong, & Hepburn, 2005) frequently ignoring treatment personnel employed in these same institutions. This study advanced the literature on correctional workplace stress by: (1. The goal of this paper is to synthesize what the field knows about female correctional officers and describe the evolution of their experiences from training and on the everyday situations on the job.

Chapter Outcomes

The correctional system, on an organizational level, is deeply intertwined with the patriarchal system. After you read this chapter, you will learn why:

- From the beginning, women in training, who want to become Cos, realize that the institution is built on sexist assumptions.

- Female COs are socialized to internalize the patriarchal environment of corrections in a way in which to successfully perform their duties women need to adjust their feminine behavior to be more masculine.

- Women who work in the correctional system will have more obstacles to surmount in order to be promoted over males.

- Female COs will face more physical and psychological stressors than their male counterparts.

In 1958 Gresham Sykes wrote one of the most iconic pieces for correctional scholars, in which he argues that corrections are institutions that not only incapacitate and limit the interactions of some individuals within the society, but most interestingly is a place where a society itself is created. Patriarchal societies are the norm rather than the exception and as a result, the criminal justice system (CJS) reflects

© josefkubes/Shutterstock.com

sexist constructions and norms about what is expected from men and women. Not surprisingly, correctional institutions such as jails, prisons, or even community corrections are characterized by being male-dominated fields. Interestingly, even when a new society is born inside a correctional facility (Sykes, 1958), it will follow and maintain patriarchal paradigms.

These non-natural social norms are applied to both inmates and workers within the jails and prison systems, and one way to understand how sexism operates inside this justice institution is by looking at the experiences of women who work in this field (Britton, 1997; Burdett, Gouliquer, & Poulin, 2018; Gordon & Baker, 2017; Jurik, 1985). To do so, this chapter begins by framing how patriarchy has shaped our thinking and behavior and has established 'natural' and 'traditional' roles and expectations for men and women (J. Butler, 1999; Enloe, 2014; hooks, 2014; West & Zimmerman, 1987). Then, the chapter reviews how female workers have entered the justice system and what are some of the most common obstacles women will face (Blackburn et al., 2011; Castle & Martin, 2006; Wells, Colbert, & Slate, 2006). Next, the chapter synthesizes what we know about gendered training for correctional officers (COs), the sexist expectations of female officers, how women cope with the obstacles of this male-dominated job, and the implications of its meager environment.

Women in a Patriarchal Society

Society builds social norms that establish how individuals should behave and what is expected from them. Since 1951, the French sociologist Emile Durkheim (1951) argued that people learn these norms from their social groups; conversely, Veroff (1995) proposed that people can experience despair and uncertainty without group norms. The problem is when we forget that institutions are the ones that *build* these social constructions and norms. These rules are not inescapable, nor inevitable. Regardless, people internalize and normalize social constructions to the point of forgetting that these norms are not natural and that there are possibilities outside the pre-established 'traditional' social behaviors. One example of these normalized social constructions is gender.

Patriarchy, a system of domination, has established gendered social norms (hooks, 2014). A patriarchal society determines the appropriate behaviors, performances, and expectations for a woman or a man, and it has positioned the heterosexual man on top of the hierarchical system (J. Butler, 1999; Confortini, 2006; Enloe, 2014; hooks, 2014; Pascoe, 2011; West & Zimmerman, 1987). As Bourdieu (2004) argues, structures of domination are established thanks to its historical and constant reproduction by all individuals and institutions. Therefore, in order for patriarchy to be reproduced, both the oppressor and the oppressed (actively or tacitly) legitimize the norms and limits imposed by following them without question. Bourdieu (2004) labels this process as "symbolic violence," where power and dominance can only be exercised with the contribution of the oppressed.

Social norms and traditional gender roles have been normalized due to patriarchy, a system that has made these norms look natural, normal, and expected. Patriarchal social norms have gendered behaviors; thus, gender has become *what* people do instead of *who* they are (West & Zimmerman, 1987). Performing a gender is legitimized and supported by social institutions and when people repeat these expected behaviors, they facilitate gendered norms to be perceived as 'normal' (Butler, 1999). However, none of these *built* gendered social norms are truly natural, nor traditional. These are used and repeated by societies to maintain and uphold the dominant system. Unfortunately, when people behave outside of these non-natural norms, they are in danger of being marginalized (J. Butler, 1999; West & Zimmerman, 1987).

By normalizing gendered behaviors and performances, societies are allowing everyday violence to happen; a violence that is not perceived as "deviant", but is rather accepted and customary in this oppressor-oppressed system (Scheper-Hughes & Bourgois, 2004). One way to normalize gendered violence is through the discourse and language used by societies (J. Butler, 1999; Cohn, 1993; Confortini, 2006). Cohn (1993) argues that gendered narratives, not the used words, but rather the system of meanings, shape how people experience and understand themselves as either a man or a woman. The author mentions that this rhetoric is able to outline how we see ourselves within a culture and a society, and this symbolic system results in dichotomized human characteristics (e.g. associating colors to gender such as blue for boys and pink for girls, and if a boy wears pink he would be in danger of being stigmatized). Similarly, Confortini argues that the social construct of gender "organizes social life in hierarchical, mutually exclusive categories, which are in a relationship of sub/super ordination to one another" (2006, p. 335). In other words, societies sculpt gendered expectations based on opposites and extremes where one gender is superior to the other, reflecting the roles as the oppressed and the oppressor.

Following this binary perspective, societies end up with traditional gender roles where men are perceived and expected to be the ones who work, are rational, proactive, and strong, while the women are expected to be the emotional, passive, and fragile housewives (Confortini, 2006; Enloe, 2014; C Kaplan & Grewal, 2006). These constructed gendered perceptions have been normalized throughout history and influence the everyday life of both men and women, their careers, and have imposed limitations to everyday behavior. One example of this inequality can be observed when we look at one job that has been traditionally perceived as work for men - correctional officers.

Women in the Criminal Justice System

The criminal justice field is characterized for being a patriarchal and male-dominated institution (Blackburn et al., 2011; Castle & Martin, 2006; Wells et al., 2006). The responsibility of enforcing and punishing for the law has historically laid in the hands of strong and rational male police officers, judges, district attorneys, correctional officers, and probation and parole officers.

One example of this situation is when looking at the group of individuals we first encounter in the criminal justice system, the police. In this field, the entrance of women to the job market came only after long legal battles and political action (Seklecki & Paynich, 2007). Research from the 1980s argues that women joined the job to help others and that the traditionalist, sexist male officer perceived a female partner as weak and soft (Seklecki & Paynich, 2007). Additionally, female police officers face sexual harassment, issues with maternity leave, and are working without proper sizes of equipment. As Skelcki and Paynich (2007) explain, this male-dominated profession pushes women in the field to act as men (or even 'better') to adjust to the patriarchal environment. However, there are negative consequences for this 'adjustment.' For example, when looking at female probation officers, research has found that women in this job have greater levels of stress when compared to male probation officers (Wells et al., 2006).

© LightField Studios/Shutterstock.com

The question is how are female justice officers perceived inside the criminal justice system? What are their experiences inside this male-dominated field? As Confortini (2006) argues, the patriarchal system has been in charge of portraying women with specific characteristics and roles. For instance, "women were, by nature, upbringing, and/or by virtue of being mothers and caretakers, morally superior to and more peaceful than men" (Confortini, 2006, p. 333). Following this idea, does this mean that the CJS is including female officers because the institution believes the value of women lies solely on the fact that they are the opposite of men? (Seklecki & Paynich, 2007). In other words, based on the sexist assumption that females are the opposite of men, is the justice system neglecting the value of female officers simply for *who* they are?

As hooks (2014) and Bordieu (2004) argue, to avoid perpetuating gendered social constructions and its expected behaviors, it is important to bring to consciousness these issues and shift away from systems of domination. In order to begin this process in the CJS, this paper explores and describes the experiences of one group of officers within the justice system: female correctional officers. The goal is to describe the experiences of women officers and initiate the conversation that perhaps the CJS is including women officers in the correctional system under the pretenses of a patriarchal and sexist system that sees the value of women in the field only when compared to men.

The Rise of Female Correctional Officers

The percentage of women working in corrections has grown dramatically from less than 10% in 1970 to approximately 40% in 2010 (Management & Training Corporation Institute, 2008). This 30% increase has appeared to cause a calming effect between inmates and officers over the past several decades (J. Gordon & Baker, 2017). For example, the presence of female officers produced more positive interactions inside prisons. Regardless, female COs face unique challenges in this primarily male job due to biased policies and infrastructure, spillover of gender role stereotypes, sexist resistance and prejudices, negative self-perceptions, and a poor work-life balance that results in health-related complications (Martin & Barnard, 2013).

Gendered Training: Inherently Designed for Males

In correctional settings, the reinforcement of gender inequality through gender neutral policies and practices, such as training, are practically inevitable (Britton, 1997). Female officers interviewed in Britton's (1997) study recall that during training everyone is referred to as a "correctional officer", assuming there is no difference among these justice officers. Justice jobs assume a male audience in which men's needs and skills are the only ones on the table, allowing neutrality to ignore inequality in this justice field. Britton labels this phenomenon a "gendered organizational logic" (1997, p. 797), where the field of corrections attempts to seem gender neutral, but in fact, the CO career is inherently reflecting a patriarchal system.

While training, whether facilitated by a male or female instructor, appears gender-neutral at first, during training sessions, a gendered theme will develop (Britton, 1997). For example, classroom and role-play exercises will solely reference male COs working in male prisons or jails. This fosters an atmosphere that leaves all women, both as a COs and as inmates, out of the narrative. A bulk of the trainings also revolve around the violent aspects of correctional work (e.g. encounters with violent or distressed offenders) and fail to discuss the potential sexual harassment that females' COs are likely to face on the job (Britton, 1997; Burdett, Gouliquer, & Poulin, 2018). Female officers consistently report dealing with more harassment than males COs, such as witnessing masturbation, verbal abuse, threats, and taunting by inmates (Britton, 1997). The problem is that the CJS is not offering adequate, if any, guidance to the female officers on how to navigate these situations and women must learn and develop coping strategies themselves (e.g., ignoring incidents, taking recreational substances, seeking professional help, physical exercise) (Burdett et al., 2018).

Inadequate formal training forced female officers to rely and depend more on informal training offered to them by senior officers who were most likely men and had the idea that women were less capable officers (Jurik, 1985). As a result, women COs become acutely aware that *doing* masculinity is required to succeed in this justice career (Britton, 1997; Prokos & Padavic, 2002). Unfortunately, as Bordieu (2004) argues, women adjusting and internalizing the expectations that a patriarchal society establishes contributes to symbolic and everyday violence in which the oppressed contributes and is complicit to the maintenance of the dominant system. Moreover, when women COs believe that performing masculinity is better than their femininity, they are reinforcing and even legitimizing patriarchy (J. Butler, 1999).

Women are negatively socialized into this male-dominated work, and scholars have found that this might result in fearless male COs and fearful females COs (Alvi, Schwartz, DeKeseredy, & Maume, 2001; Day, 2001). This sexist environment also influences and has negative implications on social cohesion and a sense of belonging amongst officers, which have been shown to improve job-related stress, satisfaction, burnout, and overall commitment to the organization (Britton, 1997; J. Gordon & Baker, 2017; Griffin et al., 2005).

The 'Normalized' Role of Female Officers

Once female correctional officers 'survive' training, they are assigned to a post which is often predicated on supervisors' and peers' perceptions of women's ability to deal with violence on the job (Britton, 1997). Jurik (1985) found that the possibilities of work assignments for female officers were more limited than for males. These decisions were usually based and centered on assumed physical weaknesses of women and rights to privacy for male inmates. Some specific duties within correctional work are often labeled as "safe" or "unsafe" positions for female officers (Britton, 1997). In other

© ChameleonsEye/Shutterstock.com

words, regardless of women's abilities and skills in justice work, females will be inevitably allocated to do and perform in gendered positions determined by a patriarchal field (J. Butler, 1999; Enloe, 2014).

The restrictions in routine work assignments are not only an issue because these reflect a patriarchal system, but limitations can also generate a practical problem for women COs. Female officers experience restricted promotional possibilities due to lack of experience working in the yard or in housing units, and thus found it difficult to be promoted to higher-security-level facilities or into the counseling officer track (Jurik, 1985; Matthews, Monk-Turner, & Sumter, 2010; Burdett, Gouliquer, & Poulin, 2018). Furthermore, restrictions led to resentment of male officers for 'special treatment' awarded to women (Jurik, 1985). These consequences caused by a patriarchal system ultimately allow this dominant-male work to maintain its gendered discrimination and limit the success of women (Enloe, 2014).

One's socialization into an organization (such as the justice system) and its environmental factors, weigh heavily on how one positions themselves in their role within a team and if they believe they fit. The 'outsider's' perspective of female officers leaves them in a stressful position, questioning their place in corrections, which could explain their low numbers in the field. Again, these circumstances reflect a sexist system in which women who act and behave outside their traditional gendered roles will be marginalized (Britton, 1997; Burdett et al., 2018; West & Zimmerman, 1987).

The discussion of gender is particularly important when tasks are unpredictable, complex, or difficult to measure. As Zimmer argues, "In the prisons, where accomplishments like reducing tension, de-escalating conflict, and averting riots cannot be quantified, or even observed," (1987, p. 427) it is difficult to suggest and normalize that women, when compared to men, are uncapable of adequately performing the job. It is not surprising that in correctional settings, women officers are evaluated on the "basis of how closely their performance approximates that of men" (Zimmer, 1987, p. 425). As Cullen and colleagues (1989) found, female officers were no more likely than male officers to have a rehabilitative approach to inmates.

Gendered Job Experiences

Female officers tend to have less contact with inmates, but this does not mean their experiences on the job are easier when compared to male officers. In a study by Burdett, Gouliquer, and Poulin (2018), researchers found several complications faced by female officers. These included a lack of institutional support, social exclusion from peers, gender performativity standards favoring males, sexualized hostile work environment, and health problems stemming from work-related stress. However, when women tried to make sense of their workplace environments through a gendered lens, it always came back to their physical inferiority (Burdett et al., 2018). Yet, inmates' perceptions of female officers' job performances rated them as equally or more capable than male officers at handling high custody offenders (Cheeseman, Mulllings, & Marquart, 2001). Some inmates also rated their treatment by staff as fairer when more female officers worked at the prison (Beijersbergen, Dirkzwager, Molleman, van der Laan, & Nieuwbeerta, 2015).

Women overwhelmingly attributed resistance they experienced at work with biased attitudes on women's reliability in violent situations and with the behavior of individual male officers and supervisors (Jurik, 1985). These gendered attitudes assumed three ideas about women: greater physical weaknesses; mental weaknesses; and becoming sexually involved with inmates (Jurik, 1985). Adversely, male officers tended to see their own position in another light. Most officers felt that performance ratings used in promotion decisions were affected by favoritism; this reinforced the beliefs that evaluations of women were based either on physical appearance or on the promise of sexual favors (Jurik, 1985). Due to this, female officers feared on one side, retaliation if they defended themselves against sexual harassment from supervisors, and on the other side, the risk of not being promoted. When women were promoted, they felt the need to prove their qualifications and disprove "sexual" favoritism (Jurik, 1985).

Female officers face the risk of being victimized by inmates as well. Women and non-White COs are more likely to perceive fear of victimization initiated by inmates than White male officers (J. Gordon & Baker, 2017; J. Gordon, Proulx, & Grant, 2013). As a generalized example, a study of COs in men's institutions explored the emotional and cognitive fears of COs (J. Gordon & Baker, 2017). On one hand, findings suggest that the emotional and cognitive fears of male COs were driven by a combination of the race of the officer, frustration with the organization, lower education, and institutional security level. On the other hand, women's emotional fear was driven by the race of the officer, while cognitive fear was caused by facility frustration and disorganization.

Female COs cognitive fear seems to be derived solely from structural issues within the correctional organization, while for men both fears are caused by a combination of personal and organizational factors. This could suggest that differences lie within the socialization process of correctional officers (Alvi et al., 2001; Day, 2001; J. Gordon & Baker, 2017). It is also important to consider that emotional female fear might be caused by racial prejudice or discrimination, which might be related to the culture and climate of correctional facilities (J. Gordon & Baker, 2017).

Other organizational factors that can influence the experiences of female officers must be targeted and addressed. For instance, female officers report higher levels of job stress than their male officer counterparts (D. Butler, Tasca, Zhang, & Carpenter, 2019; Dial, Downey, & Goodlin, 2010; Lambert, Hogan, & Griffin, 2007), yet they report more organizational commitment (D. Butler et al., 2019). Furthermore, role problems, lack of autonomy, procedural justice, and instrumental communication significantly increases female COs' job stress (Lambert et al., 2007; Lambert, Kim, Keena, & Cheeseman, 2017). Age and tenure however make a difference; female officers with higher tenure were generally less stressed from work (Lambert et al., 2015), while female officers from Generation X (i.e., born between 1965 to 1981) were more stressed (Dial et al., 2010).

The most common coping strategies to deal with the sexist correctional environment are ignoring sexist comments, positive thinking, advocating for rights to supervisors, toning down femininity and increasing assertiveness, physical activity outside of work, professional behavioral health help, and self-medicating with substances (Burdett et al., 2018). Regardless of how women adjust to the male-dominated environment, females have continued to face structural violence established by the patriarchal system: if they do well on the job they are stigmatized and labeled abnormal or lesbians, but if they appear too weak or feminine, they may be viewed as unable to do their job well (Britton, 1997; J. Butler, 1999; Cohn, 1993; Confortini, 2006).

© 1968/Shutterstock.com

Overall, it is clear that "women's experiences as correctional officers indicate that they are still viewed as inferior in ways grounded in biological determinism and gendered patriarchal stereotypes" (Burdett, Gouliquer, & Poulin, 2018, p. 343). In other words, women are perceived as not capable due to female stereotypes, and therefore unable to hold the title and duties of a correctional officer. Tokenism of female officers and apparent 'neutral' organizational practices and procedures need to be re-evaluated and reformed by the American correctional system to avoid sexist environmental conditions, and the legitimation and maintenance of a patriarchal society (J. Butler, 1999; Jurik, 1985).

Conclusion

Patriarchy has deeply engrained gender norms into society and has narrowed the scope of attention to how people *perform* a gender instead of valuing people simply for *who* they are. Over time, women have started to dismiss and reject traditional sexist roles and have taken on 'male-dominated' roles with courage. Unfortunately, within the correctional system, our feminist curiosity (Enloe, 2014) falls short and we still do not know enough about what female officers face inside those walls. In order to fully understand their plight, and to jumpstart policy and procedural changes, it is paramount to address their concerns. One, continue to do research on this group of women (considering that most of our current knowledge dates back to 1980s studies) and two, include an intersectional approach to inform change regarding non-white female officers and their particular experiences. In order to shatter the status quo of our gendered society, it is not enough to bring to consciousness and squash the 'box' that establishes limits to females' capabilities, it is also imperative to maintain our feminist curiosity and shift away from a system that generates a sexist environment (Bourdieu, 2004; Enloe, 2014).

Discussion Questions:

1. Are women officers included in the correctional system under the pretenses of a patriarchal system that sees the value of women only when compared to men?

2. Where do female officers fit in the social space of the correctional system?

3. Why do female COs minimize their feminine behavior?

4. What is problematic about gender neutral trainings?

5. Why is it more arduous for a female CO to be promoted than a male CO?

References

Alvi, S., Schwartz, M., D., DeKeseredy, W., S., & Maume, M., O. (2001). Women's fear of crime in Canadian public housing. *Violence Against Women, 7*(6), 638–661. https://doi.org/10.1177/10778010122182640

Armstrong, G. S., & Griffin, M. L. (2004). Does the job matter? Comparing correlates of stress among treatment and correctional staff in prisons. *Journal of Criminal Justice, 32*(6), 577–592. https://doi.org/10.1016/j.jcrimjus.2004.08.007

Beijersbergen, K. A., Dirkzwager, A. J. E., Molleman, T., van der Laan, P. H., & Nieuwbeerta, P. (2015). Procedural justice in prison: The importance of staff characteristics. *International Journal of Offender Therapy and Comparative Criminology, 59*(4), 337–358. https://doi.org/10.1177/0306624X13512767

Blackburn, A. G., Fowler, S. K., Mullings, J. L., & Marquart, J. W. (2011). When boundaries are broken: Inmate perceptions of correctional staff boundary violations. *Deviant Behavior, 32*(4), 351–378. https://doi.org/10.1080/01639621003748837

Bourdieu, P. (2004). Gender and Symbolic Violence. In N. Scheper-Hughes & P. Bourgois (Eds.), *Violence in War and Peace: An Anthology* (pp. 339–342). Malden, MA: Blackwell Publishing.

Brasch, S. (2017). *Inmates headed for court inside the Pueblo County Jail* [photo]. Retrieved from URL: https://www.cpr.org/news/story/pueblo-s-overcrowded-jail-is-the-worst-of-a-statewide-problem

Britton, D. M. (1997). Perceptions of the work environment among correctional officers: Do race and sex matter? *. *Criminology, 35*(1), 85–106. https://doi.org/10.1111/j.1745-9125.1997.tb00871.x

Brough, P., & Williams, J. (2007). Managing occupational stress in a high-risk industry: Measuring the job demands of correctional officers. *Criminal Justice and Behavior, 34*(4), 555–567. https://doi.org/10.1177/0093854806294147

Burdett, F., Gouliquer, L., & Poulin, C. (2018). Culture of corrections: The experiences of women correctional officers. *Feminist Criminology, 13*(3), 329–349. https://doi.org/10.1177/1557085118767974

Butler, D., Tasca, M., Zhang, Y., & Carpenter, C. (2019). A systematic and meta-analytic review of the literature on correctional officers: Identifying new avenues for research. *Journal of Criminal Justice, 60*, 84–92. https://doi.org/10.1016/j.jcrimjus.2018.12.002

Butler, J. (1999). *Gender trouble: feminism and the subversion of identity.* New York: Routledge.

Caster, P. (2013). *Lewis County Corrections Officer Ona Felker completes her hourly checkup of one of the pods at the Lewis County Jail on Monday morning in Chehalis* [photo]. Retrieved from URL: http://www.chronline.com/news/lewis-county-jail-in-need-of-female-corrections-officers/article_3b3718e8-3040-11e3-8a34-001a4bcf887a.html

Castle, T. L., & Martin, J. S. (2006). Occupational hazard: Predictors of stress among jail correctional officers. *American Journal of Criminal Justice, 31*(1), 65–80. https://doi.org/10.1007/BF02885685

Cheeseman, K., Mulllings, J., & Marquart, J. W. (2001). *Inmate Perceptions of Security Staff Across Various Custody Levels. 5*(2), 41–48.

Cohn, C. (1993). War, wimps and women: Talking gender and thinking war. In *Gendering War Talk* (pp. 227–246). Princeton: Princeton University Press.

Confortini, C. C. (2006). Galtung, violence, and gender: The case for a peace studies/feminism alliance. *Peace & Change, 31*(3), 333–367. https://doi.org/10.1111/j.1468-0130.2006.00378.x

Day, K. (2001). Constructing masculinity and women's fear in public space in Irvine, California. *Gender, Place & Culture, 8*(2), 109–127. https://doi.org/10.1080/09663690120050742

Dial, K. C., Downey, R. A., & Goodlin, W. E. (2010). The job in the joint: The impact of generation and gender on work stress in prison. *Journal of Criminal Justice, 38*(4), 609–615. https://doi.org/10.1016/j.jcrimjus.2010.04.033

Durkheim, E. (1951). *Suicide.* New York: Free Press.

Enloe, C. (2014). *Bananas, Beaches and Bases: Making Feminist Sense of International Politics.* Univ of California Press.

Farkas, M. A. (2000). A typology of correctional officers. *International Journal of Offender Therapy and Comparative Criminology, 44*(4), 431–449. https://doi.org/10.1177/0306624X00444003

Gordon, J., & Baker, T. (2017). Examining correctional officers' fear of victimization by inmates: The influence of fear facilitators and fear inhibitors. *Criminal Justice Policy Review, 28*(5), 462–487. https://doi.org/10.1177/0887403415589630

Gordon, J., Proulx, B., & Grant, P. H. (2013). Trepidation among the "keepers": Gendered perceptions of fear and risk of victimization among corrections officers. *American Journal of Criminal Justice*, *38*(2), 245–265. https://doi.org/10.1007/s12103-012-9167-1

Gordon, M. S. (2006). Correctional officer control ideology: Implications for understanding a system. *Criminal Justice Studies*, *19*(3), 225–239. https://doi.org/10.1080/14786010600764526

Griffin, M. L. (2006). Gender and stress: A comparative assessment of sources of stress among correctional officers. *Journal of Contemporary Criminal Justice*, *22*(1), 5–25. https://doi.org/10.1177/1043986205285054

Griffin, M. L., Armstrong, G. S., & Hepburn, J. R. (2005). Correctional officers' perceptions of equitable treatment in the masculinized prison environment. *Criminal Justice Review*, *30*(2), 189–206. https://doi.org/10.1177/0734016805284306

Hauck, N. (2016). *Attacks on Wisconsin Corrections Officers Reach Crisis Level* [photo]. Retrieved from URL: https://www.afscme.org/now/attacks-on-wisconsin-corrections-officers-reach-crisis-level

Hooks, bell. (2014). *Feminism is for Everybody: Passionate Politics*. New York: Routledge.

Jurik, N. C. (1985). An officer and a lady: Organizational barriers to women working as correctional officers in men's prisons. *Social Problems*, *32*(4), 375–388. https://doi.org/10.2307/800759

Kaplan, C, & Grewal, I. (2006). Social and historical constructions of gender. In Caren Kaplan & I. Grewal (Eds.), *An Introduction to Women's Studies: Gender in a Transnational World* (pp. 1–5). McGraw-Hill Humanities/Social Sciences/Languages.

Lambert, E. G., Hogan, N. L., & Griffin, M. L. (2007). The impact of distributive and procedural justice on correctional staff job stress, job satisfaction, and organizational commitment. *Journal of Criminal Justice*, *35*(6), 644–656. https://doi.org/10.1016/j.jcrimjus.2007.09.001

Lambert, E. G., Kim, B., Keena, L. D., & Cheeseman, K. (2017). Testing a gendered models of job satisfaction and work stress among correctional officers. *Journal of Crime and Justice*, *40*(2), 188–203. https://doi.org/10.1080/0735648X.2015.1074092

Management & Training Corporation Institute. (2008). *Women Professionals in Corrections: A Growing Asset*. Retrieved from https://www.mtctrains.com/wp-content/uploads/2017/06/Women-Professionals-in-Corrections-A-Growing-Asset.pdf

Martin, P., & Barnard, A. (2013). The experience of women in male-dominated occupations: A constructivist grounded theory inquiry. *SA Journal of Industrial Psychology*, *39*(2), 01–12.

Merriman, J. (Freelance photographer). (2010) *Correction Officers* [photo]. Retrieved from URL: http://www.justinmerriman.com/photographyblog/2010/08/correction-officers.html

Oza, N. (2017). *A homemade aerial drone carrying drugs and cell phones flew over Arizona State Prison Complex-Lewis in Buckeye crashed in a security zone inaccessible to inmates* [photo]. Retrieved from URL: https://www.azcentral.com/story/news/local/southwest-valley/2017/11/16/drone-carrying-drugs-phones-crashes-buckeye-prison-yard/870429001/

Pascoe, C. J. (2011). *Dude, You're a Fag: Masculinity and Sexuality in High School*. University of California Press.

Prokos, A., & Padavic, I. (2002). 'There oughtta be a law against bitches': Masculinity lessons in police academy training. *Gender, Work & Organization*, 9(4), 439–459. https://doi.org/10.1111/1468-0432.00168

Scheper-Hughes, N., & Bourgois, P. (2004). Introduction. In *Violence in War and Peace* (pp. 1–32). Malden, MA: Blackwell Publishers.

Seklecki, R., & Paynich, R. (2007). A national survey of female police officers: An overview of findings. *Police Practice and Research*, 8(1), 17–30. https://doi.org/10.1080/15614260701217941

Sykes, G. M. (1958). *The Society of Captives: A Study of a Maximum Security Prison*. Princeton University Press.

The Journal.ie (2018) *What is it like to be a female prison officer?* [screenshot] Retrieved from URL: https://www.youtube.com/watch?v=bjHZC-g5TxE

Veroff, V. B. (1995). *An Integration of Friendship and Social Support: Relationships with Adjustment in College Students*. Doctoral dissertation. Concordia University.

Wells, T., Colbert, S., & Slate, R. N. (2006). Gender matters: Differences in state probation officer stress. *Journal of Contemporary Criminal Justice*, 22(1), 63–79. https://doi.org/10.1177/1043986205285381

West, C., & Zimmerman, D. H. (1987). Doing gender. *Gender & Society*, 1(2), 125–151. https://doi.org/10.1177/0891243287001002002

Whilden, J. (2018) *I'm the Talking Ass* [photo]. Retrieved from URL: https://www.imdb.com/title/tt7435422/mediaviewer/rm1143948544

Williams, J. C. (2013). *In the new Suffolk County Correctional Facility in Yaphank, one correction officer mans this entire pod* [photo]. Retrieved from URL: https://www.newsday.com/long-island/suffolk/new-yaphank-jail-wing-stirs-rave-concerns-1.5244441

CHAPTER 13

#ThemToo: Examining Sexual Harassment among Female Correctional Officers

TaLisa J. Carter, Ph.D. | American University
Chrysanthi Leon, Ph.D. | University of Delaware

Contributed by TaLisa J. Carter and Chrysanthi Leon. Copyright © Kendall Hunt Publishing Company.

Overview

The #MeToo movement has drawn attention to the pervasive nature of sexual harassment in various aspects of society. In corrections, the sexual harassment of incarcerated populations has received increasing scholarly attention. The sexual harassment of correctional staff, however, is far less discussed. Considering the documented differential experiences of female correctional officers and the masculine nature of correctional facilities, it is surprising the sexual harassment faced by female staff is largely overlooked. This chapter addresses this gap in scholarship by bridging two bodies of research: criminal justice and sociolegal literature. Sociolegal and criminal justice scholarship are then integrated to investigate ways correctional officers navigate sexual harassment on-the-job. As women who have spent time in correctional facilities in different roles: teacher, researcher, consultant and correctional officer, we also fuse our prison experiences to inform these connections. We conclude with the policy and translational implications of considering correctional employees, law enforcement personnel, and other sexual harassment survivors who may be less visible due to their occupations as members of the #MeToo movement.

Chapter Outcomes

- Students will understand how gender relates to correctional employment.
- Students will understand how female correctional officers can experience sexual harassment.
- Students will be introduced to the research which challenges our assumptions about when law will be useful to solve problems like sexual harassment.
- Students will be able to reflect on how workplace dynamics operate in correctional settings.

Introduction

To help women and girls of color who experienced sexual violence, Tarana Burke, a survivor of sexual violence, coined the phrase "Me Too" in 2006 (C. A. Johnson & Hawbaker, 2018). Since that time, "Me Too" transformed into an international movement of solidarity for victims of sexual harassment, violence, and inappropriate behavior. Around the world, individuals self-identify as victims of sexual misconduct with #MeToo hashtags on social media in their native tongue including, #BalanceTonPorc (French), #YoTambien (Spanish), and #Ana_kaman (Arabic) (Zacharek, Dockterman, & Edwards, 2017). The #MeToo community is incredibly diverse, spanning age, sex, race/ethnicity, sexuality, social class, and occupation. Entertainers, medical professionals, educators, nuns, support staff for politicians and others have all identified as members of the #MeToo community in search of social change and justice for sexual misconduct that plagues society.[1]

Correctional officers are survivors of inappropriate sexual behavior, sexual harassment and sexual violence. However, mainstream society has yet to acknowledge correctional officers as members of the #MeToo community. Charged with ensuring the safety and security of carceral facilities, correctional officers face challenges every day yet remain largely invisible to the public. These obstacles can be heightened for female correctional officers who work in an environment dominated by men.

In short, correctional officers—particularly female officers—need the same systems of social support, change and justice which the #MeToo movement invokes. We need to consider #ThemToo. This chapter examines the sexual harassment of female correctional officers through criminological and sociolegal literature. While scholarship informs our understanding of key issues, lived experience offers insights as well. Having worked as a correctional officer, the first author integrates her personal experiences to illustrate the sexual harassment faced by female correctional officers.[2]

Corrections & Gender

In 1882 the United States appointed the first female correctional matron in the state of Maryland (Crank, 2015). Matron was the term for female correctional professionals that preceded officers. Correctional matrons were hired to supervise female inmates in response to complaints of physical and sexual abuse by male guards. Furthermore, matrons instructed their charges on how to perform domestic work and led bible study (Crank, 2015). In the nearly 200 years since the first matron was hired, female correctional officers have gained equity in title, but not in number. The gender disparity among correctional professionals is significant. In 2018, only 29.6% of correctional officers, bailiffs and jailers were female (BLS, 2019). Nearly 93% of the correctional population housed in state and federal facilities were male (BOP, 2019), illustrated in Figure 1. That is, female correctional officers also supervise a majority of the male population. In a profession that is known for a wealth of challenges including high levels of stress, burnout, difficulties with work-life balance, and elevated risk of assault (Crawley, 2004; Ferdik & Smith, 2017; Thompson & Prottas, 2006), we must improve corrections for all employees regardless of identity. However, the suitability of women to serve as correctional officers remains debated.

Critics question the role and impact of female officers in prison (Martin & Jurik, 2006). Female officers may receive simpler or less physical assignments such as writing reports or processing incoming detainees because of doubts about ability (Britton, 2006). This restriction on task assignment reduces

---

[1] The Equal Employment Opportunity Commission (EEOC) is the federal agency that oversees workplace discrimination. In defining "sexual harassment" they explain: it is unlawful to harass a person (an applicant or employee) because of that person's sex. Harassment can include "sexual harassment" or unwelcome sexual advances, requests for sexual favors, and other verbal or physical harassment of a sexual nature. Harassment does not have to be of a sexual nature, however, and can include offensive remarks about a person's sex. For example, it is illegal to harass a woman by making offensive comments about women in general. Both the victim and the harasser can be either a woman or a man, and the victim and harasser can be the same sex. Although the law doesn't prohibit simple teasing, offhand comments, or isolated incidents that are not very serious, harassment is illegal when it is so frequent or severe that it creates a hostile or offensive work environment or when it results in an adverse employment decision (such as the victim being fired or demoted). The harasser can be the victim's supervisor, a supervisor in another area, a co-worker, or someone who is not an employee of the employer, such as a client or customer.
This definition is helpful for its clarity, but as we will discuss, how it manifests in practice and how workers respond is much more complex.
[2] These experiences are recounted with the direct and explicit language that is commonplace in many workplaces, including corrections.

Figure 1

Statistics from BOP, 5/18/2019

Inmate Gender

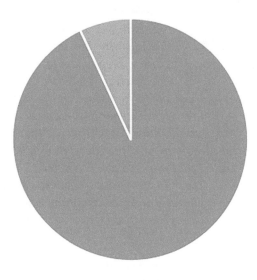

■ Male   ■ Female

opportunities for women to advance in their profession; the institution praises physical and more complex tasks more often than their respective counterparts. Additionally, correctional officers who have positive informal relationships with their supervisors and colleagues are in better positions for career advancement and have higher levels of job satisfaction (Britton, 2006). Essentially, in corrections it isn't just *what you know* but also *who you know*. Correctional institutions are "good old boy" systems, or informal networks that promote career advancement by favoring males and prioritizing traditionally masculine characteristics (Britton, 2006). In the good old boy system, female correctional officers are further hindered from career advancement because they often do not have access to the same informal relationships that are forged between their male peers.

In short, working in corrections is demanding regardless of gender. However, female correctional officers face unique obstacles on the job. Males outnumber them both in terms of peers and those they supervise. The formal and informal arrangements to advance in corrections creates a dynamic for female officers in which their male colleagues and supervisors are more likely to be in positions of power. Power dynamics may play a major role in sexual harassment at the workplace. The U.S. Equal Employment Opportunity Commission defines sexual harassment as "unwelcome sexual advances, requests for sexual favors, and other verbal or physical harassment of a sexual nature" (EEOC, 2019). Female correctional officers, therefore, may be at a higher risk for experiencing sexual harassment in carceral environments. In other words, existing formal and informal structures, such as assigned tasks and the good old boy network, create gendered-obstacles female correctional officers must contend with to be successful, including the sexual harassment that female correctional officers endure.

> *I saw most of the dick play in the Delta unit. It housed male inmates who were considered highest risk, so at least two officers were assigned there at a time. One worked in the central glassed-in booth, answering inmate buzzers through an intercom (a system they used to make requests and complaints) and maintaining logs*

© Michael Mong/Shutterstock.com

of visitors or other individuals entering or exiting the unit. The other worked in the wing itself and had face-to-face interaction with the men, primarily through their flaps—small rectangular openings with metal doors—and windows… The buzzer rang without ceasing…After a few shifts in Delta, a male officer finally explained to me why the intercom rang so constantly. "They keep buzzing because they're pleasing themselves to your voice," he said. I was dumbfounded. I was educated and had the highest score on the state exam of any cadet at that time. But training didn't prepare me for that moment. And I honestly didn't really get it. First off, gross. Second, how and why would that be a thing they want …? Reading the utter disbelief on my face, the officer proved his point by answering the next few buzzers. Repeat callers would ask, "Where's Carter?" and he'd reply, "She's out. It's me now." In less than 10 minutes, the buzzers all went silent. So, I eased off the intercom. I became self-conscious about my voice. When I did answer, I tried to sound strong and relay a no-nonsense attitude to the caller. But the masturbation was just beginning (Carter, 2018).

The first author (Dr. Carter) was assigned to a more challenging housing unit but given a less physically demanding task that had the least interaction with the detained. Although such a task is important to the functioning of the wing, these duties are unlikely to be formally commended by the institution due to the sheltered nature of the booth and minimal contact with detainees. As the only female in the wing, she was outnumbered by men in every respect, coworker and detainees. Although striving to do the job well, her naivete regarding male masturbation behind bars required reliance on a more experienced male colleague for guidance and institutional knowledge. Based on this newly acquired information, her approach to working in the booth changed, exemplifying how female officers strategize around sexual harassment and misconduct to do their jobs in a more efficient and effective way. It is possible that the detained buzzed frequently because as a new officer, Dr. Carter was not institutionalized. She was eager to do the job well without knowing how things worked. That is, she was not yet numb to or tired of prisoner grievances and other requests; Dr. Carter was willing to listen and find a middle ground.

Scholars repeatedly find that having excellent communication skills is a critical part of being a correctional officer (R. Johnson & Price, 1981); this is also evident in corrections training across the United States and Canada where communication skills are emphasized in 98% of programs (Anonymous, 2005). Although communication skills are valued, Dr. Carter's inexperience put her at increased risk for sexual harassment.

In sum, female correctional officers face unique conditions on-the-job that may put them at an elevated risk to experience sexual harassment. As Dr. Carter's professional experience highlights, female correctional officers are required to navigate these challenges and may rely on the guidance of male and/or more experienced colleagues to do so.

Inmate-on-Officer Sexual Harassment

Scholarship related to sexual assault and misconduct in carceral settings has increased dramatically since the implementation of the Prison Rape Elimination Act (PREA) in 2003. The goal of PREA is to eradicate instances of prisoner rape and sexual harassment within correctional facilities across the United

States by creating a culture of Zero Tolerance through data collection, rule enforcement, and training (BJA, 2019). As the definition implies, researchers and practitioners primarily apply and explore this law to protect the detained from abuse. It is vital to also apply these principles to the experiences of correctional staff. Literature on prison sexual misconduct focuses primarily on inmate-on-inmate assault and staff-on-inmate misconduct (Levan Miller, 2010; Medina, 2018; Struckman-Johnson & Struckman-Johnson, 2006).

© Andrey_Popov/Shutterstock.com

One day after lunch . . . we were busy tending to after-chow responsibilities, such as processing paperwork and visitors, and other daily tasks. The buzzer rang. The caller was in a cell directly across from the booth, a straight shot from our window to his. I glanced toward him. Hanging from his open flap was his dick. I clicked the intercom and told him to "Put that shit away." Then I called down to the floor officer to close the inmate's opening. I wrote the guy up, but all the while I was thinking: How the hell did I end up with this job? That was the first actual jack-off write-up for me—the first of many. At one point it got so bad that I whenever I saw an inmate masturbating, I would look away or pretend not to see it, so I didn't have to do all the paperwork. Besides, I soon realized that for some men housed in isolated segregation, the punishment they would get—another day or so in seg—was no deterrent for this kind of misconduct.

Dr. Carter's experience mirrors other female correctional officers. Recently, six current and former female correctional officers won a case for 2.5 million dollars after settling in a sexual harassment and discrimination case against 23 male guards in New Mexico (Terrell, 2018). Although the Corrections Department continued to deny the allegations, the settlement was reached in order to avoid a costly legal battle. The D.C. Department of Corrections settled a similar lawsuit for 8.5 million dollars in 1999 (Chandler, 2018). Even prior to training to become a correctional officer, women who are interested in this profession can find a range of information on the risk of sexual harassment online. Six of the top ten results from a Google search of the question "What's it like to be a female correctional officer?" discussed the sexual harassment female correctional officers face from inmates and peers and/or shared advice on how to avoid being inappropriately involved with inmates.[3]

Although there is a substantial amount of both experiential knowledge and litigation that demonstrate the risk of sexual harassment for female correctional officers, some people believe that female correctional officers should not complain but accept that sexual harassment is simply part of the territory.

- *Why would any female want to be a corrections officer around a bunch of male convicts?! They are certainly not going to be gentlemen!*

- *Didn't (you) figure that out BEFORE you took the job?*

---

[3] Google Search Terms "What's it like to be a female correctional officer" on May 14th, 2019. Results on file with the first author.

- *I personally don't think it's appropriate for women to be in that environment. It has nothing to do with them being able to handle themselves either...I don't think you can expect to go into that type of environment and not expect to be subjected to such events. It's the nature of the beast so to speak.*

After publishing her experiences, Dr. Carter received a variety of comments and messages, including those excerpted above.[4] Although anecdotal, they illustrate a predominant belief that correctional employment comes with inherent risk such as sexual misconduct, and that female officers can resign and find other employment if they cannot handle prison conditions. This perspective speaks to the complexities of women in male dominated professions, particularly correctional employment. The #MeToo Movement and its span across professions symbolizes societal intolerance for individuals in certain occupations to face sexual harassment. We argue that correctional professionals must be included in this conversation. Sexual harassment happens in prison, inmate-on-inmate, officer-on-inmate, officer-on-officer and, as discussed in this chapter, inmate-on-officer. Sociolegal literature sheds light on inmate-on-officer sexual harassment and societal perceptions of this issue.

Sociolegal Research on Sexual Harassment

Naming "Harassment" and Mobilizing the Law

The American approach to the protection of civil rights is a reactive one: instead of detailed rules and regulations as the best path to justice, the U.S. relies on individuals to litigate and force institutions to react. Twentieth century civil rights history highlights landmark legal cases that have changed policy, practice and social norms around our rights and liberties. However, critical legal theorists, drawing on the tradition of critical race scholars, challenge the assumption that the assertion of rights leads to substantive gains (Alexander-Floyd, 2010; Crenshaw, 1989). As Cheryl I. Harris explains, "The challenge for scholars of color in the academy . . .

© Mohd Shahrizan Hussin/Shutterstock.com

is to render the invisible visible and tangible, to move what is in the background to the foreground; to tell a different story that is neither known or familiar and indeed may be disturbing, annoying, and frightening. . . . The work of the scholar of color involves the task of exposing the jurisprudence that oppresses in order to work towards articulating a jurisprudence that resists subordination and empowers (Harris, 1992, 333)."

Other scholars question whether the backlash and retrenchment that follow landmark cases are worth the costs to individuals and social movements (Rosenberg, 1991). Rather than "real rights," these critiques draw attention to the "myth of rights" and call for more nuance in our interpretation and in our reform efforts (Feeley, 1992; McCann, 1992; Munger, 2004; Scheingold, 2010).

Sociolegal literature draws on these critiques and amplifies the struggles victims of civil rights violations face when trying to mobilize those rights through legal channels. Contrary to the assumption that Americans will typically use the law to address wrongs, empirical research shows that people often perceive that they are better off NOT invoking the law, and that this is particularly true for people who experience structural disadvantages like poverty, racism and sexism (Crenshaw, 1989; Munger, 2004).

---

[4] Comments were edited for grammar. De-identified comments on file with the author.

Bumiller emphasizes that " the link between economic, social, psychological, sexual, and legal roles creates an ethic of survival that precludes the protective role of law" (Bumiller, 1987, 423–424). As Bumiller and numerous scholars since have documented, people who experience discrimination weigh the costs and benefits of pursuing legal protection, and often find that the costs far outweigh the benefits. In addition, the relative power and privilege of victims matters in how and whether people mobilize the law.

© Zolnierek/Shutterstock.com

Scholars have also documented the range of strategies women in particular use to respond to workplace sexual harassment, which most often involves deciding not to pursue a formal complaint, sometimes because they know that grievance processes are better at protecting the organization than the individual. Detailing a range of women's experiences in addressing sexual harassment in the workplace, Marshall finds that "women's understanding of sexual harassment reflected the adversarial nature of the complaint process, shrinking to include only those behaviors they could prove" (Marshall, 2005, 114). Women also experienced negative consequences from reporting harassment, as "worse than witnessing inaction, women also found themselves to be targets of retaliatory action" (Marshall, 2005, 106).

Using the law to address discrimination requires naming experiences as wrong or as harassment or discrimination: but in many cases, women do not apply these labels (Marshall, 2005; Nielsen, 2000). This may be due to the normalization of highly-sexualized work environments (McGinley, 2006) or a gap between informal assumptions about what "counts" as harassment or abuse and what the law is designed to address. A number of scholars demonstrate that women report experiencing unwanted sexual attention but will not label it sexual harassment (Solomon & Williams, 1997; Vaux, 1993). Welsh et. al find that White women with full citizenship rights most easily identify with existing legal understandings of sexual harassment and believe they have the right to report their harassment (Welsh, Carr, MacQuarrie, & Huntley, 2006). For women of color and women without full citizenship rights, racialized sexual harassment[5] emerges as central in their harassment experience.[6] The authors argue that intersectional analyses are needed to understand women's harassment experiences and their ability to complain and seek legal recourse.

Altogether, empirical and critical perspectives make it clear that getting justice for workplace sexual harassment is far more complicated than just calling out the behavior or even of filing a complaint. How do we then reconcile an emerging awareness of the ways the correctional workplace allows sexual harassment with realistic suggestions for reform that are grounded in the experiences of officers?

---

[5] Welsh et. al. explain that the terms gendered racism or racialized sexual harassment used to describe the harassment of women of color focus on how sexual discrimination and race are intertwined. See also (Texeira, 2002)

[6] Further, Welsh et. al.'s robust sample allows them to specify that Black women with full citizenship rights question whether the term sexual harassment captures their experiences and Filipinas working as live-in caregivers on limited visas demonstrate how racism and lack of citizenship changes definitions of sexual harassment: their experiences of harassment combine elements of isolation due to their lack of citizenship, racialized sexual harassment, and abuse (Welsh, Carr, MacQuarrie, & Huntley, 2006).

Organizations and Sexual Harassment Policy

A significant body of sociolegal research has documented the ways in which organizations resist top-down efforts to change their practices (Edelman, Krieger, Eliason, Albiston, & Mellema, 2011; Edelman, Uggen, & Erlanger, 1999). Employers may adapt "law-like" processes or procedures to show that they are doing something to address claims of discrimination or sexual violence, such as providing information for employees that give definitions of prohibited conduct and that encourage reporting; they may also use numerical tallies of reported incidents as a way to show they take the issues seriously (Edelman et al., 1999; Grossman, 2003; Leon, 2015). In a related phenomenon, correctional institutions have demonstrated "compliant resistance" when ordered by judges to make changes, doing just enough to demonstrate compliance but neglecting to fully engage in systematic reform (Reiter, 2012) (although these have more commonly focused on inmates' rights and not on correctional workers). Reform is far more successful when leaders and front-line workers within the correctional institution participate in the reforms and truly "buy in" to changes (Reiter, 2016).

Studies of workplace sexual harassment have not focused on correctional environments, but some lessons learned by free world employers likely translate. Specifically, evidence points to some success in addressing sexual harassment in the workplace when training is provided (Grossman, 2003). Having policies in place that explain sexual harassment can shape whether people view behavior as actually "counting" as sexual harassment or otherwise problematic and worthy of redress. But the content of these policies matter: examining perceptions of sexual harassment through a factorial survey with a series of vignettes, Weinberg & Nielsen (2011) find that only strict workplace policies would lead ordinary people to view a scenario to qualify as "sexual harassment."

Implications & Recommendations

Throughout a wide range of workplace contexts and facing all kinds of troubling situations, research tells us that workers are often likely to "look away" as Dr. Carter discusses in her excerpt above. Importantly, this is not just an individual decision, but in fact is structured by the way organizations respond to "problems" of all kinds by creating bureaucratic burdens related to documentation (Sykes, 1958). Prisons in particular are called upon to fulfill so many complex and contradictory functions that officers by necessity cannot write up every infraction and must use their discretion to decide when it is "worth it" (Sykes, 1958). Combining this insight with the reality that female workers know their discrimination claims will rarely be successful (see Bumiller, 1987 and others mentioned in this chapter), we can locate *female correctional officers* at the intersection of several strands of research that explain why employment law and the workplace protections now in place will not be used or found adequate. What should organizations do to address sexual harassment in corrections? The research and our experience in correctional facilities all point to the need to shift towards a broader recognition of what counts as sexual harassment and to avoid top-down mandates.

Although some employers fear that providing training will increase sexual harassment claims (and therefore financial liability) (Grossman, 2003), there is general agreement in the value of putting more and better resources into quality training. We particularly commend "Mental Health in the Correctional System: Making Choices for Safety & Well-Being"—a free, online training curriculum for delivery to correctional officers made available through the University of South Carolina School of Social Work. The detailed training modules were created through an extensive process that included needs assessment interviews and focus groups, review of best practice literature, an advisory board of professionals who work with persons who are incarcerated, consultation with experts and persons who were formerly incarcerated, and pilot testing of content and delivery. Their current curriculum addresses officer stress but does not specifically address sexual harassment. Future efforts could create a case study and module specific to corrections' sexualized atmosphere and address Correctional Officer on Correctional Officer as well as Correctional Officer and inmate interactions.

As teachers, we look to our students for current insights into what may work. Some of our students indicate that new generations of officers are more open to discussing trauma and other mental health and well-being related aspects of their work. Our best hope may thus be generational change: as new officers bring their less-stigmatized views on well-being and help-seeking, officer culture may bend towards a healthier environment. The larger atmosphere around #MeToo may also be determinative; although it remains to be seen whether long-term change or backlash (or both) will result from the broader movement, and how this may or may not impact the lives of working people without the celebrity or resources of #MeToo.

While other scholars of sexual harassment policies call for legal incentives that would mandate sexual harassment training and procedures in order to avoid only superficial compliance (Grossman, 2003), our experience with correctional workplaces and the research on correctional reform contradicts a top-down approach. Instead, making resources available like the MHCS project, and empowering officers through professional organizations to lead education efforts, will likely result in more meaningful change.

In some cases, individual or class action lawsuits that document sexual harassment in correctional environments may be necessary to draw attention to truly recalcitrant institutions. But individuals cannot be expected to bear the high financial, emotional and other costs of litigation in order to achieve change. Celebrities involved in #MeToo have channeled some of their resources into a legal fund for ordinary working people; perhaps feminist or correctional organizations might dedicate specific funds for correctional officers. But in addition to the calculation of costs and benefits that all victims of discrimination must engage in, women in corrections may also worry that invoking the formal law might have unintended outcomes on women's access to employment. This concern is amplified by the existing good old boy network within correctional departments, in which informal relationships influence employment success. These informal relationships already exclude marginalized correctional officers (women, people of color, LGBTQ, etc.) and would be even more strained if combined with the label of a sexual harassment victim. If employers feel that hiring women or other minoritized groups in male facilities creates liability for future lawsuits, they may amplify biased hiring decisions that limit professional options for women in corrections and sacrifice the benefits of cross-gendered supervision of inmates.

Rather than burdening and further stigmatizing individuals, corrections could look to other professions that directly acknowledge the fact that their work exposes them to bodily functions and to racism, sexism, and harassment in the care of others, such as nursing and physical therapy (Doyle & Timonen, 2009; Nielsen, 2000). Training for correctional officers should include such frank acknowledgement as part of the formal curriculum rather than leaving it up to the informal mentoring of more seasoned officers. Supervisors can be encouraged to create a working environment which feels safe for employees to bring up their concerns and seek solutions together, without fear of retaliation or negative impacts on promotion. By acknowledging that correctional officers are worthy of our respect and support, we can improve their experiences on-the-job, as well as broader problems such as recruitment and retention. It is critical to include correctional employees, law enforcement personnel, and other sexual harassment survivors who may be less visible due to their occupations as members of the #MeToo movement, because sexual harassment impacts #ThemToo.

Compliant resistance   Prison Rape Elimination Act

Myth of rights   Sexual harassment

Discussion Questions:

1. When you think of a correctional officer, what image comes to your mind? Has this mental image changed since reading this chapter or other chapters in this book?

2. When you first heard about #MeToo, who did you think it applied to? Have your views changed?

3. In general, do you think people use the law too much or not enough? Are there particular circumstances in which you think people should use the law more?

4. Do you think female and male correctional officers contribute differently to the prison environment? In what ways?

5. Based on this chapter, what advice would you give to a friend entering the correctional field about what to expect in terms of sexual harassment? How would your friend's gender, race or other characteristics influence your advice?

6. How do you think correctional administrators should respond to sexual harassment allegations among employees? In what way, if any, should this response differ from the way sexual harassment is handled among inmates?

7. When do you think people should "police themselves" and when do you think outsiders should come in and insist on reforms?

8. What else should correctional professionals do to ensure that workplaces are welcoming to all?

References

Alexander-Floyd, N. G. (2010). Critical race Black feminism: A "Jurisprudence of Resistance" and the transformation of the academy. *Signs, 35*(4), 810–820. https://doi.org/10.1086/651036

Anonymous. (2005). Correctional officer education and training. *Corrections Compendium, 30*(3), 10–22.

BJA, B. of J. A. (2019). Prison Rape Elimination Act (PREA). *U.S. Department of Justice.* Retrieved from https://www.bja.gov/ProgramDetails.aspx?Program_ID=76

BLS, B. of L. S. (2019). Employed persons by detailed occupation, sex, race, and Hispanic or Latino ethnicity. Retrieved May 28, 2019, from https://www.bls.gov/cps/cpsaat11.htm

BOP, F. B. of P. (2019). BOP statistics: Inmate gender. Retrieved May 28, 2019, from https://www.bop.gov/about/statistics/statistics_inmate_gender.jsp

Britton, D. M. (2006). *At work in the iron cage: The prison as gendered organization.* New York: New York University Press.

Bumiller, K. (1987). Victims in the shadow of the law: A critique of the model of legal protection. *Signs, 12*(3), 421–439.

Carter, T. (2018). *Blinded bars: Race and social control among corrections employees* (ProQuest Dissertations Publishing). Retrieved from http://search.proquest.com/docview/2130942894/?pq-origsite=primo

Chandler, M. A. (2018). Women working in male prisons face harassment from inmates and co-workers. *The Washington Post.* Retrieved from https://www.washingtonpost.com/local/social-issues/women-working-in-male-prisons-face-harassment-from-inmates-and-co-workers/2018/01/27/21552cee-01f1-11e8-9d31-d72cf78dbeee_story.html?utm_term=.88db43764211

Crank, B. V. (2015). Corrections. *In Women in the criminal justice system: Tracking the journey of females and crime.* Boca Raton: CRC Press.

Crawley, E. (2004). *Doing prison work: The public and private lives of prison officers.* Willan.

Crenshaw, K. (1989). Demarginalizing the intersection of race and sex: A Black feminist critique of anti-discrimination doctrine, feminist theory and antiracist politics. *University of Chicago Legal Forum*, 139–167.

Doyle, M., & Timonen, V. (2009). The different faces of care work: understanding the experiences of the multi-cultural care workforce. *Ageing & Society, 29*(3), 337–350. https://doi.org/10.1017/S0144686X08007708

Edelman, L. B., Krieger, L. H., Eliason, S. R., Albiston, C. R., & Mellema, V. (2011). When organizations rule: Judicial deference to institutionalized employment structures. *American Journal of Sociology, 117*(3), 888–954. https://doi.org/10.1086/661984

Edelman, L. B., Uggen, C., & Erlanger, H. S. (1999). The endogeneity of legal regulation: Grievance procedures as rational myth. *American Journal of Sociology, 105*(2), 406–454. https://doi.org/10.1086/210316

EEOC. (2019). Sexual Harassment. Retrieved May 27, 2019, from https://www.eeoc.gov/laws/types/sexual_harassment.cfm

Feeley, M. M. (1992). Hollow hopes, flypaper, and metaphors symposium: The supreme court and social change. *Law and Social Inquiry, 17,* 745–760.

Ferdik, & Smith, H. (2017). Correctional officer safety and wellness literature synthesis. *Washington, DC: U.S. Department of Justice, Office of Justice Programs, National Institute of Justice.*

Grossman, J. L. (2003). The culture of compliance: The final triumph of form over substance in sexual harassment law. *Harvard Women's Law Journal, 26,* 3.

Harris, C. (1992). Law professors of color and the academy: Of poets and kings. *Chicago-Kent Law Review, 68*(1), 331.

Johnson, C. A., & Hawbaker, K. T. (2018). Me too: A timeline of events. *Chicago Tribune.*

Johnson, R., & Price, S. (1981). The complete correctional officer: Human service and the human environment of prison. *Criminal Justice and Behavior, 8*(3), 343–373. https://doi.org/10.1177/009385488100800307

Leon, C. S. (2015). Law, mansplainin', and myth accommodation in campus sexual assault reform. *University of Kansas Law Review, 64,* 987.

Levan Miller, K. (2010). The darkest figure of crime: Perceptions of reasons for male inmates to not report sexual assault. *Justice Quarterly, 27*(5), 692–712. https://doi.org/10.1080/07418820903292284

Marshall, A.-M. (2005). Idle rights: Employees' rights consciousness and the construction of sexual harassment policies. *Law & Society Review, 39*(1), 83–124. https://doi.org/10.1111/j.0023-9216.2005.00078.x

Martin, S. E., & Jurik, N. C. (2006). *Doing justice, doing gender: Women in legal and criminal justice occupations.* SAGE.

McCann, M. W. (1992). Reform litigation on trial symposium: The supreme court and social change. *Law and Social Inquiry, 17,* 715–744.

McGinley, A. C. (2006). Harassment of sex(y) workers: Applying title VII to sexualized industries symposium: Sex for sale. *Yale Journal of Law and Feminism, 18,* 65–108.

Medina, S. (2018). Sexual abuse of juveniles in correctional facilities: A violation of the prison rape elimination act. *The American University Journal of Gender, Social Policy & the Law, 26*(3), 947–971.

Munger, F. (2004). Rights in the shadow of class: Poverty, welfare, and the law. In *The Blackwell companion to law and society* (p. 330). Malden, MA: Blackwell Pub.

Nielsen, L. B. (2000). Situating legal conciousness: Experiences and attitudes of ordinary citizens about law and street harassment. *Law & Society Review, 34,* 1055–1090.

Reiter, K. (2016). *23/7: Pelican Bay Prison and the Rise of Long-term Solitary Confinement.* Yale University Press.

Reiter, K. A. (2012). The most restrictive alternative: A litigation history of solitary confinement in U.S. prisons, 1960?2006. In *Studies in Law, Politics and Society: Vol. 57. Studies in Law, Politics, and Society* (Vol. 57, pp. 71–124). https://doi.org/10.1108/S1059-4337(2012)0000057006

Rosenberg, G. N. (1991). *The hollow hope: can courts bring about social change?* Chicago: University of Chicago.

Scheingold, S. A. (2010). *The Politics of Rights: Lawyers, Public Policy, and Political Change.* University of Michigan Press.

Solomon, D. H., & Williams, M. L. M. (1997). Perceptions of social-sexual communication at work: The effects of message, situation, and observer characteristics on judgments of sexual harassment. *Journal of Applied Communication Research, 25*(3), 196–216. https://doi.org/10.1080/00909889709365476

Struckman-Johnson, C., & Struckman-Johnson, D. (2006). A comparison of sexual coercion experiences reported by men and women in prison. *Journal of Interpersonal Violence, 21*(12), 1591–1615. https://doi.org/10.1177/0886260506294240

Sykes, G. M. (1958). *The Society of Captives: A Study of a Maximum Security Prison.* Princeton University Press.

Terrell, S. (2018). NM settles female COs' sexual harassment case for 2.5M. *CorrectionsOne.Com.* Retrieved from https://www.correctionsone.com/ethics/articles/480071187-NM-settles-female-COs-sexual-harassment-case-for-2-5M/

Texeira, M. T. (2002). "Who protects and serves me?": A case study of sexual harassment of African American women in one U.S. law enforcement agency. *Gender & Society, 16*(4), 524–545. https://doi.org/10.1177/0891243202016004007

Thompson, C. A., & Prottas, D. J. (2006). Relationships among organizational family support, job autonomy, perceived control, and employee well-being. *Journal of Occupational Health Psychology, 11*(1), 100–118. https://doi.org/10.1037/1076-8998.10.4.100

Vaux, A. (1993). Paradigmatic assumptions in sexual harassment research: Being guided without being misled. *Journal of Vocational Behavior, 42*(1), 116–135. https://doi.org/10.1006/jvbe.1993.1008

Weinberg, J. D., & Nielsen, L. B. (2011). Examining empathy: Discrimination, experience, and judicial decisionmaking. *Southern California Law Review, 85*, 313.

Welsh, S., Carr, J., MacQuarrie, B., & Huntley, A. (2006). "I'm not thinking of it as sexual harassment": Understanding harassment across race and citizenship. *Gender & Society, 20*(1), 87–107. https://doi.org/10.1177/0891243205282785

Zacharek, S., Dockterman, E., & Edwards, H. S. (2017). The silence breakers. *Time Magazine.*

Web Links

- https://www.themarshallproject.org/2018/02/08/
  my-sexual-harassers-were-behind-bars-i-was-their-guard

- http://cmhtraining.sc.edu/

- https://nwlc.org/times-up-legal-defense-fund/

- https://metoomvmt.org/

Acknowledgements

The authors wish to thank the many collaborators who have supported our personal and professional paths and shaped our analysis, including the colleagues and students we have worked with in correctional and university settings, including Aneesa Baboolal and Emily George. Additionally, we appreciate support from Vice and The Marshall Project.

CHAPTER 14

Women, Criminal Justice Professionals, and Leadership Styles

Leon T. Geter | *Benedict College*

Learning Outcomes

After engaging this chapter, you will be able to:

- Understand the challenges women as criminal justice professionals face as leaders.
- Recognize various types of leadership styles.
- Explain the components of full-range leadership.
- Describe how leadership style contribute to leadership effectiveness in criminal justice.
- Explain the influences of leadership style on follower behavior and performance.
- Identify selected impacts of full-range leadership on organizational performance and employee behavior.
- Summarize the strengths and weaknesses of women's leadership styles impact on outcomes.

Overview

The purpose of this chapter is to explore the relationship between women criminal justice professionals and leadership styles in relation to organizational mission, goals, and performance outcomes, within a criminal justice construct. This chapter is important because of the collective body of information it provides to criminal justice students, educators, policymakers, researchers, professionals, practitioners, and society into the role of women and how leadership styles play a role in relation to successful organizational outcomes. In addition, it is important to gain a precise understanding of what leadership styles are most effective for criminal justice professionals and the field.

This chapter sets forth the hypothesis that transformational women leaders in criminal justice achieve more positive outcomes than men through the motivation of others, development of a shared vision, increased worker commitment and inspiration toward the achievement of common organizational goals. At its core, leadership is about influencing others in a given situation (Cordner, Scarborough, & Sheenan, 2004). Based on a broad body of research and experiences, history has revealed that men and women leadership styles do differ in measurable ways. Women are more naturally drawn to care about the overall well-being of others and have an instinctive desire to connect on a personal level when compared to men in most instances (Science-People). Research found that female leaders are more than likely less hierarchical than men in most leadership circumstances, more good-natured, and exhibits greater degrees of authentic concern for others (Eagly & Johannesen-Schmidt, 2001). A University of San Diego study (2019) found that women possess professional qualities often sought by leadership in the criminal justice field. Eagly et al. (2001) asserted that women more likely than men display a relational and self-governing pattern of leadership style, while men often display an autocratic style of leadership when engaging subordinates within an organizational situation.

Criminal Justice System

The United States Criminal Justice System comprises all law enforcement, courts, corrections, and public policy institutions on local, state, and a national level that facilitate the justice system for the nation. In 2014, the annual arrest rates in the United States were 11,207,143, which included all offenses (Synder, Cooper, & Mulako-Wangota, 2019) and reflects an active criminal justice system. Whereas, each arrest case must be handled by one of the 2,300 prosecutor officers throughout the country. In 2016, there were an estimated 6,613,500 individuals under some form of correctional supervision in the United States (Kaeble & Cowhig, 2016). Although, the overall prison population did experience a slight decrease from 2015 to 2016, the overall correctional populate unfortunately remains relatively high. On an annual basis, 44% of released prisoners were re-arrested after one year, while 34% of released prisoners were re-arrested within three years after being released (Bureau of Justice Statistics Press Release, 2018). The available data presents a large volume of criminality and justice administration needs that must be mitigated across the criminal justice continuum to ensure a healthier system with high-quality public safety for all.

Leadership

Leadership is a practice in which an individual personally influences another person or a broader group in-order to achieve a mutual aim based on a clearly articulated vision (Burns, 1978; Northouse, 2019; Geter, 2010). Leadership is a progression of behaviors that result in a positive or negative action. A leader is needed to ensure that a sought-after goal is achieved whether within an individual or a team construct. Leadership will have a direct impact on an organization's performance, workforce commitment, and effective outcome. Basically, successful leaders ensure that things get done right. The first role of a respectable leader, in most cases, is to effectively communicate and to describe the vision for the group, while inspiring individuals toward the realization of superior goals (Bennis, 1988).

Leaders habitually exhibit qualities such as self-assurance, determination, and an elevated level of interpersonal skills that are formed early in one's life-course and subsequently influence followers (Conger, 2004; Geter, 2010). Leaders who are trustworthy, honest, and exhibit compassion for the well-being of others will more likely develop a better relationship with followers in most instances (Geter, 2010) and produce superior outcomes and performance within an organizational setting. However, there is a measurable difference between leaders and effective leaders. From a practical and theoretical perspective, leaders may or may not get positive things accomplished, while an effective leader will more than likely inspire followers to be more ethical than is natural for them during the process of elevated goal attainment.

CASE STUDY: LEADERSHIP WITH SUBSTANCE

A former director of prisons learned good leadership skills by observing others. He would ask himself, 'What is good; what is bad; what do I want to put in my bag?'

One leader he personally observed was Colin Powell, Gen (Ret). The director considered Powell a level 5 leader on John Maxwell's scale (people follow a level 5 leader because of who they are and what they represent, not because they have to (level 1), because they want to (level 2), because of what the leader has done for the organization (level 3), or because of what the leader has done for them (level 4). 'Powell was cool, calm, and collected and when something was not going according to plan, he would ask subordinates for their input instead of blaming someone else. He was different than other military leaders who made proclamations without getting input. Level 5 leaders are hard to find. When you do, people flock to them.'

The director carried through on Powell's philosophy when he faced a prison incident. He did not believe in 'beating up' on people when mistakes happened. Instead he would ask questions such as, 'What systems do we have in place to prevent this?' Were they applied? What needs to be changed?'

He concluded, 'Corrections is the ultimate people business. If you take care of people, everything around you fall into place'

Source: Cebula, N., Craig, E., Eggers, J., Fajardo, M. D., Gray, J., and Lantz, T. (2012). Achieving performance excellence: The influence of leadership on organizational performance. Washington, DC: U.S. Department of Justice, National Institute of Corrections. As presented in Maxwell, J. C. 2011. The 5 Levels of Leadership. New York: Center Street.

Leadership Styles Matter

Leadership, but moreover leadership styles, play a major role in organizational performance and outcomes. How a leader treats and influences a follower or subordinate is a major factor in evaluating the style of leadership exhibited by the leader in the first instance. The leader sets the expectation, presents the attitude, and value-system needed for high performance.

From a leadership style construct, this chapter presents that transformational leadership and transactional leadership are the better forms of leadership styles that individuals should aspire to exhibit. A solid body of research has established that female leaders are more often transformational in temperament in comparison to male leaders (Eagly & Johannesen-Schmidt, 2001). While on the other-hand, men often exhibit a transactional or an active and passive management by exception style of leader (2001), that is often less product in inspiration and positive goal attainment in comparison to a transformational leadership style. Moreover, men time and again present more of a laissez-faire style of leadership compared to women (2001). Transformational women leaders in the field of criminal justice habitually achieve positive outcomes through the motivation of others, development of a shared vision, increased worker commitment, and inspiration for the achievement of common organizational goals.

At its core, leadership is about power, authority, and the power to influence others and organizations toward a common aim.

Born or Made Leaders

Like the chicken and the egg conundrum, questions of whether leaders are made or born have filled volumes of literature and debates. Today, the deliberations continue to be vigorously argued by scholars and laymen alike. Just as often, on any given day, one could hear a law enforce commissioner re-count a story of how he or she led a little league team to a local championship, or how he or she started a successful home business during their teens. This law enforcement commissioner would tell these and other stories to support the assumption that he or she was a born or natural leader. While another law enforcement commissioner would tell illustrative stories of how he or she took the initiative to lead, which exhibited them to be a self-made leader based on life-course experiences. Which begs the question, are leaders born or made? Conger (2004) argued that leaders are both: born and made. There are many factors that make one an effective leader that include, but not limited to, hereditary, underlying personality, talent, skills, desire, determination, and life-course experiences. Leadership is not regulated to trait or process but is a combination of trait and process for the most part (Dunst, Bruder, Hamby, Howse, & Wilkie, 2018).

It has been well established that women are just as talented as men, but obstacles to opportunities for women in many industries still exist (Pew Research Center, 2015). From the athletic field to the corporate boardroom, women must always seem to prove themselves in direct comparison to men in most instances. In relation to traits, a Pew Research Center study (2015) found that women and men are more than likely equal when it comes to core leadership characteristics, such as aptitude and ingenuity, which are essential factors for effectiveness. In addition, research has established that in most measured instances, women are more naturally compassionate in comparison to men, which is a core feature of a transformational leadership style.

Gender and Leadership

The gender of a leader is often argued to make a measurable difference in organizational outcomes. As such, there are various gender-based stereotypes that result in various expectations in leadership roles for men and women (Padgett, Caldwell, & Embry). However, stereotypes do not hold true to form in most occasions. Discrimination and sexism remain major impediments for women and other minorities in the workforce, where hitting the preferable glass-ceiling is a daily reality for many women. Despite the challenges, it is well established that women do make remarkable leaders for an abundance of measurable reasons.

Effectiveness

An effective leader ensures that a program's mission, goals, or objectives are realized. Effective leaders ensure that barriers to successful communications within a program setting are mitigated. Effective leaders exhibit genuine concern for others in the process of goal attainment (Dunst et al., 2018). This indicates the importance to having a leader who is effective in vision, inspiration, attitude, and behavior. Effective leaders give subordinates and others hope for a better future within a program environment. An effective leader works vigorous to ensure that goals and objectives are met in an efficient and effective manner (Northouse, 2019), while at the same time inspiring others based on a mutual aim.

The most important factors for a criminal justice leader's success is sound decision-making abilities with the authority, power, and vision to effect organizational change. Effective leaders make sound decisions to the betterment of the group (Maciariello, 2008). Therefore, within an organization, a leader must take care to make sound decisions at every level: systems, human capital; strategic planning, engagement of subordinates, mission, goals, and movement toward an achievable vision of the future (Geter, 2010). An organization that fails to have self-control of strategy and decision-making from the leader will more than likely end up in an organizational crisis (Geter, 2010).

Qualities and Traits

Qualities of Effective Leaders include, but aren't limited to honesty, high intelligence, strong commitment to a task, flexible, integrity, inspirational, high energy levels, strong internal locus of control, self-confidence, and emotional maturity. In addition, effective leaders should be courageous, energetic, adaptable, resolute, and flexible within and organizational setting (Simon and Stautzenback, 2003). Effective leaders most often have the characteristics of being highly intelligent, self-assured, and exhibit a genuine willingness to take initiative (Rowley, 1997).

Whether leading another individual, a high impact team, and or a nation state, the following five competencies are central for any leader to be effective and successful toward goal attainment. First, a leader must be willing to fail in the face of opportunity and uncertainty. Failure is just another learner opportunity (Dunst et al., 2018). Second, a leader must have the courage to battle for what is right, good, and moral. A true leader champions a cause for the greater good (2018). Third, a leader must have a genuine compassion for others and seek to do no harm. Authentic leadership offers a solid foundation for longer term success (2018). Fourth, a leader must be a good communicator, which is built on a foundation of active listening (2018). To hear and understand what is expected provides a leader with a mental blueprint for high performance. A leader must have the clarity of vision to see possibilities when others do not and to be able to inspire others throughout the process of goal accomplishment (2018). Hence, a leader that exhibits these five competencies daily will be more effective in comparison to leaders that do not exhibit these five competencies.

Leadership Verse Management

What is leadership verses what is management is an often-discussed comparison construct. At its core, leadership is about prioritizing things that need to be done for direct goal attainment, while management is more about following procedures.

Ethical Leadership

Leadership is based within a morality construct where ethics is central. The leadership role is based on having a responsibility to do what is right for followers, the organization, and society in the operation of any organization. An ethical leader is more likely to ensure that ethical principles are engrained into an organization's environment to ensure that the vision and goals of the organization are always realized. Ethical leaders are more likely to develop and nurture better relationships with subordinates and to make sound decisions for the most part (Northouse, 2019). Ethical leaders more readily exhibit honesty, trustworthiness, altruistic behavior, and a genuine concern for subordinates (2019). Moreover, ethical leaders are more likely to model the behavior of accountability that they expect followers to emulate (2019).

Transformational Leadership

Established research reveals that a transformational leadership style, at its core, inspires, motivates, and presents a clear vision toward a common goal (Conger, 2004; Geter, 2010; Dunst et al., and Northouse, 2019). Transformational leadership is the process wherein morality, vision, motivation, and vision are clearly exhibited by the leader in all instances (Burns, 1978, Geter, 2010). Transformational leadership offers an emotional connection between leaders and subordinates in a given situation (Lee and Change, 2006; Geter, 2010). The transformational leader will often enhance the performance level of subordinates based on inspirations and a clearly articulated vision toward common goal attainment. Transformational leaders motivate others to higher levels in relation to personal attitude, behavior, and performance outcomes in an organizational environment.

Transformational leadership consists of four central components: charisma or idealized influence (attributed or behavioral), inspirational motivation, intellectual stimulation, and individualized consideration (Bass, 1998). The core element of transformational leadership is the fact that the construct is framed as an envisioning construct that consistently looks to move a group and or organization toward a mutually more beneficial future. Transformational leadership is principally concerned with the ethical path to goal attainment that is based in justice and equality for all (Burns, 1978). Transformational leaders articulate a brighter and potentially obtainable future for followers and the organization at large. Research into several criminal justice offender reentry programs found that subordinates viewed their supervisors as being transformational, because those leaders requested worker perspectives and talked optimistically about the future of the organization, while instilling a sense of pride within those employees (Geter, 2010).

Transformational leaders motivate subordinates to do more than expected by (1) enhancing subordinates consciousness level concerning what is critical and valuable toward goal attainment where goals are idealized, (2) encouraging followers work beyond their normal threshold and make sacrifices for the great good of the team or enterprise, and (3) inspiring followers to a higher order to achievement (Northouse, 2019). Transformational leadership motivates followers through a sense of empowerment and inspiration (Geter, 2010, Northouse, 2019). As such, the theory of congruence supports the hypotheses that a transformational leadership style will produce a high level of organizational performance.

Transactional Leadership

Transactional leadership is based on a something for something paradigm. Transactional leadership has three core constructs in a leader's role: contingent reward, management by exception (active), and management by exception (passive). Whereas, transactional leadership within an organizational setting is built upon a quid-pro-quo relationship between the leader and his or her subordinates where there is a value-exchange relationship (Burns, 1978; Geter 2010, Northouse, 2019). Research found within several criminal justice reentry programs that worker at time saw their respective supervisor to be more transactional in nature. Whereas those leaders were primarily focused the achievement of stated performance targets, talked more enthusiastically about what needs to be accomplished toward outcomes; and expressed satisfaction after goal are achieve.

Laissez-Faire Leadership

Laissez-faire leadership is based on the construct that real and meaningful leadership is absent in a given situation. A laisses-faire leader, in most instances, neglects to motivate or inspire subordinates and avoid leadership responsibilities within an organizational setting (Bass, 1985). For example, the Warden is, seemingly, always absent when core decisions or actions need to be made within prison. As such, staff lead themselves in operating the facility to the best of their ability. Laissez-faire leadership is often a contributing factor in prison riots or other breakdowns within the criminal justice on many levels.

Research found that laissez-faire leaders within a criminal construct happens when the supervisor or leader avoids getting involved when important issue arise. The leader is often absent, and delays handling urgent issues within the organization, which is a leadership that differs from both transformational and transactional. Laisses-faire leaders are more likely to create role ambiguity among organization staff that subsequently impacts in a negative manner work's morale, commitment, and performance. A laissez-faire leader impacts an organization's culture and internal environment in a negative manner. Therefore, it is critical to have leaders that do not have a laissez-faire leadership style, attitude, nor behavior. In most instances, an organization with a laissez-faire leader more likely ensures that a program's vision, mission, goals, or objectives will not be realized (Dunst et al., 2018; Northouse, 2019).

Whereas, a transformational leader or a transactional leader's style is better suited for positive outcomes and performances. The transformational leader based on the inspiration of subordinates and a clear and articulated vision toward common goal attainment provides hope for a better future within an organizational environment (Geter, 2010; Dunst et al., 2018; Northouse, 2019). Understanding what style of leadership is most effective within an offender reentry program environment is important for the development of a high level of staff commitment, the creation of more effective programs, and increased public safety (Geter, 2010).

Authentic Leadership

The actions of an authentic leader are to influence the behavior of subordinates within a true moral construct toward the achievement of common organizational outcomes. The focus of the authentic leader should truly center around doing what is always right for followers, the organization, and society in securing positive outcomes that are in-line with organization's vision, mission, objectives, and goals (Geter, 2010; Dunst et al., 2018; Northouse, 2019). Whereas, the authentic leader must ensure that the objectives are clear, deliberate, and achievable for followers based in a principled framework (Northouse, 2019). Authentic leaders who sincerely know themselves well and deliberately improve their leadership abilities throughout their life-course will be of higher ethics and more effective in the end (Geter, 2010; Dunst et al., 2018; Northouse, 2019). Furthermore, authentic leaders must take full responsibility for their own moral existence and development, rather than relying entirely on their organization to set the standard.

Expectancy Theory

Expectancy theory is based on the construct that individuals or group are more likely motivated and perform at a higher level based on the expectation for goal attainment that is reflected in the amount of effort expended to achieve a given task (Northouse, 2007; Geter, 2010). There are four central elements (Northouse, 2007) that support expectancy theory:

1. A certain association exists between effort and results.
2. Unquestionable efforts yield sought-after rewards
3. Earned rewards are fulfilling
4. Meaningful outcomes based on need.

Followership

In-order to be a true leader, one must have at least one or more followers in a given situation or task working toward a mutual goal. Followership is a construct where one or more person freely consents to the influence of a leader to accomplish a desired collective goal (Northouse, 2019). Followership as a process can be either positive or negative depending on the outcome (2019). Nevertheless, successful leaders will more than likely get a higher level of effort and commitment from subordinates (Peak, 2007). Effective leaders empower workers to produce greater results (Stojkovic, Kalinich, and Klofas, 2003) in most situations. Leaders ensure that the path and means for goal attainment are unobstructed and realizable for followers (Northouse, 2019). True leaders more than likely treat subordinates as partners and focus on the good of the individual, team, or organization (Hesselbein and Shrader, 2008).

Leadership Development

Leadership development programs have the ability in some instances to create an environment where as a leader can gain a better awareness of his or her own inspirational and visionary abilities. There are many instances where a potential leader must learn how to realistically lead and get followers to be more productive. Whereas, it becomes important for an individual to learn how to implement a strategic plan, evaluate subordinates, get the most out of a team, and communicate more effectively in goal attainment. Therefore, leaders, men or women, should seek to increase their knowledge, experiences, and skills through formal professional development programs, mentorship opportunities, and ongoing training over one's professional life-course (Northhouse, 2019) to become better leaders.

In related to women and professional development, barriers persist for women in all industries. In-order to benefit from various professional development opportunities, an individual must have a sound work-home balance that doesn't create undue challenges. As such, within a criminal justice construct, there should be broader opportunities for women to increase both their skill and leadership opportunities throughout each stage of the criminal justice process (Geter, 2010), Develop mentoring programs to cultivate younger women professions, while increasing both recruitment and job retention that leads to solid career advancement and promotions (2010).

Commitment and Performance

There are many factors within an organization that impact worker commitment, performances, and overall effectiveness. However, effective leadership is the number one factor that must be in place in-order to ensure that the vision is clear, and the articulated goals are achieved. Therefore, the better the relationship is between the leader and his or her subordinates the better the chances are for effective outcomes. A higher performing criminal justice system based in effective leadership will result in reduced recidivism, increased public safety, reduced costs.

Leaders should be focus on issues such as staff qualification, ongoing training, leadership accountability, performance appraisals, and retention strategies to develop a culture where staff commitment and perception of effective increases to a higher level of organizational performance. Accessing adequate resources is central to the delivery of services to clients or program participants. In most instances, jail-based, prison, correctional, and community-based programs deal with a challenging population: offenders and ex-offenders. Within a reentry program environment, staff are charged daily with supervising, counseling's, treating, or providing various resources and services to violent and non-violent offenders. Staff are expected to be professional, skilled, and motivated to work with various groups. Through the efforts of effective leaders, committed staff are expected to produce better outcomes regarding program participants. Moreover, public safety is ultimately increased when organizational staff commitment is high (Dunst et al., 2018).

Conclusion

This chapter adds to the discourse concerning whether leadership styles has a measurable impact on organizational outcomes and workforce performance with the criminal justice construct. Leadership matters, but all leadership is not equally effective in all instances. Therefore, having the appropriate leadership is critical for any organization growth, success, and effectiveness. Leadership is about personal influence at its core. While leadership style is the methods used to influence others toward a common aim within the construct of an articulated vision. Leadership styles reflect a level of care that a leader has for subordinates and the organization.

Increased leadership style awareness will help individuals develop into more effective leaders in the end. Additionally, given leadership style will offer a greater opportunity to achieve common goals based on a clear and articulated vision that inspire followers. Few studies today focus on the role of the leadership style of women professionals in criminal justice, therefore gaining a broader understanding would be critical to criminal justice safety and a more efficient operation.

Leadership style, as a construct, serves to allow people to better mitigate challenges, influence others, and to develop strategies for goal attainment. Leadership skills that are critical for meaningful success or a higher level of performance include, but not limited to, preparation, mentorship engagement, relationship building, critical-thinking, and sound organizational skills (Cebula, Craig, Eggers, Fajardo, Gray, and Lantz, 2012). A transformational leadership style within the criminal justice system is a benefit, because such styles create a safer culture for subordinates and those people who are being processed through the continuum. A more motivated criminal justice workforce will more than likely perform at a higher level (Cebula, et al., 2012).

Leaders may have a positive or negative association with organizational commitment and perceptions of effectiveness within the field of criminal justice. Research supports the argument that a measurable association exist among selected leadership styles, organization commitment, and outcomes performance (Geter, 2010, Dunst et al., 2018). Therefore, better understanding which leadership style is most effective within the field of criminal justice is vital for developing a continuum of justice processes in-order to ensure public safety. Wherefore, having more transformational women leaders in throughout the criminal justice system will result in more positive outcomes through the motivation of others, development of a shared vision, increased worker commitment, and inspiration for the achievement of common goals of justice.

Authentic Leadership

Authorative Leadership

Common Goals

Contingency Theory

Corrections

Courts

Criminal Justice
  Administration

Criminal Justice Reform

Expectancy Theory

Full-Range Leadership

Great Man Approach

Hersey and Blanchard's
  Situational Theory

Law Enforcement

Lazzia -faire Leadership

Leader-Member Exchange

Leadership

Leadership

Leadership Development

Leadership Styles

Management

Offender Reentry

Organizational Commitment

Path-Goal Theory

Performance Outcomes

Public Policy

Relationship-Oriented
  Leader

Self-confidence

Servant Leader Leadership

Task-Oriented – Leader

The Leadership Grid

Transactional Leadership

Transformational Leadership

Vision

Discussion Questions:

1. Why is it important for criminal justice leaders to know their own leadership style?

2. What are the similarities and differences between leadership and management in criminal justice?

3. Describe the best leadership style that you have witnessed or experienced within an organizational environment. How did this leadership style inspire you?

4. What is the best style of leadership for someone working in the criminal justice field? Why?

5. Do you think that leadership style makes a measurable difference based on the leader's gender? Why or why not? Give examples to support your argument.

Web Links

National Criminal Justice Reference Services - https://www.ncjrs.gov/

U.S. Department of Justice - https://www.justice.gov/

Police Executive Research Forum (PERF) - https://www.policeforum.org/about-us

The International Association of Chiefs of Police (IACP)- https://www.theiacp.org/

National District Attorneys Association (NDAA)- https://ndaa.org/

National Center for State Courts (NCSC)- https://www.ncsc.org/

American Society of Criminology - https://www.asc41.com/

Academy of Criminal Justice Sciences - https://www.acjs.org/default.aspx

References

Aruda, W. (2019. There difference between managers and leaders. University of Notre Dame, Mendoza College of Business. Retrieved from https://www.notredameonline.com/resources/leadership-and-management/the-difference-between-a-manager-and-a-leader/ on May 28, 2019.

Bass, B. M. & Steidlmeier, P. (1998). Ethics, character, and authentic transformational leadership. Retrieved on March 11, 2019, from http://cls.binghamton.edu/BassSteid.html.

Bennis, W. (1988, January 21). University of Cincinnati, University of Maryland symposium. Retrieved on March 20, 2006, from http://www.legacee.com/Info/Leadership/Definitions.html

Burns, J. M. (2003). Transforming leadership: A new pursuit of happiness. New York: Grove Press.

Business News Daily. (2019). 17 Reason Women Make Great Leaders. The Time Intelligence Company. Retrieved from https://www.replicon.com/blog/17-reasons-women-make-great-leaders/amp/ on May 26, 2019

Cebula, N., Craig, E., Eggers, J., Fajardo, M. D., Gray, J., and Lantz, T. (2012). Achieving performance excellence: The influence of leadership on organizational performance. Washington, DC: U.S. Department of Justice, National Institute of Corrections.

Conger, J. A. (2004). Developing leadership capability: what's inside the black box? *Academy of Management Executive, 18*(3), 136-139.

Cordner, G. W., Scarborough, K. E., & Sheehan, R. (2004). Police administration. (5th ed). Anderson Publishing.

Department of Justice (DOJ). Office of Justice Programs. 5 out of 6 state prisoners were arrested within 9 years of their release. Bureau of Justice Statistic Press Release. May 23, 2018.

Dunst, C. J., Bruder, M. B., Hamby, D. W., Howse, R., & Wilkie, H. (2018). Meta-analysis of relationships between different leadership practices and organizational, teaming, leader, and employee outcomes. Journal of International Education and Leadership. Vol. 8 Issue 2. Fall 2018.

Eagly, A. H., Johannesen-Schmidt, M. C. (2001). The leadership styles of women and men. *Journal of Social Issues, 57*(4), 781-797.

Geter, L. (2010). A quantitative study on the relationship between transformational leadership, organizational commitment, and perception of effectiveness. University of Phoenix (UOP). ProQuest LLC. UMI Dissertation Publishing.

Hesselbein, F. & Shrader, A. (2008). *Leader to leader: Enduring insights on leadership.* San Francisco, CA: Jossey-Bass.

Kaeble, D. & Cowhig, 2016. Correctional Population in the United States, 2016. Bureau of Justice Statistics.

Karabell, S. (2016). 10 Commandments for Women in Leadership. Forbes.com. Retrieved April 9, 2019. from https://www.forbes.com/sites/shelliekarabell/2016/05/14/10-commandments-for-women-in-leadership/#1ff5dc6172e0

Maciariello, J. A. (2008). Mastering peter drucker's the effective executive. In Hesselbein, F. & Shrader, A. (Eds.). Leader to leader: Enduring insights on leadership. San Francisco, CA: Jossey-Bass.

Northouse, P. G. (2007). Leadership: Theory and practice. (4th ed.). Thousand Oaks, CA: Sage Publications.

Northouse, P. G. (2019). Leadership: Theory and practice. (8th ed.). Thousand Oaks, CA: Sage Publications.

Padgett, M. Y., Caldwell, C. B., & Embry, A. (2008) Can leaders step outside of the gender box? An examination of leadership and gender roles stereotypes. Scholarship and Professional Work-Business, 71.

Peak, K. J. (2007). Justice administration: police, courts, and corrections management. Upper Sadler River, NJ: Pearson Prentice Hall.

Pew Research Center. Social & Demographic Trends. (2015). Women and leadership: Public say women are equally qualified, but barriers persist. Retrieved from https://www.pewsocialtrends.org/2015/01/14/women-and-leadership/ on May 3, 2019.

Rowley, J. (1997). Academic leaders: made or born? *Industrial and Commercial Training. 29*(3), 78–84.

Simon, M. A. & Stautzenbach, T. E. (2003). Leaders are made, not born: the role of theAmerican orthopaedic association leadership traveling fellowships and leaderships and leadership development programs. Journal of Bone and Joint Surgery, *85-A*(9), 1833-1836.

Stojkovic, S. & Farkas, M. A. (2003). Correctional leadership: a cultural perspective. United States: Thomson Wadsworth.

Synder, H. N., Cooper, A. D. & Mulako-Wangota, J. Bureau of Justice Statistics. (Annual Table, 2014) Generated using the Arrest Data Analysis Tool at www.bjs.gov 2019.

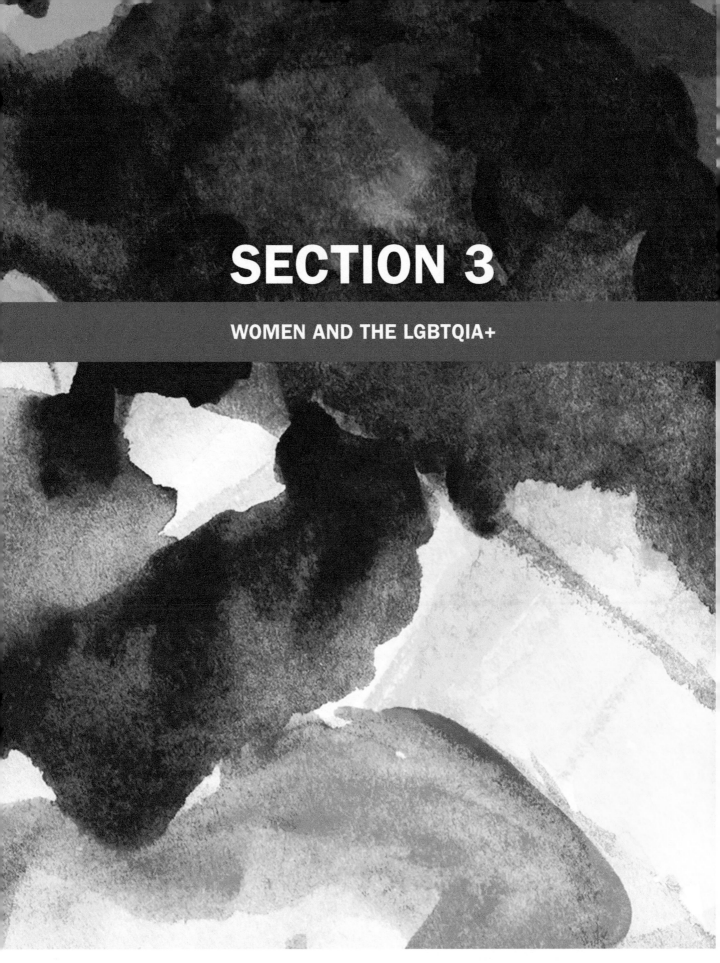

SECTION 3

WOMEN AND THE LGBTQIA+

CHAPTER 15

Squaring the Circle: Exploring Lesbian Experience in a Heteromale Police Profession

Lauren Moton, M.S. & Kwan-Lamar Blount-Hill, J.D. | *John Jay College, CUNY*
Roddrick Colvin, Ph.D. | *San Diego State University*

Chapter Outcomes

- Students should understand the major themes in the literature on lesbian police officers.
- Students should understand some of the major "gaps in our knowledge" about lesbian police officers.
- Students should understand some of the challenges associated with gathering data about lesbian police officers.
- Students should understand the role that intersectionality has played in the research on lesbian police officers.
- Students should understand the relationship between the positive and negative effects of coming out as a lesbian police officer.

Introduction

Across disciplines, policing and police officers have long been an area of interest for research. Central to this research has been a quest to better understand police officers, and the environments - both internal and external to policing - in which they operate. Officers' personal characteristics are often considered significant factors affecting their police work. The earliest studies examine such characteristics as age, education, relationship status, and military experience (Friedrich, 1980; Worden, 1990; Terrill and Reisig, 2003; McElvian and Kposowa, 2008). These studies were also based on samples that were overwhelming White, male and heterosexual, reflective of the homogeny among police forces at the time. Since these studies were conducted, however, changes in the workforce composition necessitate a second look at the experiences of present-day police officers. Shifting demographics within the police occupation has arguably chipped away at the hegemony of traditional notions of patriarchal power dynamics in Western culture, along with the hypermasculine nature of the occupation (Sklansky, 2005). Those changes include a growing number of women.

Presently, only 12.1% of our nation's law enforcement agencies are comprised of women, which is up from 8% in 1987 (Reaves, 2015). Large police departments (serving communities over 250,000 habitants) have higher portions of women employees than smaller departments (Reaves, 2015). It is not immediately clear why so few women have entered policing given significant increase in female participation in the workforce. However, coinciding with this discrepancy is an exclusionary police culture that pervades every facet of the job and has consequential effects on women's navigation of the field. Over the years - as society has

© John Roman Images/Shutterstock.com

become more pluralistic, and police departments have become more (though not sufficiently) representative - research on officer characteristics has expanded inquiry into additional characteristics, including gender, race and sexual orientation. Moreover, recent research has begun to consider also the identity intersectionality and its influence on the officer, her/his police work and the communities s/he serves.[1]

Despite a more expansive research agenda, our knowledge of lesbian police officers is extremely limited. In the last 25 years, there have been fewer than 60 articles and books that directly consider their contributions to policing. Still more concerning is the small number of individuals upon which our knowledge is built. Reviewing over 25 major works on this field, we estimate that our entire body of knowledge about lesbian police officers is based on a combined sample of less than 800 women. Of the 437 women from single study, which was Jones' UK focused work, *Who forgot lesbian, gay, and bisexual police officers? Findings from a national survey* (Jones, 2014), the remaining women come from other sources, none of which exceed a sample of 40 lesbian officers. While the majority of these articles are rich in qualitative data and insights, they—and the few quantitative studies existing—are severely limited in their generalizability (Colvin, 2009; Jones, 2014).

Aside from small sample size, another glaringly apparent limitation in our knowledge of lesbian officers' stems from our general lack of research into officer intersectionality. Research that includes holistic analyses of gender, race, class, or other dimensions are virtually absent in the literature about police officers (Sklansky, 2005; Hassell and Brandl, 2009). Given the unique intersectional approach that only lesbian officers can bring to policing through their womanhood and queer status, it is necessary to investigate how their identities unite, and how that impacts their work as well as their livelihood. In this chapter, we review the literature for insights into lesbian officer experience, noting areas of general consensus and directions for further research. In the following section, we position our review in the context of both policing and queer studies.

Disciplinary intersectionality: The need to understand lesbian officer experience

An exploration of the experiences of lesbian police officers is a critical frontier in policing scholarship. Myriad studies have now shown that female police officers are as capable as male officers. They receive less complaints, resort to force less often, and facilitate reporting of gender-sensitive crimes, such as the sexual assault of a woman (Brandl & Stroshine, 2013; Dejong, 2005; Hoffman & Hickey, 2005; Paoline & Terrill, 2004). In addition, the employment of female police officers also addresses society's ethical concerns around equity, including the desire for a force that represents our diversity and provides equal opportunity for professional success to men and women alike (Prenzler and Drew, 2013). However, as the literature base shedding light on female officers is expanding, a focus

---

[1] Kimberlé Crenshaw proposed in 1991 that the intersectionality between race and social class generates different experiences for individuals. The effects of these experiences are often confounding based on various identities the person embodies. From Crenshaw's perspective, intersectional identities create differences in people's positionality—that is, social locations and perceptions—within society (Frontiers, 2019).

on the intersectional perspectives of lesbian officers is still needed. Heterosexual and lesbian women have very different experiences that may further diverge in the hypermasculine police environment. This should be explored.

© iofoto/Shutterstock.com

Study of lesbian police officers should also further our understanding of policing diverse constituencies. Policing, as a profession, has historically had a strained relationship with the queer community (Williams and Robinson, 2004; Cherney, 1999). In a survey of local chapter members of Stonewall, a gay rights organization in the United Kingdom, 59% of men and 51% of women who were surveyed felt "unprotected by the law," while 39% of men and 18% of women felt they had been directly "discriminated against or harassed by the police" (Williams and Robinson, 2004, p. 223). This mirrors tensions between police and other marginalized identity groups, and lessons from the study of one set of strained police-constituent relations may inform thought, policy and practice about another. Colvin (2015) suggests that the queer officers shape the larger queer community's perceptions of police by sharing their individual experiences and perceptions, either helping or hurting the departments' image—a theory of *shared perceptions*. Thus, we expect that building police departments that mimic the true population may improve police community relations, particularly those that have strained relationships with law enforcement.

Research in this area is also an important extension of work on queer experience. Policing is "particularly susceptible" to hostility towards sexual minorities due to "the historical enforcement of anti-homosexual-related laws by police, its paramilitary structure and culture, and its overwhelming male majorities" (Colvin, 2015, p. 334). This has led to reluctance on the part of LGB victims to report crimes committed against them. This is especially problematic, as recent years have averaged just over 1,000 hate crimes—those targeting victims *because of their identity*—against queer individuals, and there is good reason to believe those numbers are significantly underreported (Pezzella, Fetzer, and Keller, 2019; Williams and Robinson, 2004; Herek, 2009). Notably, hate crimes against lesbians were significantly more likely to result in serious bodily injury (Pezzella and Fetzer, 2019).

Prior scholars have noted the dominance of gay men as the center of discussions around LGBTQIA+ issues (Williams and Robinson, 2004), and this includes policing studies.[2] Nonetheless, distinction between gay males and lesbian women experiences is vital to academic research. Lesbian and gay officers tend to be lumped together in current scholarship but have very different experiences not only based on their gender, but also differences in the stereotypes attributed to lesbian women and gay males. The few studies of LGB officers that discuss lesbian experiences show important differences between these officers that should be further illuminated (Burke, 1994). In the following section, we review the current state of research on lesbian police officers to highlight major themes in the literature, identify gaps, and make recommendations for expanding our knowledge about this population.

---

[2] Throughout, we use the acronym LGBTQIA+ to refer to the full lesbian, gay, bisexual, transgender, queer, questioning, intersex, androgynous and asexual population and their respective communities (+ unspecified non-heterosexual individuals). Unfortunately, smaller communities within this collective have been studied even less frequently than lesbians, gays, and bisexuals and most studies have been only of these three. In those cases, we revert to "LGB" or "sexual minorities," and enlarge the acronym when applicable to include other communities.

Reviewing the literary landscape

Hegemonic Masculinity and Police Culture

An overarching theme within policing studies is the idea of "hegemonic masculinity." According to Connell (1992; 1995), hegemonic masculinity involves the legitimation and maintenance of male dominance in societal social structures while subordinating feminine identities, as well as un-masculine or gay identities. It is characterized by a Western, capitalistic understanding of masculinity conjoined with authority, aggressiveness, technical competence, and heterosexist desire to dominate women. Hegemonic masculinity is entrenched within police cultures because it upholds the patriarchal dominance of White, heterosexual males who have traditionally been the majority not only in policing, but in all of Western industrialized culture. Resulting feelings of White entitlement make it difficult for persons of any marginalized population to succeed or exist comfortably in law enforcement.

All police officers are trained to adopt police culture, conform and emphasize shared values of law enforcement over individual identities (Loftus, 2010; Cherney, 1999). This is true for LGBTQIA+ officers as well, though the process is more difficult for identities deviating from hegemonic masculinity (Mennicke et al., 2018; Colvin, 2015). A line of scholarship has found that perceptions of lesbian masculinity make it easier for them to navigate police machismo culture and that they are preferred over gay male officers (Mennicke et al., 2018; Colvin, 2015; Williams and Robinson, 2004; Cherney, 1999l Burke, 1994).

Diversifying police forces offer some hope that a wider array of views will be incorporated into future policing (Sklansky, 2005). In an ethnographic study of an English constabulary, Loftus (2010) found that women embraced viewing the public as "customers" who should be served by the police and have their needs tended to more so than male officers. However, even among women, he found that the crime control ethos predominated commitment to customer service. Results such as these suggest that pressures internal to police work and culture makes it more likely that minority officers' worldviews will conform, rather than replace, the values of hegemonic masculinity.

Sexual Deviance and Police as Moral Agents

Traditionally, police culture internalized society's negative views about sexual minorities, seeing them as deviant identities (Miller and Lilley, 2014; Williams and Robinson, 2004). An earlier study found that, in fact, approximately 25% of anti-gay hate crime occurs at the hands of police officers themselves. Some have argued that police are particularly susceptible to bigotry against sexual minorities because of the profession's role in upholding society's moral codes (Miller and Lilley, 2014; Loftus, 2010; Williams and Robinson, 2004).

© John Roman Images/Shutterstock.com

As moral agents and defenders of what is 'right', officers may be apprehensive to relent to challenges to absolutist morality, including calls for sexual liberality (Burke, 1994). This explanation fits well with Herek's (2009) theoretical framework on *sexual stigma*. He argues that anti-homosexual prejudices result from the internalization of societal norms against sexual deviance, and that they arise as felt stigma (an awareness of stigma), enacted stigma (actions premised on that awareness), and internalized stigma (acceptance of stigma as right and proper, i.e. legitimate). Once internalized, individuals may be resistant to changing deeply held "legitimate" beliefs, and especially so if their professional purpose is to uphold those beliefs.

In a recent analysis of qualitative interviews with attendees to a LGBT law enforcement conference in 2012, Mennicke and colleagues (2018) found that respondents felt some of their colleagues saw them as "predatory and sexually insatiable" (p. 718). While respondents' perception of their professional experience might have encompassed events that took place years prior, that current and active police officers do not report a sea-change in police attitudes shows these concerns remain relevant today.

In a survey study that included 243 respondents from the United Kingdom's Gay Police Association, a significant portion of LGB officers (over half of the lesbians surveyed) reported overhearing homophobic talk in their workplace (Colvin, 2015). Similarly, Belkin and McNichol (2002) and Mennicke and her colleagues (2018) found that most of their qualitative samples had heard offensive remarks made about homosexuality in the workplace. In accordance, studies suggest that White heterosexual male officers may feel particularly aggrieved that LGB officers are treated with the benefits that come with being "a special class," along with racial minorities and women (Miller & Lilley, 2014; Belkin & McNichol, 2002).

A qualitative study of the Australian Federal Police force revealed that, as a general culture of tolerance toward sexual minorities have emerged, officers more often experienced subtle, indirect harassment due to their sexual identities (Cherney, 1999). Microaggressions can make the workplace uncomfortable and even hostile for individuals on the receiving end, and this is true for officers of other minority groups (Bolton, 2003) and minorities in other professions (Blount-Hill and St. John, 2017).

The Psychological Toll of Managing and Divulging Conflicting Identities

In law enforcement, sexual minorities may opt to suppress their queer identity in order to gain acceptance from their colleagues. The LGBTQIA+ individual who assumes both a law enforcement and queer identity is forced to manage identities which, at times, conflict with others in their identity group (e.g., cops who hate gays, or gays who hate cops) and possibly with the individual's own self-conception (e.g., ambiguity towards self or self-hate, arising from Herek's (2009) concept of internalized). Burke (1994; 1995) was first in the field to characterize LG officers as having dual, conflicting identities and experiencing marginality as officers and as non-heterosexuals (i.e. double marginality). He compared this to the *double consciousness* introduced by DuBois (1903) to explain Black American experience. Although Burke (1994) did not parse out his results by sex or sexual orientation, he did note that female officers might experience additional challenges in the sense that their status as women is also considered deviant in the policing profession.

This reality often forces officers to lead "double lives." Burke's (1994) qualitative study revealed that many officers attempted to "pass" as heterosexual, or "cover" their identity, making efforts not to draw any attention to themselves even where their sexual minority status is known. 53% of those participants responded that they were leading double lives on two fronts, keeping coworkers unaware of their sexual identity, and their LGB friends ignorant of their

© Nic Neufeld/Shutterstock.com

profession as a police officer. Specifically, Burke found that lesbians were not interested in revealing their sexuality because they already faced roadblocks based on their womanhood. Disclosing would add yet another identity that could work against them within the policing bureaucracy. This sentiment has been replicated in study after study since (Cherney, 1999; Belkin and McNichol, 2002; Miller and Lilley, 2014).

This precarious existing - always at risk of discovery and persecution - causes deleterious health and wellbeing impacts: Over one third (36%) felt keeping up the façade had a negative effect on their work performance and 39% felt leading a double life negatively affected their ability to maintain long-term relationships (Burke, 1994).

Interestingly, Cherney (1999) also found that those who reported being open about their sexuality reported that their colleagues' responses had been largely positive, a finding replicated in Belkin and McNichol's (2002) study and by Mennicke and her colleagues (2018; see also Sklansky, 2006). Galvin-White and O'Neal (2016) also found that disclosure of LGB officers' sexual orientation had a positive influence on working relationships with heterosexuals. In these cases, LGB officers reported that perceptions of their competence and skill—being a "good cop"—often outweighed discomfort with their sexual orientation. In Colvin's (2015) study, 70.8% of respondents reported being "out" at work. This could also be potentially attributed to the progression of sensibilities toward LGB individuals over time (though approximately one-third of Colvin's (2015) sample reported having been "outed" against their wishes).

Willingly divulging one's sexual minority status is largely based on individual and environmental characteristics that are unique to that person and situation. Specifically, in the case of lesbians, having other "out" (i.e. not closeted) officers around and environments open to different levels of disclosure create the most welcoming environments for lesbian officers to be open about their sexuality (Galvin-White & Neal, 2016). In Belkin and McNichol's (2002) mixed-sex San Diego study, respondents described a gradual process of coming out, on an individual-by-individual basis when trust and circumstances lined up to make the disclosure "appropriate" (p. 77). Lesbian officers are much more likely to be "out" than their gay male counterparts, largely attributed to the association of lesbianism with masculinity and its greater acceptability because of this perception (Mennicke et al., 2018). Here, the differential experiences of lesbian and gay male officers justify parsing study samples for gender-specific insights.

Performing Masculinity in a Masculine Hegemony

Historically, police officials resisted calls for women officers, both by attacking the physical capability of women to perform at levels expected of a man, and also by attacking their sexuality. Women who challenged traditional gender roles in the workplace were often suspected of challenging traditional sex roles and being homosexual. For example, in her case study of the 1920s London Metropolitan Police Department, Doan (1997) documents how powerful forces used government and legal processes to resist gender equality in policing by expanding the crime of 'gross indecency' beyond male homosexual activity to include female-with-female intercourse. In the United States, criminalization of their sexual inclinations was a common obstacle for LGB officers (Burke, 1994) until homosexual conduct was declared protected by the United States Supreme Court in *Lawrence v. Texas*.

Research into current departmental environments shows that lesbian women are more likely to face harassment or discrimination on the basis of their sex rather than their sexuality (Cherney, 1999). Female sex is seen as the problematic aspect of lesbian identity, in the context of policing, because it is feminine, while sexual attraction towards women, a traditionally masculine trait, might actually mitigate some of the mismatch between women officers and the "ideal" masculine officer. This may explain why studies find disproportionate numbers of lesbians among female police officers, in comparison to the general female population (Swan, 2016). A former police officer union president put it this way: "This is still a male profession and it is a macho-male profession. In most people's mind the gay men do not fit that mold …. [G]ay men have less of an opportunity to advance than gay women. I think that is pretty factual" (Belkin and McNichol, 2002, p. 85).

In a recent study, Swan (2016) found that (54%) of women reported performing masculine stereotypes, and this included a large proportion of heterosexual women. An interesting wrinkle was that those women who identified as *androgynous* were more satisfied with their jobs than those who reported being *masculine*, and lesbians disproportionately identified as masculine. The researcher opines that this is because of the "othering" effect of heterosexuals' negative views of homosexuals, but it may be, more specifically, that androgyny allows female officers to both avoid the feminine attributes that evoke resistance from police culture while also avoiding sexual deviance. Nonetheless, Swan (2016) found high overall levels of job satisfaction in her female sample that heavily skewed from feminine identification.

A relatively consistent finding is that lesbian officers face lower levels of discrimination when compared to male gay officers. Burke (1994), in his study of 36 current or retired LGB police officers, discusses a distinct disparity in the acceptance of these officers within the police culture. According to the LGB stereotypical archetypes, gay men are generally viewed as effeminate while lesbians assert a masculine persona. Both groups of officers are exposed to the harsh realities of hegemonic masculinity; however, lesbians experience it differently than gay officers. Lower perceived levels of discrimination, including in "areas of discretion" like performance evaluation, may translate into greater professional opportunities for lesbian officers (Colvin, 2012) as well as better organization integration as officers (Galvin-White and O'Neal, 2016). Prior studies have also found less strain between lesbian communities and the police than between the police and gay male communities (Williams & Robinson, 2004), meaning that lesbian officers likely bring a different preconception of policing than do queer males.

However, the exact parameters of difference in experience are not entirely clear. In one of the few quantitative studies of gay and lesbian officers, discriminatory experiences across the sexes did not differ statistically significantly, suggesting that perceptions of difference may be more disparate than actual experiences warrant (Colvin, 2015). Still, while the sexes' experiences were more similar than different, male gay officers did experience these more intensely, with the exception of harsher evaluation and trouble finding mentorship. Notably, however, lesbian officers also reported fewer instances of their identity being a benefit than did male gay officers. Though lesbian officers may assimilate more smoothly within the masculine police profession, they may also feel pressure to live up to and exude the masculinity expected of them. This can pose a problem to lesbian officers because, even if they prove successful, masculine performance denies women their femininity (Burke, 1994).

Gaining Acceptance and Building A Community

Recent scholarship shows that excelling in police work can mitigate, to some degree, the negative connotations surrounding sexual minority identity (Cherney, 1999; Belkin and McNichol, 2002). In fact, LGB respondents gave very strong support for merit-based systems of assignment and promotion in Belkin and McNichol's (2002) qualitative case study of the San Diego Police Department. On the other hand, reliance on demonstrations of competence in order to gain acceptance places disproportionate pressure on LGB officers to excel, a sentiment found across a number of studies (e.g., Mennicke et al., 2018; Miller and Lilley, 2014).

Work on LGBTQIA+ officers highlight the importance of peer support (Cherney, 1999). Sklansky (2006) notes that, in general, greater diversity has resulted in the emergence identity-based police organizations—*social fragmentation*—that provide support for individuals as well as competing power bases which facilitate "the decline of the monolithic police subculture" (p. 1231). In the interviews with lesbian officers, Burke (1994) reported that several respondents discussed their unique ways to find solidarity and kinship within the police force. They alluded to a more close-knit network of coworking lesbians that gay males do not necessarily have access to. His respondents were less likely to become involved in formal associations such as the Lesbian and Gay Police Association because they 'suss' each other out through more discrete avenues. For example, in the particular police agency from which Burke's sample was drawn, it was a clandestine secret that the lesbian officers purposely joined the department hockey team for networking.

Evidence suggests that, broadly, affirmative action policies have facilitated greater diversity within police departments, and this includes with respect to sexual minorities (Sklansky, 2006). Anti-discrimination and inclusion policies can help reduce discriminatory behavior (Mennicke et al., 2018). However, the mere existence of a supportive policy is not enough; policies must be enforced. Belkin and McNichol (2002) likewise found that, when conflicts arose due to their sexuality, officers tended to resort to intra-unit resolution, given the lengthy and psychologically-taxing nature of formal personnel complaint processes.

Even when policies exist, underlying attitudes are often less malleable, and policies are most influential in shaping how individuals entering the field are trained to incorporate these norms into their conception of what it means to be a police officer. Belkin and McNichol's (2002) study suggests that older officers, especially those in command positions or who are religious, are more likely to maintain a cold professionalism, seeking to minimize social contact with gay officers while not violating equal employment policies. It may be that efforts at integrating LGBTQIA+ officers can be successful, but must be given time to become culturally ingrained, particularly within open-minded generations who enter the force and are trained for tolerance.

Ultimately, sexual minorities in policing, including lesbians, may gain greater acceptance "simply" by embracing their own identity in the face of hegemonic masculinity. Belkin and McNichol's (2002) interviewees reported that other open LGB officers, in combination with supportive policies and backing from department leadership, eased previous tensions around having sexual minorities on the force (see also Mennicke et al., 2018; Miller and Lilley, 2014; Sklansky, 2006). One explanation is that trust and intimacy between lesbian and gay officers and their "straight" colleagues, fosters a more authentic *esprit de corps*. Allport's (1954) contact hypothesis states that contact with a group facilitates normalization and acceptance of them and reduces intergroup conflict; it appears that the increasing visibility of LGBTQIA+ individuals with personal connections to heterosexuals has contributed to sexual minorities' acceptance. Indeed, this process of accepting non-heterosexuality is accelerated when pre-disclosure relationships are characterized by friendship and warm feelings (Herek, 2009, citing Pettigrew, 1998), and if the heterosexual knows multiple people who have disclosed—in other words, the more lesbian officers that are open, the merrier.

Where to go from here?

The current set of studies provides only a glimpse of what is means to be a lesbian in law enforcement and much more work needs to be done. Many of the most influential studies are also from decades ago: since then, all sexual intercourse between consenting adults was legalized and same-sex marriage has become a constitutional right. Lesbians in particular have been dramatically more accepted and integrated into American civic life: just weeks before Chicago would see the inauguration of an openly lesbian Black woman as mayor, in Florida, voters choose a former police chief to be the first openly lesbian mayor of Tampa.

Still, much of the life of lesbian police officers remains unstudied. While important works on lesbian officers have been produced, with few exceptions (e.g., Colvin, 2009; 2015; Hassell and Bradl, 2009; Jones, 2015; Jones and Williams, 2015) most have been qualitative studies that lack generalizability. While seminal qualitative studies provide us with rich and detailed analyses of the lives of lesbian officers, they do so with samples that are not representative. This means that even the modicum of knowledge that we have cannot be said to represent the lesbian officers not directly involved in these studies, nor their experiences.

A larger body of work on lesbian officers lends more opportunity to explore nuance within their experience. For example, while Hassel and Brandl (2009) noted the reality and importance of intersectionality - between race, gender, and sexual orientation - few studies make mention of its centrality in understanding the lived experience of lesbian police officers. Furthermore, we are aware of no empirical studies that consider the intersectionality of these officers. While time has revealed largely positive experiences for those who openly claim queer sexuality, as recently as 2014, Miller and Lilley found LGB officers of color were more likely to stay closeted.

In a society more endorsing of civic and cultural resistance, those fighting for changes in traditional understandings and discourses have argued that merely breathing—that is, open, unapologetic existence—is a first and potent strategy for change. Sklansky (2006) posited such a view more than a decade before:

> The presence of openly gay and lesbian officers, particularly once they begin to rise through the ranks, challenges the easy, taken-for-granted homophobia of the law enforcement, and all that it has helped to foster—the nominally desexualized police workplace, the hyper-masculinized ethos of the profession, and the tacit acceptance of extralegal violence. All of this is on top of the ways in which gay and lesbian officers, like minority officers and female officers, will help to fragment the police subculture and to build identity-based bridges to groups outside of law enforcement. The social realignment of policing—the decline in the solidarity and insularity of the police—has turned out to be the most important effect of the profession's growing diversity (p. 1234).

The role of research is to explore, examine, and explain this existence and reactions to it. Theories are ways of explaining the world and, if lesbians and other sexual minorities truly do have a life experience that is peculiar, we need better ways of explaining that experience. There is a general need for expanding queer theory, but we have near none to explain the experience of LGBTQIA+ officers' experiences. Colvin's (2015) application of shared perceptions as a framework by which individual officers' experience and subsequent perceptions of a department are then shared through their intra-community networks to shape communal opinions, and vice versa, is an example of such theorizing. Further theoretical development is crucial.

Feminist epistemologies, such as standpoint theory (Harding, 1983), may offer a productive framework on how to capture the unique intersectional experience of lesbian officers. Standpoint theory challenges the positivist notion that there is one objective, knowable truth that can be discovered by research, and instead demands researchers account for the impact of social positioning on interpretations of study data. Feminist scholars take three stances in employing standpoint theory that may especially connect to exploring the lesbian experience in policing: (1) knowledge is socially situated; (2) the lived experience of the marginalized makes them more socially aware than those that have not experienced marginalization; and (3) research should emerge from the experiences of the marginalized (Doucet and Mauthner, 2006). We argue that the best theory may come from giving lesbian officers agency to tell their own story. We believe this is a foundational starting point to further develop theory that caters particularly to criminal justice and more specifically, to policing.

Key Terms:

Intersectionality	masculine hegemony	sexual minorities
lesbian officers	policewomen	

Discussion Questions

1. How does the concept of double consciousness apply to lesbian police officers?

2. What are some factors that have inhibited research about lesbian police officers?

3. What is "hegemonic masculinity" and how does it affect research related to lesbian police officers?

4. How has intersectionality been applied to this research area?

5. What are some privileges and oppressions lesbian officers face?

6. According to the literature, what barriers or challenges do lesbian police officers face on the job?

Web Links

National Center for Women & Policing: http://womenandpolicing.com/default.asp

Out to Protect: https://www.comingoutfrombehindthebadge.com/

The International Lesbian, Gay, Bisexual, Trans and Intersex Association (ILGA): https://ilga.org/

Serving with Pride Canada: https://www.servingwithpride.ca/

European Gay Police Association: https://www.lgbtpolice.eu/

Gay Officer Action League: http://www.goalny.org/

Center for Policing Equity: https://policingequity.org/

References

Barratt, C. Bergman, M. & Thompson, R. (2014), Women in federal law enforcement: The role of gender role orientations and sexual orientation in mentoring. *Sex Roles, 71*(1-2), 21-32.

Belkin, A and McNichol, J. (2002). Pink and blue: Outcomes associated with the integration of open gay and lesbian personnel in the San Diego Police Department. *Police Quarterly, 5*(1), 63-95.

Berrill, K. T. (1992). Organizing against hate on campus: Strategies for activists. Hate crimes: Confronting violence against lesbians and gay men, 259-269.

Blount-Hill, K. and John, V. S. (2017). Manufactured "mismatch": Cultural incongruence and Black experience in the academy. *Race and Justice: An International Journal, 7*(2), 110-126.

Bolton Jr, K. (2003). Shared perceptions: Black officers discuss continuing barriers in policing. *Policing: An International Journal of Police Strategies & Management, 26*(3), 386-399.

Brandl, S. G. & Stroshine, M. S. (2013). The role of officer attributes, job characteristics, and arrest activity in explaining police use of force. *Criminal Justice Policy Review, 24*(5), 551-572.

Buhrke, R. (2013). A matter of justice: Lesbians and gay men in law enforcement, Psychology Press. (New York: NY) Routledge.

Burke, M. (1994). Prejudice and discrimination: The case of the gay police officer. *The Police Journal. 67*(3), 219-229.

Burke, M. (1994). Homosexuality as deviance: The case of the gay police officer. *The British Journal of Criminology, 34*(2), 192-203.

Burke, M. (1995). Identities and disclosures: The case of lesbian and gay police officers. *The Psychologist, 12*(8), 543-547.

Charles, M. Arndt, L. & Rouse. (2013). Gay-and lesbian-identified law enforcement officers: Intersection of career and sexual identity. *The counseling psychologist, 41*(8), 1153-1185.

Cherney, A. (1999). Gay and lesbian issues in policing, Current Issues in Crim. Just. 11, 35.

Colvin, R. (2009). Shared perceptions among lesbian and gay police officers: Barriers and opportunities in the law enforcement work environment. *Police Quarterly, 12*(1), 86-101.

Colvin, R. (2015). Shared workplace experiences of lesbian and gay police officers in the United Kingdom. *Policing: an international journal of police strategies & management, 38*(2), 333-349.

Connell, R. W. (1992). A very straight gay: Masculinity, homosexual experience, and the dynamics of gender. *American sociological review*, 735-751.

Connell, R. W. (1995). Masculinities, (Berkeley) University of California Press.

Department of Justice. (2016). Full Time Law Enforcement Employees. FBI Criminal Justice Information Services Division. Retrieved from: https://ucr.fbi.gov/crime-in-the-u.s/2016/crime-in-the-u.s.-2016/tables/table-25.

DeJong, C. (2005). Gender differences in officer attitude and behavior. *Women & Criminal Justice, 15*(3–4), 1-32.

Doan, L. (1997). 'Gross Indecency Between Women': Policing Lesbians or Policing Lesbian Police?. *Social & Legal Studies*, 6(4), 533-551.

Doucet, A. and Mauthner N. (2006). "Feminist Methodologies and Epistemologies" in C. D. Bryant and D. L. Peck (Eds.) Handbook of 21st Century Sociology (36-42). Thousand Oaks, CA: Sage.

DuBois, W. E. (1903). The souls of Black folk: Essays and sketches. Chicago: AC McClurg, 8.

Friedrich, R. J. (1980). Police use of force: Individuals, situations, and organizations. *The Annals of the American Academy of Political and Social Science*, 452(1), 82-97.

Frontiers (2019). Intersectionality and Identity Development: How Do We Conceptualize and Research Identity Intersectionalities in Youth Meaningfully? Retrieved 13 June 2019, from https://www.frontiersin.org/research-topics/9001/intersectionality-and-identity-development-how-do-we-conceptualize-and-research-identity-intersectio

Galvin-White, C. & O'Neal, E. (2016). Lesbian police officers' interpersonal working relationships and sexuality disclosure: A qualitative study. *Feminist Criminology*. 11(3), 253-284.

Harding, S. (1983). Why has the sex/gender system become visible only now?. In Discovering reality (pp. 311-324). Springer, Dordrecht.

Hassell, K. & Brandl, S. (2009). An examination of the workplace experiences of police patrol officers: The role of race, sex, and sexual orientation. *Police Quarterly*, 12(4), 408-430.

Herek, G. M. (2009). Sexual stigma and sexual prejudice in the United States: A conceptual framework. In Contemporary perspectives on lesbian, gay, and bisexual identities (pp. 65-111). Springer, New York, NY.

Hiatt, D. & Hargrave, G. (1994). Psychological assessment of gay and lesbian law enforcement applicants. *Journal of Personality Assessment*, 63(1), 80-88.

Hoffman, P., & Hickey, E. (2005). Use of force by female police officers. *Journal of Criminal Justice*, 33(2), 145-151.

Jones, M. (2014). Who forgot lesbian, gay, and bisexual police officers? Findings from a national survey. *Policing: A Journal of Policy and Practice*. 9(1), 65-76.

Jones, M. & Williams, M. (2015). Twenty years on: Lesbian, gay and bisexual police officers' experiences of workplace discrimination in England and Wales. *Policing and society*, 25(2), 188-211.

Jordan, K. (1998). The effect of disclosure on the professional life of lesbian police officers. Unknown.

Loftus, B. (2010). Police occupational culture: classic themes, altered times. *Policing and society*, 20(1), 1-20.

Lyons Jr, P., DeValve, M. & Garner, R. (2008). Texas police chiefs' attitudes toward gay and lesbian police officers. *Police Quarterly*, 11(1), 102-117.

McElvain, J. P., & Kposowa, A. J. (2008). Police officer characteristics and the likelihood of using deadly force. *Criminal justice and behavior*, 35(4), 505-521.

Mennicke, A., Gromer, J., Oehme, K., & Macconnie, L. (2018). Workplace experiences of gay and lesbian criminal justice officers in the United States: A qualitative investigation of officers attending a LGBT law enforcement conference. *Policing and Society*, 28(6), 712-729.

Miller, S., Forest, K. & Jurik, N. C. (2003). Diversity in blue: Lesbian and gay police officers in a masculine occupation. *Men and masculinities, 5*(4), 355-385.

Miller, S. L., & Lilley, T. G. (2014). Proving themselves: The status of LGBQ police officers. *Sociology Compass, 8*(4), 373-383.

Myers, K., Forest, K. & Miller, S. (2004). Officer friendly and the tough cop: Gays and lesbians navigate homophobia and policing. *Journal of homosexuality, 47*(1), 17-37.

Paoline, E. A., & Terrill, W. (2005). The impact of police culture on traffic stop searches: An analysis of attitudes and behavior. *Policing: An International Journal of Police Strategies & Management, 28*(3), 455–472.

Pettigrew, T. F. (1998). Intergroup contact theory. *Annual review of psychology, 49*(1), 65-85.

Pezzella, F. S., Fetzer, M. D., & Keller, T. (2019). The Dark Figure of Hate Crime Underreporting. American Behavioral Scientist, 0002764218823844.

Prenzler, T., & Drew, J. (2013). Women Police in Post-Fitzgerald Queensland: A 20 Year Review. *Australian Journal of Public Administration, 72*(4), 459-472.

Reaves, B. A. (2015). Local police departments, 2013: Personnel, policies, and practices. Washington, DC: Bureau of Justice Statistics.

Rennstam, J., & Sullivan, K. R. (2018). Peripheral inclusion through informal silencing and voice – A study of LGB officers in the Swedish Police, Gender, Work & Organization. *25*(2), 177-194.

Sklansky, D. (2005). Not your father's police department: Making sense of the new demographics of law enforcement. *J. Crim. L. & Criminology, 96*, 1209.

Swan, A. (2016). Masculine, feminine, or androgynous: The influence of gender identity on job satisfaction among female police officers. *Women & Criminal Justice, 26*(1), 1-19.

Terrill, W., & Reisig, M. D. (2003). Neighborhood context and police use of force. *Journal of research in crime and delinquency, 40*(3), 291-321.

Thompson, R., & Nored, L. (2002). Law enforcement employment discrimination based on sexual orientation: A selective review of case law. *American Journal of Criminal Justice, 26*(2), 203-217.

Watson, D. (1995). The assimilation of openly gay and lesbian police officers into the law enforcement culture: Technical report., Commission on Peace Officer Standards and Training. (Sacramento, CA) Commission on Peace Officer Standards and Training.

Williams, M. L., & Robinson, A. L. (2004). Problems and prospects with policing the lesbian, gay and bisexual community in Wales. *Policing and Society, 14*(3), 213-232.

Worden, R. E. (1990). A badge and a baccalaureate: Policies, hypotheses, and further evidence. *Justice Quarterly, 7*(3), 565-592.

Wright, T. (2011). A "lesbian advantage"? Analysing the intersections of gender, sexuality and class in male-dominated work. *Equality, Diversity and Inclusion: An International Journal, 30*(8), 686-701.

CHAPTER 16

Justice Served? An Examination of Courtroom and Incarcerated Transgender Individuals' Treatment within the Criminal Justice System

Chastity Blankenship, Ph.D. and Emma Leahy

Contributed by Chastity Blankenship. Copyright © Kendall Hunt Publishing Company.

Overview

The current chapter discusses some of the experiences of transgender persons as they interact with other actors in the criminal justice system. First, we define and estimate the number of transgender individuals living within the United States today. We then discuss one of the ways most individuals interact with the criminal justice system—contact with the police as the victims of crimes or as the alleged offenders committing crimes. We also address some of the discrimination transgender individuals face within the courtroom from social workers, attorneys, court officials, and judges. We will cover correctional facilities housing policies and the interactions reported between transgender inmates, other incarcerated individuals, and correctional staff. Last, we discuss some barriers faced by transgender former inmates and suggest ways to move forward as we become an increasingly non-gender binary society.

Defining Transgender and Gender Dysphoria

According to the Diagnostic and Statistical Manual of Mental Disorders (DSM-5), *transgender* refers to individuals who transiently or persistently identify with a gender different from their biological sex at birth (2013, p.451). Additionally, transgender individuals may also suffer from gender dysphoria, which is the incongruence between their expressed gender and assigned gender for at least six months. Only a portion of transgender or gender nonconforming people experience gender dysphoria (World Professional Association for Transgender Health, 2011). *Gender dysphoria* is manifested by experiencing at least two of the following conditions: a strong desire to be rid of their primary (e.g., vagina or penis) or secondary sex characteristics (e.g., breasts), a strong desire for primary and/or secondary sex characteristics of another or alternative gender, a strong desire to be or be treated as another or alternative gender, and/or a strong belief they have feelings and/or reactions of another gender (DSM-5, 2013, p.452). Gender dysphoria was previously referred to as Gender Identity Disorder until 2013 when the DSM-5 was updated to more accurately reflect current scientific knowledge. Transgender and gender dysphoria are also separate from *intersex*, which is a medical classification for those born with chromosomes, gonads, or genitalia that are ambiguous or contain characteristics of both male and female characteristics.

Chapter Outcomes

- Students should understand how gender identity is just one of many intersectional characteristics that influence criminal justice interactions and legal outcomes.

- Students should identify obstacles transgender individuals face in all aspects of the criminal justice system.

- Students should summarize current legal precedents and how these judicial decisions will influence institutional policies.

Based on these definitions (i.e., transgender and gender dysphoria), it is difficult to estimate the number of transgender individuals in the United States. More specifically, there may be many more individuals who do not conform to cultural gender norms and who also do not self-report themselves as transgender or gender non-conforming. Of those individuals who do count themselves as transgender or intersex, some estimate that these groups consist of only 1% of the population in the U.S. (Stohr & Walsh, 2018). The World Professional Association for Transgender Health (WPATH) estimates more male-to-female transgender individuals (1:45,000) and in comparison, to female-to-male (1:200,000) persons worldwide (2011). This is a low-end estimate of transgender individuals worldwide since the WPATH measure only includes individuals who have experienced gender dysphoria (2017).

Intersectionality: Race, Social Class, and Trans-Identity

Transgender individuals consist of a diverse group of people representing all races and social class backgrounds. In one study of transgender individuals who self-reported their race, 76% were White, 5% were Black, 5% were Hispanic, or Latino/a, and 11% were multiracial or mixed race (Grant et al., 2011). In this same study, transgender individuals had much lower household incomes that the U.S. population as a whole with 15% reporting making under 10,000/year and an additional 12% making less than $20,000 (Grant et al., 2011). In another study, 29% of transgender individuals reported living in poverty, which was twice the rate of the U.S. population during the same year (James et al., 2016). Living in poverty is almost certainly related to their employment status. Transgender individuals' unemployment is three times higher (15%) than the general population, with 16% losing a job due to their gender identity (James et al., 2016). Additionally, the unemployment rate was much higher for people of color—20% for Black respondents and 35% for Middle Eastern participants (James et al., 2015).

Due to their disproportional chances of living in poverty and being unemployed, 19–30% of transgender individuals have experienced homelessness at some point in their lifetime (Grant et al., 2011; James et al., 2016). In a study of transgender people in California men's prisons, 47% reported being homeless at some point, with 20% reporting they had been homeless just before *incarceration* (i.e., confined in jail or prison) (Center for American Progress, 2016). Among homeless youth, 20–40% are LGBTQ who may have run away from home, where they experienced verbal and/or physical abuse (Majd, Marksamer, & Reyes, 2016). While homeless, transgender people reported challenges in finding a shelter that will willingly and safely accommodate them. More specifically, 25% of transgender people reported being turned away from a shelter, and another 55% reported harassment by other residents or shelter staff when they were able to find temporary housing (Center for American Progress, 2016; Grant et al., 2011). Lastly, 25% of homeless transgender people reported being physically assaulted at a shelter (Grant et al., 2011).

In addition to race and social class, another intersectional factor that can impact the likelihood of contact with the criminal justice system is educational attainment. Among all race groups, those with the least educational attainment (i.e., high school dropouts) have the highest rates of incarceration (Raphael, 2011). However, the proportion of incarcerated Black male high school dropouts (19%) is much higher in comparison to White men (5%) (Raphael, 2011). As evidence of some of the discrimination, or unfair treatment of an entire group of people suffers based on a shared characteristic, the pattern of educational attainment related to incarceration is less clear for transgender persons. Among transgender individuals, they typically report higher levels of educational attainment than the U.S. population. In one study, 27% of transgender people reported earning a college degree, and 20% went on to graduate or professional school (Grant et al., 2011).

Overall, transgender people are more likely to come into contact with the criminal justice system because they are more likely to be victims of violent crime or harassment and be homeless, among other issues (Grant et al., 2011). However, the intersection of demographic characteristics (i.e., race, class, and gender identity) is also related to the likelihood a person will come into contact with the criminal justice system. Contact with the criminal justice system mostly affects those who are multiple-marginalized by their race, social class, and gender identity (Agbemenu, 2015). In other words, if a transgender person is also poor and a person of color, they are more likely to report contact and more specifically, discrimination by the criminal justice system (Agbemenu, 2015).

Contact with the Police

Overall, transgender individuals report being hesitant to call the police for help and report higher rates of dissatisfaction with police services than the general public. In one study, 57% of transgender respondents were not comfortable asking the police for help if they needed it (James et al., 2015). In Grant et al.'s study, 20% of transgender individuals reported denial of equal service by police (2011). Race was a significant factor when reporting mistreatment after interacting with police. More specifically, transgender people of color were more likely to report being treated with a lack of respect in comparison to Whites, such as being referred to as the wrong gender pronouns (James et al., 2015). Further, Black and Hispanic or Latino/a transgender people of color were more likely to report verbal harassment from the police in comparison to Whites (James et al., 2015).

Beyond contact with the police due to attempting to report victimization, low-income, and transgender people of color disproportionately report being targeted by the police (Center for American Progress, 2016). For example, many transgender women report stories of being stopped and aggressively frisked by police officers while being questioned about their destination and reasons for being out (Center for American Progress, 2016; Minter & Daley, 2003). Perhaps due to these negative interactions, over 90% of transgender youth reported employing some tactic to avoid police contact (Dank et al., 2015). During contact with the police, some transgender people claim they were inappropriately touched to "establish their true gender" (Minter & Daley, 2003). In addition to stop-and-frisk, under programs like the Priority Enforcement Program (PEP), police officers can check fingerprints of those arrested against immigration databases. These fingerprint checks can result in Immigration and Customs Enforcement (ICE) taking custody of transgender individuals regardless of whether they committed a crime (Center for American Progress, 2016).

Being stereotyped or profiled as a sex worker is an experience homeless transgender youth (and adults) point to as a way for police to initiate a stop-and-frisk procedure or invasive questioning (Center for American Progress, 2016). Young transgender women of color are the most likely to be profiled by police as being a sex worker with the "evidence" being carrying condoms (Dank et al., 2015). Fifteen percent of LGBTQ people stopped by police, claimed that condoms were used to justify lengthy questioning or sex work arrests made by police (Center for American Progress, 2016). This practice may discourage transgender individuals from carrying condoms, which undermines safe sex practices. Additionally, the police may classify an individual as a known prostitute and issue stay away orders from a particular physical location regardless of the non-criminal reasons a transgender person may have for being in the area (Center for American Progress, 2016).

Discrimination in Court Proceedings

There are few recently documented cases of discrimination during legal proceedings by a judge or court official against gender non-conforming individuals. The discrimination is seen through social policy, institutional discrimination, and narrow legal interpretations that continue to perpetuate heteronormative standards instead of a judge ruling against an individual based on their unrelated gender identity. Just because transgender discrimination is difficult to document does not mean it does not exist. It may be challenging to support a claim of discrimination by a judge or court official unless it is blatantly apparent. In one study, 7% of transgender men and women reported harassment by a judge or court official (Grant et al., 2011).

In rare cases, discrimination during legal proceedings by a court official is clear. For example, in 2011 and 2012, Oklahoma Judge Bill Graves refused to grant a name change for two transgender females (Brown, 2014). In one decision, Graves wrote that granting a name change would be assisting fraud and he commented to the Associated Press, "We can't change our sex, the way God made us" (Brown, 2014). In both cases, the Oklahoma Court of Civil Appeals eventually granted these requests allowing name changes for both individuals. Graves found the ruling disappointing and claimed sex changes were counterfeit; however, he did obey the ruling (Ford, 2014). More broadly and within the LGBTQ community, Stern and Oehme (2016) claim that anti-LGBTQ bias in the courtroom is relatively common, especially during child custody disputes. As a recent example, in 2015, a Utah judge ordered a baby girl to be removed from her lesbian foster parents because their sexual orientation would be detrimental to the child (Stern & Oehme, 2016).

In other documented instances, heterosexual men charged with murdering transgender women have claimed the *trans panic defense* (Wodda & Panfil, 2014). More specifically, according to Wodda and Panfil (2014), only heterosexual men murdering transgender women have attempted to use this defense to date (no other types of victim-offender relationships). While this claim is similar to one of temporary insanity, it is not an official defense. The trans panic defense is when a defendant argues that he was deceived or tricked into sexual contact and his rage and violence are justified upon learning this woman was a "man" (Wodda & Panfil, 2014). Michael Magidson and Jose Merel, two of the four men who beat and strangled transgender woman Gwen Araujo in 2002 attempted to use this defense. They argued that Gwen deceived her murderers and challenged their masculinity by not disclosing she was a transgender woman (Buist & Stone, 2014). Ultimately Magidson and Merel were convicted of second-degree murder.

According to Buist and Stone (2014), there is a lack of research on transgender defendants in criminal cases. In one case, CeCe McDonald, a Black transgender woman, murdered Dean Schmitz in 2011 (Buist & Stone, 2014). McDonald and her friends walked past Dean Schmitz, Molly Flaherty, and several other bar patrons who began yelling homophobic, racist, and transphobic slurs at the group (Pasulka, 2012). Flaherty broke a beer bottle and cut McDonald's face, who then tried to leave the scene. As McDonald left the fight, Schmitz followed her. McDonald pulled a pair of scissors out of her purse, and allegedly a scuffle ensued with Schmitz getting stabbed in the process (Buist & Stone, 2014; Pasulka, 2012). McDonald and her defense attorney argued she had reason to believe Schmitz intended to hurt her and she acted in self-defense. Eventually, McDonald accepted a plea bargain of second-degree murder in exchange for agreeing to serve 41 months in a male prison (Pasulka, 2012). Now an LGBTQ activist, some see McDonald as a folk hero who survived a hate crime and cruel punishment by the criminal justice system (Qian, 2017).

McDonald's case and trial are similar to two others—Ky Peterson and Eisha Love. All of these defendants were charged with murder for what they described as life-threatening altercations in which they feared for their life and claimed self-defense during their trails. All three were the victims of violent attacks, and were either punched (Love), cut (McDonald), or raped (Peterson), while the perpetrator yelled homophobic, transphobic, and/or racist comments (Blickensderfer, 2014; Buist & Stone, 2014; Center for American Progress, 2016; Pasulka, 2012).

Within the juvenile justice system, some court officials take on parental attitudes and may discriminate against LGBTQ youth, believing they have their best interests in mind.

One prosecutor claimed he was more likely to petition the court and push forward with charges, "to get family counseling in order to address the relational stress that LGBTQ issues cause on many families" (Majd et al., 2016, p. 89). In other words, court officials may willingly file a case or encourage youth to plead guilty to guarantee some form of mental health services. While this may be positive, it also distorts the purpose of the system and deprives youth of due process (Majd et al., 2016). In some cases, LGBT individuals may want to keep this information from professionals or family members. One juvenile reported she did not want anyone working on her case to know she was a lesbian and for this information to be revealed because she was afraid of her parents (Majd et al., 2016).

Lastly, gender nonconformity and pronoun use within the courtroom is an emerging issue. Transgender individuals reported lawyers, probation officers, judges, and detention workers would refuse to call them their preferred pronoun (Dank et al., 2015; Majd et al., 2016). According to the Center for American Progress (2015), up to 12% of transgender and gender non-conforming individuals have reported mistreatment by legal services, courts, and judges. Additionally, up to 33% heard a lawyer, court official, or judge make a negative remark about an individual's gender expression, identity, or sexual orientation (Center for American Progress, 2015). In one case, a 16-year-old Black transgender girl was referred to as a young man by her court-appointed attorney who refused to call her anything else (Majd et al., 2016).

Incarceration of Transgender Individuals in the United States

There are several estimates of the number of transgender individuals currently incarcerated within the United States. One study of California Prisons found there were 385 transgender inmates receiving hormone therapy (Queally, 2015). As stated earlier, only a portion of transgender individuals report taking hormones at some point in their lives, which means this is a low-end estimate of the actual population (Bassichis, & Spade, 2007). In a different study, Meenvijk and Sebelius's found approximately 0.25% of the inmate population self-reported as transgender (2017). Lastly, the U.S. Department of Justice estimates there are over 3,000 transgender inmates serving time in state and federal prisons, and around 2,000 in jail (Beck, 2014).

In the United States, inmates are primarily housed based on their biological sex in separate male or female institutions (Sumner & Sexton, 2016). Further, a transgender individual who has not undergone sex reassignment surgery is most likely to be housed based on their biological sex regardless of how long they may have been living as another gender (Buist & Stone, 2013). In 2012, The U.S. Department of Justice banned facilities from housing inmates based only on biological sex under Standard 115.42(c). However, the Trump administration changed housing guidelines after several female inmates in Texas filed a federal lawsuit arguing their privacy is violated and it could be dangerous for them to share facilities with transgender inmates (Leventis Lourgos, 2018). These new guidelines roll-back some of the criteria for housing making biological sex the initial determination for facility assignments and only using gender identity in rare cases (Leventis Lourgos, 2018). Additionally, correctional facility staff may claim there is nowhere else to place transgender individuals, which means the inmate would be housed based on their biological sex.

In addition to the Department of Justice's policies regarding transgender inmates, there may be other state or county level regulations. For example, offenders are housed based on their gender identity in San Francisco (Queally, 2015). In Harris County, Texas, where Houston is located, a Gender Classification Specialist conducts interviews with an inmate to discuss gender issues (U.S. Department of Justice, Harris County Sheriff's Office (HCSO), 2013). This Gender Classification Specialist, regardless of the inmate's biological sex, helps to determine if the offender will be housed with other LGBTQ inmates. However, many institutions have yet to put a formal policy or specialist in place to secure the safety of transgender inmates. When institutions do not have a particular unit for LGBTQ inmates, some facilities use solitary confinement as a means to protect transgender inmates from the general population.

According to Sumner and Jenness (2014), many issues transgender inmates face once incarcerated are related to the interpretation of the Eighth Amendment's Cruel and Unusual Punishment Clause and the Fourteenth's Equal Protection Clause. Due to the vagueness of what may constitute excessive, cruel, or unusual punishment, there are a variety of interpretations of the Eighth Amendment. Few court cases weigh-in on an inmates' Fourteenth Amendment rights, or the Equal Protection Clause, which requires equal protection of laws. In Figure 1, we highlight some legal outcomes primarily centered on transgender inmate's Eight and Fourteenth Amendments rights.

As established by some of the court cases displayed in Figure 1, gender dysphoria has been established as a serious medical condition in which some form of treatment within correctional facilities is required. As a requirement for treatment within many correctional facilities, an inmate must be diagnosed by a medical professional with gender dysphoria. What type of medical treatments for gender dysphoria that are required have yet to be firmly decided. According to Nylund and Waddle (2015) until very recently, many institutions only continued hormone therapy if a transgender person entered prison already taking hormones (i.e., "freeze-frame policies). In other words, court cases regarding transgender inmates' Eighth and Fourteenth Amendment rights have only set a lower or minimal determination of care. In some extreme cases, inmates have resorted to actions such as attempted suicide and genital

Figure 1

Court Precedents for Transgender Inmates

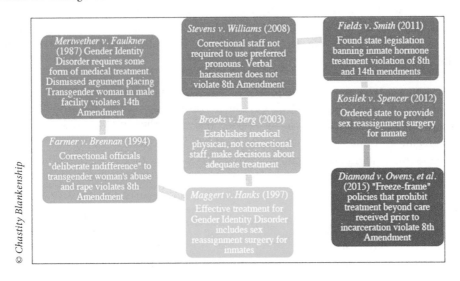

self-mutilation, such as castration, in order to pressure correctional staff to take them seriously (Agbe-menu, 2015; Nylund & Waddle, 2015). Self-mutilation and other extreme behaviors to call attention to indifference by correctional staff may exacerbate mental health issues of inmates. Thus, inmates with no prior mental health interventions will require mental health services at some point during incarceration (Nylund & Waddle, 2015). Legal precedent has medicalized gender and requires medical professionals to act as gatekeepers to gender nonconformity (Tarzwell, 2006).

Mistreatment of Transgender Inmates within Correctional Facilities

Overwhelmingly, research focuses on the experiences of transgender women in men's correctional facilities (Bassichis, & Spade, 2007; Gibbons & de Belleville Katzenbach, 2006; Sumner & Sexton, 2016). A lack of research on female-to-male inmates is not surprising considering that within the U.S. general population male-to-female transgender individuals are more common. Within the research literature, transgender inmates have consistently reported higher levels of mistreatment, abuse, and sexual assault in comparison to other detainees. Similar experiences were reported for transgender inmates regardless of correctional facility type (i.e., jail or prison).

In one study, transgender inmates who spent time in jail reported they were slightly more likely to be harassed by correctional officers (37%) in comparison to other inmates (35%) (Center for American Progress, 2016). Beyond verbal and physical harassment, transgender inmates are much more likely to experience sexual assault or rape. Fifty-nine percent of transgender inmates claimed they experienced reported or unreported sexually assault while incarcerated (Jenness, Sexton, & Sumner, 2011). As a comparison, reported sexual victimization among all inmates is around 3-4% for correctional facilities (Nylund & Waddle, 2015). In response to high rates of sexual assault within correctional facilities of LGBTQ inmates, the Prison Rape Elimination Act (PREA) was passed by Congress (2003). Broadly, PREA states correctional facilities must attempt to protect inmates that are likely to be sexually victimized by other inmates (2016).

PREA and Solitary Confinement

In order to protect inmates and meet PREA standards, some institutions began using administrative segregation (solitary confinement) to separate certain groups from the general population. In addition to being housed based on sex (or possibly gender), inmates are often classified based on other factors, which could increase vulnerability in the general population (Sumner & Jenness, 2014). For example, known gang activity, sexual identity or orientation, physical stature, and/or committed offense can be some of the many reasons inmates may be separately housed. Policies that separate inmates based on these factors were created in order to prevent violations of the Eight Amendment regarding Cruel and Unusual Punishment. In other words, the state determines what punishment, retribution, or rehabilitation is appropriate for prisoners. Allowing inmates to be victimized by correctional officials or other inmates could, at the very least be mistreatment and at the worst, torture.

Administrative segregation for special populations is one of the most widely used solutions due to a lack of special housing available in many facilities (Howell, 2009). However, the likelihood of being placed in a solitary confinement cell is not equal and intersects with other factors. Transgender inmates of color are more likely to be placed in administrative segregation in comparison to White inmates. Around 40% of Black and 21% of Hispanic or Latino/transgender inmates reported being held in a cell due to their gender identity or expression alone (Grant et al., 2011). Higher proportions of inmates of color may be placed in administrative segregation due to their increased likelihood of abuse and rape by others within correctional institutions.

The use of administrative segregation permits the institution to comply with PREA standards while only temporarily addressing transgender inmates' need for personal safety. Placing inmates in administrative segregation adversely affects transgender inmates' mental health and restricts their access to programs and services available to other inmates (Caramico, 2017). For example, most inmates in administrative segregation cannot use facilities such as the library, educational classes, and recreational facilities (Howell, 2009). Ashley Diamond, one of the most well-known transgender female inmates incarcerated in a male prison, reported she was locked in administrative segregation for 24 hours a day, without access to light, exercise, or running water (Matricardi, 2015; Southern Poverty Law Center, 2015).

Further, there is evidence that being confined in administrative segregation causes violence between staff and prisoners (Gibbons & de Belleville Katzenbach, 2006). According to Gibbons & de Belleville Katzenbach (2006) transgender inmates in administrative segregation experience more idle time, which in turn increases misconduct and recidivism. Gibbons & de Belleville Katzenbach (2006) also found that inmates who participate in the programs those in administrative segregation do not have access to had lower recidivism rates after release.

Juvenile Justice System

One in five transgender youth claimed that if they needed help, they had no one go to and cited a lack of support from family and friends as the main reason (Dank et al., 2015). Family rejection is the most significant predictor of future involvement with the criminal justice system for LGBTQ youth (Majd et al., 2016). Transgender youth may experience abuse or a lack of acceptance in their family or foster care home. Thus, some transgender youth who are involved in the juvenile justice system may be trying to flee an abusive or unwelcoming home life. The vast majority of offenses for which transgender youth are arrested and charged can be linked to being homeless or impoverished (e.g., trespassing, survival sex) and other misdemeanors (e.g., drug possession, shoplifting) (Dank et al., 2015).

Further, it has been well documented that transgender youth may enter the underground economy for survival with some selling drugs or engaging in sex work for money or a place to stay (Dank et al., 2015; Grant et al., 2011). While sex work makes up the most significant percentage of transgender people, who worked in the underground economy, only 11% reported having sex for money (Grant et al., 2011). In other words, the stereotype of transgender homeless youth as sex workers or prostitutes is excessively inflated.

Migrant Detention Centers

The immigration system in the United States functions as its own criminal justice system in many ways; however, many of their programs rely on local law enforcement to help enforce state and local immigration policies. This is the case for programs such as the Priority Enforcement Program in which immigrants are transferred by local law enforcement to immigration enforcement officials (Center for American Progress, 2016). Immigration detention centers serve a variety of functions and hold both documented and undocumented immigrants. Documented transgender immigrants can be detained and have deportation proceedings commenced against them for convictions of specific categories of crimes. Undocumented immigrants who are detained by immigration officials may be held in detention facilities while awaiting deportation proceedings or asylum applications.

Undocumented transgender immigrants may be more likely to come into contact with police (i.e., see above section on police contact), which could initiate deportation proceedings in comparison to heteronormative undocumented immigrants. "Technically, if someone is undocumented and entered the country after January 2014, they are considered a high priority for criminal deportation, even if they have committed no other offense" (Wiltz, 2016). Being more likely to be stopped and questioned by police could, in turn, lead to transgender immigrants being disproportionally more likely to be held in migrant detention centers. Additionally, transgender women are overrepresented in immigration detention centers because they may come to the United States to escape persecution and to seek asylum (Center for American Progress, 2016).

Similar to what transgender inmates face in other correctional facilities, transgender immigrants held in immigration detention centers are more likely to be victimized in comparison to non-LGBTQ immigrants (Center for American Progress, 2016). Immigration and Customs Enforcement detention centers reported less than 10% of detainees were transgender; however, they comprised 20% of substantiated sexual assault claims (Center for American Progress, 2016). Placing transgender detainees in solitary confinement or LGBTQ housing may be the only safe option to prevent physical and sexual assault; however, the number of beds in these units is limited. Beyond a lack of access to programs and services, not all LGBTQ detainees want to be singled out, stigmatized, and separated from the general population. Recently, in March 2019, the American Civil Liberties Union of New Mexico sent a letter to immigration authorities and the warden of Otero County Processing Center, which stated transgender migrants were being mistreated (Stelloh). In particular, transgender migrants were placed in solitary confinement and were being threatened for complaining about conditions within the Otero facility (Stelloh, 2019).

© Chelsea Manning Shutterstock.com

Military Disciplinary Barracks: Chelsea Manning

Military disciplinary barracks follow stricter inmate guidelines for gender expression in comparison to civilian jails and prisons. Further, there are few documented transgender individuals serving time within military facilities. Chelsea Manning is perhaps one of the most famous transgender individuals who was formerly incarcerated in the United States Disciplinary Barracks at Fort Leavenworth (Strangio, 2015). Manning was convicted of violating the Espionage Act for sharing classified government documents related to national security practices (Hackl, Becker, & Todd, 2016). At the time of her conviction, Manning was sentenced to the longest sentence in U.S. history for the transmission of government information (Hackl et al., 2016). During her time, she had to follow military rules regarding grooming and hygiene standards, which required her to have her hair cut every two weeks that may not exceed two inches (Strangio, 2015). Eventually, Manning was permitted to grow her hair long and received hormone treatment during her incarceration after several suicide attempts and a lawsuit, which brought attention to her treatment. Manning served seven years of her 35-year sentence before being released (Stack, 2019).

Transgender Individuals' Barriers to Re-Entry

Transgender individuals convicted of crimes face many barriers to re-entry. Some of these barriers are shared and cut-across inmate demographics such as finding stable employment and housing. These topics have been well-covered within research literature (Greenberg & Rosenheck, 2008; Holzer, Raphael, & Stoll, 2003). Above and beyond these barriers, transgender former inmates face a lack of adequate re-entry programs and limited access to certain identity documents.

Name Changes and Accurate Identity Documents

Accurate identity documents and name changes are especially challenging for transgender individuals convicted of a criminal offense. Only 21% of transgender individuals report being able to update all of their identity documents to their new gender (Grant et al., 2011). Of those who are transgender and presented identification that did not match their gender expression, 40% reported being harassed, and 15% reported being asked to leave (Grant et al., 2011). In other words, accurate identity documentation is necessary for individuals to successfully re-enter society after incarceration.

Three states, Kansas, Ohio, and Tennessee prohibit changing a birth certificate to match an individual's current sex (Aviles, 2019). These state laws can be problematic for transgender individuals who are attempting to use their license for employment, health, education, and housing. As an example, the Tennessee Vital Records Act states that a birth certificate shall not be changed as the result of a sex change surgery (Aviles, 2019). As of April 2019, in the court case, Gore V. Lee, four transgender individuals are challenging this Tennessee statue. Tennessee does allow transgender residents to change their driver's license or identification card; however, in order to obtain certain documents, some institutions require a birth certificate (Aviles, 2019).

Beyond these restrictions, transgender individuals on parole or probation face additional barriers to accurate identity documents. For example, a judge may require written consent from their parole or probation officer before they may change their name (Center for American Progress. 2016). Additionally, over 50% of transgender individuals live in states that have restrictions for individuals attempting to change their name with a criminal record (Center for American Progress, 2016).

Barriers for Transgender Immigrants

As stated earlier, some transgender immigrants may be seeking asylum in the United States to escape persecution in their home country. When a transgender person seeks asylum, they are required to complete an asylum application within a year. In addition to this requirement, there are other barriers asylum seekers face during their application. Asylum seekers are ineligible for most public assistance programs and cannot work legally for at least 180 days after filing their application (Center for American Progress, 2016). Without substantial financial and emotional support from organizations, friends, or family, these barriers make it difficult for transgender immigrants to be able to follow the legal path to citizenship successfully.

Where Do We Go From Here?

As gender non-conformity continues to increase in the U.S. population, we can expect to see increased contact between members of this group and the criminal justice system. Much of this chapter focused on the experiences of defendants and inmates within the criminal justice system. What was not addressed within this chapter is the experiences of LGBTQ court officials, lawyers, and judges. Do they face the same issues of mistreatment and discrimination reported by defendants and inmates within this system? It would be shocking if their experiences did differ, as this group faces prejudice and misunderstanding in many areas of life. Within the criminal justice system, advocates and oversight are needed to help reduce discrimination of this vulnerable population. Oversight and accountability should come from new research by social scientists, and by outside agencies monitoring training and documenting interactions that take place in these institutions.

Change requires judges to make decisions that secure the safety and security of transgender individuals, while also taking into account how policies with the best of intentions may exacerbate mental health issues. Laws that prohibit the changing of birth certificates create unnecessary barriers for transgender individuals trying to be officially recognized as the sex that most accurately reflects their expressed gender. The incongruence between birth certificate sex and expressed gender when applying for employment, high school transcripts, or other benefits is outdated and based on policies from a time when the vast majority of society believed sex equaled gender. Hopefully, as electronic identity records become more accurate and shared between jurisdictions, having a prior criminal offense will cease to be a barrier for inmates who paid their debt to society. Accurate linking of identity records would allow for the small number of transgender former inmates to be recognized with the name they have chosen for themselves without public fear that convicts are trying to escape their previous records.

Whatever changes ultimately take place, they need to be at the institutional level and include changes in social policy. Institutions such as the criminal justice system should meet constitutional standards by treating all individuals in a fair and just manner. While individual change can be significant, we need to create policies that are equitable and inclusive. Improved institutional practices to address the overwhelmingly negative experiences many transgender individuals face when interacting with others in the criminal justice system is one step in the right direction.

Key Terms:

Gender dysphoria   **Intersex**   **Transgender**

Incarceration

Discussion Questions:

1. Beyond race and social class, are there any other intersectional factors that may influence legal outcomes for transgender individuals? If so, what are they? How might they play out in the criminal justice system?

2. Does housing trans-women in female correctional facilities violate inmate privacy? Justify and explain your position.

3. What change(s) in courtroom procedures or language may be beneficial for transgender petitioners or defendants?

4. If solitary confinement is restricted to only the most violent offenders who disrupt the safety and security of correctional institutions, what can facilities with limited space do to house transgender inmates?

5. What changes in technology do you foresee that may reduce discrimination when actors within the criminal justice system interact with transgender people?

References

Agbemenu, E. (2015). Medical Transgressions in America's Prisons: Defending Transgender Prisoners' Access to Transition-Related Care. *Colum. J. Gender & L.*, *30*, 1.

Aviles, G. (2019, April 24). Transgender plaintiffs sue Tennessee to change birth certificate gender. *NBC News*. https://www.nbcnews.com/feature/nbc-out/transgender-plaintiffs-sue-tennessee-change-birth-certificate-gender-n997996

Beck, A., (2014). Sexual victimization in prisons and jails reported by inmates, 2011–12—Supplemental tables. U.S. Department of Justice, Office of Justice Programs, Bureau of Justice Statistics, http://www.bjs.gov/content/pub/pdf/svpjri1112_st.pdf.

Blickensderfer, G. R. (2014, September 17). Trans* woman claims self-defense in case. *Windy City Times*. Retrieved from http://www.windycitymediagroup.com/lgbt/Trans-woman-claims-self-defense-in-case/49008.html

Brooks v. Berg, 270 F. Supp. 2d 302 (N.D.N.Y. 2003).

Buist, C. L., & Stone, C. (2014). Transgender victims and offenders: Failures of the United States criminal justice system and the necessity of queer criminology. *Critical criminology*, *22*(1), 35–47.

Caramico, G. (2017). Thank You Sophia Burset: A Call on the Federal Bureau of Prisons to Break Free of the Chains of Tradition in Order to Protect Transgender Inmates. *Geo. J. Gender & L.*, *18*, 81.

Center for American Progress. (2016, May). *Unjust: How the broken criminal justice system fails transgender people*. Washington, DC. Retrieved from http://www.lgbtmap.org/file/lgbt-criminal-justice-trans.pdf

Dank, M., Yu, L., Yahner, J., Pelletier, E., Mora, M., & Conner, B. (2015). Locked in: interactions with the criminal justice and child welfare systems for LGBTQ youth, YMSM, and YWSW who engage in survival sex.

Diamond v. Owens et al., No. 5:2015cv00050 (M.D. Ga. 2015).

Farmer v. Brennan, 511 U.S. 825 (1994).

Fields v. Smith, 653 F.3d 550 (7th Cir. 2011).

Gibbons, J. J., & de Belleville Katzenbach, N. (2006). Confronting confinement-A report of the commission on safety and abuse in America's prisons. *Wash. UJL & Pol'y*, *22*, 385.

Grant, J. M., Mottet, L., Tanis, J. E., Harrison, J., Herman, J., & Keisling, M. (2011). *Injustice at Every Turn: A Report of the National Transgender Discrimination Survey*. National Center for Transgender Equality.

Greenberg G.A., & Rosenheck, R.A. (2008). Jail incarceration, homelessness, and mental health: A national study," *Psychiatry Services*. Retrieved from ps.psychiatryonline.org/doi/full/10.1176/ps.2008.59.2.170.

Hackl, A. M., Becker, A. B., & Todd, M. E. (2016). "I Am Chelsea Manning": Comparison of Gendered Representation of Private Manning in US and International News Media. *Journal of Homosexuality*, *63*(4), 467–486.

Holzer, H.J., Raphael, S., & Stoll, M.A. (2003). Employment Barriers Facing Ex-Offenders. The Urban Institute. Washington, DC. Retrieved from urban.org/sites/default/files/publication/59416/410855-Employment-Barriers-Facing-Ex-Offenders.PDF.

Howell, A. W. (2009). A comparison of the treatment of transgender persons in the criminal justice systems of Ontario, Canada, New York, and California. *Buff. Pub. Int. LJ, 28*, 133.

James, S. E., Herman, J. L., Rankin, S., Keisling, M., Mottet, L., & Anafi, M. (2016). *The Report of the 2015 U.S. Transgender Survey*. Washington, DC: National Center for Transgender Equality.

Jenness, V., Sexton, L., & Sumner, J. (2011). Transgender inmates in California's prisons: An empirical study of a vulnerable population. *Report submitted to the California Department of Corrections and Rehabilitation.*

Kosilek v. Spencer, No. 12-2194 (1st Cir. 2014).

Majd, K., Marksamer, J., & Reyes, C. (2016). *Hidden Injustice: Lesbian, Gay, Bisexual and Transgender Youth in Juvenile Courts.*

Maggert v. Hanks. (1997). United States: United States Court of Appeals for the Seventh Circuit.

Matricardi, D. (2015). Binary imprisonment: Transgender inmates ensnared within the system and confined to assigned gender. *Mercer L. Rev., 67*, 707.

Medina-Tejada v. Sacramento County, No. CIV. S-04-138 FCD/DAD (E.D. Cal. Feb. 27, 2006).

Meriweather v. Faulkner, 821 F.2d 408 (7th Cir. 1987).

Nylund, D., & Waddle, H. (2015). Breaking out of the gender binary: Liberating transgender prisoners. In Afuape, T., & Hughes, G. *Liberation practices: Towards Emotional Wellbeing Through Dialogue.* (140-148). Routledge.

Qian, S. (2017, November 11). Activist CeCe McDonald takes allies to task in public talk. *The Chronicle*. Retrieved from https://www.dukechronicle.com/article/2017/11/171129-qian-cece-mcdonald

Queally, J. (2015, September, 10). San Francisco jails to house transgender inmates based on gender preference. *Los Angeles Time.* Retrieved from http://www.latimes.com/local/lanow/la-me-ln-transgender-san-francisco-jails-20150910-story.html

Raphael, S. (2011). Incarceration and prisoner reentry in the United States. *The ANNALS of the American Academy of Political and Social Science, 635*(1), 192-215.

Stelloh, T. (2019, March 25). Transgender, gay migrants allegedly suffer 'rampant' abuse at New Mexico ICE facility. *NBC News.* Retrieved from https://www.nbcnews.com/news/us-news/transgender-gay-migrants-allegedly-suffer-rampant-abuse-new-mexico-ice-n987286

Stack, L. (2019, May 9). Chelsea Manning is released from jail, but she may return soon. *The New York Times.* Retrieved from https://www.nytimes.com/2019/05/09/us/chelsea-manning-jail.html

Stern, M. J., Oehme, K., & Stern, N. (2016). A test to identify and remedy anti-gay bias in child custody decisions after Obergefell. *UCLA Women's LJ, 23*, 79.

Stevens v. Williams, 05-CV-1790-ST (D. Or. Mar. 27, 2008).

Stohr, M. K., & Walsh, A. (2018). *Corrections: From Research, to Policy, to Practice.* Sage Publishing: Los Angeles.

Strangio, C. (2015, November 16). Government to Chelsea Manning: 'We're denying your treatment for your own good'. American Civil Liberties Union. Retrieved from https://www.aclu.org/blog/lgbt-rights/transgender-rights/government-chelsea-manning-were-denying-your-treatment-your-own

Sumner, J., & Jenness, V. (2014). Gender integration in sex-segregated US prisons: the paradox of transgender correctional policy. *In Handbook of LGBT Communities, Crime, and Justice* (pp. 229–259). Springer, New York, NY.

Tarzwell, S. (2006). The Gender Lines are Marked with Razor Wire: Addressing State Prison Policies and Practices for the Management of Transgender Prisoners. *Colum. Hum. Rts. L. Rev., 38,* 167.

The Chelsea Manning Case: A Timeline. (2017, May 9). American Civil Liberties Union. Retrieved from https://www.aclu.org/blog/free-speech/employee-speech-and-whistleblowers/chelsea-manning-case-timeline

Transgender inmate Ashley Diamond released from Georgia prison after pressure from SPLC lawsuit. (2015, August 31). Southern Poverty Law Center. Retrieved from https://www.splcenter.org/news/2015/08/31/transgender-inmate-ashley-diamond-released-georgia-prison-after-pressure-splc-lawsuit

U.S. Const., amend. XIV.

U.S. Department of Justice, Harris County Sheriff's Office (HCSO) (Houston, TX). (2013). *Lesbian, Gay, Bisexual, Transgender and Intersex, (L.G.B.T.I.) Training Program and Agency Policy.* Retrieved from https://nicic.gov/lesbian-gay-bisexual-transgender-and-intersex-lgbti-training-program-and-agency-policy

U.S. Department of Justice, National PREA Resource Center. (2016, March 24). *Does a policy that houses transgender or intersex inmates based exclusively on external genital anatomy violate Standard 115.42(c) & (e)?* Retrieved from https://www.prearesourcecenter.org/node/3927

Wiltz, Teresa. (2016, December 21). What Crimes Are Eligible for Deportation? Pew Research Center. Retrieved from https://www.pewtrusts.org/en/research-and-analysis/blogs/stateline/2016/12/21/what-crimes-are-eligible-for-deportation

Wodda, A., & Panfil, V. R. (2014). Don't talk to me about deception: The necessary erosion of the trans panic defense. *Alb. L. Rev., 78,* 927.

World Professional Association for Transgender Health. (2017). *Standards of Care for the Health of Transsexual, Transgender, and Gender-Nonconforming People, Version 7.* Retrieved from https://www.wpath.org/publications/soc

CHAPTER 17

Understanding Crimes Against and Amongst LGBTQ through an Intersectionality Lens

Dr. Michelle Boone-Thornton | *Saint Leo University*

Overview

The LGBTQ population encompasses a large number of individuals whose sexual identities dictates how they view themselves and attempts to answers the question, "Who am I?' LGBTQ struggles are unique and specific because changing ones sexual identity influences all prior relationships and social constructs. Some members emigrate from other countries were they are persecuted without justice. Social inequalities experienced by the group promotes crimes against and by its members. Characteristics such as homelessness, rejection, and isolation makes them easy targets for violence and victimization. Collecting data is difficult due to under reporting, fear of retaliation, being transient, and their inability to obtain and/or maintain regular employment. LGBTQ survival behaviors are a criterion for criminal activity. Survival behaviors focus on meeting necessities such as food, shelter, clothing, safety, and the money or support needed to secure these items. Many LGBTQ persons exhibit a "Do whatever it takes" mentality that includes using drugs, prostitution, illegal weapons, stealing, and robbery. The impact of legislation passed during the Obama administration and support from Hollywood has brought awareness to many of the hardships that LGBTQ members face but it has made minimal progress in the area of social justice.

Learning Outcomes

- Bring about awareness and discussion about crimes as it relates to the LGBTQ population.
- Discuss the "Systems Failure" that members of the LGBTQ population experience.
- Students should understand how hate and homophobic behaviors are the catalyst to crime in the LGBTQ community.
- Students should develop a greater understanding of the self-identity crisis as it relates to sexual orientation, gender identity, and gender expression amongst LGBTQ members.

The LGBTQ View of Crime

This chapter provides an introduction to a unique perspective on criminal activity as it relates to the LGBTQ population. The author does not condone crime in any form as being acceptable; however, there are some instances when crime becomes a vicious cycle of survival. The vulnerability of the LGBTQ community makes them victims on both sides of the law (some of which we will discuss in this chapter). Although, data cannot conclusively support that all members of the LGBTQ population are negatively impacted by their gender and sexual identity choices as it relates to crimes against their persons but to some degree, they all experience discrimination and prejudices due to heteronormativity. Media channels detail several accounts of violent acts against members of the LGBTQ community due to homophobia. This irrational fear is primarily based on stereotypes, ignorance, and lack of knowledge. It has led to a hatred, aversion, and/or dislike of lesbians, gay, bisexual, transgender, queer people who are discriminated against solely because they are different and their homosexuality.

Although some members within the group are impacted more severely than others, prejudices extend across race, age, gender identity, and ethnicity. After being ostracized by society, friends and family; members resort to crime to meet basic needs and/or support their new way of life. They often struggle with self-identity and homelessness. LGBTQ members endure hate crimes, health disparities, and a multitude of obstacles that makes the vulnerable to a variety of injustices. The information provided herein utilizes an intersectionality approach to bring about awareness and understanding of crime from the victim/perpetrator framework that is embedded in the LGBTQ community.

The Crime of Non-Conformity

Self-identify refers to the attributes, characteristics, qualities and abilities that people use to define who they are as it relates to their surroundings and the world around them. According to Rosario, Schrimshaw, Hunter & Braun (2006) most members of the LGBTQ community struggle with coming to grips in determining "Who I am". Unlike heterosexual individuals who use social cues and constructs in their environment to help shape and reinforce their alignment with the world around them, members of the LGBTQ community's paradigms are distorted. They know that they are different and are constantly being pressured by society, their environment, parents, and friends and feel they must conceal their true identity and conform to heteronormal expectations so they can be accepted (Ryan, 2003).

Heteronormativity occurs when you live outside of the framework of boy/girl, man/woman, and husband/wife that is dictated by society. Erikson's fifth stage of development, identity versus role confusion, mirrors much of what LGBTQ members endure while they continuously search for self for extended periods of time. For members of the LGBTQ community self-identity is a process that involves disorganized thinking, procrastination, and avoidance of issues and action. There is an inability to connect to the heterosexual community as well as isolation from the LGBTQ community for fear of association (Ryan, 2003). Learning when and how to safely disclose their identity is a costly decision for the LGBTQ community. Members are guarded about sexuality and gender identity to include keeping the truth from parents and siblings. This state of constant turmoil and stress can lead to "Coming Out" and/or may even take its toll on the psyche (Rhoades, Rusow, Bond, Lanteigne, Fulginiti, & Goldbach, 2018). At this point, members no longer have to hide who they truly are, can openly connect with members of the LGBTQ community, and begin the uninhibited process of self-identity. However, "Coming Out" is a doubled edge sword. It can positively impact self-esteem but increases the risk for abuse, harassment, discrimination and rejections.

The Crime of Abandonment

Homelessness amongst the LGBTQ population is impacted by members who emigrate to the United States to escape persecution by their country of origin. There are several countries that impose criminal penalties to include death, for engaging in "homosexual acts" (Dworkin & Yi, 2003). In addition, many youth turn to life on the streets after being excluded by peers and rejected by their families. Unfortunately, in the U.S. many homeless LGBTQ members are turned away by shelters (Haas, Herman & Rodgers, 2014).

Data collected by the Williams Institute indicates, 40% of the homeless youth served by agencies identify as LGBT. A breakdown of the agencies reveal, 43% of clients served by drop-in centers (open in daytime provides food and other services) identified as LGBT; 30% of street outreach (food, clothing, shelter, and medical care and a list of resources

The Crime of Abandonment

provided by counselors who go into areas looking for homeless people) clients identified as LGBT, and 30% of clients utilizing housing programs (temporary/short-term housing) identified as LGBT. This transient lifestyle (moving from relative to relative, city to city and shelter to shelter) is perpetuated by the constant search for stable housing along with employment, healthcare and a multitude of other necessities. In addition, youth who are placed in group homes and in foster care experience abuse at the hands of their foster parents and group home residents and service providers due to stigmatization, prejudices, and rejected by the dominate society (Love, 2014). Homelessness lends itself to a variety of crimes against members of the LGBTQ community to include abuse, sexually exploitation, and human trafficking. Living on the streets without food and shelter increases the predisposition for crime as members rob, steal, beg, borrow and do what they have to do to survive.

Crime and Violence in LGBTQ Community

Violence in the LGBTQ community are evident in a multitude of areas but for this chapter we will explore, hate crimes, intimate partner violence, and bullying. The FBI (2019) defines a hate crime as a "criminal offense against a person or property motivated in whole or in part by an offender's bias against a race, religion, disability, sexual orientation, ethnicity, gender, or gender identity." According to Waters and Yacka-Bible (2017) the number of homicides of LGBTQ cisgender (person identifies with their birth sex) men increased 400% from 2016 (four incidents) to 2017 (20 reported homicides). The rates of violence crimes involving weapons, sustained injuries and requiring medical attention increased, as well. Forty-six

percent of LGBTQ people who experienced hate violence sustained an injury (up from 31% in 2016), 42% sought medical attention (up from 23% in 2016) and 27% reported that their attackers used weapons (up from 13% in 2016). Although these numbers show an overall increase, they still may not represent all offenses because many hate crimes go unreported for fear of retaliation. Hate crimes and violence against members of the LGBTQ community occurs worldwide. Identifying as LGBTQ is judged as being outside of societal the norms and/or religion. This violation is

Crime and Violence in LGBTQ Community

not tolerated by mainstream society and members of the LGBTQ community can be subjected to imprisonments, brutally and even death (Dworkin & Yi, 2003).

Intimate Partner Violence

According to Morin (2014) intimate partner violence (IPV) formerly called domestic violence occurs at the same frequency in the LGBTQ community as with heterosexual partners. It includes but is not limited to, physical violence, rape, and/or stalking. Violence is classified as four categories: threatening behavior, sexual violence, physical violence, and psychological or emotional abuse. However, legislation and enforcement of laws differs from state to state in the level of severity and punishment based on the sexual identity of the victims. Disparities in treatment for IPV crimes that occur between LGBTQ and heterosexual partners is adversely impacted by gender orientation and sexual identity. Members of the LGBTQ community report that they are subjected to homophobic reactions by the police, social services providers, and the courts. This behavior perpetuates fear in reporting IPV, seeking treatment, and or therapy for the trauma that is experienced (Morin, 2104).

Intimate Partner Violence

Bullying and Cyberbullying

Haas et al. (2014) utilized the National Transgender Discrimination Survey to collect data from LGBTQ youth which indicated that 50% of the youth who participated in the survey indicated that they were bullied at school. Stomp-Out Bullying is a non-profit organization working to bring awareness and prevent bullying in schools. The non-profit reports that during the 2017-2018 school year, nine out of ten LGBTQ students reported being harassed, excluded, threatened, and bullied. Most of the research over the past few years indicates that schools are unsafe, faculty are not adequately training to support LGBTQ students, and the educational system is failing to keep lesbian, gay, bisexual, transgender and queer students safe. Bullying can occur in all school components to include, before and after school programs, and school buses.

Bullying and Cyberbullying

Cyberbullying is just as detrimental as negative images, homophobic and threatening messages are shared on social media twitter, email, text and a multitude of other formats. Bullying negatively impacts LGBTQ students, school attendance, graduation, grades/GPA, and the desire to pursue higher education programs (Kosciw, Greytak, & Diaz, 2009). There are national bullying and various educational campaigns to address violence in schools as well as, counseling programs, legislation, and non-profits that have been developed to support LGBTQ students in school, students in the LGBTQ community turn to suicide in an effort to try to end the relentless persecution that they are subjected to (Rhoades et al., 2018). The American Foundation for Suicide Prevention and the Williams Institute at UCLA School of Law analyzed survey data and reported that the prevalence of suicide attempts was highest amongst 18-24-year-old's at (45%). The study concluded that this group were most vulnerable due to, rejection by family and friends, discrimination, violence, and mental health problems. Bullying and cyberbullying are crimes that occur daily in the LGBTQ community.

Health Disparities in the LGBTQ Community

The cost of and obtaining basic healthcare is an issue for many Americans and is even more of a problem for the LGBTQ community. Findings from the William Institute 2014 revealed that 60% of the LGBTQ population surveyed said that health care providers refused treatment. This type of discrimination can discourage members from seeking healthcare as it relates to sick visits, preventative treatment, or follow-up care. Most members visit community health centers, and health departments to avoid the discrimination and humiliation (Mirza & Rooney, 2018). In addition, their lifestyle places them at a greater risk for the human immunodeficiency virus (HIV) and acquired immunodeficiency syndrome (AIDS) which can have severe consequences if left untreated and can be spread unknowingly. LGBTQ members who disclosed that they were HIV positive reported being denied medication. Homeless youth are at risk for sexually transmitted diseases (STD's), alcohol and drug abuse, mental health problems, and other serious health conditions. They receive no regular medical check-up, prevention care, or treatment for cold, viruses, or physical injuries (Rhoades et al., 2018).

Members of the transgender population undergo hormone therapy. This treatment helps them match their outward appearance to the gender that they identify with. Black market sex-change hormones are a thriving and very lucrative business. Many in the transgender community use this illegal source to get pills and injections in exchange for money, drugs, and or sexual favors. Of course, these are not the only issues that LGBTQ members have to deal with when it comes to health disparities, but these topics were highlighted to showcase the absorbent cost of treatment, discrimination that members of the community encounter, and the propensity for crime.

Inequalities within the LGBTQ Community Perpetuate Crime

There are many social injustices and issues of inequality that encompass the LGBTQ community. Gay, transgender, and gender nonconforming youth are at a significantly higher risk of being victims of crimes because they experience a total systems failure. They have been abandoned by their families, denied treatment by the health systems, victimized by the educational system, experiencing homelessness, discriminated against by employers, and overrepresented in the criminal justice system. Approximately 300,000 gay and transgender youth are arrested and/or detained each year, and many are on track for entering the school-to-prison pipeline (Hunt & Moodie, 2012). These injustices are not just specific to youth but occur in the LGBTQ community across race, gender, ethnicity, and age. The Obama administration championed the LGBTQ community. There were legislations passed to protect against bullying, discrimination in employment, housing, and improve health care. The administration supported same-sex marriage and worked to advance and protect the rights of LGBTQ persons around the world (Perry & McCormick, 2015). However, even with the recent legislation that has been passed on behalf of the LGBTQ community and increasing acceptance by the general population, there is still a tremendous need for advocacy work, lobbyist, leadership, and the creation of new laws to protect the rights LGBTQ individuals (Brubaker, Harper, & Singh, 2011).

Summary

When you factor the many hardships experienced by the LGBTQ population, crime is an aftermath. This chapter provides just a glimpse of information from an intersectionality perspective about the LGBTQ community as it relates to crime. There are many aspects that are not explored, however, those that have been explored are quite compelling. Crime weaves itself throughout the LGBTQ community and is multifaceted. This topic deserves more exploration and should be studied and investigated. There are many resources available to include; organizations, agencies, non-profits, and government funded programs throughout the United States that support and provide services and research/statistics on the LGBTQ community. They can help provide more insight and knowledge about this phenomenon.

Discussion Questions:

1. Why is homelessness a serious problem in the LGBTQ community especially with teenagers?

2. What are some of the problems LGBTQ youth face in school and how does it impact educational outcomes?

3. How does the process of self-identity differ for members of the LGBTQ community and what are some of the problems LGBTQ members face as a result of "Coming Out"?

4. Many people in the U.S. face problems as it relates to receiving adequate health care but what makes the LBGTQ population different as it relates to medical treatment, regular check-ups, preventative care and follow-up.

5. Explain the impact that a heteronormative society has on the LGBTQ population and what can be done to change the negative effects.

References

Brubaker, M. D., Harper, A., & Singh, A. A. (2011). Implementing multicultural-social justice leadership strategies when advocating for the rights of lesbian, gay, bisexual, transgender, queer, and questioning persons. *Journal for Social Action in Counseling & Psychology*, 3(1), 44–58.

Dworkin, S., & Yi, H. (2003). LGBT identity, violence, and social justice: The psychological is political. *International Journal for the Advancement of Counselling*, 25(4), 269–279.

FBI: What We Investigate-Civil Rights. Retrieved February 27, 2019 https://www.fbi.gov/investigate/civil-rights/hate-crimes

Haas, A. P., Herman, J. L., and Rodgers, P. L. (2014) American Foundation for Suicide Prevention The William Institute UCLA School of Law Suicide Attempts among Transgender and Gender Non-Conforming Adults: FINDINGS OF THE NATIONAL TRANSGENDER DISCRIMINATION SURVEY

Hunt, J., Moodie, A. C. (2012) The Unfair Criminalization of Gay and Transgender Youth: An Overview of the Experiences of LGBT Youth in the Juvenile Justice System, Center for American Progress 1-8 (brief), June 29, 2012

Kosciw, J. G., Greytak, E. A., & Diaz, E. M. (2009). Who, what, where, when, and why: Demographic and ecological factors contributing to hostile school climate for lesbian, gay, bisexual, and transgender youth. *Journal of Youth & Adolescence*, 38(7), 976–988. https://doi-org.saintleo.idm.oclc.org/10.1007/s10964-009-9412-1

LOVE, A. (2014). A room of one's own: Safe placement for transgender youth in foster care. *New York University Law Review*, 89(6), 2265–2300.

Mirza, S A., & Rooney, C. (2018) Discrimination Prevents LGBTQ People from Accessing Health Care. Center for American Progress https://www.americanprogress.org/issues/lgbt/news/2018/01/18/445130/discrimination-prevents-lgbtq-people-accessing-health-care/

Morin, C. (2014). Re-traumatized: How gendered laws exacerbate the harm for same-sex victims of intimate partner violence. *New England Journal on Criminal & Civil Confinement*, 40(2), 477–497.

Perry, R. K., & McCormick II, J. P. (2015). LGBT politics and rights through the Obama era: President Barack Obama's evolution on LGBT issues. *Research in Race & Ethnic Relations*, 19, 49–75.

Rhoades, H., Rusow, J., Bond, D., Lanteigne, A., Fulginiti, A., & Goldbach, J. (2018). Homelessness, mental health and suicidality among LGBTQ youth accessing crisis services. *Child Psychiatry and Human Development*, 49(4), 643–651.

Rosario, M., Schrimshaw, E. W., Hunter, J., & Braun, L. (2006). Sexual identity development among lesbian, gay, and bisexual youths: Consistency and change over time. *Journal of Sex Research*, 43(1), 46–58.

Ryan, C. (2003). Lesbian, gay, bisexual, and transgender youth: Health concerns, services, and care. *Clinical Research & Regulatory Affairs*, 20(2), 137–158

Stomp Out Bullying: Culture the Change
https://www.stompoutbullying.org/get-help/about-bullying-and-cyberbullying/lgbtq-bullying

Waters, E., Yacka-Bible, S. (2017) A Crisis of Hate: A mid-year report on lesbian, gay, bisexual, transgender and Queer Hate Violence Homicides, National Coalition for Anti-Violence programs, New York City Gay and Lesbian Anti-Violence Project, Inc. https://avp.org/ncavp/

Wikipedia (2019) History of violence against LGBT people in the United States https://en.wikipedia.org/wiki/History_of_violence_against_LGBT_people_in_the_United_States

CHAPTER 18

Against the Grain: Women in Policing

Dr. Debbie Mims | Saint Leo University
Dr. Karin May | Saint Leo University

Contributed by Dr. Debbie Mims and Dr. Karin May. Copyright © Kendall Hunt Publishing Company.

Overview

This chapter examines the emergence of police women throughout history in a predominately male dominated profession. Historically, women in law enforcement were assigned stereotypical tasks that involved dealing with issues related to children and women. Early police women fought hard to break out of the traditional stereotypical feminine roles and into the dominated White heterosexual profession. Women and advocacy groups have helped to facilitate changes in the labor force through the Equal Pay Act and the Civil Rights Act of 1964, development of the National Organization for Women in 1966, Title IX Education Amendments of 1972 and the Pregnancy Discrimination Act of 1979. In spite of these historical rulings, policewomen today are still haunted by many of those traditional stereotypes. Lesbian, gay, bi-sexual, transsexual and queer (LBGTQ) individuals further challenge the traditional police officer stereotypical role when entering the profession. This chapter will look at these challenges and discuss the culture of the thin blue line and the future of women in policing.

Learning Outcomes

- Students should understand the profile of modern policing in America
- Students should identify the early roles of women in law enforcement
- Students should recognize the characteristics of what is considered the police sub-culture
- Students should comprehend the dynamics of being a lesbian police officer

History of Women in Policing

Since the mid-1800's the emergence of modern policing in America has remained a predominately male profession. Unfortunately, even with the many advances in police reform and increased representation of women and racial/ethnic minorities, it still remains a White-male-dominated profession (Novak, Smith, Cordner & Roberg, 2016). Despite the approximate 18,000 federal, state, county and municipal law enforcement agencies throughout the United States, females make up roughly only 15% of the law enforcement workforce, compared to their 85% male counterparts (Bureau of Justice Statistics, 2018). Of the 15 % of female law enforcement officers, only 9.6% hold supervisory roles within their agencies. These numbers indicate that although women have "come a long way baby" in the profession of law enforcement it remains a predominately male vocation (Bureau of Justice Statistics, 2018).

© Everett Collection/Shutterstock.com

Throughout the last fifty years, women who wanted to pursue a career in law enforcement were faced with sexual harassment, sexist jokes, insults, downgrading remarks, propositions, and blatant forms of locker room gossip (Rabe-Hemp, 2009). Often, they were assigned to stereotyped dead-end positions of meter maid, working with juveniles and positions within the school's system; often being denied the privilege of working in coveted assignments like canine, SWAT, homicide, air patrol, marine patrol, and motorcycle squads. Although the rate of female police officers has not grown exponentially over the past decade as expected, policing in America has become more diverse over the past decade, and women in law enforcement are better off today than they were fifty years ago (Archbold & Schultz, 2012).

In 1905, Lola Baldwin became the first sworn "policewoman" to be hired by the Portland Oregon Police Department. Baldwin's role as a policewoman (patrolling in plainclothes) was restricted to special social work type cases involving primarily women, children and juveniles. Always in plainclothes, Baldwin was assigned to "patrol" areas in which juveniles might congregate, places like movie theaters, dance halls, and train stations, being on the lookout for promiscuous behavior (Archbold & Schulz, 2012). It wasn't long before Baldwin's work within the community, helping to prevent juvenile delinquency, was noticed by other law enforcement agencies. Soon, agencies across the country were emulating Portland's example and began to hire women in specialist roles investigating sexual assaults, detecting shoplifters and pickpockets (Eisenberg, Kent, & Wall, 1973; Walker, 1977).

In 1910, Alice-Stubbins-Wells was hired by the Los Angeles Police Department to assist women and delinquent youth who were in trouble with the law. Shortly after that, Stubbins-Wells became the voice for the national policewomen's movement, founding the International Association of Policewomen, an association that petitioned for the employment of policewomen (Walker, 1977). From 1910 to 1916, the role of women in law enforcement would begin to increase as women were put into positions as social workers and jail matrons (Owings, 1925). Although women's' presence in police work began to increase between 1916 and 1965, their roles continued to be disregarded and downplayed by the male dominated field of police officers and often taunted as "mothers with badges." Stereotypical metaphors of women police officers remained throughout much of the 60s and into the early 70s maintaining that women were not competent to handle the wide-range everyday police work of their male counterparts. According to Wilson and McLaren (1963), men were more effective as supervisors and administrators and "were less likely to become irritable and overly critical under emotional stress" (p. 334).

By the early 1960s, the roughly 2,400 police women employed in municipal police agencies across the United States began to challenge their pre-determined roles. However, history wasn't made until 1968, when the Indianapolis Police Department assigned the first of two women (Betty Blankenship and Elizabeth Coffal) to patrol duties, putting them on an equal status with their male colleagues (Archbold & Schultz, 2012; Milton, 1972; Novak, Smith, Cornder, & Roberg, 2016). Employment discriminatory lawsuits like the Equal Pay Act and the Civil Rights Act of 1964, development of the National Organization for Women in 1966, Title IX Education Amendments of 1972 and the Pregnancy Discrimination Act of 1979 helped to ease some of the challenges women faced going into the police force. In 1972, the Civil Rights Acts of 1964 extended the requirements to government entities, and combined with the Crime Control Act of 1973, specifying that agencies would be denied federal funds if they implemented any employment discriminatory practices and job assignments. The local units of government were excluded from this requirement until the passage of the

Equal Employment Opportunity Act of 1972; women could finally see a breakthrough in equal treatment for women police officers (Garmire, 1978; Archbold & Schultz, 2012). These acts, in conjunction with Executive Order 11478, issued by President Richard Nixon in 1969, eliminating discriminatory practices in federal employment related to age, race, religion, sex, ethnicity, or disability; contributed to a steady increase of women applying for police officer positions in both federal and local agencies. The U.S. Civil Service Commission, in 1971 extended the firearms exception to allow women to be able to carry a firearm and by 1986 women police officers could be seen in the U.S. Secret Service, U.S. Postal Inspection Service, special agents, and assignments in field operations (Schultz, 2009).

© iofoto/Shutterstock.com

Over the next few years many of the nation's largest law enforcement agencies began to integrate women onto their police force and "by 1979, the percentage of policewomen assigned to patrol was approximately 87 in city departments serving populations larger than 50,000" (Novak, Smith, Cornder,& Roberg, 2016 p. 383). Unfortunately, although women were carrying firearms and patrolling alongside their male counterparts, there remained many critics who contended that women were not physically or emotionally capable of handling the demands of police work, thus making it difficult for female police officers to be taken seriously (Hindman 1975; Vega & Silverman 1982). No empirical evidence supported this perception. To research gender-based policing, Bloch and Anderson (1974) conducted a study on the first generation of female police officers on patrol. Their study revealed that although both genders performed similarly, women police officers were less aggressive, made fewer arrests and were more successful in diffusing potentially violent situations than their male colleagues (Novak, Smith, Cornder, & Roberg, 2016).

Since the study by Bloch and Anderson in 1974, numerous research studies have been conducted on the effectiveness of gender performance in patrol officers. These studies have continually revealed that women police officers excel in many areas of policing and are as competent, efficient and skilled as their male colleagues. Furthermore, studies have shown that citizens' encounters with female police officers tend to have less citizen-police complaints, less use of excessive and deadly force, and a positive influence on community relations (Robinson, 2000; Novak, Brown, and Frank, 2001; Sun 2011). Studies have also shown that the role of a police officer, in general, can be more mentally challenging than physically; nevertheless, the subject of physical strength and the ability to perform in a physical confrontation continues to confront women in policing. Traditionally, the police sub-culture has placed value on machismo, physical strength, sexism, chauvinist characteristics and power and control; not characteristics formally connected to women (Franklin, 2005). Conversely, if a female police officer wants to be accepted and treated with respect, she has to embody the persona and traits of her hegemonic counterparts which oftentimes conflicts with the cultural expectations of females (Galvin-White & O'Neal, 2015; Morash & Haarr, 2011; Rabe-Hemp, 2009).

Although women police officers are better off today than their female predecessors, the male cop persona is still largely alive and well. Due to mandatory department diversity training, much of the blatant harassment and sexist jokes have given way to more subtle forms of discrimination. If anything, time has shown that women police officers make:

> "a unique contribution to law enforcement, and a preponderance of studies show that they do the job with the same effectiveness as men—even when the task involves physical aggression which is only about 10% of the time" (Kirschman, 2009, p. 201).

LGBT Issues in Policing

As women have gained a foothold into the predominately White, male profession of law enforcement we have seen an increase in women who have identified as lesbian join in the rank and file of law enforcement across the nation (Gavin-White & O'Neal, 2015). When female officers join the force, they face the stereotypical beliefs of being the "weaker sex," timid, and incapable of performing the duties associated with law enforcement. Furthermore, if either a heterosexual or homosexual female officer attempt to dispel this notion by adopting the police officer persona of being tough, competent and qualified, she risks being viewed as a "bitch," or perceived as a "dyke," or butch (Miller & Lilley, 2014; Rabe-Hemp, 2009). It was not until 1981 that the New York Police Department, Sergeant Charles Cochran, made history by openly acknowledging that he was gay (Barlow & Barlow, 2000). Studies by Cannon (2005) and Olivera & Murataya (2001) revealed that undergraduate students pursuing a criminal justice major were less accepting of lesbian and gay individuals and held strong opinions regarding the hiring of gay and lesbians as police officers.

A qualitative study by Miller, Forest and Jurik (2003) surveyed both gay and lesbian (GL) police officers examining how this population coped with homosexuality within the police subculture and what strategies the GL police officers utilized to manage their sexual orientation within the police environment. Perhaps because of the controversy generated by the "Don't Ask, Don't Tell" policy relative to the military, when President Clinton decided to include homosexually oriented persons among the ranks of federal law enforcement officers.

Gay law enforcement officers in states that do not recognize sexual orientation as a protected class are dependent upon the good will of their colleagues or upon their ability to keep their sexual orientation private. Community-oriented policing is likely to be most effective at the local level, the benefits of doing so, state and local law enforcement agencies, have been somewhat slow to follow the lead of federal agencies in admitting lesbians and gay men into their ranks. Leinen (1993), Buhrke (1996), and Barlow and Barlow (2000) all describe numerous struggles faced by gay and lesbian police officers imposed upon them by their departments, and indeed by organizations ostensibly created to represent the interests of officers (Lyons et al., 2008).

A study conducted in 1988 by the National Center for Women and Policing, suggested 80% of female police officers have been sexually harassed at work, including explicit lesbian-baiting and lewd commentary by male colleagues (Garcia, 2003). Homosexual police officers regardless of race, ethnicity, or gender are subordinated by the production of hegemonic masculinity. In this regard, lesbian officers face barriers similar to those confronting racial-ethnic minorities and White women in policing, yet there are significant differences (Leinen 1993; Buhrke 1996).

© Motortion Films/Shutterstock.com

Research suggests that homosexuals are the social group most disliked by police (Burke, 1994). Such beliefs persist despite empirical evidence that lesbian officers perform police duties as well as heterosexuals. It is also still legal to deny employment on the basis of sexual orientation in most jurisdictions. With 24 states still criminalizing consensual same-gender sexual acts, gay and lesbian officers also occupy the ironic position of having to enforce penal codes that they violate themselves (Leinen, 1993). As a result, lesbians and their allies in criminal justice fear for their jobs and sometimes even their lives. The decisions to be "out," as well as other workplace strategies, are a separate decision shaped not only by an individual's social location (e.g., gender, race, and ethnicity) but also by situational factors, such a time on the job. Unfortunately, this single decision sometimes comes with immeasurable consequences that can include harassment or discrimination. According to Kirschman (2007) author of *I Love a Cop: What Police Families Need to Know,* interviewed openly gay and lesbian officers who stated that despite the obstacles of having to prove themselves, suffering harassment, insults, and stereotypical reputations of being a bitch; most officers believed the rewards of "coming out" exceeded the risks of staying in the closet.

Organizational and community climates of support or hostility for gay/lesbian rights also shape individual and collective strategies for constructing sexual identity (Buhrke, 1996; Bernstein, 1997). For example, fears about co-worker and supervisor hostilities, termination, loss of promotional opportunity, or denial of backup lead some officers to conceal their sexual orientation. Tensions between the police and lesbian and gay communities encourage some officers to hide their occupation from gay and lesbian friends as well as acquaintances. This behavior insinuates that once gay and lesbian officers prove their abilities, they will be accepted by their peers—as were White women and racial-ethnic minorities (Martin, 1992). As more police departments discover the advantages of community policing models, the gay and lesbian police officer's inclusion may represent more than a human rights effort; these nontraditional police officers may bring a range of roles and skills that can increase the flexibility of police work without sacrificing its crime-fighting mission.

Collected data from approximately 1,923 sworn law enforcement officers in the United States showed that female police (e.g., LGBTQ) reported more stress at work. Research suggests that female, LGBTQ officers, and other minority officers from racial and ethnic groups face additional issues within their chosen occupation. These issues include on-going stress or accumulative stress related to police work and ostracism within the police subculture. A woman may feel pressured to perform better than her male colleagues, in part because she thinks that a woman's performance will reflect positively or negatively on all women (Anderson & Papazoglou, 2015).

A study with gay and lesbian officers in the United States found that LGBTQ officers had to try harder than the typical White male officers to prove to their fellow officers that they were capable of the same job. In another study 1,100 police officers from a large metropolitan police department found that African-American female officers experienced burnout in significantly higher levels than non-minority officers. Policewomen have reported higher amounts of sexual harassment and feeling like an outsider when reporting incidents because male officers indicated that the harassment was warranted because it was their fault. Women working in criminal justice occupations may also encounter sexual harassment in a variety of forms. Such harassment may contribute to a hostile work environment in which submission to unwelcome sexual advances and comments becomes a condition of employment. Women who complain may be ostracized by their colleagues (Anderson and Papazoglou, 2015).

Minority female, LGBTQ officers, are more likely to experience discrimination than non-minority individuals. On the one hand, if women socialize with male colleagues, they may be perceived to be sexually available, which reflects negatively on women's professionalism. On the other hand, if women do not socialize (either by choice or by exclusion), they risk not learning information related to their job or promotion opportunities and may be labeled as "cold" or "lesbians." It is unclear if discrimination suffered by male coworkers or civilians contribute to the burden or reduce the likelihood that minority officers

© aquatarkus/Shutterstock.com

would experience discrimination from their work (Anderson and Papazoglou, 2015).

A qualitative study by Galvin-White and O'Neal (2015) examined interpersonal relationships among 15 lesbian police officers. Their research revealed the unspoken thin blue line conduct among law enforcement was one in which the "don't ask, don't tell" code prevailed. However, the study divulged the decision of whether to reveal one's sexuality within the workplace was an individualized and personal choice. Many of the study participants' indicated their individual and private decision to disclose their sexuality had a direct reflection on their perceived feelings of respect and overall success as a law enforcement officer. The decision to openly display one's sexuality is a personal matter, but those individuals who elected to come forward expressed relief and an unexpected show of support from coworkers and the community (Kirshman, 2007).

In conclusion, both gay and lesbian police officers have existed within the police subculture of the thin blue line for years. However, since ethnicity, race, and gender are visually obvious, a gay or lesbian police officer's sexual orientation is only apparent if the officer wants to make it known (Wilson, Longmire, Swymeler, 2009). Police agencies today are much more culturally diverse than those of yesterday. Openly gay and lesbian police officers are part of the increasing diversity seen in law enforcement agencies today, and the future progress of social reform looks promising.

Future of Women in Policing

Women are entering the field of law enforcement in increasing numbers and play a critical role in the development of modern policing (Lonsway, 2007). Today, there are higher levels of female police officers that play a role in community policing than ever before. Police agencies that have a greater commitment to community policing have shown to have more female police officers than agencies with less community policing initiatives. Currently in America, there are approximately 82,418 full-time sworn female police officers (Schuck, 2014). Women make up more than half of the U.S. population, but fewer than 13% of law enforcement officers are female (Path, 2019). Although men traditionally make up the vast majority of police officers in the country, agencies have taken note of the unique and indispensable qualities that women bring to the profession. Women in law enforcement are still under represented. Despite significant research and the evidence showing the profound impact female police officers have on the culture of policing, women still account for only approximately 15% of law enforcement officers. According to an article in the Law Enforcement and Public Safety Leadership titled *Why We Need More Women Working in Law Enforcement*, law enforcement departments realize how beneficial female officers are and the unique skills they bring to an agency. As the law enforcement profession becomes more standardized, the chance for advancement for female law enforcement officers will increase with promotion and improvements. Women in supervisory roles have been seen as symbols of organizational change. Many female police officers have received promotions into leadership positions within law enforcement agencies. However, women are underrepresented, especially in small and medium-sized police agencies (Schuck, 2014). The typical male leadership has given way to a more consultative style of law enforcement leadership. A significant challenge for police agencies is to make the organization aware of the advantages involved in incorporating a feminine leadership style (Silvestri, 1998). A change exists in the field of policing for women. As female officers continue to make great strides in achieving professional success by breaking down barriers, will play a big part in ensuring opportunities for future generations for women in policing.

Key Terms:

discriminatory practices	gay and bi-sexual police officers	policewomen
diversity		sexual orientation
female police officers	lesbian	stereotypes

Discussion Questions:

1. Discuss the role of early female police officers and compare and contrast that role with female officers of today.

2. Examine what is meant by the thin blue line and discuss how it affects the role of the female police officer.

3. Explain and discuss the obstacles that lesbian police and LGBT officers have had to overcome in the past and how diversity training within police agencies has helped to facilitate change.

4. Describe significant differences in female representation between county, and state law enforcement agencies and discuss what measures law enforcement agencies can take to promote recruiting and retaining female officers.

5. Explain some issues that are keeping female law enforcement officers from advancing to high-ranking positions within their agencies.

Web Links

https://journals.sagepub.com/doi/pdf/10.1177/1098611103254315?casa_token=EjIYG5XUApgA-AAAA:Jd9vef0BHiPDC9iruezcUsLEIwazlymmhNF5qMycSMqmR3yip7j5y6C23UGU-GRVzmBAqgkDyA

https://www.n-r-c.com/gender-balance-law-enforcement/#:~:text=Women%20in%20Law%20Enforcement%201%20Diversity%20in%2021,Legitimizing%20Law%20Enforcement%20Careers%20to%20Diverse%20Workforces.%20

https://www.ncjrs.gov/pdffiles1/nij/252963.pdf

https://www.allcriminaljusticeschools.com/law-enforcement/women-in-law-enforcement/

https://www.bing.com/videos/search?q=women+in+policing&qpvt=women+in+policing&FORM=VDRE

https://www.prisonpolicy.org/blog/2019/05/14/policingwomen/

http://iawp.org/

https://www.policefoundation.org/publication/on-the-move-the-status-of-women-in-policing/

https://justiceclearinghouse.com/resource/women-in-policing-performance-and-outcomes/

References

Andersen, J. P., & Papazoglou, K. (2015). *Compassion fatigue and compassion satisfaction among police officers: An understudied topic. among minority officers*

Archbold, C & Schulz, D. (2012). Research on women in policing: A look at the past, present and future. *Sociology Compass. 6.* 694-706. 10.1111/j.1751-9020.2012.0050

Barlow, D. E. & Barlow, M. H. (2000). *Police in a multicultural society: An American story.* Prospect Heights, IL: Waveland Press, Inc.

Bloch, P., and Anderson, D. (1974). *Policewomen on Patrol: Final Report.* Washington, DC: Police Foundation.

Buhrke, R. (1996). *A matter of justice: Lesbians and gay men in law enforcement.* Routledge.

Bureau of Justice Statistics. 2018. Local Police Departments, 2018. Washington DC: Bureau of Justice Statistics.

Cannon, K. D. (2005). Ain't no faggot gonna rob me!": Anti-Gay attitudes of criminal justice undergraduate majors. *Journal of Criminal Justice Education, 16*(2), 226-243,379. Retrieved September 27, 2007, from Criminal Justice Periodicals database Document ID: 991646611

Eisenberg, T., Kent, D. and Wall, C. (1973). *Police Personnel Practices in State and Local Government.* Washington, DC: Police Foundation.

Galvin-White, Chistine & O'Neal, Eryn. (2015). Lesbian police officers' interpersonal working relationships and sexuality disclosure: A qualitative study. *Feminist Criminology. 11.*10.1177/1557085115588359.

Garcia, V. (2003). Difference" in the police department: Women, policing, and "doing gender. *Journal of Contemporary Criminal Justice, 19*(3), 330-344.

Hassell, K. D., & Brandl, S. G. (2009). An examination of the workplace experiences of police patrol officers: The role of race, sex, and sexual orientation. *Police quarterly, 12*(4), 408-430.

Hindman, R. E. 1975. 'Survey Related to use of Female Law Enforcement Officers.' *Police Chief, April 4:* 58–9.

Kirschman, E. (2007). *I love a cop: What police families need to know.* New York, NY: Guilford Press

Law Enforcement and Public Safety Leadership (nd) https://onlinedegrees.sandiego.edu/women-in-law-enforcement

Leinen, S. H. (1993). *Gay cops.* Rutgers University Press.

Lonsway, K. A. (2007). Are we there yet? The progress of women in one large law enforcement agency. *Women & Criminal Justice, 18*(1-2), 1-48.

Lyons Jr, P. M., DeValve, M. J., & Garner, R. L. (2008). Texas police chiefs' attitudes toward gay and lesbian police officers. *Police Quarterly, 11*(1), 102-117.

Martin, S. E. (1996, July). Doing gender, doing police work: An examination of the barriers to the integration of women officers. *In Paper to the Australian Institute of Criminology Conference: First Australasian Women Police Conference.* Sydney (Vol. 29, p. 30).

Milton, C. (1972). *Women in Policing.* Washington, DC: Police Foundation.

Miller, S. L., & Lilley, T. G. (2014). Proving themselves: The status of LGBQ police officers. *Sociology Compass, 8,* 373-383.

Miller, S. L., Forest, K. B., & Jurik, N. C. (2003). Diversity in Blue: Lesbian and gay police officers in a masculine occupation. *Men and Masculinities, 5*(4), 355-385. http://dx.doi.org/10.1177/0095399702250841

Morash, M., & Haarr, R. N. (1995). Gender, workplace problems, and stress in policing. *Justice Quarterly, 12,* 113-140.

Novak, K., Brown, R. and Frank, J. (2011). Women on Patrol: An Analysis of Difference in Officer Arrest Behavior. Policing: *An International Journal of Police Strategies and Management 34*(4): 566-587.

Novak, K., Smith, B., Cornder, G., Roberg, R. (2016). *Police & Society.* New York, NY: Oxford University Press.

Olivero, J. M. & Murataya, R. (2001). Homophobia and university law enforcement students. *Journal of Criminal Justice Education 12,* 271-81.

Owings, C. (1925). *Women Police.* New York: Hitchcock.

Rabe-Hemp, C. (2008). Survival in an all-boys club: Policewomen and their fight for acceptance. *Policing: An International Journal of Police Strategies Management, 31*(2), 251-270.

Rabe-Hemp, C. (2009). POLICEwomen or policeWOMAN? Doing gender and police work. *Feminist Criminology, 4,* 114-129.

Robinson, A. (2000). Effects of a Domestic Violence Policy Change on Police Officers' Schemata. *Criminal Justice and Behavior, 27,* 600-624.

Schulz, Dorothy Moses 2005. '*Women in Federal Agency Law Enforcement.*' Pp. 908–911 in Encyclopedia of LawEnforcement 2, edited by Larry E. Sullivan and Dorothy Moses Schulz. Thousand Oaks, CA: Sage Reference.

Schulz, Dorothy Moses. 2009. 'Women special agents in charge: The first generation.' *Policing: An International Journal of Police Strategies and Management, 32,* 675-93.

Silvestri, M. (1998). Visions of the future: The role of senior policewomen as agents of change. *International Journal of Police Science Management, 1*(2), 148-161.

Sun, I. (2011). Policing domestic violence: Does officer gender matter? *Journal of Criminal Justice, 35*(6), 581-595.

Vega, Manuel and Ira Silverman. 1982. 'Female police officers as viewed by their male counterparts.' *Police Studies, 5,* 31-9.

Walker, S. (1977). *A Critical History of Police Reform.* Lexington, MA: Lexington Books.

Wilson, F, Longmire, D & Swymeler, W. (2009). The absence of gay and lesbian police officer depictions in the first three decades of the core cop film genre: Moving towards a cultivation theory perspective. School of Criminal Justice, University at Albany. *Journal of Criminal Justice and Popular Culture, 16* (1).

CHAPTER 19

Intersectionality of Women and Crime: Queer Women of Color's Experience in Law Enforcement

Sapphire Beverly | *Tarleton State University*

Overview

Historically, there has been a lack of women of color representation in law enforcement. There also has been limited research done on marginalized women's positions and personal experiences working in the law enforcement (Wilson, 2016). According to the Bureau of Justice Statistics, women in general only account for 15% of police officers (NRC, 2019). LGBT officers are facing issues regarding equal employment opportunities, which can contribute to the perception of racial and gender identity as well. The behavioral bias is a huge problem in police departments (Colvin, 2015). There is also underrepresentation of women of color in law enforcement which can be linked to cultural and organizational barriers (Greene, 2000). In the future, researchers should take into account the demographic, economic, social, and political barriers as well as personal experiences female officers in marginalized communities face (Greene, 2000). The purpose of this article is to identify the needs that have not been met, how environmental and social factors contribute to lack of representation in law enforcement, and the issues queer women of color face within law enforcement. The goal is to call attention to what needs to be done to improve the experiences of queer women of color in law enforcement.

Policing and Sexuality

To understand the mistreatment and lack of representation of queer Black women in the criminal justice system the social institution of policing has to be analyzed through a sociological lens. The occupation of policing is hypermasculine and male-dominated. There are ideas of heterosexual masculinity practices and social interactions within law enforcement (Miller, 2003). According to Miller (2003), "despite the structural barriers of homophobia and sexism that tempered these officers' full acceptance and access to the police subculture, lesbian and gay officers struggled to balance job demands with their sexual orientation, gender, race-ethnicity, and other dimensions of their identities." The struggle of social acceptance does not only extend for prohibiting hate crimes, same-sex marriages, and adoptions for LGBT individuals (Miller, 2003). The social institutions, such as policing, have varied tremendously in their acceptance of LGBT individuals. The criminal justice system is dominated by White, masculine, and heterosexual ethos (Miller, 2003). Marginalized groups, such as people/women of color and sexual minorities threaten the dominant groups and are faced with tremendous obstacles when going into law enforcement (Miller, 2003). Gender, sexual orientation, and other social differences serve as organizing features of work organizations (Miller, 2003). According to Joan Acker, "organizational policies and interactions control, segregate, exclude, and construct hierarchies of workers."

Furthermore, certain qualifications for jobs include unconscious and conscious images associated with race, gender, and identity to better the "appropriate" applicants' chances of getting the job. The socially deviant workers are more visible than those with a dominant social type (Miller, 2003). The members of the dominant group may exclude deviant types while reminding them of their differences, stereotypes, and microaggressions (Miller, 2003). The job expectations and performances often times reflect the dominant social type. Norms of heterosexuality pervade in systems, such as the criminal justice system. Policing is culturally seen as a job only masculine heterosexual men can handle. Historically, police work was associated with the images of working-class masculinity that emphasized physical strength and aggressiveness (Miller, 2003). Due to the nature of the job, criminal justice officers develop a close-knit subculture that emphasizes loyalty (Mennicke, 2016).

History of Black Women in Law Enforcement

To talk about the experience of a queer Black women's law enforcement experience, there has to be a historical background analysis on Black women's roles in law enforcement. Historically, in the mid to late 1860s, as a result to the Fifteenth Amendment, it guaranteed the right to vote for Black Americans. The earliest known cities to hire Black officers included Selma, Alabama, Jacksonville, Florida, Houston, and Galveston, Texas (Thompson, 2017). The Black women in law enforcement played a role beginning in the late 1800s. Georgia Ann Robinson became the first African-American female police officer in Los Angeles, California (Thompson, 2017). She began her career as a police officer at the age of 37. Robinson's desire to serve, led her to become involved with different community organizations (Thompson, 2017). A few years later, she became involved with homicide and juvenile cases. The only positions available that Robinson could hold was a jail matron and a juvenile crime prevention (Thompson, 2017).

The portrayal of Black female law enforcement officers in mainstream media started off as Blaxploitation Films such as Cleopatra Jones (Thompson, 2017). There was also the portrayal of Foxy Brown and Coffy, which were both undercover Black female police detectives. They were portrayed as the "jezabels" with tight clothes and high heels. These shows did inspire many Black women to become police officers because the embodiment of the women portrayed on the show were of strong and intelligent Black women (Thompson, 2017). Young Black girls could relate to them because they grew up in a neighborhood surrounded by drugs and had a strong connection to the community (Thompson, 2017). These women on television showed Black power and ideas of feminist thought. For example, Cleopatra Jones was seen as both feminine and fashionable, but at the same time she was talented and driven, even more than the men on the show. Back in that time period, Black women were seen as mammies, jezebels, and welfare queens, while White women were seen as pure and submissive (Thompson, 2017). This portrayal of Black women causes hostility in the workplace.

Queer Law Enforcement Treatment

To address the intersectionality of Black queer women the experiences of LGBT officers must also be represented. Previous research suggests that discrimination against LGBT officers is alarming. The discrimination is related back to their sexual orientation. A 2009 report by William Institute, found that

40% of LGBT-based discrimination in public employment came from the fields of law enforcement (Mennicke, 2016). With that being said, as it was highlighted previously the criminal justice values traditional masculinity which have led to the unfavored work experiences with those who identify as lesbian, gay, bisexual, and transgender. Gendered expectations, such as explicit laws, policies, and implicit culture has led to an environment where many LGBT officers have reported discrimination within the workplace (Mennicke, 2016). The sad thing is this does not account for the intersectionality identity of the officers which can be oppressed in the criminal justice system collectively such as the triple jeopardy of being female, Black, and queer.

There is emphasis in the diversification of law enforcement agencies reflecting the populations and communities in which they serve. The police agencies should help make sure the interests of all groups are considered when hiring. The only reason for the increase of LGBT hiring in law enforcement was because of affirmative action policies which led to racial and sexual diversification in law enforcement with the varying success depending on the geographic region (Mennicke, 2016). This shift has resulted in some improved relations and increased credibility within minority communities (Mennicke, 2016).

The integration of women has had different results. As more women became employed in law enforcement agencies the culture of criminal justice did not become more feminine (Mennicke, 2016). The criminal justice values masculine gender expressions, leading women to emphasize their masculine qualities (Mennicke, 2016). Women tend to access masculine capital by acting more masculine when in a male-dominated space. The female/masculine gender experience is rewarded through recruitment, promotion, and retention for being a represented as a masculine woman (Mennicke, 2016). However, women's leadership capabilities are undermined by the glass cliff, which is a theory that "women are put into positions of power and authority in times of chaos and crisis, setting them up to fail," (Mennicke, 2016). When women do fail at these leadership positions their leadership capabilities are challenged (Mennicke, 2016).

The recruitment of LGBT officers is mainly important for repairing community sanctions between LGBT and policing communities (Mennicke, 2016). LGBT liaison units have sprung up to attempt to improve relations but the research shows while the knowledge to programming is high and the access is low (Mennicke, 2016).

Black Women Officer Treatment

The issue with Black women officer's discrimination is the presence of discrimination in law enforcement (Thompson, 2017). This is identified by 92% of Black women officers feeling discrimination compared to, 50% of discrimination felt by White women officers (Thompson, 2017). Black women feel they have to demand respect while White women do not. Black women have reported that their bosses do not send White women into crime areas (Thompson, 2017). Black women have reported that they have no one to help them secure assignments, special training sessions or promotions (Thompson, 2017). Black women report verbal racial insults more frequently than White women (Thompson, 2017). Also, Black women say they have more trouble with racial discrimination from law enforcement colleagues than from the public (Thompson, 2017). Black women have greater rates of discrimination than White women in law enforcement and Black women see themselves as discriminated against because of their race and gender (Thompson, 2017). Black women experience their work in law enforcement differently than White women. Black women today express high levels of cynicism in policing and argue for the job.

Black and Queer Officer Experience

There is a lack of intersectional research surrounding queer Black women's experience in law enforcement with discrimination and challenges. Breaking it down by each marginalized identity is the best way to explain this. First, as a queer woman of color, in their career there will be many obstacles to overcome. As a Black woman, the officer will have to workplace discrimination such as microaggressions, stereotypes, and stigmas. Black women experience a higher level of workplace stressors and issues, such as language harassment, sex discrimination, and lack of mentors. Research shows, 40% of Black women have their judgement questioned in their area of occupation (Gadsden, 2018). One particular problem Black women face is being the only women of color at work which "the impact of being an 'only' is a phenomenon affecting 20% of all women and twice that for women of color where they feel uniquely alone, plus having the scrutiny for representing a whole group," (Gadsden, 2018).

Black women feel more microaggressions in the workplace because of their feeling of being the "only" woman of color or woman at all. When there is a lack of diversity representation in the workplace, there are often times biases and filters they may not be aware of (Gadsden, 2018). A Lubbock Black woman police officer explained "On certain calls that I went on, I have received comments from certain people on calls, racial slurs, I've been called out of my name," (Main, 2019). This shows that Black women have to deal with physical, sexual, and racial discrimination while in law enforcement. A lot of Black women also have to "code-switch" which involves embracing dominant culture among certain groups then switching to a more authentic self when around friends and family (Cheeks, 2018).

As a woman there are double standards and issues involving balancing family and career. There is a lack of peer acceptance when operation with a male-dominated police organization. Many female officers report feeling they have to work twice as hard to prove themselves and to be accepted, while male officers can just show up and gain acceptance. Women must overcome societal prejudice of being the "weaker" sex. The practice of retaining and hiring more women will lessen a police department's liability by reducing the underrepresentation of female officers.

As a queer, individual workplace discrimination seems to be widespread and distinct from heterosexual discrimination in workplaces (Mennicke, 2016). Sexual minorities are often stereotyped as defying traditional gender roles (Mennicke, 2016). An individual's failure to accept gender norms is met with negative assumptions about their ability to perform job duties (Mennicke, 2016). Therefore, an officer must be hypermasculine to be accepted. The lower rates of discrimination are linked to impression management (Mennicke, 2016). LGBT officers report less outright discrimination than LGBT workers, but that being said LGBT officers might report less discrimination because they have not been open about their sexual identities (Mennicke, 2016). The ongoing process of coming out at positive but LGBT officers can have negative consequences if they do come out (Mennicke, 2016). It is possible that those who disclose their identity do so because they work in an environment where their staff is more open minded. Those who are closeted are reading the norms of the police agency they work at (Mennicke, 2016). Agencies who openly hire and integrate LGBT officers have fewer negative consequences for effectiveness, performance, recruiting, and well-being (Mennicke, 2016).

Conclusion

In conclusion, the identities of being Black, queer, and a woman is a recipe for increased obstacles while working in law enforcement. Not only is she discriminated because she is a woman, but also because she is queer and Black. That makes for a triple jeopardy when dealing with the issues of intersectionality of a Black woman. There is a need for more ongoing research for the intersectionality of queer Black women in law enforcement and their experiences. This will help us better understand their experiences, identities, and how they change (Bridges & Moore, 2018). Also, it could help cater to a Black woman's need for better diversity training, intersectionality, training, etc. Accurate research can continue to learn more about the members of this group reflect, reveal, and reinforce forms of discrimination and inequality that shapes their lives as queer, Black women (Bridges & Moore, 2018).

Key Terms:

Marginalized   **Queer**   **Underrepresentation**

References

Avenue, N. (2018, November 06). The Troubling News About Black Women In The Workplace. Retrieved from https://www.forbes.com/sites/nextavenue/2018/11/06/the-troubling-news-about-black-women-in-the-workplace/#1c07b9f2605

Cheeks, M. (2018, March 26). How Black Women Describe Navigating Race and Gender in the Workplace. Retrieved from https://hbr.org/2018/03/how-black-women-describe-navigating-race-and-gender-in-the-workplace

Clintonyates. (2016, July 11). A black police officer's perspective. Retrieved from https://theundefeated.com/features/a-black-police-officers-perspective/

Colvin, A. (n.d.). Mandatory Arbitration and Inequality of Justice in Employment. Retrieved from https://digitalcommons.ilr.cornell.edu/articles/1004/

Magazine, C. (n.d.). Young Women of Color and Shifting Sexual Identities. Retrieved from https://contexts.org/articles/young-women-of-color-and-shifting-sexual-identities/

Main, K. (2019, February 26). Only black female police officer in Lubbock shares experience. Retrieved from http://www.kcbd.com/2019/02/26/only-black-female-police-officer-lubbock-shares-experience/

Mennicke, A., Gromer, J., Oehme, K., & MacConnie, L. (n.d.). Workplace experiences of gay and lesbian criminal justice officers in the United States: A qualitative investigation of officers attending a LGBT law enforcement conference. Retrieved from https://www.tandfonline.com/doi/full/10.1080/10439463.2016.1238918

Miller, S. L., Forest, K. B., & Jurik, N. C. (2003). Diversity in Blue. *Men and Masculinities, 5*(4), 355-385. doi:10.1177/0095399702250841

Thompson, M. (n.d.). TRIPLE THREAT: BLACK, FEMALE, WITH A BADGE—cji.edu. Retrieved from https://www.cji.edu/site/assets/files/1921/triple_threat-black-female-withabadge.pdf

V. (n.d.). Thin Rainbow Line. Retrieved from https://sites.psu.edu/thinrainbowline/

Wilson, A. A., Dr. (n.d.). Female Police Officers Perceptions and Experiences with . . . Retrieved from https://scholarworks.waldenu.edu/cgi/viewcontent.cgi?referer=&httpsredir=1&article=4051&context=dissertations

Women in Law Enforcement. (2017, December 29). Retrieved from https://www.n-r-c.com/gender-balance-law-enforcement/

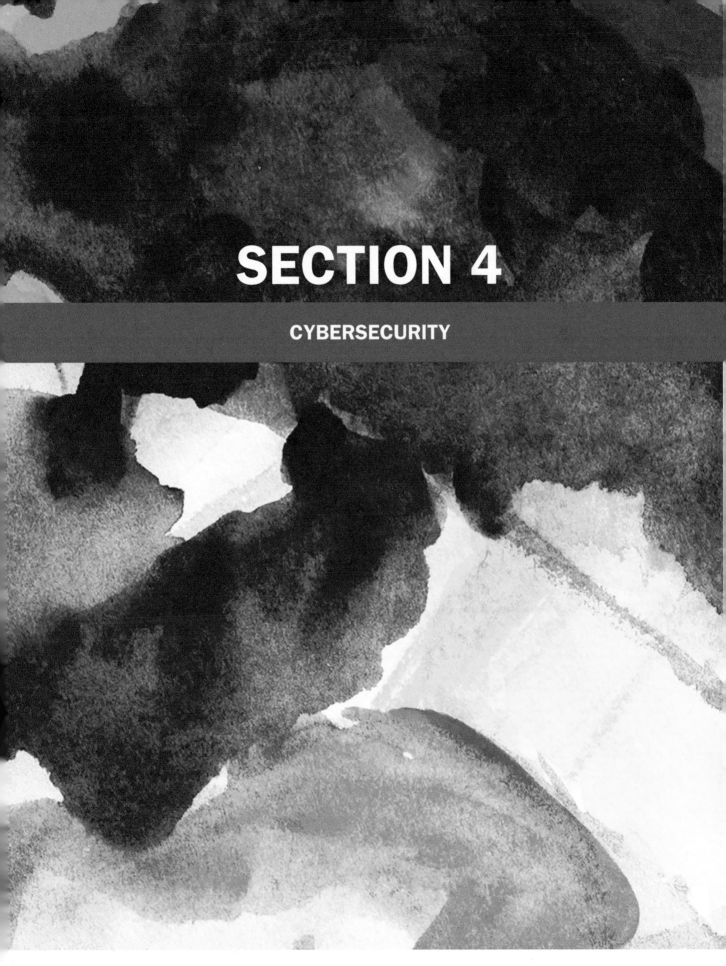

SECTION 4

CYBERSECURITY

CHAPTER 20

Cyber Connectivity, Cybercrime, and Cyberspace Regulations

Prit Kaur, Ph.D. | Auburn University at Montgomery
Shanta Varma, Ph.D | Auburn University at Montgomery.

Abstract

Human dependence on critical infrastructure and computer technology via cyberspace has made people highly vulnerable to cyberattacks and cyber hacking. Threats from cyberspace are among the most critical security challenges faced in the 21st century. This is raising serious concerns about the preparedness of individuals, organizations, and criminal justice institutions to counter the challenge (Mesko, 2018).

This chapter is based on a review of the existing information on cyber connectivity and the evolving nature and impact of cybercrimes on individuals and society at large. It also examines issues such as hacking, hacking groups, ransomware, and the role of both legal protection and artificial intelligence in empowering humans to thwart cyber threats.

Chapter Objectives

This chapter has three specific objectives:

- To discuss cyber connectivity and its relationship to the nature and impact of cybercrimes, including hacking and popular hacking groups,
- To discuss the role of macro (global), meso (national), and micro(state/local) laws, policies, procedures, and frameworks for responding to cybercrime,
- To discuss preventive measures to thwart cybercrime.

Introduction

Perhaps the inventors of the computer (1945), the Internet (1969), and the World Wide Web (1989) did not anticipate the impact of their inventions on the nature and extent of criminality via enhanced global human connectivity. Cybercrimes evolved with the expansion of the Internet, but the benefits of the technology overshadowed the criminal possibilities.

One of the most significant effects of the Internet is enhanced human connectivity. Currently, over 40% (3.4 billion) of the world's population enjoys some form of benefit of Internet connectivity (Pick & Sarkar, 2015). The ability to email, text, find information about goods and services, read the news, and use financial services have made Internet access indispensable. In 2017, the United States had more than 230 million Internet users (74.5% of the country's population), and the highest number of Internet providers. An analysis of the top 20 social media sites by Kessler (2017) shows that there are over 100 million active users (someone who has used the service within the last 30 days) in the United States alone. Most social media platforms are available globally, but are associated with the country where they were created, as seen in Table 1.

Instances of cybercrime, such as hacking, ransomware, and identity theft, have become increasingly common as humans have increased their connections via the Internet, which has led many to believe that cybercrime will become the most serious problem in the future. Nearly two-thirds of online users (more than two billion) have their personal data stolen or compromised. Over one million users fall prey to some form of cybercrime every day (European Commission, 2015; Europol, 2016). According to research by Lewis (2018) for McAfee and the Center for Strategic and International Studies, among crimes with a global impact, cybercrime ranks third, following closely behind government corruption and narcotics. Cybercrime costs almost $600 billion, or 0.8%, of the global GDP. In relation to the global Internet economy—$4.2 trillion in 2016—cybercrime can be viewed as a 14% tax on growth.

TABLE 1: SNAPSHOT OF GLOBAL CYBER CONNECTIVITY

Type of Media	Count	Country	Description
Facebook	1.71 billion	US	Online social networking
WhatsApp	1 billion	US	Mobile encrypted instant messaging
Facebook Messenger	1 billion	US	Instant messaging
TencentQQ	877 million	China	Instant messaging
WeChat	762 million	China	Mobile text/voice-messaging
Tencent Ozone	648 million	China	Social networking
Instagram	500 million	US	Mobile multimedia sharing
Twitter	310 million	US	"The SMS of the Internet"
Tumblr	307 million	US	Microblogging
Skype	300 million	Estonia	Video chat/call service
Baidu Tieba	300 million	China	Communications platform
Sina Weiba	261 million	China	Microblogging
Viber	249 million	Israel	Mobile instant messaging (voice)
LINE	218 million	Japan	Proprietary instant communications
Google+	212 million	US	Social networking
YY	122 million	China	Online chat/streaming media
LinkedIn	106 million	US	Social networking
Snapchat	100+million	US	Photo sharing
Pinterest	100 million	US	Visual discovery
Telegram	100 million	Germany	Instant messaging

(Source: Kessler, 2017)

Since 2016, the average cost of cybercrime for businesses has increased 22.7%, reaching an average of $11.7 million globally. In that time, data leaks have increased by 27%, as have the frequency of ransomware attacks. The Wannacry ransomware attack in May 2017, for example, hit more than 200,000 users in 150 countries (and more than 400,000 computers) in just a few days. According to Beale (2015), in 2014-15, the costs associated with dealing with digital crime quadrupled, and it is predicted that the cost of cybercrime will cross $2 trillion by 2019. According to Signe & Signe (2018), there could be up to 16,000 data breaches a year by 2020, and which will cost countries $2.5 trillion. Companies of all sizes, sectors, and location comprise most victims of cyberattacks, and attacks are becoming more common daily (Signe & Signe, 2018). The Federal Bureau of Investigation's (FBI) Internet Crime Report 2017 shows that the Internet Crime Complaint Center (IC3) received more than 300,000 complaints with reported losses exceeding $1.4 billion. The report shows that these numbers have been increasing since 2013. On average, IC3 has received 284,000 complaints per year (a total of 1,420,555 in five years) with a total loss of $5.52 billion.

Understanding Cybercrimes and Cyber Hacking

"Cybercrime" refers to criminal, unlawful activities carried out by means of computers and the Internet that target other wired devices or individuals. There are three distinct forms of cybercrimes: First, on the one hand, there are cyber-dependent acts that exist purely within the virtual realm and can only be committed using a computer, the Internet, or other technology. Such acts are directed toward other computer networks. These can include hacking, spreading viruses, or denial of service attacks (UNODC, 2017; Wall, 2007). Second, some cyberattacks remain focused on personal information, such as identity theft, online money laundering, and purchasing drugs online (UNODC, 2017; Brown, 2015). In addition to these two types of Internet crimes, the UNODC added a third category that includes specific crime types such as online child sexual exploitation and abuse, bullying, and/or stalking.

Scholarly interest in cybercrime originated in the beginning of the 21st century. The goal was to understand these activities by using criminological theories. First, a group of scholars concluded that online crimes were committed due to rational choice and the lack of legal consequences. They argued that restricted moral development and the presence of a personality disorder could encourage a person's online criminal activity. They tried to make sense of digital criminality by using subcultural, learning, and social control theories, but did not come to meaningful conclusions. They also explained acts of terrorism and politically backed hacking through political theory.

Scholars have also tried to explore the differences between traditional crime and cybercrime. First, several researchers, including Goucher (2010), Grabowsky (2001), Yar (2005), and Taylor, Caeti, Loper, Fritsch, and Liederback (2006), believed that cybercrimes were traditional unlawful acts but committed through a new technology. They suggested that these acts were driven by the same intrinsic human emotions that underlie real world crime. Grabosky described cybercrime as "old wine in new bottles" (2001), while Yar called it "old wine in bottles of varying and fluid shape" (2005). Taylor et al. (2006) cited the routine activities theory (Cohen & Felson, 1979) and asserted that the basic tenets of motivation, opportunity, and the absence of a capable guardian are as applicable to cyberspace as they are to street crime. Nevertheless, in their analysis of studies on victimization using routine activities as a theoretical framework, Luekfeldt and Yar (2005) found divergence among diverse types of cybercrimes and the impact of each tenet. For example, the examination of victim impact factors (opportunity) found that women, people with higher educational qualifications, and those with paying jobs were exposed to the greatest risk of hacking and malware, whereas the risk of identity theft had no correlation with any of these factors. The authors therefore questioned whether cybercrimes had changed the traditional elements of the routine activities theory to the extent that they can no longer explain victimization. Similarly, Bossler and Holt (2009) identified that strong computer skills and careful password management did not reduce the threat of malware infection, suggesting that the presence of a capable guardian has little influence over cybercrime victimization. They applied the routine activities theory and concluded that the lack of guardians to protect Internet users led to the speedy growth of cybercrime.

Meanwhile, Harvey (1989), Shields (1996), Capeller (2001), Brenner (2010), and Goucher (2010) considered cybercrime as a unique construct focusing on the social-structural aspects of the environment in which it occurs. Furnell (2002) and Brenner (2010) argued that conventional spatial-temporal theories are unable to comprehend activities such as hacking, virus spread, or DDoS (distributed denial of service) attacks since they exist purely within the infrastructure of information technology systems. In this novel environment, the scale and scope of offense is inexorably transformed, as are the relationships between victims and offenders (Capeller, 2001). Here, attention is given to the sociological accounts of globalization as a form of time-space compression (Harvey, 1989), with Internet theorists suggesting that near-instantaneous encounters between spatially distant actors in cyberspace render us vulnerable by creating new methods of connection and exchange (Shields, 1996). In discerning their ontological structures, it is suggested that while people, objects, and activities can be located easily in the fixed and ordered "real world," such assets are chronically disorganized in cyberspace. Thus, the ecologically oriented theories of crime that require convergence between likely perpetrators and suitable targets in time and space are of limited value in explaining cybercrime (Yar, 2005). Goucher (2010) noted that cybercrime is different from traditional crimes because cybercrime is not influenced by who the attacker is or where they are located.

Other studies focus on the mechanisms used by criminals, such as malware, viruses, website defacement, and sabotage. Studies have also looked at legal mechanisms and the roles of law enforcement, society, and individuals in preventing cybercrime (Hoar, 2005; Janczewski & Coarik, 2007; Schmalleger & Pittaro, 2009). Some research has advocated for the use of widespread communication and education programs, creation of legislative measures, and training of law enforcement officers to prevent and address cybercrime (Asokhia, 2010; Nykodym, Taylor, & Vilela, 2005).

It can be said that, although the intent of criminals remains mostly the same—to make money—free and open access to information has altered the traditional modes of crime and victimization and has created new demands on the criminal justice system. Controlling cybercrime is more difficult than its real-world counterpart because the victim and the victimizer do not need to be at the same location for the act to occur. Perpetrators are generally free of any social responsibility or consequences and can therefore operate more aggressively. According to the United Nations Office on Drugs and Crime:

> *The complex nature of cybercrime, as one that takes place in the borderless realm of cyberspace, is compounded by the increasing involvement of organized crime groups. Perpetrators of cybercrime and their victims are often located in different regions, and its effects ripple through societies around the world. This highlights the need to mount an urgent, dynamic, and international response."*

Impact of Cybercrime

Cybercrime affects all of society's activities and infrastructure. Crime has evolved since the 1990s, attaining new dimensions and creating an array of new challenges and demands on the criminal justice system (Brown, 2015; Pyrooz, Decker, & Moule, 2013; Brenner, 2010). While cybercrime is mostly targeted at organizations, but it is not a victimless crime. These attacks cause national security breaches, social discontent and unrest, and loss of property. They create a culture of fear for individuals and cause serious damage to organizational reputation and trust.

The impact of a cybercrime can be judged by evaluating its effect on human interactions as well as the actual cost incurred on its prevention, detection, and investigation. Although the United States and Europe have incurred the most financial damage from cybercrime, every region in the world has been affected. According to Konradt, Schilling, and Werners (2016), the combined losses from cyberattacks have had a significantly negative impact on the economy ($445 billion in 2013). Furthermore, case studies have shown an immense increase in costs for organizations due to investments in improving their Internet security measures (Pnemon Institute, 2013).

However, the social costs of cybercrimes may be hard to define, as the lack of reliable empirical data means that no study can ever be definitive (Levi, 2012). Research has been conducted on the social aspects of cybercrimes. For instance, in the United Kingdom, approximately 16,500 young people aged between 11 and 15 years were absent from school in 2010. When asked, bullying was the main factor cited for their absenteeism (Brown, Clery, & Ferguson, 2011). Of the total number who experience bullying, 65% report some form of cyberbullying (Ditch the Label, 2016). A longitudinal study found that Britons who were bullied in childhood had poorer cognitive functioning and lower education levels at the age of 50, with male victims more likely to be unemployed and earn less (Takizawa, Maughan, & Arseneault, 2014). The spread of online child pornography worldwide exposes children to the dangers of sexual assault and repetitive re-victimization that occurs in the knowledge that their images are kept alive through the Internet (Taylor & Quayle, 2003). Examples of cybercrimes can be broadened further to include cyber stalking, corporate espionage, and cyber terrorism (Brenner, 2010).

Cybercrime has added a new dimension to traditional crime. The nature of online criminal activities means that skilled attackers have acquired a transnational reach to conduct illicit intrusions into computer networks to gather information, deface websites, and carry out DDoS attacks. Cyber hackers have created new business models such as ransomware-as-aservice, which means that attackers are finding it easier to scale their cybercrimes globally to extort money. The cyber component has made criminal activity more difficult and complex to understand, detect, and investigate, such as when fraud specialists employ social engineering techniques including spamming, spoofing, domain squatting, and phishing to manipulate peoples' actions (Broad Hurst, Grabosky, Alazab, & Chon, 2014).

Cyber Hacking and Cyber Hackers

Over the years, with the continuous rise of Internet users and Internet service providers, cybercrime has expanded into a global organized criminal enterprise with serious financial consequences. These exceed the damages generated by illegal trafficking in drugs and people (Europol, 2016). Technology will continue to evolve to meet the global demand for faster results, more power, ever-expanding electronic commerce, and social networking. On the other hand, technically skilled motivated criminals have identified inherent technical and social vulnerabilities to exploit. Their methods are tech-smart and strategic methods designed to infect, compromise, and take over computer systems at the personal, corporate, and governmental level. These criminals are well-organized, more apt to work together as hacking groups, partners, and subcontractors, and they communicate anonymously through sophisticated dark channels that continue to evolve and pose global threats. Manky (2013) offered an insight into cyber criminality when he said that cybercrime offenders are highly skilled individuals acting in pursuit of their own goals. They work for countries, companies, counties and/or individuals for monetary gains and aim to expand their criminal enterprises to a larger scale. To this end, they've even begun offering cybercrime-as-a-service.

While defining cybercrimes, Kessler (2017) said that IoT has three primary classes of communication: machine to machine (M2M), people to machine (P2M), and people to people (P2P). The number of devices, individuals, companies, governments, and society as a whole are potentially at risk. Data show that there is a rise in the membership of online hacking groups. Some of these groups are state-sponsored, some are loosely affiliated with various agendas, and some are directly affiliated to a single cause. These groups engage in cyberattacks for the purpose of stealing money or information, disrupting services, and more. They operate somewhat like gangs and drug lords in physical spaces, using their specialties and selling their services to make money (The Cyberpunk Project, 2003). According to an FBI report, cyber criminals operate as a group, with each member having an area of specialty related to one or the other aspect that is necessary for the commission of cybercrimes. Each group usually has one coder or programmer, a distributor or vendor, a techie, a hacker, a tracker, a cashier, a few tellers, and a leader (Chabinsky, 2010). Kessler (2017) listed some of the popular and active hacking groups as below:

- Chaos Computer Club: Chaos Computer Club was formed in 1980 and is one of the largest hacking groups in Europe.

- Lizard Squad: Lizard Squad is most known for the hacks on Facebook and Sony.

- LulzSec: A spinoff of Anonymous, LulzSec's major hacking victims includes the CIA, Fox, and Sony.

- Syrian Electronic Army: The Syrian Electronic Army is run by active supporters of Syrian President Bashar al-Assad. They target enemies of the official regime. Although they act on behalf of Assad, they are not believed to be directed by the Syrian government.

- TeaMpOisoN: TeaMpOisoN was formed in the UK in 2010. They have hacked into the North Atlantic Treaty Organization (NATO), the UK Daily Mail, and Facebook, and have evolved into a group of white hat hackers.

- Tarh Andishan: Tarh Andishan is a state-sponsored Iranian hacking group that primarily targets security systems, military installations, utilities and critical infrastructures, hospitals, transportation agencies, and airports around the world.

- Unit 61398: A unit of the People's Liberation Army, Unit 61398 is a military initiative of the People's Republic of China and specializes in advanced persistent threat attacks on dozens of countries in North America, Western Europe, and Asia.

- United Cyber Caliphate (UCC): The Islamic State Hacking Division, also called the UCC, is the hacker team of the ISIS. The group comprises a skilled set of hackers who have successfully attacked targets in several countries, including Australia, France, US, and the UK. The DCC routinely uses social media and other websites to disseminate information and post threats against both individuals and agencies around the world.

- Anonymous: Anonymous is perhaps the best-known hacker group. Formed in 2003, it operates as a group without a leader, an organization, a membership list, a mission statement, a charter, and a political affiliation. Anyone can say that they are affiliated with Anonymous. There are many YouTube videos of a person wearing a Guy Fawkes mask, speaking through a digitized voice, and often ending his statement with the words, "We are Anonymous. We are Legion. We do not forgive. We do not forget. Expect us." The lack of political affiliation makes it hard to categorize Anonymous, although the claim to generally advocate liberal causes, privacy, anti-censorship, and support of the underdog seems common. Their targets have included

  ▫ The US government

  ▫ NATO

- The Catholic Church
- The Church of Scientology
- The Labour Party in Ireland
- many Arab government sites
- Iranian government officials' websites
- copyright enforcers in India
- any adversary of WikiLeaks
- sites in Zimbabwe
- the Westboro Baptist Church
- and other sites and individuals around the world.

After the Charlie Hebdo attacks in Paris in 2015, Anonymous claimed responsibility for several anti-ISIS projects, including #OpParis, #OpiSIS, and #PrayForParis. Part of this initiative provides tools that can be used to troll the Internet for ISIS sites that Anonymous hackers can then attack.

Case of Cyber Hacking of Information for Ransomware

This case shows a typical example of how cyber criminals can, with one opportunity, impact millions of people. Equifax is one of the three main credit reporting agencies of the US. On September 8, 2017, Equifax disclosed that hackers had broken into its files and stolen personal information that compromised as many as 143 million Americans (around 44% of the population). Among the information pilfered were drivers' licenses, social security records, credit card numbers, birth dates, names, and addresses.

Case of Ransomware for the Denial of Access to Information

Ransomware is a form of malware that targets both human and technical weaknesses in organizational and individual networks to deny the availability of critical data and systems. Hospitals, school districts, state and local governments, law enforcement agencies, and businesses can be impacted by ransomware. Keeping organizations from accessing their data can be catastrophic; sensitive or proprietary information can be lost; regular operations can be disrupt; and the organization may suffer both financial losses and harm to their reputation.

Home computers are just as vulnerable to ransomware. An attack can lead to the loss of personal and often irreplaceable items such as family photos, videos, and other data. Ransomware attacks are not only proliferating but are also becoming progressively more sophisticated. Several years ago, ransomware was delivered through emails, but because email systems are now better at filtering out spam, cyber criminals have resorted to spear phishing emails. In newer instances of ransomware, some attackers bypass email and instead simply seed legitimate websites with malicious code. This defacement typically occurs when the website owner isn't maintaining their own security.

One such ransom attack was reported by *The Washington Times* on September 26, 2017 (Blake, 2017). Montgomery, Alabama's capital city, paid more than $40,000 in Bitcoin to regain access to their data after a ransomware infection brought local operations to a standstill. The infection was discovered on September 19, 2017, and had sidelined nearly every agency in Montgomery County.

County officials initially tried to avoid paying the ransom by recovering the data from backup files. Unrelated technical issues made this impossible; the county ultimately voted to pay the ransom and regain access, including releasing enough funds to purchase 9 Bitcoins, worth about $32,000, according to *The Advertiser*. "You don't think about these things until they happen," Elton Dean, Chairman of Montgomery County Commission, told the *Montgomery Advertiser*. "When you are talking about losing about $5 million worth of files, that's kind of like an emergency situation." The county paid the ransom in two installments and regained access to some of their data after each payment went through, as indicated in the report.

Montgomery County was lucky; there have been cases where organizations paid the ransom but never got a decryption key. Because of this, some experts suggest not paying the ransom, especially since compliance emboldens existing cyber criminals to target more organizations. But when companies do not maintain proper backups or ensure that those backups are retrievable, there may be few other options.

GPS Hacking in a Domestic Violence Case

Global Positioning Systems (GPS) and other phone tracking technologies have unexpectedly made it easier for abusers to track their victims. A US Justice Department report last year estimated that over 25,000 adults in the US are victims of GPS stalking annually, including through their cell phones. Consumers who surf the Internet unintentionally surrender all kinds of personal information to marketing firms online that use invisible tracking technology to monitor the consumers' online activity.

Modern cell phones add a tracking feature to cell phones; this has proven very useful. Tracking technology has helped rescue lost drivers, authorities find kidnap victims, and enabled parents to keep tabs on their children. However, this technology is also abused by stalkers to track their victims. One stalking incident was highlighted in the literature as early as 1995. One morning that summer, Glenn Helwig threw his then wife onto the floor of their bedroom in Corpus Christi, Texas, according to her allegations in police reports. She packed her 1995 Hyundai and drove to a friend's home, not expecting her husband to find her.

The day after she arrived, she said that her husband had shown up suddenly. According to police reports, he barged in and knocked her onto the floor, and then took off with her car. Helwig later acknowledged that he used a cell phone service to track his wife sometimes without her knowledge.

The new type of criminality has neither replaced traditional crime nor perpetuated it. Rather, it has providing tools and created more opportunities for crime to be committed. Studying cybercrime has also provided clarity to the goals of cybercriminals: they clearly establish targets so they can steal confidential data, breach the integrity of the data, or make the data unavailable. As the Internet raises new risks for criminal victimization, it inevitably raises questions about safety as well. It is argued that repression in the physical world is realized through the regulation of cyberspace, in what has been described as the " soft line" mode of social control Cohen (1985). The difficulty in managing Internet safety may be increased by an underreporting of cybercrime from the public and businesses, as well as the lack of transparency and comparability from industry sources (McGuire & Dowling, 2013). Wall (2007) argued that the global impact of the Internet has altered traditional modes of criminality and has created new demands on the police because "new blended criminality" has complicated crime by providing tools, such as "anonymity" and clear targets and by raising the boundaries of the crime space.

Legal Measures: Global (Macro), National (Meso), and State/Local (Micro)

This section discusses the existing global, national, and local level laws, policies, procedures, and frameworks in place for responding to cybercrime and for protecting enhanced cyber connectivity.

The Macro: A Multilateral Response to Cybercrime

Publicly available cyberspace has been both an instrument and a target of criminal activities since the early 1990s. At that time, the bulk of the growth of Internet use was in North America, Western Europe, and the Asia-Pacific region. Since the early 2000s, the largest growth in Internet use has occurred in Africa, Eastern Europe, and the Middle East. With this growth, we have seen cyberspace become a vector for many types of offensive and defensive actions, including crime, terrorism, ideological activism (hacktivism), war/information operations, diplomacy, espionage, sabotage, stalking, bullying, and more. Cyberspace also faces the issue of enforcement. If there is a cyberattack, who is responsible for investigating and punishing the criminals? Is it the victim's country or the country where the criminals reside? In the absence of international cybersecurity laws, this issue has become very serious. The Council of Europe passed the Budapest Convention on Cybercrime to establish a uniform law that applied to all 50 signatory countries. All countries agreed to develop their own cyber laws and cooperate with each other in handling cybercrimes. It remained more of a symbolic law, however, and the signatory countries did not take steps to prevent cybercrimes.

In June 2016, the NATO officially recognized cyberspace as an operational domain, adding the cyber dimension to existing arenas of warfare, namely air, sea, and land. This recognition also formalized the fact that cyberspace now became a vector that could initiate an Article 5 response to an adversarial action. However, some scholars believe that the strength of the Convention in terms of its potential to deliver cyber security depends on the cooperation among countries. However, on the contrary, nations are becoming less cooperative and more isolationist (The Economist, 2016). In this context, achieving the multilateral regulation of cyberspace may necessitate the creation of a common framework with the capacity to move beyond like-minded coalitions. New institutions and structures are necessary at the national and international levels, in the form of a uniform international cyber law. This law would define what constitutes a cybercrime, re-adjust existing principles of international law, establish an international regulatory body to monitor cyber activities under a UN framework, and the establish an international cyber court to try cyber offenses of an international character (Hurwitz, 2014; Williams, 2011).

The Meso Level Response to Cybercrime

To effectively deal with cybercrime within any country, proper coordination is required among national and state agencies at all levels. For instance, Wheeler (2018) pointed out that "Cybersecurity is not something; it is everything." He said that all major federal agencies must get their electronic devices certified because all systems are interconnected.

National cybersecurity requires cooperation among all levels of law enforcement, from federal to state to local. After 9/11, when it was found that there had been communication issues between the CIA and the FBI, the role of communication and collaboration among law enforcement agencies was reexamined

- The National Security Agency (NSA): The NSA was created with the exclusive responsibility of intelligence interception and interpretation and decryption of information. The NSA leads the

US Government in cryptology, encompassing both Signals Intelligence (SIGINT) and Information Assurance (IA) products and services. It also enables Computer Network Operations (CNO) to gain a decision-making advantage for the nation and its allies under all circumstances. The NSA secures all systems that handle classified information and intelligence in the main arenas of cyberspace. They intercept intelligence and detect foreign threats, and mitigate or prevent attacks on US Government networks.

- Department of Homeland Security (DHS): The DHS was created in a major reorganization effort after the attacks of September 11, 2001.

- Federal Bureau of Investigation (FBI): In recent years, the FBI has built a set of technological and investigative capabilities and partnerships in which they are as comfortable chasing outlaws in cyberspace as they are chasing down back alleys and across continents. The FBI includes:

  - The Internet Crime Complaint Center (IC3) and the National White Collar Crime Center (NW3C), which provide preventive measures for cybercrime and also support victims of cyber and white collar crimes. The list of services they provide can be found on their websites.

  - Operation Wellspring (OWS) was implemented through a close collaboration with FBI field officers and the IC3. It helps the states and local law enforcement agencies build capacity to counter cybercrimes.

  - A Cyber Division at the FBI Headquarters to address cybercrime in a coordinated and cohesive manner

  - Specially trained cyber squads at FBI headquarters and in each of the 56 field offices, each staffed with agents and analysts who protect against and investigate computer intrusions; theft of intellectual property and personal information; child pornography and exploitation; and online fraud

  - New Cyber Action Teams that travel around the world on a moment's notice to assist in computer intrusion cases and to gather vital intelligence to help identify cybercrimes that are most dangerous to national security and the economy

  - There are 93 Computer Crimes Task Forces nationwide that combine state-ofthe-art technology and resources of the federal, state, and local counterparts

  - A growing partnership with other federal agencies including the Department of Defense, the DHS, and others that share similar concerns and resolutions to combat cybercrimes.

Micro Level Efforts to Control Cybercrimes

The evolution of policing in the US can be traced over three prominent eras. Kelling and Moore (2005) described the three eras as follows: the political era (from 1840 to the early 1900s), when policing aimed to preserve political order through moral control and social service; the reform era (from the 1930s to the late 1970s), when the eradication of corruption was sought through professionalism and crime control; and finally, the community era (from the 1980s to the present day), in which community support services were developed through the deployment of prevention and problem-solving strategies. In post-9/11 America, scholars believed that the community era was insufficient for handling the prevailing threats of terrorism, and beginning September 11, 2001, a fourth era began, namely one of homeland security or information policing driven by research evidence, diverse forms of intelligence, and predictive strategies.

The biggest chunk of law enforcement is concentrated at the local level. As the impact of networked technologies on human social connectivity and behavior increases (Burford & Park, 2014; Misra, Cheng, Genevie, & Yuan, 2014), new and emerging forms of cyber criminality have constantly being added to the list of conventional problems that law enforcement must continue to deal with (Brenner, 2014). It has always been a challenge to train local law enforcement to respond to new criminal methods. In local policing, officers are most likely to respond to what they can see. Since cybercrime is difficult to detect, victims may receive less support (Leukfeldt, Veenstra, & Stol, 2013).

Studies have confirmed that police officers in the US are less aware of the serious impact of cybercrime. Half of the frontline officers surveyed had no opinion on the subject of cybercrimes, with only 18% agreeing that cybercrimes should be dealt with by local law enforcement (Bossler & Holt, 2012). Similarly, research on an English metropolitan force suggested that only 21% of the frontline officers agreed that "in their current role they should be dealing with incidents or crimes which are the result of the way someone has behaved on the Internet" with three-quarters remaining neutral or disagreeing that they were "clear about the definition of cybercrime."

Additionally, at the beginning of their careers, police officers were assigned to serve in a specific neighborhood or town to teach them that the role of policing is tied to a physical space (Huey, Nhan, & Broll, 2012). Evidence also suggests that recruits often join the police force because they want a practical and physically demanding job that is predominantly outside. The professionalization of policing is further supported by the concept of evidencebased policing (EBP) practices through practitioner-led research and evaluation (Thomas, 2014). Without a dedicated "cyber force," police are unable to respond appropriately. The reality is that most cybercrime victims are not supported by their local police. Research reveals a disturbing lack of empathy and resistance to owning the problem among the police force itself (Brenner, 2014). This is particularly serious since the increasing use of the Internet raises the risk of victimization. Thus, as the capacity of traditional law enforcement is outpaced, a number of private actors ranging from citizens to large businesses are starting to play a role in the administration of online security (Wall, 2007). This phenomenon is described as the privatization of cybercrime control. Privatization of cybercrime is good as a short-term solution but law enforcement agencies themselves have to develop their specialized units and personnel to effectively respond to the digital citizenry of today.

Preventive Measures to Thwart Cyber Crime

This chapter reviewed the existing literature in order to analyze the effect of the computer and the Internet on crime. It also evaluates the capacity and capability of the prevailing criminal justice system to confront new risks and forms of cyber victimization. The introduction of the computer and Internet has been marked as a cultural revolution in the acquisition and diffusion of information that surpasses all previous manifestations of human connectivity. This enhanced human connectivity appears to correspond with changes in criminal behavior, with increases in offenses where online facilitation has made it possible. With the rising cybercrime rates, the focus is now on developing a proper connection among law enforcement, citizens, and technology to prevent cybercrimes in the future.

Having reviewed information published in the media such as news sources and newspapers as well as on the websites of numerous agencies working under the department of justice of the US, it appears that cybercrimes have continued to expand almost exponentially since the development of computer systems and Internet connectivity. Technology will continue to evolve to meet the global demand for faster results, more power, ever-expanding electronic commerce, and social networking. These attributes provide opportunities for criminals who will continue to exploit such systems in the future. There will be continuous expansion in cybercrimes due to the environment of anonymity. Criminals will identify technical and social vulnerabilities that they can then use to infect, compromise, and take over computer systems at the personal, corporate, and government levels. Therefore, the following recommendations are made to effectively counter cyber attackers and cyber hackers:

- **Technological empowerment of consumers.** To live in the "third wave" of the information society, consumers must educate themselves to stay safe and to keep their devices secure before adopting any technology and technology-driven devices. Individuals committing cybercrimes are no longer the relatively uneducated "crooks" of the past. Rather, they are fully attuned to the intricacies of computers, databases, and technology. They have the necessary means to defeat security systems placed on digital connections. Local police may or may not be able to protect people from these threats all the times. Consumers must become educated digital citizens and understand how to protect themselves.

- **Encourage consumers to file complaints with the IC3 in the US, and encourage other countries to develop similar organizations.** Because cybercrime is global in nature, nations should develop their cyber frameworks and encourage cyber reporting to understand and deal with the cybercrime. Individuals and organizations must also report the crime. IC3 accepts online complaints of cybercrimes either from the actual victim or from a third party. Complaints must be filed with the following information:

  ◦ Name, address, telephone number, and email of the complainant

  ◦ Financial transaction information (e.g., account information, transaction date and amount, details of who received the money)

  ◦ Subject's name, address, telephone, email address, website, and IP address

  ◦ Specific details on how the individual or organization were victimized Any other relevant information that the individual or organization may believe is necessary to support the complaint. Keeping the global nature of cybercrimes in mind, IC3 centers can also assist each other at the international level.

- **Artificial intelligence (AI)** is prevalent in many systems, a few of which include the Internet of Things, big data sifting which creates product recommendations and shopper profiles, and systems that recommend certain candidate profiles in specific situations. It is believed that AI not only reduces bias and abuse of power but also reduces the chances of human error and violations. AI may be used in the future by providing alerts in advance to take adequate and timely preventive measures. Cyber hacking, cyberattacks, and cybercrimes can be defeated or their impacts can be reduced if systems have the capability of protecting themselves. Individual consumers of technology, legal frameworks and laws, and AI must remain actively involved in changing and improving the process of cybersecurity to protect their cyber connectivity.

Artificial Intelligence	**Dark Web**	**Global Cyber Connectivity**
Currency	**Digilantism**	**Ransomware**
Cyber Hacking	**Digital**	**TOR**

Discussion Questions:

1. What are the recent trends in cybercrimes?

2. Identify and describe the major gateways to vulnerabilities faced by users of the Internet. Which of these pose the greatest risk and why?

3. What role do social media play in promoting or stopping cybercrime?

4. How can one stay safe in cyberspace?

5. Describe some of the cyber hacking techniques and models in trend and any possible solution to mitigate them? Provide examples.

6. How can one encourage victims of cybercrime to report the crime to the police?

References

Anderson, R., Barton, C., Böhme, R., Clayton, R., Van Eeten, M. J., Levi, M., & Savage, S. (2013). Measuring the cost of cybercrime. In *The economics of information security and privacy* (pp. 265–300). Springer, Berlin, Heidelberg.

Armin, J., Thompson, B., & Kijewski, P. (2016). Cybercrime economic costs: No measure no solution. In *Combatting cybercrime and cyberterrorism* (pp. 135–155). Springer, Cham.

Asokhia, M. O. (2010). Enhancing national development and growth through combating cybercrime/ Internet fraud: A comparative approach. *Journal of Social Sciences, 23*(1), 13–19. doi:10.1080/09718 923.2010.11892806

Bassiouni, M. (2006). The history of universal jurisdiction and its place in international law. In S. Macedo (Ed.), *Universal Jurisdiction: National Courts and the Prosecution of Serious Crimes Under International Law* (pp. 39–64). Pennsylvania: University of Pennsylvania Press.

Blake, A. (2017). Alabama officials pay ransom to recover county data held hostage. (Online) 09/26/2018 Washington Post. https://www.washingtontimes.com/news/2017/sep/26/alabamaofficials-pay-ransom-recovercountydatah/?utm_campaign=shareaholic&utm_medium=email_this&utm_source=emailhttps

Bossler, A., & Holt, T. (2009). On-line activities, guardianship and malware infection: An examination of routine activities theory. *International Journal of Cyber Criminology, 3*(1), 400–420.

Bossler, A., & Holt, T. (2012). Patrol officers' perceived role in responding to cybercrime. *International Journal of Police Strategies & Management, 35*(1), 165–181. doi:10.1108/13639511211215504

Brenner, S. (2010). Cybercrime: *Criminal threats from cyberspace*. Oxford: Praeger.

Brenner, S. (2014). Cyberthreats and the Decline of the Nation State. Abingdon: Routledge.

Broadhurst, R., Grabosky, P., Alazab, M., & Chon, S. (2014). Organizations and cybercrime: An analysis of the nature of groups engaged in cybercrime. *International Journal of Cyber Criminology, 8*(1), 1–20.

Brown, C. (2015). Investigating and prosecuting cybercrime: Forensic dependencies and barriers to justice. *International Journal of Cyber Criminology, 9*(1), 55–119. doi:10.5281/zenodo.22387

Brown, V., Clery, E., & Ferguson, C. (2011). *Estimating the Prevalence of Young People Absent from School Due to Bullying*. (Online) 06/12/2019, NATCEN. http://www.natcen.ac.uk/media/22457/estimating-prevalence-young-people.pdf

Burford, S., & Park, S. (2014). The impact of mobile tablet devices on human information behaviour, *Journal of Documentation, 70*(4), 622–639. doi:10.1108/JD-09-2012-0123

Capeller, W. (2001). Not such a neat net: Some comments on virtual criminality. *Social and Legal Studies, 10*(2), 229–242. doi:10.1177%2Fa017404

Chabinsky, S. R. (2010, March). The cyber threat: Who's doing what to whom. In *Government Security/ FOSE Conference, March* (Vol. 23).

Cohen, S., & Felson, M. (1979). Social change and crime rate trends: A routine activity approach. *American Sociological Review, 44*(4), 588–608.

Cohen, S. (1985). Visions of social control: Crime, Punishment and classification. Cambridge: Blackwell Publishers.

Ditch the Label. (2016). The *Annual Bullying Survey* 2016. (Online) 06/12/2019 http://www.ditchthelabel.org/wp-content/uploads/2016/04/Annual-Bullying-Survey-2016-Digital.pdf

European Commission, 2015. The European agenda on security. Strasbourg: European Commission. http://ec.europa.eu/dgs/homeaffairs/elibrary/documents/basicdocuments/docs/eu_agenda_on_security_en.pdf.

Europol 2014. The Internet Organised Crime Threat Assessment (iOCTA). The Hague: Europol.

Europol 2016. The relentless growth of cybercrime. Retrieved from https://www.europolo.europa.eu/newsroom/news/relentless-growth-of-cybercrime

Federal Bureau of Investigation Internet Crime Report (2017). https://www.fbi.gov/news/stories/2017-internet-crime-report-released-050718

Furnell, S. (2002). Cybercrime: Vandalizing the information society. London: Addison Wesley.

Goodman, M. (2010). International dimensions of cybercrime. In S. Ghosh and E. Turrini (Eds.), *Cybercrimes: A Multidisciplinary Analysis* (pp. 311–339). Heidelberg: Springer Publishing.

Goucher, W. (2010). Being a cybercrime victim. Computer Fraud and Security, 10(2010), 16–18. Doi:10.1016/S1361-3723(10)70134-2

Grabowsky, P. (2001). Virtual criminality: Old wine in new bottles? *Social & Legal Studies, 10*(2), 243–249. Doi:10.1177%2Fa017405

Harvey, D. (1989). *The condition of postmodernity*. Oxford: Blackwell.

Hoar, S. B. (2005). Trends in cybercrime: The Darkside of the Internet. *Criminal Justice, 20*(3), pp. 4–13

Horsman, G. (2017). Can we continue to effectively police digital crime? *Science and Justice, 57*(6), 448–454. doi:10.1016/j.scijus.2017.06.001

Huey, L., Nhan, J., & Broll, R. (2012). 'Uppity Civilians' and 'Cyber Vigilantes': The role of the general public in policing cyber-crime. *Criminology & Criminal Justice, 13*(1), 81–97. Doi:10.1177%2F1748895812448086

Hurwitz, R. (2014). The play of states: Norms and security in cyberspace. *American Foreign Policy Interests, 36*(5), 322-331. doi:10.1080/10803920.2014.969180

Internet Crime Complaint Center, Federal Bureau of Investigation. (n.d.). Internet Crime Prevention Tips. (Online). 06/12/2019. http://www.ic3.gov/preventiontips.aspx

Janczewski, L. J., & Colarik, A. M. (2007). Cyber warfare and cyber terrorism. Ida Group, Hersshey, PA.

Kelling, G., & Moore, M. (2005). The evolving strategy of policing. In T. Newburn (Ed.), *Policing: Key Readings* (pp. 88–108). London: Routledge.

Kessler, G. C. (2017). Technologies in cyberspace: A context of threats and defenses. In, Identification of Potential Terrorists and Adversary Planning, by T.J. Gordon et al (Eds.) IOS Press.

Kessler, G. C. (2017). Technologies in CyberSpace: A Context of Threats and Defenses. Identification of Potential Terrorists and Adversary Planning: Emerging Technologies and New Counter-Terror Strategies, 132, 60.

Konradt, C., Schilling, A., & Werners, B. (2016). Phishing: An economic analysis of cybercrime perpetrators. *Computer and Society, 58*(2016), 39–46. doi:10.1016/j.cose.2015.12.001

Lewis, J. (2018). *The economic impact of cybercrime: No slowing down.* McAfee. *Cybercrime Economic Costs: No Measure No Solution.* Paper presented at 10th International Conference on Availability, Reliability and Security (pp. 701–710).

Leukfeldt, E., Veenstra, S., & Stol, W. (2013). High volume cybercrime and the organisation of the police: The results of two empirical studies in the Netherlands. *International Journal of Cybercriminology, 7*(1), 1–17.

Levi, M. (2012). Measuring the cost of cybercrimes. *Cybercrime and Policy Issues, 90,* 12–13. Doi:10.1007/978-3-642-39498-0_12

Manky, D. (2013). Cybercrime as a Service: A very modern business. *Computer Fraud & Security, 2013*(6), 9–13. Doi: 10.1016/S1361-3723(13)70053-8

McGuire, M., & Dowling, S. (2013). Cybercrime: A review of the evidence, research report 75. London: HMSO.

Mesko, Gorazd (2018). On Some Aspects of Cybercrime and Cybervictimization. European Journal of Crime, Criminal Law and Criminal Justice 26(2018).

Misra, S., Cheng, L., Genevie, J., & Yuan, M. (2014). The iPhone effect: The quality of in-person social interactions in the presence of mobile devices, *Environment & Behaviour, 48*(2), 275–298. Doi:10.1177%2F0013916514539755

National White Collar Crime Center. (n.d.). Cyber Crime Links. (Online). 06/12/2019. http://www.nw3c.org/services/research/cyber-crime-links

Nykodym, N., Taylor, R., & Vilela, J. (2005). Criminal profiling and insider cybercrime. *Computer Law and Security Review, 21*(5), 408–414. doi:10.1016/j.diin.2005.11.004

Pick, J., & Sarkar, A. (2015). *The global digital divides: Explaining change.* London: Springer.

Ponemon Institute. (2011). Second annual cost of cybercrime study: Benchmark study of U.S. Companies. Michigan, USA: Ponemon Institute LLC.

Pyrooz, D., Decker, S., & Moule, R. (2013). Criminal and routine activities in online settings: Gangs, offenders and the Internet. *Justice Quarterly, 32*(3), 471-499. doi:10.1080/07418825.2013.778326

Rosenbaum, D. (2010). Police research: Merging the policy and action research traditions. *Police Practice & Research, 11*(2), 144–149. doi:10.1080/15614261003593203

Schmalleger, F., & Pittaro, M. (2009). *Crimes of the Internet.* Prentice Hall, Upper Saddle River, NJ.

Shields, R. (1996). Cultures of the Internet: Virtual spaces, real histories, living bodies. London: Sage.

Signe, L., & Signe, K. (2018). Global cybercrimes and weak cybersecurity threaten businesses in Africa. (Online). Brookings. 03/01/2019. https://www.brookings.edu/blog/africa-infocus/2018/05/30/global-cybercrimes-and-weak-cybersecurity-threaten-businesses-in-africa/

Takizawa, R., Maughan, B., & Arseneault, L. (2014). Adult health outcomes of childhood bullying victimization: Evidence from a 5-decade longitudinal British cohort. *American Journal of Psychiatry, 171*(7), 777–784. doi: 10.1176/appi.ajp.2014.13101401

Taylor, M., & Quayle, E. (2003). *Child pornography: An Internet crime.* London: Routledge.

Taylor, R., Caeti, T., Loper, D., Fritsch, E., & Liederbach, J. (2006). *Digital crime and digital terrorism.* New Jersey: Pearson Prentice Hall.

Tehrani, P., & Manap, N. (2013). A Rational jurisdiction for cyber terrorism. *Computer Law & Security Review, 29*(6), 689–701. doi:10.1016/j.clsr.2013.07.009

The Cyberpunk Project. (2003). A Portrait of J. Random Hacker. (Online), 06/12/2019. http://project.cyberpunk.ru/idb/portrait_of_j_random_hacker.html

The Economist. (2016, November). Trump's World: The new nationalism. (Online) 06/12/2019. https://www.economist.com/leaders/2016/11/19/the new-nationalism

Thomas, G. (2014). Research on policing: Insights From literature. *Police Journal: Theory, Practice and Principles, 87*(2014), 5–16. Doi:10.1350%2Fpojo.2014.87.1.646

UN Police Training Tool Crime Reduction Kit (2017)

Unicef. (2011). *Child Safety Online: Global Challenges and Strategies.* (Online). UNICEF Innocenti Research Centre. 06/12/2019. https:// www.unicef-irc.org/publications/pdf/ict_eng.pdf

Wall, D. (2007). Policing cybercrimes: Situating the public police in networks of security within cyberspace. *Police Practice & Research, 8*(2), 183–205. Doi:10.1080/15614260701377729

Wheeler, T. (2018, February). Cybersecurity is not something; it is everything. (Online), 06/12/2019. Brookings. https://www.brookings.edu/blog/techtank/2018

Williams, C. (2011). Police governance: Community, policing and justice in the modern UK. *Taiwan in Comparative Perspective, 3*, 50–65.

WTHR, Tapping your cell phone (2008, November 14) https://www.youtube.com/watch?v=uCyKcoDaofg

Yar, M. (2005). The Novelty of 'Cybercrime': An assessment in light of routine activity theory. *European Journal of Criminology, 2*(4), 407–427. Doi:10.1177%2F147737080556056

CHAPTER 21

Women and Cybersecurity: An Analysis of Workforce Gaps

Leon T. Geter | *Benedict College*

Chapter Outcomes

After engaging this Chapter, Students should be able to:

- Discuss the correlation between women and cybersecurity job gaps.
- Recognize selected cybersecurity threats and challenges.
- Discuss the talent gaps of skilled professionals in cybersecurity and related areas.
- Gain a broader understanding of the role of gender, inclusion, and diversity in today's cybersecurity workforce.
- Recognize the need for increased education, training, and certification opportunities for females in cybersecurity.
- Assess workplace challenges and opportunities for women in the cybersecurity Workforce.
- Gain a broader understanding of cybersecurity career pathways and the workforce pipelines.

Introduction

In this chapter, we introduce you to cybersecurity, cybercrime, and the workforce gaps that exist with a focus on the need for more skilled professionals, especially women, in the cybersecurity field. We will briefly discuss cybersecurity, cybercrime, workforce shortages, and highlight the role women should play in helping to fill some of the many employment job openings that now and in the projected future. We will also delve into selected aspects of career development for women in cybersecurity.

By the year 2021, it is expected that there will be as many as 3.5 million global cybersecurity job openings (Nesmith, 2018) that will need to be filled. An increase in the number of women entering the cybersecurity workforce could serve to reduce the job gaps by producing more skilled professionals ready to enter the field. Moreover, as presented in a Market and Markets Analysis 2017 report, the cybersecurity global market worth will increase to an estimated $248.26 billion by the year 2023 (Cybersecurity Market, 2019).

According to Bradford (2018), cybercrime worldwide will reach an estimated $6 trillion by 2021. Cybersecurity threats, risks, and vulnerabilities are global phenomenon that have the potential to impact the lives of millions daily. Therefore, a lack of skilled cybersecurity professionals and the growing workforce gaps in cybersecurity becomes a real National Security threat. It is important to understanding that cyber-criminals are skilled in their areas of nefarious activities. We a need a ready, talented, and skilled cybersecurity workforce to technologically combat all current and future threats from a global perspective.

Cybersecurity

Cybersecurity is the process or system designed to protect individuals, networks, organizations, and governments information or sensitive data from being illegally accessed. Combating cybersecurity involve an ongoing process of prevention, detection, investigation, and responding to all risks and potential threats in a fast and efficient manner. Proactive action is the best course in all instances as a proper cyber defense for individuals, businesses, and society. An August 2018 survey conducted by **Information Systems Audit and Control Association** (ISACA) found that only 78 percent of manufacturing companies have a formal cybersecurity infrastructure prevention and response strategy in place and only 68 percent have a ransomware attack anticipation and protection engagement policy (Batas, 2020). Cybersecurity defense preparation is essential and should not be taken lightly in the face of the mounting worldwide cybersecurity threats. According to the FBI's 2018 Incident Crime Report, cybercrime resulted in an estimated $2.7 billion in losses due to internet crimes worldwide (IC3 Annual Report, 2019). Virtually every major global organization experienced some level of information or data breach due to illegal intrusions in 2018.

The cybersecurity industry is one of the fastest expanding sectors in innovation and technology universally. Cybersecurity spending in relation to prevention, detection, and responding is projected to surpass $1 trillion by 2021 (Morgan, 2016). The global threats from various cyber-attacks, such as phishing, malware, and ransomware, continues widespread and will cost millions to prevent and respond. For example, in March 2019, Norsk Hydro company was the victim of a massive ransomware attack that cost company over $40 million to bring their infrastructure and related system back on-line after the hacker attack. A ransomware incident often damages critical internal networks of an organization. Whereas, revenue losses, operation uncertainties, and or a damaged company reputation is often the result of a cyber breach. Many companies are irreversibly impacted and crippled into extinction after a cybersecurity penetration. Fortunately, despite the potential risks of cybersecurity breaches, many companies are going full steam ahead with industry and technological innovations that will be better protected with the assistance of a skilled cybersecurity workforce.

Cybercrime

Cybercrime is the use of any computer or network to engage in any level of fraudulent or criminal behavior. Cybercrime can be committed an individual, group, organization, industry, and or Nation-States. Cybercrime impacts all markets, industries, financial institutions, and governments worldwide. As the world becomes more technologically advance, so do the potential for cybersecurity breaches and technologically-based crimes. Andrews (2019) asserted that 19 percent of charities and 43 percent of businesses domestically experienced some level of cyber security breach.

According to the FBI's 2018 Internet Crime Complaint Center, more than 350,000 cybersecurity related complaints were received. On average, the Center received 900 call complaints per day in 2018.

In addition, the Center reported that between 2014 - 2018, the nation's lose to cybercrime ranged from $800.5 million in 2014 to $2.7 Billion in 2018 (Wilczek, 2019).

Cybercriminals vastly outnumber the available and skilled cybersecurity professional needed to combat the increasing threats. Gartner reported that $114 Billion was spent to strengthen cyber security efforts. However, attacks and breaches continue at an increasing rate. World-wide billons of dollars are lost each year due primarily to cybercriminal and security network breaches by hackers (Crumpler and Lewis, 2019). Cybersecurity financial losses increase almost daily for targeted individuals and or organizations. For example, in 2013, Target suffered an organizational breach of sensitive records that cost the company an estimate $202 million.

Data breaches, in 2018, compromised the personal information, financial records, a broad-birth of Organizational network systems, and various amounts of person identifiable data of millions worldwide. Some of the noted cybercrime victims in 2018 were Aadhaar, Marriott, MyHeritage, and Facebook. The largest data breach in 2018 was experienced by Aadhaar where 1.1 billion users' information and data were stolen by hackers. The hacked information and data included, but wasn't limited to unique 12-digit numbers, banking details, and user private information.

Workforce Shortages

From a global perspective, the cybersecurity skills and talent shortages are at an all-time high despite increased salaries and promotion opportunities. According to a recent ESG brief, the shortage of skilled cybersecurity talent presents a real state of emergency for society (Cyberbit.com, 2016). Over 50 percent of IT and cybersecurity professionals recently surveyed asserted that there is a major gap in being able to hire skilled cybersecurity specific workers (Armstrong-Smith, 2018). The 2017 Global Information Security Workforce (GISW) report found that many organizations are not adequately staffed with a cybersecurity workforce to combat the current threats (NeSmith, 2018). In addition, job turnover is another actual challenge for the industry in keeping workers in a competitive job market. As such, cybersecurity employee recruitment and retention are major problems for most businesses (Rayome, 2018).

Almost at every department within the security networking industry, the is a major need for new hires with high level technical skills (Crumpler and Lewis, 2019). In 2010, a CSIS report found that the United States is in a hiring crisis due to the extreme number of open cybersecurity positions that need to be filled as soon as possible. There is a major need for individuals with the skills and abilities to create innovative secure security systems, compose safer computer codes and programming, and to design better means and processes to prevent, detect, mitigate, and recover from various breaches (The California Community Colleges Centers, 2019).

Bring in more women into the cybersecurity field would serve to reduce the current job gaps. Women are an underrepresented population within the cybersecurity sector. Although there has been marginal growth of women in the cybersecurity workforce, there is a need for more comprehensive strategies to enhance the number of women entering the field. Increasing the number of women in the cybersecurity filed would produce professionals, who are fully capable of impacting the field in meaningful ways. In many instances, women don't often see themselves in technology careers, but need to be encouraged to enter the field at an earlier period (Poster, 2018).

Many cybersecurity positions remain open at least three months until filled and most of those position is technical in nature (State of cybersecurity, 2019). In many instances, the lack of job openings awareness is major reason that contributes to the workforce gaps. Since people are just aware of the opportunities that could be beneficial to them if sought. In addition, many people believe that cybersecurity jobs are only for the technically skilled, however that is not the case. There are many qualities technical as well as non-technical positions in need of qualified and motivated workers.

There are job gaps in all sections of criminal justice: local, state, and federal. According to Cyberseek, there are various open positions for digital forensic analyst, cyber IT/forensics/security incident responders, digital forensics technician, and cybersecurity forensics analyst. There are an estimated 777 job openings nationally just of the cybercrime analyst/investigator position with a starting salary of $85,000. See figure 2. At least 70% of the positions within this section require at least a bachelor's degree and skills such as computer forensics, Linux, Network Security, Python, Malware Analysis, forensics tools, and malware engineering. Some of the top certifications that organization seek in new hires include but aren't limited to: Certification Information Systems Security Professional (CISSP), Global Information Assurance Certification (GIAC) Certified Incident Handler, GIAC Certified Forensic Analyst, and EnCase Certified Examiner (EnCE) (Cyberseek, 2019). There are a variety of certifications on the market, so it is critical to do your homework concerning a given industry's need and expectations.

Women and Cybersecurity

Women hold approximately 11 percent of cybersecurity positions, despite representing half of the global population (Frost and Sullivan, 2018). More needs to be done to attach women into the field (NeSmith, 2018). K through 12 and various Science, Technology, Engineering, and Math (S.T.E.M.) programs could assist with introducing girls and young women to various aspects of computer science, coding, programming, math, and cybersecurity. Girls and women need to have ready access to both technology-based education and career pathways in-order to really increase the number of skilled workers this the cyber space (Garlinghouse, 2019).

Women entering the field must exhibit a high-level self-confidence in-order to avoid discouragement along the career pathway. Securing a professional mentor would be value-added for women and reduce the chances of them losing interest in the field. Sustaining an interest through the years will serve to strengthen the cybersecurity pipeline and increase the number of people interested and subsequently skilled enough to make a measurable impact in the field.

CASE STUDY 1: WOMEN IN TECHNOLOGY - GRACE HOPPER

Grace Brewster Murray Hopper (1960–1992) was a technology forerunner and a renowned computer professional and a U.S. naval officer for most of her career. During Hopper's academic journey, she earned both a master's degree and a Ph. D in mathematics from Yale University in 1930 and 1943 respectively. Hopper was distinguished as a computer science innovator for the important contributions in the areas of software development, computer programming, and the dynamic creation of various programming languages.

While employed, in 1949, with the Eckert-Mauchly Computer Corporation in Philadelphia, PA., Hopper worked on the first commercial electronic computer. Later, Hopper led the way with automatic programming and innovations in coding. Hopper's efforts were foundational in many of the programming languages used today. Hopper, in 1956, led a team to create the first word-based programming language called FLOW-MATIC. Hopper's efforts greatly added to the body of programming knowledge that, globally, serves the coding, programming, and computer science community.

Through Hopper's professional career, she continued to make significant contributions to the field. Hopper worked on a team that created a Common-Business-Oriented-Language, now better known as COBOL. Hopper continued to work and to make meaningful contributions to the field until her passing in 1992. Hopper was the first American women to receive the Distinguished Fellow of the British Computer Society Award in 1973 and former U.S. President George H. Bush bestowed onto Hopper the National Medal of Technology as acknowledgement of her groundbreaking work in the advancement of computer programming languages for which much of the world benefits. The U.S. Presidential Medal of Freedom was posthumously awarded to Hopper in 2016 in full recognition of her lifelong contributions to the computer science field.

Source: https://president.yale.edu/biography-grace-murray-hopper

Creating a workforce pipeline of young, talented, and skilled people with the proper qualifications will serve to benefit the overall cybersecurity community and society in both short and long terms (State of cybersecurity, 2019). The ability to understand the corporate side of cybersecurity is an important skill, because high level career advancement will require broader knowledge and abilities beyond basic coding and programming.

An early interest in Science, Technology, Engineering, and Math (S.T.E.M.) or any related technological field is a benedict for those interested in a cybersecurity career path. In many instances, teenagers are just unaware of the broad range of educational, training, and career opportunities that exist within the field of cybersecurity that could place them on a more rewarding career pathway. Therefore, having more women to enter the cyber workforce would greatly help to reduce both the job and gender gap.

Challenges Faced by Women in Cybersecurty

The number of women majoring in computer science is at a very low 18 percent in comparison to the once high rate of 37 percent in 1984 (Poster, 2018). The U.S. is seemingly not producing a high enough level of skilled S.T.E.M. workers (Griffey-Brown, 2019). Job ready skills are in short supply for many of those entering the job market. An innovation continues at a steady pace, the learning curve for securing new and competitive skills continue to be a challenge for many people. Early education, training, networking, and career development is essential to help build a true cybersecurity pathway. Having the perspective of more women in the technology and cybersecurity field would be value-added (Kapin, 2019). There is an increase in women leading technology start-ups, but much more is needed (Kapin, 2019). Women are far less likely than men or other minorities to receive a job referral and this increases the level of inequality (Garlinghouse, 2019)

CASE STUDY 2: WOMEN IN TECHNOLOGY - DIANA INITIATIVE

Diana Initiative was created in 2017 as an information security organization primarily steadfast in their focus to hold up women who are interested in building a career pathway in data security, while fostering diverse workplaces, and helping to transform for the better workplace culture so that organizations can be more accommodating of the workforce regardless of gender (The Diana Initiative, 2019). Visit the Diana Initiative for more information at https://www.dianainitiative.org/

Source: The Diana Initiative

Gender

By all accounts, cybersecurity is a male dominate field and having more women in the cybersecurity field is good for business, society, and national security (Bradford, 2018). There is a growing need to better recruit, train, hire, promote, and retain more women in cybersecurity and related technological fields. Women naturally bring certain qualities, skills, perspective, and leadership that is a plus on all fronts. Academia, business, and organizations should be encouraged to recruit and retain more women as a standard practice (Horowitz, Igielnik, & Parker 2019).

The lack of gender diversity at all level in the technology field continues, primarily because of a high rate of unconscious bias related to concepts such age, gender, race, sexual orientation or international status. Women are often not offered the same job opportunities and career advancement pathways as men in most instances (State of cybersecurity, 2019). Senior leadership must be come champions for women in the workplace in-order for measurable and positive changes to be observed (Armstrong-Smith, 2018).

Inclusion and Diversity

In the United States, minority groups are the rapidest growing population, therefore it becomes a value to have many of those within these population to consider a career path in S.T.E.M. and cybersecurity. Globally, all organizations should work hard to ensure that inclusion and diversity are a core strategy of their respective enterprise model. Moreover, there is a great need to recruit more women into the field in-order to benefit from the perspective and talent that women would bring into the industry. Research has widely established that a more inclusive and divers organization produce higher performing enterprises (Geter, 2010).

However, in many organizations, unconscious discrimination is an unfortunate part of a career pathway (Williams, L. Y. (2018) and such bias can be experienced within any corporation and at any level of the hierarchy. Although, a larger percentage of women in cybersecurity are white, there is a dire need for more women of color to balance the workforce by introducing varying perspectives, skills, talents, and leadership (Geter, 2010; Bradford, 2018). The scope of cybersecurity breaches and the growing rate of cybercrime dictate the we include every skilled women, man, minority, young professional, and seasoned veteran to fill some of the many cybersecurity jobs at every stage to better ensure personal protections and National security.

Recruitment and Retention

Cybersecurity breaches and related cybercrimes are at an all-time high. Therefore, organizations worldwide are in a rush to recruit, hire, and retain the top cybersecurity talent. The most skilled and talented workers have broad choices when it come to deciding on what job to accept and at what salary package (Rayome, 2018). Professionals with expert level skills in areas such as intrusion detection, reverse-engineering, secure software development, and cyber-attack mitigation are in the highest demand (Crumpler and Lewis, 2019).

Recruitment and retention efforts should, also, focus in a deliberate manner on recruiting more skilled women into the field at all levels. Whereas, inclusion and diversity should become a priority to create a culture that is more supportive of women and minorities (Evans & Reeder, 2010). Building a workplace environment that offers one-to-one mentoring, innovative peer support models, re-training opportunities can lead to a reduce employee gap for many organizations (Armstrong-Smith, 2018). In most cases, cybersecurity workers leave an organization for better financial packets with a full range of incentives and bonuses, promotion and development opportunities that become harder for many other organizations to compete with in recruiting and retaining top talent (State of cybersecurity, 2019). Retention is also strained, because many other workers seek more flexible work schedules, less stress in a given workplace, and an increased desire to work with the latest innovations and technologies. On-the-other-hand, people leave a given organization due to burnout or the perceived lack of potential career advancement (Horowitz et al., 2019)

Nevertheless, women continue to fall behind when it comes to pay, incentives, promotions, and project assignments. In addition, women deal with ongoing issues of discrimination and harassment in the workplace that men rarely experience (Horowitz et al., 2019). Organizations need to put-forth more clear and deliberate effort in the recruitment process in-order to a reach a broader population of potential candidates to fill cybersecurity and related positions.

Education

Colleges and universities, around the globe, are challenged to more effectively prepare and to rapidly produce enough workers to make a meaningful dent in the current job gaps. In the U.S., a major National Security concern is the ability to secure enough highly skilled and talented professionals to work across the technology and cybersecurity continuum. Unfortunately, the educational systems in the U.S. have found it difficult to produced well-skilled, highly educated, and talented cybersecurity professionals to meet the current need. (Geter, 2010; Crumpler and Lewis, 2019). Employers have expressed their respective dissatisfaction with the lack of practical experiences and hands-on skills exhibit by entry level cybersecurity workers (Crumpler and Lewis, 2019). Many of the Nation's computer science degree offering programs do not require any type of cybersecurity course as a core component of the curriculum. Evidently, a great deal more needs to be done in-order to strengthen various S.T.E.M. related curriculum to include cybersecurity courses to expand student's awareness, knowledge, and skills.

Training and Certifications

According to the Annual ISACA Global State of Cybersecurity Survey conducted in 2018, found not enough people have the prerequisite skills or talent to be readily hired in the cybersecurity field above entry position (State of Cybersecurity, 2019). For people seeking jobs in cybersecurity, re-training maybe the most expedient pathway. Even with a college degree in computer science, there may be a need for prospective hires to invest and earn a cybersecurity certificate. Organizations are seeking workers with the proper qualifications and experiences that clearly exhibit that the potential hire can do the work beyond just having a theoretical understanding of the job. In most cases, organizations are seeking workers with transferable skills that require less re-training in the first instance (State of Cybersecurity, 2019). In 2018, ISACA found that 61% percent of organizations surveyed believed that fewer than half of all new hire applicants for open cybersecurity positions were qualified for the job (Crumpler and Lewis,

2019). Therefore, it is imperative for those individuals interested in entering the cybersecurity career pathways that they demonstrate a clear and deliberate manner the expert level ability to do the work as expected by the various enterprises.

Closing the Talent Gaps

The cybersecurity career pathways will need to be strengthened from K thru 12, colleges, universities, and continuing education programs in-order to have a meaningful impact in produced higher level of skilled workers ready to enter the cybersecurity field. Closing the skills shortage and talent gaps in cybersecurity will require a strong commitment to better prepare the desired workforce that is needed to fill the job gaps. Academia, organizations, technology industry, and government, at all levels, must collaborate to strengthen the career pathways and opportunities for students and others interested in entering the cybersecurity field and related S.T.E.M. areas (Griffey-Brown, 2019).

Conclusion

In this chapter, we explored an essential aspect of cybersecurity: the workforce shortage. We examined the seriousness of cybersecurity breaches and the rising rate of cybercrime and discussed the importance of developing a workforce with the skills and abilities to combat cybersecurity threat. As such, it is critical that we produce a skilled workforce fully capable of filling many of the cybersecurity and technology position sooner rather than later. As this chapter presented, encouraging and better preparing women to enter the cybersecurity field will increase the number of women with the skill to make a meaningful difference in the field and work to close the job gaps that now exist. The chapter revealed that with increased interest, more developed skills, high levels of education, specialized trainings, and real opportunities, women would greatly help to reduce the job gaps of today and the future.

Research has established that having more women entering the cybersecurity field would go a long way in breaking barriers that now exist, which is a cause of the large job gaps in the industry (Williams, L. Y., 2018; Poster, W. R., 2018; Bradford, L., 2018). Moreover, organizations need to develop a culture of hiring women in various skilled, management, supervisory, and leadership roles. The cybersecurity and related fields need to ensure that interested women professional are wholeheartedly accepted within the organization's culture and are fully respected members of the career pipeline within every organization. The burden of increasing the number of women entering the field should not be left to women alone, men must become wholeheartedly ensure that the enterprise is more welcoming to all (Kapin, A., 2019).

Cybersecurity and many technology career fields are highly competitive, and preparation is central. Globally, companies are finding it more challenging to both recruit and retain the most skilled workers. For example, a 2018 survey revealed that 84 percent of cybersecurity professionals sought an organization change within the year for better career and financial opportunities (Bayern, 2018). In sum, all industries, organizational, and government sectors will need to do more to fill the job gaps in cybersecurity to ensure a stronger national security.

Adversaries

Adware

Anonymity

Attack vectors

Breaches

Career Pathways

Cloud Storage

Cyber-Attacks

Cybercriminals

Cybersecurity Workforce

Darknet

Distributed Denial of Service (DDOS)

Docing

Economic Espionage

Firmware

Hacker Groups

Hacker(s)

Internet of things (IoT)

Intrusions

Malware

Nation-States

Phishing

Privacy

Scareware

Security architecture

Security Risks

Smart-homes

Social Engineering

Spyware

Theft of Intellectual Properties

Threats

Vishing

Vulnerabilities

Workforce Pipeline.

Discussion Questions:

1. What should organizations do to increase their cybersecurity skilled workforce?

2. What skills and technological credentials do people need to enter the cybersecurity field?

3. What are the factors faced by women seeking to enter the cybersecurity profession?

4. What can you learn from global cybercrime incidences to better prevent cybersecurity breaches?

Chapter Activities

Cybercrime continues to be a worldwide threat to the U.S. Nation security and global markets. As a group, discuss to what extent is having a more skilled cybersecurity professional staff would provide better technological protections against cybersecurity breaches. Then, discuss how best to prevent cybercrimes against persons, against property, and against governments. Provide examples to support your argument. Each team member will be required to write a section of the final paper. Peer evaluations will need to be submitted with the final paper. Write a maximum 3,000-word empirical research paper with proper APA references.

Web Links

Cyberseek - https://www.cyberseek.org/pathway.html

National Institute of Standards and Technology (NIST) - https://www.nist.gov/

CyberPatriot - https://www.uscyberpatriot.org/

National Initiative for Cybersecurity Careers and Studies (NICCS) - https://www.niccs.us-cert.gov/ workforce-development/cyber-security-workforce-framework

SANS Institute - https://niccs.us-cert.gov/ SANS Institute

National Security Agency (NSA) - https://www.nsa.gov

MITRE Common Vulnerability Exposures Database - https://cve.mitre.org

DARKReading - https://www.darkreading.com

Diana Initiative - https://www.dianainitiative.org/

Women in Cybersecurity - https://www.wicys.org

References

Andrews. J. (2019). The hidden truth about cybercrime: Insider threats - UK Study. Retrieved from https://www.information-age.com/hidden-truth-about-cyber-crime-123478848/ on May 26, 2019.

Armstrong-Smith, S. (2018). Diversity in security: A collaborative effort. Computer Business Review. Retrieved from https://www.cbronline.com/opinion/women-cybersecurity on May 29, 2019.

Ashford, W. (2019). Small businesses hit hardest by cybercrime costs. ComputerWeekly.com. Retrieved from https://www.computerweekly.com/news/252460134/Small-businesses-hit-hardest-by-cyber-crime-costs on May 30, 2019.

Batas, S. (2020, July 09). Three ways that cybersecurity companies can close the gender gap. Retrieved August 10, 2020, from https://www.securitymagazine.com/blogs/14-security-blog/post/92794-three-ways-that-cybersecurity-companies-can-close-the-gender-gap

Bayern, M. (2019) Top 3 reasons cybersecurity pros are changing jobs. TechRepublic. Retrieved from https://www.techrepublic.com/article/top-3-reasons-cybersecurity-pros-are-changing-jobs/?ftag=TREa988f1c&bhid=28624689002611617679293417325084 on May 22, 2019.

Bradford, L. (2018). Cybersecurity needs women: Here's why. Retrieved from https://www.forbes.com/sites/laurencebradford/2018/10/18/cybersecurity-needs-women-heres-why/#71a2b74547e8 on May 23, 2019.

Brinded, L. (2016). Santander UK Chairman: We Can Attract More Women Employees By Changing the Language in Job Ads. Business Insider, 30 September 2016. Retrieved from https://www.businessinsider.com/santander-uk-chairman-shriti-vadera-on-changing-job-ad-language-for-more-women-in-banking-2016-9 on May 17, 2019.

Cloud Passage. (2016). Cloud passage Study Finds U.S. Universities Failing in Cybersecurity Education. Retrieved from on https://www.cloudpassage.com/company/press-releases/cloudpassage-study-finds-u-s-universities-failing-cybersecurity-education/May 29, 2019.

Cook, Steve (2019). Tackling cybercrime with culture of security: It's time for organizations to transform how their employees look at security. TechRadar-Pro. Retrieved from on https://www.techradar.com/news/tackling-cybercrime-with-a-culture-of-security March 27. 2019.

Coulson, T. Mason, M., & Nestler, V. (2018). Cyber capability planning and the need for an expanded cybersecurity workforce. Communications of the IIMA: Vol. 16: Iss. 2., Article 2. Retrieved from https://scholarworks.lib.csusb.edu/cgi/viewcontent.cgi?article=1401&context=ciima on May 15, 2019.

Crumpler, W. and Lewis, J. (2019). The cybersecurity workforce gap. Center for Strategic and International Studies. Retrieved from https://www.csis.org/analysis/cybersecurity-workforce-gap May 29, 2019.

The California Community Colleges Centers of Excellence for Labor Market Research (2018) Cybersecurity: Labor market analysis and statewide survey results. Retrieved from https://desertcolleges.org/docs/dsn/ict/coe-cybersecurity-labor-market-analysis-ca-employers-summary.pdf on March 13, 2019.

Evans, K. and Reeder, F. (2010). A human capital crisis in cybersecurity: Technical Proficiency Matters. CSIS Commission on Cybersecurity for the 44th Presidency. CSIS. Washington D.C. Retrieved from https://www.csis.org/analysis/human-capital-crisis-cybersecurity on March 8, 2019.

Crumpler, W. and Lewis, J. (2019). The U.S. Secretary of Commerce and the U.S. Secretary of Homeland Security, A Report to the President on Supporting the Growth and Sustainment of the Nation's Cybersecurity Workforce. Building the foundation for a more secure American future. (2018) Washington, D.C.

Lewis, J. A. (2016). Hacking the skills shortage: A study of the international shortage in cybersecurity skills. Center for Strategic & International Studies. Retrieved from https://www.csis.org/events/hacking-skills-shortage on April 9, 2019.

Cyberbit.com. (2016). ESG brief. Retrieved from https://www.cyberbit.com/resources/ on May 27, 2019.

Cybersecurity Market. (2019). Cybersecurity market worth $248.26 billion by 2023. Press Release. Market and Markets. Retrieved from https://www.marketsandmarkets.com/PressReleases/cyber-security.asp on May 3, 2019.

Tech Pro Research. (2014). Cybersecurity spotlight: The critical labor shortage. Retrieved from http://www.techproresearch.com/downloads/cybersecurity-spotlight-the-critical-labor-shortage/ on April 22, 2019.

Cyberseek. Cybersecurity Career Pathway. Retrieved from https://www.cyberseek.org/pathway.html on March 23, 2019.

Eubanks, N. (2017). The true cost of cybercrime for businesses. Forbes-YEC CommunityVoice Retrieved from https://www.forbes.com/sites/theyec/2017/07/13/the-true-cost-of-cybercrime-for-businesses/#43d44ccc4947 on May 27, 2019.

Evans, K. And Reeder, F. (2010). A human capital crisis in cybersecurity. CSIS Commission on Cybersecurity for the 44th Presidency. CSIS. Washington D.C. Retrieved from https://www.csis.org/analysis/human-capital-crisis-cybersecurity on May 5, 2019.

Frost, A. (2018). The 2017 global information security workforce study: Women in cybersecurity. Alta Associates' Executive Women's Forum, Information Security, Risk Management & Privacy. Retrieved from https://www.ewf-usa.com/page/WomenInCybersecurity on March 9th, 2019.

Garlinghouse, M. (2019). The +1 mentality: How it can close the gender and race gap. Forbes Magazine. Retrieved from https://www.forbes.com/sites/gradsoflife/2019/03/19/the-1-mentality-how-it-can-close-the-gender-and-race-gap/#2190080b3474 on May 3, 2019.

Geter, L. (2010). A quantitative study on the relationship between transformational leadership, organizational commitment, and perception of effectiveness. University of Phoenix (UOP). ProQuest LLC. UMI Dissertation Publishing.

Griffey-Brown, C. (2019). Why cybersecurity degree programs are essential. Education and Careers. Future of Business and Tech. Media Planet.

Horowitz, J. M., Igielnik, R. & Parker, K. (2019). Women and leadership 2018: Wide gender and party gaps in views about the state of female and the obstacles women face. Social & Demographic Trends.

Pew Research Center. Retrieved from https://www.pewsocialtrends.org/2018/09/20/women-and-leadership-2018/ on May 27, 2019.

Information Systems Audit and Control Association (ISACA). (2018). State of cybersecurity 2018, Part 1: Workforce Development.

ISACA. State of Cybersecurity 2019, Part 1: Current Trends in Workforce Development, USA, 2019, Security Skills Gap by the Numbers. ISACA.org (2018). Retrieved from https://www.isaca.org/go/state-of-cybersecurity-2020 on May 27, 2019.

Kapin, A. (2019). 50 Women-led startups that are crushing tech. Forbes Magazine. February 20, 2019. Retrieved from https://www.forbes.com/sites/allysonkapin/2019/02/20/50-women-led-startups-who-are-crushing-tech/#1aed430252b3 on May 2, 2019.

Lien, T. (2018). Amanda Rousseau's creative side helps her protect people from hackers. Los Angeles Times. Retrieved from https://www.latimes.com/business/la-fi-himi-amanda-rousseau-20180803-story.html on May 29th, 2019.

Market and Markets. (2019). Cybersecurity market worth $248.26 billion by 2023. Press Release. Retrieved from https://www.marketsandmarkets.com/PressReleases/cyber-security.asp on May 21, 2019.

Morgan, S. (2016). Cybersecurity spending outlook: $1 trillion from 2017 to 2021. Cybersecurity Business Report. CSO from IDG. Retrieved from https://www.csoonline.com/article/3083798/cybersecurity-spending-outlook-1-trillion-from-2017-to-2021.html on May 2, 2019.

NeSmith, B. (2018). The cybersecurity talent gap is an industry crisis. Forbes.com. Retrieved from https://www.forbes.com/sites/forbestechcouncil/2018/08/09/the-cybersecurity-talent-gap-is-an-industry-crisis/#603731eca6b3 on May 10, 2019.

Poster, W. R. (2018). Cybersecurity needs women. Nature Research Journal. Retrieved from https://www.nature.com/articles/d41586-018-03327-w on May 18th, 2019.

Rayome, D. A. (2018). Eighty-four percent of cybersecurity pros are open to switching companies in 2018. TechRepublic, 28 February 2018. Retrieve from https://www.techrepublic.com/article/84-of-cybersecurity-pros-are-open-to-switching-companies-in-2018/ on May 13, 2019.

White Paper - State of Cybersecurity. (2019). Part 1: Current trends in workforce development. Retrieved from https://cybersecurity.isaca.org/state-of-cybersecurity on May 15,2019.

Wilczek, M. (2019). FBI: cybercrime losses double in 2018. Dark Reading Retrieved from https://www.darkreading.com/vulnerabilities---threats/fbi-cybercrime-losses-doubled-in-2018/a/d-id/1334595on May 28, 2019.

Williams, L. Y. (2018). Opinion: How women can close the talent gap in cybersecurity jobs. Information and Management. Retrieved https://www.information-management.com/opinion/how-women-can-close-the-talent-gap-in-cybersecurity-jobs on May 26, 2019.

Women Who Code. Empowering women in technology. Retrieved from https://www.womenwhocode.com/ on May 27, 2019.

CHAPTER 22

Cybercrime and Law Enforcement

Carla Miller Coates Ph.D. | *North Carolina A&T State University*

Overview

The advent of "high-technology" (i.e., the Internet, the World Wide Web, computers, and mobile devices) has had a profound impact on law enforcement personnel throughout the country. In 2018, the number of Internet users worldwide was approximately 3.9 billion. What is more, between 2000 and 2018, Internet usage grew by approximately 219% (Internet World Stats, 2018). Over the last three-quarters of a century, members within the information communication technologies community (ICTC) have spent a significant amount of time developing and improving the way users gain access to information through the use of technology (Leiner et al., 2009; Taylor, Fritsch, & Liederbach, 2015). Thus, with just a few clicks of a mouse, finger, stylus, digital pencil, or pen, individuals can use an Internet-connected device to shop online, meet new people, search for employment, stream music and movies, or take photos, in a matter of seconds. At the same time, however, users can share their thoughts, view family photos, or find friends on social networking websites such as Facebook, Twitter or Instagram. In fact, "the number of those using social networking sites has nearly doubled since 2008" and approximately 240 million individuals use Facebook (Internet World Stats, 2018). Although the majority of individuals use the Internet and Internet-connected devices for legitimate reasons, some individuals use the Internet and Internet-connected devices illegitimately. For example, in 2017, there were approximately 301,580 Internet-related complaints reported to the Internet Crime Complaint Center (IC3) (Federal Bureau of Investigation, 2018). Consequently, in 2018, Facebook reported a security breach whereby hackers gained access to the accounts of approximately 50 million users (O'Sullvan, 2018). Yet, Facebook was not alone.

In 2017, the losses for economic crimes exceeded 1.4 billion dollars, with the majority of violations resulting from business email compromises, followed by ransomware, technical support fraud, and extortion (Federal Bureau of Investigation, 2018, p. 3). The latter leaves little doubt about the challenges that law enforcement officials, politicians, and justice professionals face combatting cybercrime. As such, the objective of this paper was to explore how technology and the use of Internet-connected devices have impacted law enforcement agencies. More specifically, this paper will explore how local law enforcement agencies within the United States, are addressing cybercrime. The discussion begins with a brief history of the development of the computer and the Internet and ends with a discussion about what law enforcement agencies are doing to reduce the incidence and prevalence of cybercrime. This study will, therefore, address the following research question: Are law enforcement agencies addressing the issue of cybercrime? The research question was derived from earlier studies on cybersecurity, cybercrime, and law enforcement.

Chapter Outcomes

After reading this chapter, students should understand:

- The development of the Internet;
- The definition of cybercrime;
- Criminal activity on the computer; and
- Law enforcement strategies and cybercriminality.

Understanding Cybercrime

Although there is no universally agreed-upon definition of cybercrime, defined, cybercrime, is "the destruction, theft, or unauthorized or illegal use, modification, or copying of information, programs, services, equipment, or communication networks" (Marcum, 2014, p. 3). In 2017, the Federal Bureau of Investigation (FBI) estimated that cybercrime cost the United States approximately 1.4 billion dollars (Federal Bureau of Investigation, 2018). The most commonly known types of cybercrimes are, but are not limited, to digital terrorism, identity theft, online counterfeiting, digital piracy, fraud, and intellectual property theft (Moore, 2011; Taylor, Fritsch, & Liederbach, 2015). Consequently, criminologists have argued that committing cybercrimes are often more profitable than traditional crimes. Thus, according to McGuire (2018), the revenue generated from cybercrimes can sometimes exceed profits made by "legitimate companies" (p. 16). As such, cybercrime may be extremely attractive to cybercriminals. This fact alone may be a primary explanation for the influx in computer crimes that have occurred over the past decade. The problem is, however, with the increase in cyber-crimes, technological advances, and "constitutional infringement issues" criminal justice and law enforcement agencies are experiencing multiple challenges apprehending suspects and preventing the incidence and prevalence of computer and technology-related crimes (Holt, Blosser, & Sigfried-Spellar, 2015, p. 5).

The Advent of the Computer, the Internet, and Cybercrime

In 1945, the first "electronic computer" was completed. However, the first Internet communication did not occur until 1969 after Licklider conceptualized a way to interconnect computers, globally. Licklider's ideas subsequently influenced the work of Leonard Kleinrock (see switching theory) and Lawrence Rob-

© Gorodenkoff/Shutterstock.com

erts's ARPANET, (i.e., the precursor of the Internet). It is worth mentioning that both forms of technology, the computer, and the ARPANET, were not commonly used by the general population until the advent of the personal computer; the technology was used exclusively by the military and within the scientific community (Taylor, Fritsch, & Liederbach, 2015). Today, however, approximately 89% of households have computers and 81% had Internet access (i.e., a 5% and 7% increase, respectively, since 2014) (File & Ryan, 2014, p. 2; Ryan, 2018, p. 1).

The widespread use of computers and the Internet has created a host of challenges for law enforcement due to the influx of computer-related crimes. It is well-known within the law enforcement community that policing, and the roles of police have primarily been a dynamic line of work. In fact, members of law enforcement, at all levels, have always had to tackle different waves of crime since the beginning of policing. Some of these waves include but are not limited to, the heroin epidemic of the 1900s, the prohibition era of the 1920s, the crack-cocaine epidemic of the 1980s, and the new opioid crisis, which was declared a

© Titima Ongkantong/Shutterstock.com

public health emergency in 2017 (Department of Health and Human Services, 2018). Consequently, however, an argument can be made that while similar to other types of crime, cybercrime includes an "integrated set of criminal practices" (McGuire, 2018, p. 10) that complicates traditional methods of policing. While the types of crimes committed online are not new to the police, the methods used to commit cybercrime is. Currently, however, police agencies across the nation have been inundated with reports of identity theft, Internet sex crimes, cyberbullying, and economic crimes through the use of mobile app technologies (i.e., Apps). Furthermore, when compared to traditional crime, cybercrime is unlike any other type of crime that law enforcement has had to address. For the most part, traditional policing requires physical training and the use of legal strategies to prevent a particular crime. However, with the growing number of cybercriminals, law enforcement officers will need training in cybersecurity, cybercrime, and digital forensics. This training will not only inform law enforcement officers about the fundamentals of cybercrime and cybersecurity, it will enhance their understanding of how to conduct a proper investigation on digital evidence, criminal and procedural law, and various cybersecurity infrastructure protocols that would aid in the prevention of online criminal activities.

Criminal Activity and the Computer

According to Moore (2011), there are three primary ways to discuss criminal activities involving a computer. First, "the computer [can be used] as an instrument of the crime" since the computer is used during the criminal act (p. 3). The second way that crimes are committed using a computer is when the "computer is the focus of a crime" (Moore, 2011, p. 3). He also posits that "the computer is the intended target of criminal activity and is not necessarily used in the commission of the act." An example of this type of cybercrime involves the following (1) committing offenses such as theft of intellectual property, (2) retrieving data on customers and pricing, and (3) gaining access to tax documents or criminal justice records (Moore, 2011, p. 3). The final type of computer crime involves using the computer as a "repository of evidence." For example, cybercriminals may use the computer to store illicit photos or to store illegally downloaded music or movies (Moore, 2011, p. 3). With the exception of the theft of computer equipment, the computer crimes described above have not

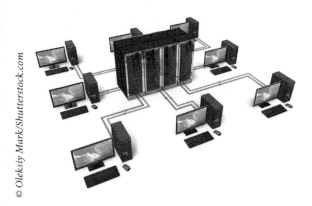

© Oleksiy Mark/Shutterstock.com

traditionally been the types of crimes that law enforcement officers have encountered. As such, traditional law enforcement tactics will not suffice when addressing crimes involving the computer. One reason is due to the highly complex nature of cybercrime. Keep in mind that cybercrime is more than just online bullying or stalking (i.e., cyberstalking) someone's social media page and the cybercriminal is more likely to be a skilled user of computer software and can possess the skills needed to navigate the Internet with ease. Consequently, some cybercriminals have spent years learning hardware and software manipulation in order to use the computer and the Internet to violate the law (Moore, 2011). In fact, in 2016, cyber-attacks against financial institutions increased by approximately 56% in Distributed Denial of Service (DDoS) attacks alone (Fiorentino et al, 2018). This increase is due to the large financial gains that cybercriminals receive from DDoS and other types of attacks (Synamtec, 2015).

The multitude of computer crimes, the lack of reporting cyber victimization to police, and jurisdiction issues are confirmation of how policing in a "high-technology" society can be problematic. For instance, traditional criminological research is replete with studies on the traditional methods in which gangs grow their criminal enterprise. Some of those traditional methods include sex and drug trafficking, and money laundering, to name a few. In the past, gangs worked the "streets" to conduct business. However, with the advent of technology and the Internet, street gang members have become computer savvy and have traded in their "timberland boots" for computers. For instance, Moule, Decker, and Pyrooz, (2012), reported that there was an influx in Internet gang activity and that gang members were using Internet-connected devices to commit a crime. In addition, their study found that: (1) gang members were more likely to use the Internet and "social networking sites just as much, if not more, than nongang members," (2) gang members have a greater overall propensity for online crime and deviance than former and nongang respondents, and (3) the Internet is rarely used to further the instrumental goals of gangs, instead appealing to the symbolic needs of gangs and gang members (Moule, Decker & Pyrooz, 2012, p.152).

Law Enforcement Strategies Used to Combat Cybercrime

Due to the exponential growth in cybercrime as well as the need to secure our nation's critical infrastructure, law enforcement agencies throughout the nation have realized the urgency to make cybercrime and cybersecurity a top priority. In fact, multiple law enforcement agencies have joined forces to address the seriousness of cybercrime and have subsequently created a task force of stakeholders throughout the nation (Wexler, 2014). According to Wexler (2014), an important strategy to problematize some of the issues that many agencies faces were to identify some of the issues and answer questions about cybercrime. Using the Police Executive Research Forum (PERF) Cybercrime Survey, law enforcement officers answered several questions about what role local law enforcement agencies could assume (i.e., 213 out of 498 law enforcement agencies or a response rate of approximately 43%) in preventing and investigating cybercrime. The results indicated that approximately 42% of those surveyed already had a cybercrime unit. In addition, approximately 96% of the law enforcement agencies participating in the survey indicated that they have programs in place to provide personnel with specialized training in cybercrime. What is

© studiostoks/Shutterstock.com

more, when participants were asked about some of the challenges that may impact the agency's ability to address cybercrime, respondents listed the following: (1) the lack of staff members (54%), (2) the lack of funding (31%), and (3) the lack of in-house expertise (29%) (Wexler, 2014, p. 6).

Agency leaders also mentioned that: (1) there needs to be a clearer picture of the cybercrime problem, (2) there are not enough arrests being made for low-level cybercriminals and as a result, they are not being brought to justice, and (3) police need proficiency in three areas of cyber-intelligence including understanding cybercrime, crime prevention, and investigation techniques (Wexler, 2014, p. 3). In fact, the concerns mentioned above are not unique to the law enforcement agencies participating in the survey. According to Holt (2018), many other law enforcement agencies have expressed similar concerns including providing training and improving training methods for offenses committed using technology and the Internet including addressing what constitutes a cybercrime and how to investigate cybercrime, given the jurisdictional constraints (Holt, 2018). Consequently, however, Wall (2010) has posited several reasons as to why there is a general lack of understanding of what cybercrime is. According to Wall (2010), the following factors contribute to the lack of understanding of what cybercrime is: (1) the way that the term is described in the media, (2) the way institutions of higher learning describes and defines cybercrime, and (3) the manner in which cybercrime has been defined and interpreted by law enforcement agencies (Wall, 2010, p. 185). In fact, in order to gain a better understanding of cybercrime, cybercrime must be "defined in terms of the informational, networked, and globalized transformation of deviant or criminal behavior by networked technologies." As such, Wall (2001) created four general types of cybercrime that can be correlated with criminal offending: (1) cyber trespass (e.g., hacking attempting to perform network penetration), (2) cyber-deception and thefts (e.g., engaging in fraud or sending mass messages via email), (3) cyber-pornography (e.g., sexual content), and (4) cyber-violence (e.g., cyberbullying, harassing messages, and hate crimes) (pp. 3-7). Wall's criminal offending typologies places different levels of cybercrime into context and can eliminate some of the confusion about what is and what is not cybercrime at a very novice level. Of significance, based on the findings from the PERF Cybercrime Survey, law enforcement professionals have expressed a lack of interest in cybercrime, in part due to their belief that cybercrime is victim precipitated (Holt, 2018). To this end, the lack of training, the lack of resources including qualified staff, and the lack of interest creates significant disadvantages for law enforcement personnel to take proactive measures against cybercrime.

Conclusion

Cybercrime is one of the fastest-growing crimes globally and until recently, many law enforcement agencies throughout the United States did not consider cybercrime a top priority. The findings from the review of the literature suggests that cybercrime is a high priority among law enforcement agencies across the nation. In addition, there is a critical need for agencies to train law enforcement officers on the prevention, mitigation, detection, investigation, and prosecution of crimes committed using technology and the Internet (Holt, 2018; Wall, 2010). What is more, multiple reports from Symantec, the Federal Bureau of Investigation (FBI), and the Police Executive Research Forum (PERF) on cybercrime, suggests that law enforcement agencies across the country recognize the critical necessity to combat cybercrime and are making a concerted effort to combat cybercrime. At the same time, however, although most law enforcement officers associate cybercrime with the unauthorized access to computer systems and networks, Holt (2018), found that some law enforcement officers believed that individual behavior (i.e., carelessness, lack of knowledge about the use of technology and the Internet, and visiting "risky" websites) significantly contributes to cybercrime.

While it is true that there are some basic precautions that individuals can take to minimize or reduce their chances of being a victim of cybercrime including but not limited to: (1) using full-service internet security suite, (2) creating strong passwords, (3) performing regular updates on software, (4) managing social media settings, and (5) strengthening your home network using a strong encryption password as well as a virtual private network (VPN), ("Eleven ways to help protect yourself against cybercrime," 2019), consideration must also be given to the multiple network system vulnerabilities and risks, since vulnerabilities are found in every system. As demonstrated, the complexity of cybercrime extends far beyond the training that a traditionally trained law enforcement officer receives. Therefore, there is a critical need for law enforcement agencies to create cybersecurity units, develop training programs for law enforcement officers, and hire qualified cybersecurity professionals in order to reduce the incidence and prevalence of computer-related offenses.

Key Terms:

Computer

Cyberbullying

Cybercrime

Distributed Denial of Service (DDoS) Attacks

Encryption

Hardware

Internet

Law Enforcement

Network

Password

Police Executive Research Forum (PERF)

Software

Virtual Private Network

Discussion Questions:

1. What is the Internet?

2. Define Cybercrime.

3. What is a virtual private network?

4. What is encryption?

5. Define cyberbullying.

6. What is distributed denial of service attack (DDoS)

7. What is the Police Executive Research Forum (PERF)?

8. What is a network?

Web Links:

https://www.khanacademy.org/computing/computer-science/internet-intro/internet-works-intro/v/what-is-the-internet

https://www.khanacademy.org/computing/computer-science/internet-intro/internet-works-intro/v/the-internet-wires-cables-and-wifi

https://www.khanacademy.org/computing/computer-science/internet-intro/internet-works-intro/v/the-internet-cybersecurity-and-crime

https://www.khanacademy.org/partner-content/nova/nova-labs-topic/cyber/v/cybersecurity-101

https://www.khanacademy.org/partner-content/nova/cybersecurity/cyber/v/the-secret-lives-of-hackers

https://www.khanacademy.org/computing/ap-computer-science-principles/the-internet/cybercrime-and-prevention/a/computer-vulnerabilities

https://www.khanacademy.org/computing/ap-computer-science-principles/the-internet/cybercrime-and-prevention/a/computer-vulnerabilities

References

Eleven ways to help protect yourself against cybercrime. (2019, June 9). How to. Eleven ways to help protect yourself against cybercrime. Retrieved from https://us.norton.com/internetsecurity-how-to-how-to-recognize-and-protect-yourself-from-cybercrime.html

Federal Bureau of Investigation. (2016). *Cyber incident reporting.* Retrieved from https://www.fbi.gov/investigate/cyber

Federal Bureau of Investigation. (2018). *2017 Internet crime report.* Retrieved from https://pdf.ic3.gov/2017_IC3Report.pdf

File, T., & Ryan, C. (2014). *Computer and Internet use in the United States: 2013. American community survey.* ACS-28, U.S. Census Bureau, Washington, DC. Retrieved from https://www.census.gov/history/pdf/2013computeruse.pdf

Hampton, K., N., Goulet, L. S., Rainie, L., & Purcell, K. (2011). *Social networking sites and our lives. How people's trust, personal relationships, and civic and political involvement are connected to their use of social networking sites and other technologies.* Pew Research Center. Washington: DC. Retrieved from http://www.pewinternet.org/2011/06/16/social-networking-sites-and-our-lives/

Holt, T. J., Blosser, A. M., & Siegfried-Spellar, K. C. (2015). *Cybercrime and digital forensics: An introduction.* New York, NY. Routledge.

Hughes, L., & DeLone, G. (2014). Viruses, works, and trojan horses. Serious crimes, nuisance, or both. *Social Science Computer Review, 25*(1), 78-79.

Internet World Stats. (2018, March). Usage and population statistics. Retrieved from https://www.internetworldstats.com/stats14.htm#north

Klinger, D., Rosenfeld, R., Isom, D., & Deckard, M. (2015). Race, crime and the microecology of deadly force. *Criminology & Public Policy, 15,* 193-222. doi:10.1111/capp.2016.15.issue-1/issuetoc

Leiner, B, M., Kahn, R.E., Postel, J, Cerf, V. G., Kleinrock, L, Roberts, L., G., Clark, D., D., Lynch, D. C., & Wolff, S. (2009). A brief history of the Internet. *Computer Communication Review, 39,* 22-31. Retrieved from http://www.cs.ucsb.edu/~almeroth/classes/F10.176A/papers/internet-history-09.pdf

Marcum, C. (2014). *Cyber Crime.* New York, NY: Wolters Kluwer.

McGuire, M. (2018, March 17). Into the web of profit: An in-depth study of cybercrime, criminals, and money. Retrieved from https://www.scribd.com/document/377159562/Into-the-Web-of-Profit-Bromium-Final-Report

Moore, R. (2011). *Cybercrime: Investigating high-technology computer* crime (2nd ed.). New York, NY. Routledge.

Moule R., K., Decker, H., & Pyrooz, D., C. (2012). Social capital, the life-course, and gangs. In *the handbook of life-course criminology: Emerging trends and directions for future research.* C. L. Gibson and M. K. Krohn (Eds). New York, New York: Springer.

O'Sullivan, D. (2018, March 16). *Facebook just had its worst hack ever-and it could get worse.* Retrieved from https://www.cnn.com/2018/10/04/tech/facebook-hack-explainer/index.html

Ryan, C. (2018, March 17). *Computer and Internet use in the United States: 2016. American community survey reports.* ACS-28, U.S. Census Bureau, Washington, DC, 2018. Retrieved from https://www.census.gov/content/dam/Census/library/publications/2018/acs/ACS-39.pdf

Symantec Corporation. (2016, March 15). *Internet security threat report, 21.* Retrieved from http://www.symantec.com/threatreport/

Taylor, R. W., Fritsch, E. J., & Liederbach, J. (2015). *Digital crime and digital terrorism* (3rd ed.) Upper Saddle River, NJ: Pearson.

U.S. Census Bureau. (2012). *Electronic ownership by household.* Washington, D.C.: Government Printing Office. U.S. Census Bureau. (2012). Electronic ownership by household. Retrieved from http://www.census.gov/data/

Wall, D., S. (2005). The Internet as a conduit for criminal activity. In A. Pattavina (Ed.). *Information technology and the criminal justice system (pp. 77-98).* Thousand Oaks, CA: Sage.

Wexler, C. (2014, March 14). *Cybercrime. A new critical issue in the role of local law enforcement agencies in preventing and investigating cybercrime.* Retrieved from http://www.policeforum.org/assets/docs/Critical_Issues_Series_2

Index

and militarism, 6
professionalization of, 307
"rotten apples" theory of, 53
and sexuality, 289–290
sexual minorities in, 250
pornography
cyber-pornography, 333
online child pornography, 301
Powell, Colin, 231
Pregnancy Discrimination Act (1979), 279–280
prenatal sex selection, 114
pre-sentence investigation (PSI), 164
priming, concept of, 102
Priority Enforcement Program (PEP), 259, 264
prison capital, 190
Prison Rape Elimination Act (PREA, 2003), 218
for protecting inmates from sexual victimization, 263
and solitary confinement, 263–264
Prison Reform Trust, 78–80, 84
probation officers (POs), 106
women working as, 161
problem-solving strategies, 306
prostitution, 77, 85, 271
protective custody, 191
psychological toll, of managing and divulging conflicting identities, 247–248
public employment, LGBT-based discrimination in, 291
public pension system, in China, 122

Q

queer women of color, in law enforcement
Black women's law enforcement experience, 290
discrimination and racial insults, 291
discrimination and challenges faced by, 292
experiences of, 289
hiring of, 291
intersectionality of, 290, 293
lack of representation of, 289
leadership capabilities of, 291

mistreatment of, 289
policing and sexuality, 289–290
treatment of, 290–291

R

race-class-gender relations, 78
racial discrimination, 291–292
racial disparities, 189–190
racial/homophobic stigmatization, 190
racial injustice, 3
recruitment
in cybersecurity industry, 320
of LGBT officers, 291
rehabilitation and gender-responsive programming, 192
Rethink organization, 80
right to vote, for Black Americans, 290
risk assessments, 12, 107, 192
Robinson, Georgia Ann, 290
"rotten apple" theory, of police misconduct, 55
rural-to-urban migration, in China, 130

S

Saga of Anatahan?, The (movie), 113
Salem witch craze, 76
same-sex friend network, exclusiveness of, 132
same-sex friendship, 133–134
same-sex marriage, 250, 275, 289
school-based law enforcement
anti-bullying laws, 147
anti-bullying programming and strategies, 155
bullying incidents, 143
curriculum-driven programming, 146
Drug Abuse Resistance Education (D.A.R.E.), 146
Gang Resistance Education and Training (G.R.E.A.T.), 146
instances of sexual harassment, 145
literature review of, 144–148
mass shootings, 144